PRESIDENT WILSON ADDRESSING CONGRESS DURING WORLD WAR

A GUIDE TO THE AMERICAN BATTLE FIELDS IN EUROPE

PREPARED BY THE

AMERICAN BATTLE MONUMENTS COMMISSION

The Naval & Military Press Ltd

Published by

The Naval & Military Press Ltd
Unit 5 Riverside, Brambleside
Bellbrook Industrial Estate
Uckfield, East Sussex
TN22 1QQ England

Tel: +44 (0)1825 749494

www.naval-military-press.com
www.nmarchive.com

In reprinting in facsimile from the original, any imperfections are inevitably reproduced and the quality may fall short of modern type and cartographic standards.

TABLE OF CONTENTS

	Page
PREFACE	v

Chapter I

The World War to May 29, 1918:

Before the entry of the United States	1
Reasons for the entry of the United States	8
Organization of the American Expeditionary Forces	10
Military situation in June, 1917, and summary of events to May 29, 1918	14

Chapter II

American Operations in the Aisne-Marne Area:

General description	21
Described tour	33
32d Division at Juvigny	62
370th Infantry (93d Division), September 15–November 11, 1918	63
Interesting places in Aisne-Marne area not visited on tour	64
Map of area illustrating described tour	Opposite 66

Chapter III

The American Attack at St. Mihiel, and Succeeding Operations in that Region to the End of the War:

General description	67
Described tour	76
Interesting places in St. Mihiel area not visited on tour	111
Map of area illustrating described tour	Opposite 114

Chapter IV

The Meuse-Argonne Operations of the American First Army:

General description	115
Described tours—	
First day's tour	131
Second day's tour	167
Interesting places in Meuse-Argonne area not visited on tours	183
Map of area illustrating described tours	Opposite 186

Chapter V

American Operations in the Champagne Region:

Explanation of chapter	187
42d Division	189
2d and 36th Divisions	192
369th, 371st, and 372d Infantry (93d Division)	197
"Lost Battalion" of the 77th Division	198
368th Infantry (92d Division), on the left of First Army, September 26–30	200

Chapter VI

American Operations North of Paris: Page

- Explanation of chapter 201
- 27th and 30th Divisions at St. Quentin Tunnel 204
- 27th and 30th Divisions near le Cateau 209
- 11th Engineers 211
- 37th and 91st Divisions in Flanders 212
- 27th and 30th Divisions south of Ypres 215
- 80th Division with the British Third Army 217
- 33d Division with British Fourth Army 217
- 6th Engineers in Somme Defensive 220
- 1st Division at Cantigny 221

Chapter VII

Sector Occupation by American Divisions:

- General description of sector occupation 223
- Sketch indicating sectors held by American divisions between Verdun and Switzerland 228

Chapter VIII

Services of Supply (S. O. S.):

- General description of activities of S. O. S. 229
- Partial list of places in which S. O. S. establishments were located 233

Chapter IX

Operations of the United States Navy in the World War:

- General description of American Naval activities 237
- Partial list of places where American Naval establishments were located in Europe 243

Chapter X

American Military Cemeteries in Europe:

- General information 245

Chapter XI

American Project for Memorials in Europe:

- Description of memorial project, with designs of monuments 257

Chapter XII

After the Armistice 263

Chapter XIII

General Information:

- Miscellaneous information concerning the A. E. F. 267
- Distinctive insignia used in the A. E. F. ..... opposite 268
- Equivalent metric and English units 270
- Helpful information for use on described tours 271
- Glossary of military terms used in book 272

Index 275

The colour maps in this volume have been gathered at the end of the volume

PREFACE

This book has been prepared for the purpose of making available an accurate guide to the American battle fields in Europe. For the convenience of the tourist its size has been limited to one small volume.

Because of this limitation, much interesting material has been excluded. This applies not only to information concerning the American forces, but also to practically all activities of the Allied armies, whose many important battles are mentioned only incidentally or not at all. In the case of our Allies these omissions should not be construed as a lack of appreciation of the magnitude of their effort, but rather a recognition of the fact that any attempt to describe the operations of their huge armies during four years of intense fighting could not, as an incident to a book of this character, do justice to their importance. The policy followed has been to devote the available space to events which happened during the World War at places where American troops served and to make but few references to historical events which occurred at these places before the war. Information of the kind indicated as omitted from this book is available in other guidebooks and similar publications.

The first chapter of the book gives a brief summary of the war before the entry of the United States. It also gives the reasons why we declared war against Germany, a brief account of the organization of the American Expeditionary Forces, and an outline of the activities of the American forces up to the time they entered active operations in the Aisne-Marne region.

Chapters II, III, and IV deal with the three areas in which American troops in relatively large numbers engaged in battle. These are, respectively, the region between the Aisne and the Marne Rivers in the general vicinity of Château-Thierry and Soissons, the territory formerly occupied by the St. Mihiel salient, and the area northwest of Verdun between the Meuse River and the Argonne Forest. Each of these chapters consists of a short general story; a detailed description of a route through the region and an explanation of the operations which took place in the area visited; a list indicating some of the places of interest not visited on the tour; and a colored map to aid in understanding the operation and for use in following the described route.

Chapters V and VI deal with the American operations in the Champagne region of France and in the battle area generally north of Paris. In these regions the American operations were in most cases those of units not larger than a division, and the areas in which they took place are quite far apart.

Brief chapters concerning the service of American units in quiet sectors, the Services of Supply, and the activities of the Navy complete the story of American participation in the war. Other short chapters give information about the American cemeteries, the memorial project of the American Government for commemorating in Europe the services of the American forces, and the American Army activities after the armistice. A general chapter has been added which contains information of interest and certain data that will help in understanding the text. A glossary of military terms used in the book is given for the convenience of those who have not been in the service.

Most of the photographs in the book have been procured from the Signal Corps of the Army. Certain of them, however, have been obtained from the British Imperial War Museum and the German Reichsarchiv and can not be reproduced without their permission. These copyrighted pictures are identified by the symbols © B and © G, respectively.

The historical data contained herein are based on official records. Every available source has been consulted in order that the presentation of information should be accurate in all details.

The publication of this book was expedited in order to have it available for the large number of ex-service men who intend to go to Europe in the fall of 1927. It is possible that another edition may be published when this one is exhausted, and, for this reason, suggestions for its improvement from men who participated in the activities of the A. E. F. will be appreciated and carefully considered in case of any future revision.

CHAPTER I

THE WORLD WAR TO MAY 29, 1918, AND THE ORGANIZATION OF THE AMERICAN EXPEDITIONARY FORCES

THE WAR BEFORE THE ENTRY OF THE UNITED STATES

For some years prior to 1914 the great countries of Europe had been divided into two rival groups. One of these was the Triple Alliance, comprising Germany, Austria-Hungary, and Italy.

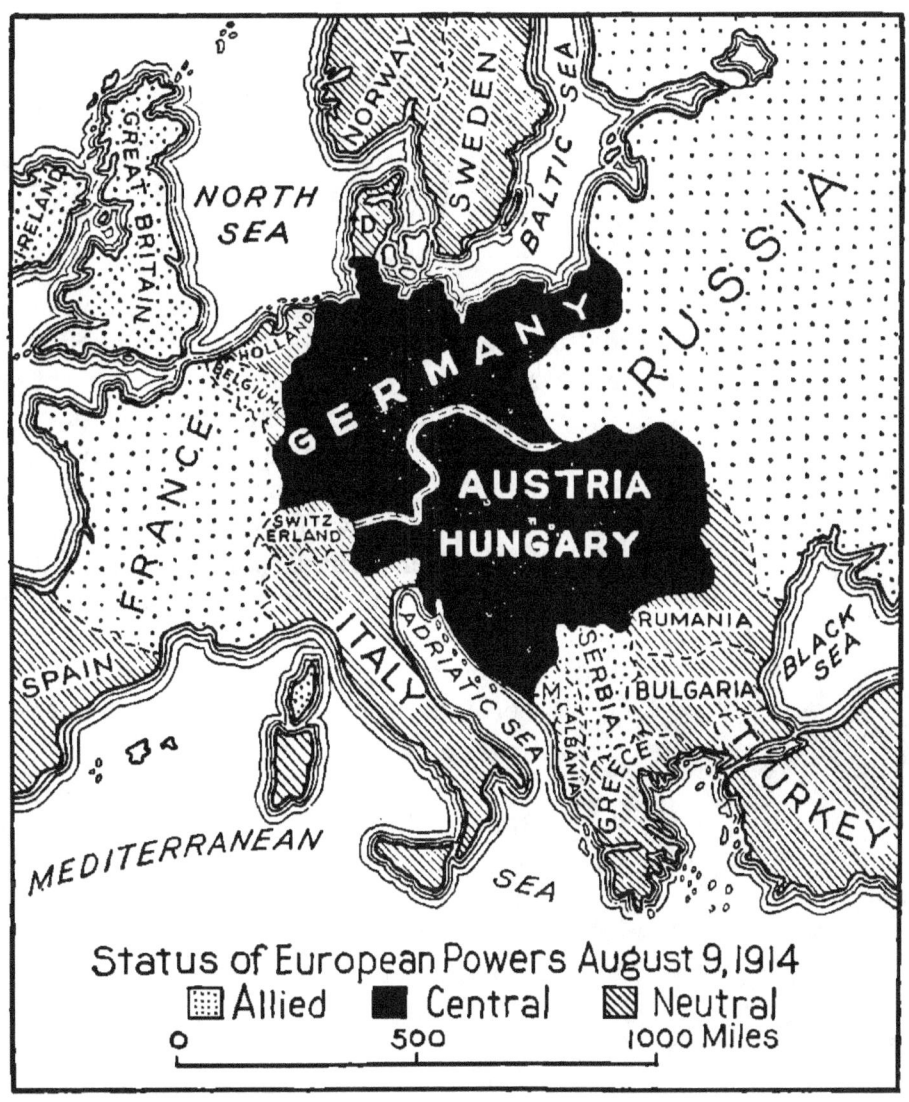

Germany, the leader of this group, had established close relations with Turkey and with some of the Balkan States.

Appreciating the danger to an individual nation when acting against a combination of powers, France, Great Britain, and Russia were naturally drawn together, and formed the other group, known as the Triple Entente.

Belgium was not identified with either group, as her neutrality had been guaranteed by Germany, France, Great Britain, Austria, and Russia.

Various incidents before 1914 had come near provoking war between the two groups and each occasion increased to some degree the strain existing between them.

GAS ATTACK ON WESTERN FRONT

The breaking point came when the Crown Prince of Austria was assassinated on June 28, 1914, while inspecting troops in the Austrian city of Serajevo, near the Serbian border. Austria at once accused Serbia of having instigated the crime and adopted an aggressive attitude in the diplomatic negotiations which ensued. Serbia went to great lengths to prevent war with her powerful neighbor, and after submitting to practically all the demands made upon her, agreed to arbitrate the others. Austria, however, sure of the support of Germany, refused to accept the Serbian proposals and declared war July 28, 1914.

LARGE GERMAN GUN ON WESTERN FRONT. © G

Austria started mobilizing her army near the Russian frontier and the Czar forthwith ordered his armies to mobilize. Germany demanded that Russian mobilization cease at once, and at the same time sent an ultimatum to France requiring that nation to state immediately her intentions in case of a Russo-German war. Receiving no reply from Russia, and the statement from France that she would do what her interests dictated, Germany declared war on Russia August 1 and on France August 3.

Italy declared that her treaties as a member of the Triple Alliance did not compel her to take part in a war of aggression, and announced her neutrality.

Great Britain declared war August 4, when it became evident that Germany had violated her treaty regarding Belgian neutrality.

By that date, therefore, Germany and Austria-Hungary, known as the Central Powers, were at war against the Allies, consisting of France, Russia, Great Britain, Serbia, and Belgium, which were joined by Montenegro a few days later. Four of these nations, France and Russia of the Allies, and both Ger-

BRITISH HOSPITAL SHIP "GLOUCESTER CASTLE"
Torpedoed in the Mediterranean, April, 1917

many and Austria, were able to place large, well-trained armies in the field at once. Serbia, Belgium, and Montenegro were relatively small, and Great Britain's organized power was, at that time, mainly centered in her great fleet.

Believing that in the event of war Russia would mobilize her forces much more slowly than France, Germany, prior to the opening of hostilities, had per-

GERMAN COLUMNS ADVANCING AT HERMIES, FRANCE © G

fected plans to crush the latter by a sudden and powerful offensive. According to these plans Austria, aided by German detachments, was to engage Russia on the east until France was defeated, after which the combined strength of the Central Powers was to inflict the same fate on Russia.

Immediately after the declaration of war, Germany began the invasion of France, using all natural avenues, including that through neutral Belgium. In spite of heroic resistance by the Belgians, and the vital aid rendered the French by Great Britain's comparatively small expeditionary force, the Allies were rapidly forced back to the general line of the Marne River. Making a determined effort in early September, they withstood further attacks and so threatened the enemy's right that his armies were compelled to retire to the Aisne.

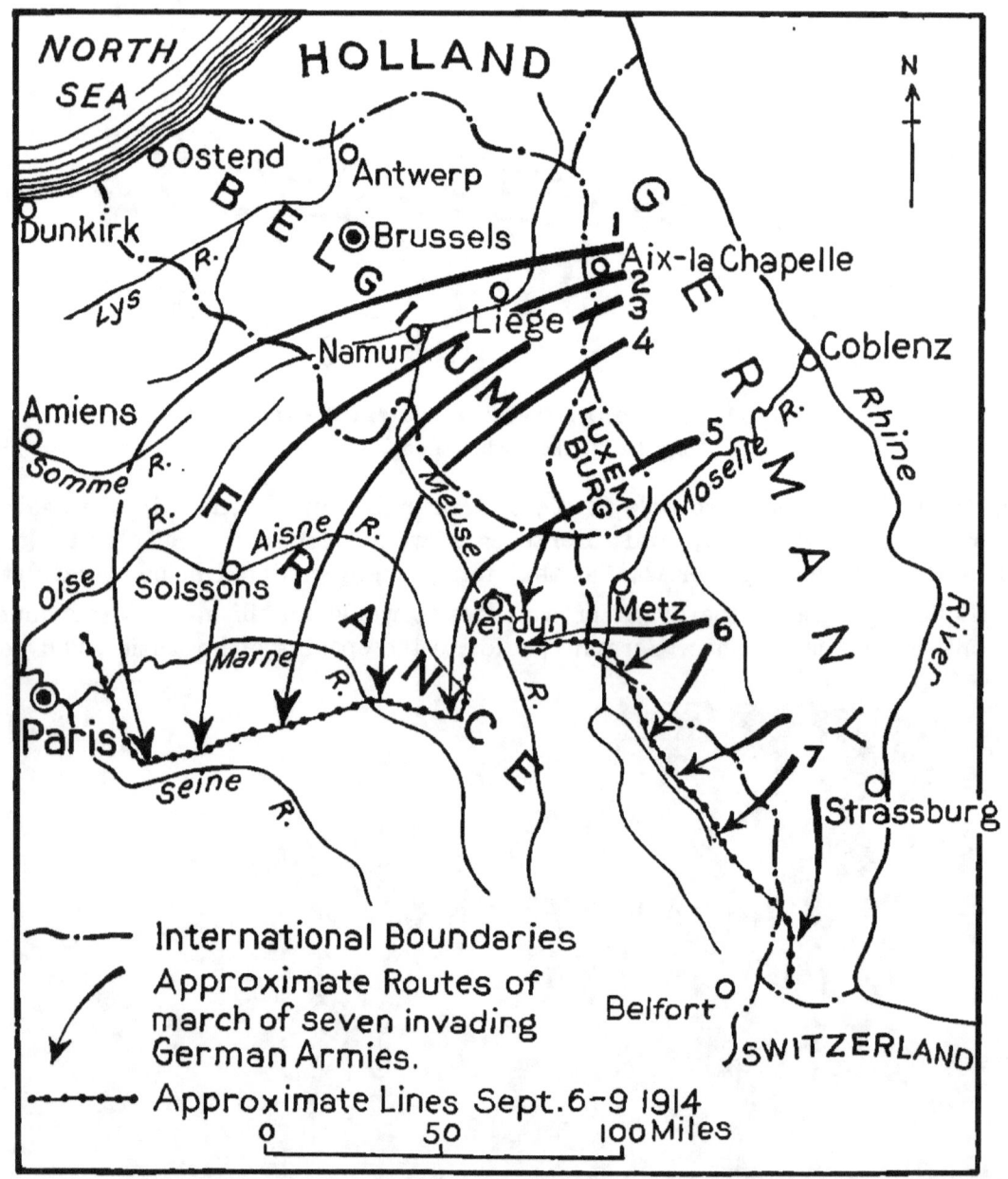

Following this battle the opposing units on the western flank of the respective lines engaged in a contest for the possession of the ports of northwestern France. If these had fallen to the Germans, not only would British military operations have been badly hampered, but the enemy would have secured excellent bases for naval activities. In this famous "race to the sea" the Allies succeeded in retaining control of the channel ports and as far to the eastward as Nieuport.

At the end of these operations neither of the contending armies on the Western Front had sufficient concentrated power to undertake a major offensive, and each began to stabilize its position by the use of every artificial means available. Elaborate systems of trenches and broad belts of barbed wire were constructed along the front, supplemented by machine guns and other quick-firing weapons in unprecedented numbers. These continuous defenses, with the hostile lines separated in many places by only a narrow strip of ground, produced the conditions which came to be known as "trench warfare."

During the advance of her armies toward Paris, Germany became alarmed at the speed of the Russian mobilization and the progress of that country's offensive

BRITISH TANK SET ON FIRE BY GERMAN FLAME THROWER
Note German trench and soldiers in foreground. © G

against East Prussia. This situation caused the German High Command to weaken the forces invading France, even before the Battle of the Marne, by withdrawing several army corps and starting them eastward to meet the Russian threat.

Hindenburg and Ludendorf came into prominence for the first time when they were ordered in August to the German Eastern Armies as Commander and Chief of Staff, respectively. The succeeding operations under their direction were characterized by rapid movements and crushing attacks, in which the losses suffered, particularly by Russia, were stupendous. The Russian armies were hurled out of East Prussia, and farther south were thrown back on Warsaw.

Turkey entered the war on the side of the Central Powers in November, 1914, thus threatening Great Britain's communications with the East by way of the

Suez Canal. As a result, many thousands of Allied soldiers, whose presence on the French front was always badly needed, were employed throughout the war in territory bordering the eastern end of the Mediterranean Sea.

Germany was in a very strong position at the close of the year. She had inflicted staggering losses on the Russians; was in possession of practically all of Belgium and areas in France which contained one-fourteenth of the French population and about three-fourths of her coal and iron deposits; and although the German colonies were virtually lost, her native resources were intact.

GERMAN 21-CM. MORTAR BATTERY FIRING ON WESTERN FRONT. © G

Italy's entry into the war in May of 1915 as one of the Allies drew approximately one-half of Austria's strength away from the eastern and southeastern theaters of war.

The French and British launched several offensives against the German front in 1915. The most important of these was the combined attack begun in September by the advance of the British near Loos, north of Arras, and by the French in the Champagne. Neither made any material change in the military situation on the Western Front.

DEPLOYMENT OF GERMAN REGIMENT FOR COUNTERATTACK. © G

Germany was again victorious against Russia in a series of desperate battles. Bulgaria, which entered the war on the side of the Central Powers in October, joined in the offensive that overran Serbia and Montenegro, while the Allied expedition to the Dardanelles was shattered and withdrawn immediately after the close of the year. The British Fleet held the mastery of the seas, but the submarine blockade which Germany had established in February was becoming a serious menace to Allied supply.

The Central Powers, believing they had nothing further to fear from Russia, planned a vigorous campaign in the west for 1916. In February they began intensive assaults against Verdun, which continued for months, only to dash themselves to pieces against French heroism. At the same time thousands of German troops were employed on the Somme to withstand the great British and French offensive in that region.

The German Fleet made a sortie in May and met the British in the Battle of Jutland, the principal naval engagement of the war. This battle resulted in the loss of several ships by each side, and terminated when the German Fleet retreated to its fortified harbors, which it did not leave again in force during the war.

Russia astonished the world by her powers of recuperation, and in June practically destroyed the Austrian Army of Galicia. When the Austrian Army in Italy was defeated in August, and Rumania entered the war against the Central Powers in the same month, it became necessary that Austria be rescued without delay. Germany quickly passed to the defensive in the west and started the eastern offensives which marked the beginning of the end for Russia, and eliminated Rumania before the close of the year.

SINKING OF "MESSANABIE"—TORPEDOED TWICE

The German High Command evidently concluded to remain on the defensive in the west during 1917 in order to complete the defeat of Russia and to help Austria crush Italy. By midsummer, aided by the revolution, the elimination of Russia was practically accomplished, and preparations were started for a powerful blow against Italy.

GERMAN CAVALRY ADVANCING. MARCH, 1918, OFFENSIVE. © G

Meanwhile the Allies had decided to undertake offensives on a large scale. In April the British began the Battle of Arras, and the French the second Battle of the Aisne. These attacks gained some ground, but the advances were inconsiderable, and the losses inflicted on the attacking troops were very great, especially in the Battle of the Aisne. The results created grave discouragement among the Allies, and were almost final proof that without additional help they would be unable to defeat the German armies on the Western Front.

Germany renewed unrestricted submarine warfare in February, 1917, and was making alarming inroads on Allied shipping when the United States entered the war.

REASONS FOR THE ENTRY OF THE UNITED STATES INTO THE WORLD WAR

The United States was in every respect a neutral nation at the beginning of the World War in 1914. The sympathies of our citizens were naturally divided, but as the causes which brought on the conflict were considered by the mass of the population to be of no direct concern to us, the attitude of the country as a whole was one of neutrality.

Early in the war, however, the activities of the warring countries on the high seas began to interfere with our maritime trade, and differences with Germany over the use of the submarine became particularly aggravating. The German Government announced in February, 1915, that the waters surrounding Great Britian would be regarded as part of the war zone in which enemy vessels of

SINKING OF AMERICAN BARK "KIRBY"

every description would be sunk, and all neutral shipping was warned to stay out of that area. The United States could not submit to such arbitrary action, and vigorously protested. As a result, Germany, while refusing to abandon her position, gave assurances that she would do her utmost to protect the lives of noncombatants and the ships of neutral nations.

However, the series of incidents that followed, including the sinking of unarmed vessels in which many American citizens lost their lives, caused a further exchange of notes with the German Government. We specifically objected to the sinking of any neutral vessels, or of any commercial vessel whatsoever when accomplished in such a way as needlessly to take the lives of noncombatants.

The events of 1915 brought about a gradual change in our attitude toward the war. The destruction of unarmed ships became more and more frequent, and finally in April, 1916, the President notified Germany that unless she at once abandoned her methods of submarine warfare against commercial vessels, diplomatic relations would be severed. Germany agreed to limit the activities of the submarines, although the sinking of commercial ships did not entirely cease.

During the remainder of 1916 our relations with Germany remained unchanged. Early in 1917, however, she announced her intention to engage in unrestricted submarine warfare, and President Wilson at once broke off diplomatic relations. He did not at that time recommend a declaration of war, stating to Congress that he could not take such an extreme step unless Germany should, by the actual sinking of ships under the conditions to which we expressly objected, clearly prove that her threats were made in earnest.

These sinkings occurred, and on April 2, 1917, the President addressed Congress, saying that under Germany's new policy "vessels of every kind, whatever their flag, their character, their cargo, their destination, their errand, have been ruthlessly sent to the bottom without warning and without thought of help or mercy for those on board." He advised that war be declared against the Imperial German Government, and Congress, with scarcely a dissenting vote, carried this recommendation into effect on April 6, 1917.

The President took great care in his speech to Congress to announce the aims and attitude of America. He said: "We have no selfish ends to serve. We desire no conquest, no dominion. We seek no indemnities for ourselves, no material compensation for the sacrifice we shall freely make. We are but one of the champions of mankind. We enter this war only where we are clearly forced into it, because there are no other means of defending our rights.

AMERICAN TROOPS MARCHING IN LONDON SOON AFTER DECLARATION OF WAR

Both the sincerity of his statement and the correctness of his interpretation of our aims and ideals were forcibly proved to the world, when, at the peace table many months later, we demanded neither one dollar of indemnity nor one square mile of territory from the defeated nations.

THE ORGANIZATION OF THE AMERICAN EXPEDITIONARY FORCES

The great task facing our Government when we entered the war was to place on the front as quickly as possible an American army sufficiently strong to give the combined American and Allied forces a decisive superiority over the Central Powers. It was evident that considerable time must elapse before we could actually have more than a nominal force in the battle lines. Our very small Regular Army was scattered in weak detachments over the country and in our outlying possessions. There were no complete and permanent units larger than regiments, and even these were not suitably organized and equipped for major operations.

GENERAL PERSHING LANDING AT BOULOGNE, FRANCE

The Allies pointed out, however, that help could be rendered almost immediately by other means, and upon their request we loaned them huge sums of money, sent them great quantities of food, and assisted them against submarines both by the use of our Navy and by building commercial ships to replace losses. They also asked that an American unit be sent over at once for the effect on Allied morale. Accordingly, the 1st Division was formed from existing organizations and shipped to France, where it landed June 26, 1917.

Major General John J. Pershing was appointed Commander in Chief of our expeditionary forces in May, 1917, and served continuously in this capacity until the war was ended and the Army demobilized. He landed in France June 13, 1917, accompanied by a small staff, and at once plunged into the preliminary work of organizing the American Expeditionary Forces.

After a thorough study of the situation, the War Department was cabled early in July that every effort should be made to have an American army in France of at least 1,000,000 men by the following May. General Pershing pointed out that this figure did not represent the total number required, and recommended that plans for the further development of our military forces should contemplate placing 3,000,000 soldiers in the field.

Decisions affecting the organization, size, and equipment of various units; methods of training to be followed; the priority in which troops and supplies of various classes should be sent; and the requirements of the army in special equipment and personnel were cabled to Washington. These cables formed the basis for the War Department's policies in mobilizing the great National Army

AMERICAN TROOPS LANDING AT ST. NAZAIRE, FRANCE

in 1917 and 1918, and enabled the authorities to proceed with their tasks in such a way as best to meet the needs of the army in France.

One decision which had a marked influence on our later operations was that all training should be conducted in preparation for offensive warfare in the open. "Trench warfare" was considered only as a special phase of military operations, which, if allowed to assume too great importance in our training, could not fail to inculcate a defensive rather than an aggressive spirit in the army.

Another important decision was that affecting the size of our combat division, which as organized for service in France was about twice the strength of any European division. This resulted in giving the American divisions a much greater driving power in the offensive than that possessed by any other.

General Pershing insisted from the start that our forces should constitute an American army under its own flag and its own commander. This policy, which later in the war proved to be a decisive factor in the defeat of Germany, was also a great governing factor in the work of organizing our expeditionary forces.

Agreements had to be reached very quickly with the Allies as to where our army should be located, in order that the necessary preparations for its development and use could be initiated. The British forces were so placed as to cover the channel ports, while the French armies were committed to the protection of Paris, and the transportation systems in these regions were heavily burdened. The necessity for the supply and movement of additional forces made it essential to choose a less crowded area where roads and railways were relatively free. The fact that there were few troops in Lorraine, and that rail facilities were available for transporting men and supplies from the French ports south of Le Havre to the Lorraine sector, largely influenced its choice as the American front.

First American Troops to Reach France, Marching in Paris, July 4, 1917

Another factor in the selection was the determination of the Commander in Chief to place our forces so that their employment would decisively affect the outcome of the war. The coal and iron mines near Metz, the essential railway systems in that vicinity, and the fortress itself, all made the area opposite the Lorraine front of paramount importance to Germany. This was the region which Germany could least afford to lose in the occupied territory of Belgium and France, for on its retention depended her ability to maintain her armies west of the Rhine. The American Army in Lorraine would, therefore, be admirably located to strike at the most vital point on the entire German front.

The insufficiency of ocean tonnage seriously retarded the transfer of our troops to France, and the question of increasing the number of vessels available was one of gravest concern to the Commander in Chief. Agreements were made by him with the British authorities at the beginning of 1918 for the use of a portion of their tonnage, but it was the crisis in March which brought out the amount of Allied shipping that made possible the remarkable increase of American arrivals to a maximum in one month of 300,000 men.

The formation of an American army was interrupted in the spring of 1918 by the succession of German drives which required the use of every available American and Allied division to avoid defeat. For this purpose General Pershing freely offered to General Foch every American man and gun in France.

When the American divisions had completed their part in preventing the catastrophe, and assisted in the resulting counteroffensives, their assembly into one force was resumed.

AMERICAN STORAGE YARD IN FRANCE ILLUMINATED FOR NIGHT WORK

Meanwhile a multitude of tasks had been accomplished in order that our forces could begin operations when the divisions became available. Staffs had been organized and trained; docks, railways, roads, depots, hospitals, bridges, and telegraph and telephone lines had been built; ammunition and supplies had been collected; intensive training schemes had been put into effect; and plans for our military operations had been studied and perfected.

AMERICAN AVIATION FIELD AT ISSOUDUN, FRANCE

The Commander in Chief, having foreseen that artillery, airplanes, and tanks necessary to a large force would not be entirely available from American sources for some time to come, had made arrangements with the Allies to meet the deficiencies, and he was thus enabled to complete the essential equipment of his forces.

Finally, after months of patient and unremitting labor, during which obstacles of every nature had been met and overcome, the American Army was ready for its first great independent effort on September 12, 1918.

MILITARY SITUATION IN JUNE, 1917, AND SUMMARY OF EVENTS TO MAY 28, 1918

The Allied situation in the early summer of 1917 had caused very serious depression and pessimism both in their armies and among their people.

Troops on Lighter Landing at Brest

The combined British and French superiority in men on the Western Front during late 1916 and early 1917 had proved insufficient to break down the German defense. In Italy, finances were in difficulties, and grave deficiencies existed in her armies, as the events of the fall of 1917 were to show.

The sacrifice by France of a large proportion of her manpower, and the presence of hostile armies on her soil for three years, had caused deep discouragement among her civil population.

Great Britain, except for morale, was scarcely better off than France. Much of her best blood had been poured out on the battle fields; and like her allies, she

Storage Dam at Savenay, France
Built by American engineers

had expended vast sums in the conflict. She retained command of the sea, but the submarine campaign was reducing food and other supplies to such an extent as to threaten her very existence.

German morale, on the other hand, was high. Practically all her offensives, with the exceptions of the Battle of the Marne in 1914 and the Verdun operations in 1916, had been crowned with great success. Her battle lines were on foreign territory, her own resources were untouched by hostile occupation, and wherever attacked by the Allies, she had inflicted severe losses upon them.

AMERICAN TROOPS AT NEUFCHÂTEAU MARCHING TO THE FRONT

At this time the Germans were frankly scornful of America's ability to exercise any real military influence in the war and they evidently believed it impossible for us to organize and transport any considerable force to France before the defeat of the Allies could be accomplished. Germany confidently expected that her armies would be victorious in 1918.

General Pershing's arrival in France, followed in two weeks by the 1st American Division, favorably affected French morale.

The Allied conception of the military situation in the summer of 1917, and of the action to be taken to meet it, are indicated in the con-

GERMAN ZEPPELIN FORCED DOWN AT BOURBONNE-LES-BAINS

clusions reached by the Commanders in Chief of the American, French, and Italian Armies, and by the Chiefs of Staff of the French and British Armies at a conference in Paris the last of July. The following is an extract from their report:

"General conclusions reached were: Necessity for adoption of purely defensive attitude on all secondary fronts and withdrawing surplus troops for duty on Western Front. By thus strengthening Western Front believed Allies could hold until American forces arrive in numbers sufficient to gain ascendency."

GENERAL PERSHING
American Commander in Chief

The Allies sought, however, to maintain the offensive on the Western Front during the latter part of 1917, as far as their strength would permit, in order to hinder Germany's conquest of Russia, and, if possible, prevent a German attack on Italy. The British captured Messines Ridge in June, and near Ypres undertook a series of operations which began on July 31 and lasted until November 10.

The French conducted limited attacks near Verdun and the Chemin des Dames. All of these Allied offensives were most carefully prepared, but only moderate gains were made. On the other hand, Russia finally collapsed in early September, and the Italians suffered a disastrous defeat in October, making it necessary to send French and British divisions to their assistance.

An analysis of these events left no doubt in the minds of Allied Commanders that Germany would soon resume the offensive in France, and in November she had actually begun the transfer of divisions from other fronts toward the west.

There were only 176,665 American troops in Europe on December 31, 1917, of which the 1st Division alone had served at the front. The British and French wished to hasten the appearance of American troops in the line if only for moral effect, and urged that our training be limited to the minimum deemed necessary for trench fighting. They also requested that our troops, in company and battalion units, be assigned to their organizations, pointing out the shortage of man power in their armies as sufficient reason. They contended that the Russian defection and the Italian defeat had so altered conditions for the worse that to withstand the expected German attacks every soldier in France should at once be made available.

The American Commander in Chief, however, held to his decision to assemble all Americans into one great independent organization. Any sort of permanent amalgamation with the Allied armies would irrevocably commit our fortunes to their hands, and there would have been no authority in France who could be held responsible to the American Government for the proper care, training, and employment of our men. Such a step would never have been approved by the American people or their troops. There was, moreover, no doubt that the effect of fresh, aggressive American units in the line would be far more depressing to the morale of the German armies and civil population than the mere presence of our soldiers in Allied regiments.

BRITISH OFFICER INSTRUCTING AMERICAN SOLDIERS IN USE OF MACHINE GUNS

The policy of eventually employing our forces as a single unit, steadfastly maintained in the face of tremendous pressure, unquestionably produced decisive results in the latter stages of the war. As a result of this policy, the American Army, welded into one powerful body, inspired by the traditions of its own country, confident in its leaders, and sure of its own ability in the offensive, was finally enabled to deliver the terrific blows toward Sedan which did so much to hasten the defeat of Germany.

AMERICAN TROOPS EN ROUTE TO THE FRONT

The Commander in Chief clearly realized, however, that the arrival of American units in the front line should be speeded up to the utmost. The 1st Division relieved a French division in a sector north of Toul by January 19. In February, the 26th entered the line with the French northeast of Soissons, and the 42d went in east of Lunéville. Of the 287,500 American troops in France on March

21, when the great German offensive started, the 1st, 2d, and 42d Divisions were in the trenches, while the 26th and 32d Divisions, the latter of which had never been at the front, were also available for service.

The German onslaught of March 21 against the British covered a front of about 50 miles, part of which had been recently taken over from the French. Within eight days the attacking troops, sweeping away all resistance, practically destroyed the British Fifth Army and penetrated to a maximum depth of about 40 miles. The Allies were greatly alarmed and many French divisions were hurriedly sent to aid the British. General Foch was charged with coordinating the action between the Allied armies, and a few days later was made Allied Commander in Chief. Fortunately the Germans were finally halted in front of Amiens, the loss of which would have practically separated the French and British Armies.

The Germans succeeded in cutting one railroad into Amiens, and in seriously impeding traffic on the other; they increased the frontage which the Allies were forced to hold with diminished numbers; they proved that they could break through highly organized defenses; they enormously increased the morale of their troops, and very seriously lowered that of the British and French. The Allies were still further depressed when on March 23 the shelling of Paris by a large gun from a distance of 70 miles was begun.

General Pershing, appreciating the gravity of the Allied position, and deferring for the moment the execution of his plan of forming an American army, went to General Foch while this first drive was in progress, and said:

MARSHAL FOCH
Allied Commander in Chief

"I have come to say to you that the American people would hold it a great honor for our troops were they engaged in the present battle. I ask it of you in my name and in that of the American people. There is at this moment no other question than that of fighting. Infantry, artillery, aviation—all that we have—are yours to dispose of as you will. Others are coming who will be as numerous as may be necessary. I have come to say to you that the American people would be proud to be engaged in the greatest battle of history."

LEARNING THE LANGUAGE

This message, expressing confident optimism and a real desire to cooperate, is a true indication of the splendid spirit which characterized the whole American Army in France throughout the war.

The battle near Amiens had scarcely died down when on April 9 the Germans broke through the British lines on a front of about 20 miles along the Lys River near Armentières. Their initial advantage was not well exploited, although they did succeed in capturing Mont Kemmel, which was then occupied by French troops, and advancing 12 miles into the British lines.

AMERICAN TROOPS ADVANCING TO ATTACK AT CANTIGNY

ENGINEERS MOVING FORWARD MATERIALS FOR ENTANGLEMENT

The 1st Division in April took over an exceedingly active portion of the line west of Montdidier. It captured Cantigny on May 28 in a brilliant operation and held that place in the face of violent and sustained counter-

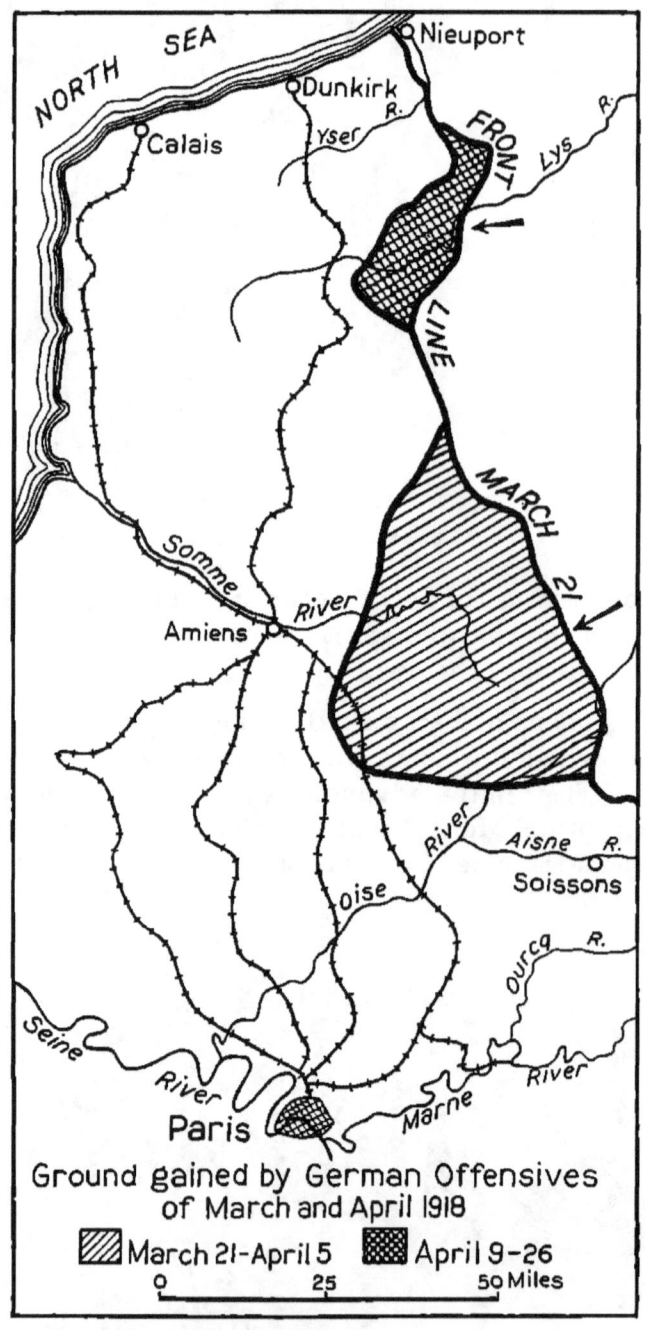

Ground gained by German Offensives of March and April 1918
March 21–April 5   April 9–26

attacks. Its creditable showing, both in offensive and defensive action, fully demonstrated the superb fighting qualities of the American soldiers, and gave the Allied population renewed hope of final victory.

CHAPTER II

OPERATIONS IN THE AISNE-MARNE AREA

The German plans at the beginning of 1918 contemplated the destruction of the British Army in the early spring, to be followed immediately by a crushing blow at the French. Their operations in Picardy and Flanders in March and April had failed to destroy the British, but in the meantime preparations to strike the French had been progressing.

GERMAN INFANTRY ADVANCING. CHEMIN DES DAMES, MAY, 1918. © G
(INSERT.) COMBAT GROUP WORKING ITS WAY FORWARD. © G

Although it appears that the German High Command was convinced that the complete defeat of the British could be accomplished in one more great offensive, the decision was made to launch first an attack against the French. The main reasons were that with the preparations already made it could be started with little delay and would use up the French reserve troops, thus preventing them from later being rushed to aid the British.

Soon after the German attack of April 9 had been stopped, the Allied Commanders felt sure that a new German offensive was about to take place, but were uncertain where it would fall. It was considered improbable that the line of the Aisne would be attacked, and many French troops had been shifted from that front to the British area. Consequently when the assault came on May 27 between Berry-au-Bac and Anizy-le-Château, it was a complete surprise.

The Germans carried the Chemin des Dames positions in the first dash and crossed the Aisne at noon on bridges the French had not destroyed. By evening they were south of the Vesle, and early on the 29th captured Soissons. They advanced rapidly toward the Marne, almost without resistance, and were in high hopes of taking Paris. The French people throughout the country were thrown into consternation, and the Government made preparations to move from the Capital.

Reserves were rushed to the front from every quarter to meet this new danger. The 2d Division was north of Paris en route to relieve the 1st near Montdidier, and the 3d Division was still in its training area. Both were turned over to the French by the American Commander in Chief, and hurried forward by forced marches and by every means of transportation.

GERMANS DEPLOYING ACROSS CHÂTEAU-THIERRY-SOISSONS ROAD, JUNE 1, 1918. © G

The motorized machine-gun units of the 3d Division reached **Château-Thierry** on May 31, where they gallantly assisted in preventing the Germans from crossing the Marne. The infantry of the division, as it came up, extended the line eastward to Jaulgonne and aided the French in holding the south bank of the river.

AMERICAN INFANTRY HURRYING FORWARD UNDER ARTILLERY FIRE. © B

The 2d Division, arriving by truck and on foot on June 1, immediately went into position. Facing northeast, with its center at **Lucy-le-Bocage,** the division established its lines across the main route to Paris, where it repulsed all attacks and effectively stopped the German advance in that direction. Thus assisted, the French were enabled to stem the onslaught, but the Germans had driven a great salient toward the Marne, roughly defined by the triangle Reims, Château-Thierry, and Soissons.

Beginning June 6, the 2d Division made a series of attacks in which it captured the exceedingly strong positions of **Belleau Wood, Bouresches,** and **Vaux.** The splendid conduct of the Americans in these severe engagements caused a new estimate of them to be published to the German Army by its High Command, which stated that "The moral effect of our own gun fire can not seriously impede the advance of the American Infantry."

When the Germans were stopped in early June, they had 40 divisions in the salient. Their failure to capture Reims had left these troops mainly dependent for supply on one railroad through Soissons. The American Commander in Chief saw that if the heights south of that city were seized and held by the Allies the Germans would be forced, on account of the impossibility of properly supplying their troops, to retire from the Marne, and the threat against Paris would be removed.

VAUX AFTER ITS CAPTURE BY 2D DIVISION, JULY 1, 1918

He proposed that this be done at once by American troops. The Allied Commander in Chief approved the idea, but felt that he was not yet ready to assume the offensive.

The German High Command realized the awkward situation of the troops in the salient, and at once undertook operations to relieve it. On June 9, two

GERMAN TROOPS DEFENDING AGAINST ALLIED COUNTERATTACK NORTH OF COMPIÈGNE, JUNE, 1918. © G

German armies made an attack southward toward Compiègne in an attempt to secure the railroad between that place and Soissons, but they were met by the French with great determination, and failed to reach their objective.

The next move of the Germans was to prepare for an offensive on both sides of Reims in the general direction of Epernay and Châlons. This attack, if successful, would not only secure another great trunk line for their use but would cut the French railway system connecting Paris and Verdun. A formidable force of three armies, powerfully supported by artillery, was assembled, and nothing was left undone to provide both the troops and material deemed necessary to break the French lines.

GERMAN TROOPS ATTACKING TOWARD COMPIÈGNE, JUNE, 1918
Note that this was taken from same spot as preceding picture. © G

GERMAN OFFENSIVE OF JULY 15, 1918
Trench mortar bombardment of Allied strongpoint. Attack with hand grenades about to start. © G

German heavy machine-gun unit advancing through captured village. © G

The Allies luckily secured precise information concerning the impending attack, which was set for the early morning of July 15. The French Fourth Army Commander's orders for the defense in the Champagne directed that the front be held only by thin lines, which were to retire before a strong attack, while the main resistance was to be made on an intermediate position 2 or 3 kilometers in the rear. As a result much of the German artillery fire of preparation on the front line fell on lightly occupied trenches.

GERMAN BATTERY FIRING NEAR MARNE RIVER. © G

During the night before the attack, the French subjected the enemy's assembly points to intense bombardments, causing heavy losses. The assaulting troops, however, advanced at the time set, but were heavily shelled upon reaching the French front-line trenches, and upon approaching the intermediate position were everywhere met with withering fire and fierce counterattacks.

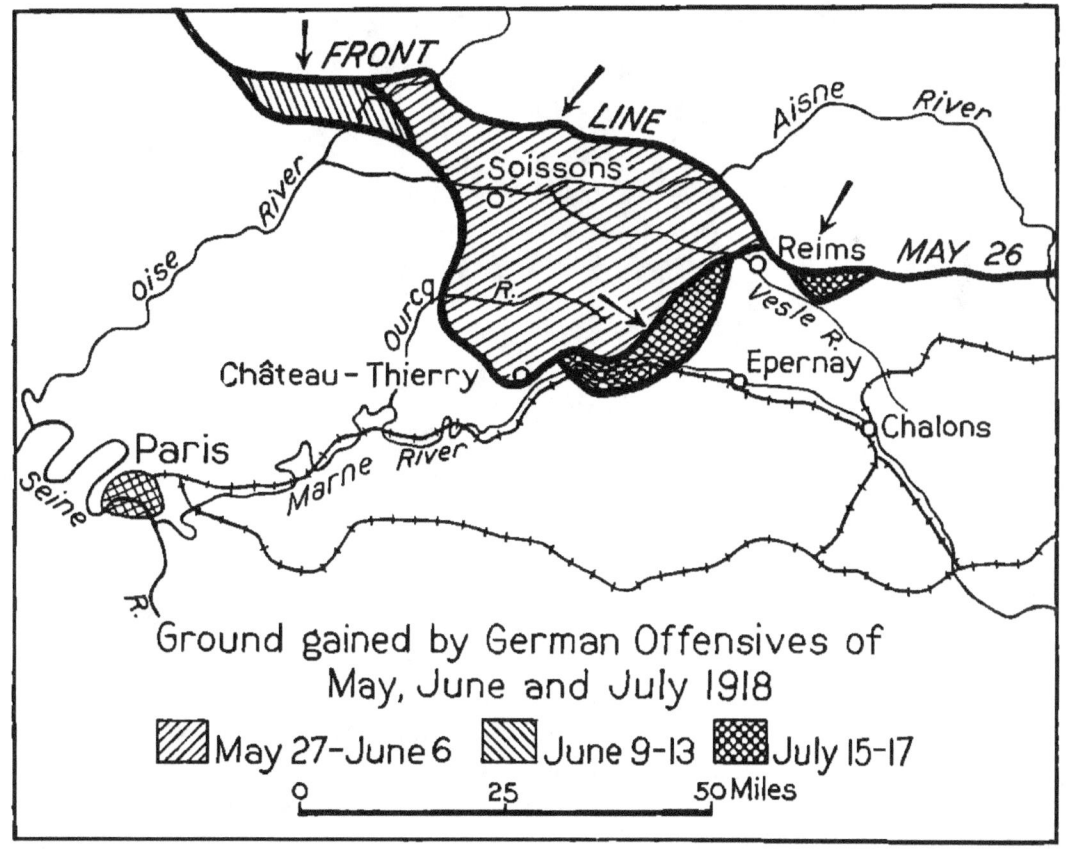

The offensive broke down all along the front, except southwest of Reims, where the Germans succeeded in crossing the Marne and made some progress on the north side of the river in the direction of Epernay. When the attack was stopped, about 10 German divisions remained south of the Marne in a small area between Mézy and Epernay.

The losses inflicted on the assaulting troops were very severe, and by the evening of July 17 Marshal Hindenburg had suspended the attacks all along the front. Not even the least of the results expected had been achieved, for instead of securing additional lines of supply in the salient, the situation was further complicated by crowding more troops into the already congested area.

In this defensive operation, American troops played an important part. The 42d Division, serving with the French Fourth Army, took part in the battle and fully measured up to the reputation the Americans were establishing as splendid fighting men. The 369th Infantry, 93d Division, was also with the Fourth Army at this time, although it was not engaged in the active fighting.

The 3d Division, still in line between **Jaulgonne** and **Château-Thierry,** was subjected to intense artillery fire and repeated assaults. The French, on its right, were compelled to give way, which made its task most difficult, but the

26TH DIVISION TROOPS IN LUCY-LE-BOCAGE, JULY 20, 1918

German troops that succeeded in crossing the Marne in its front were counter-attacked and driven back before noon of the 16th, except on the extreme right, where it was necessary for the front line to bend back to connect with the French.

Elements of the 28th Division were in the line with two French divisions on either side of the 3d, and some of its units became involved in extremely heavy fighting. The 26th, which had relieved the 2d Division, held a sector between Torcy and Vaux. The 2d and 4th Divisions were in reserve to the west of Château-Thierry and the 1st north of Paris.

In spite of this defeat the German leaders were apparently still determined to maintain the offensive, realizing without doubt that the American forces were rapidly increasing and that the victory must be won very quickly, or not at all. The troops recently repulsed were directed to be prepared to resume the attacks as quickly as practicable, and Ludendorf was sent northward to push preparations for an offensive against the British.

A graphic representation of the following operations is given in the map at the end of the chapter. It should be consulted in reading this narrative.

The Allied Commander in Chief, having decided to put into execution the American Commander in Chief's suggestion for the reduction of the salient, took immediate advantage of the check to the Germans and selected July 18 as the date for the effort.

Four French Armies, the Fifth, Ninth, Sixth, and Tenth, in line from right to left, were directed to take part, the Tenth Army, near **Soissons**, being designated to deliver the main attack. The spearhead of this army was the XX Corps, which was to capture the high ground south of Soissons. It consisted of the 1st and 2d American Divisions and the 1st Moroccan Division. The rela-

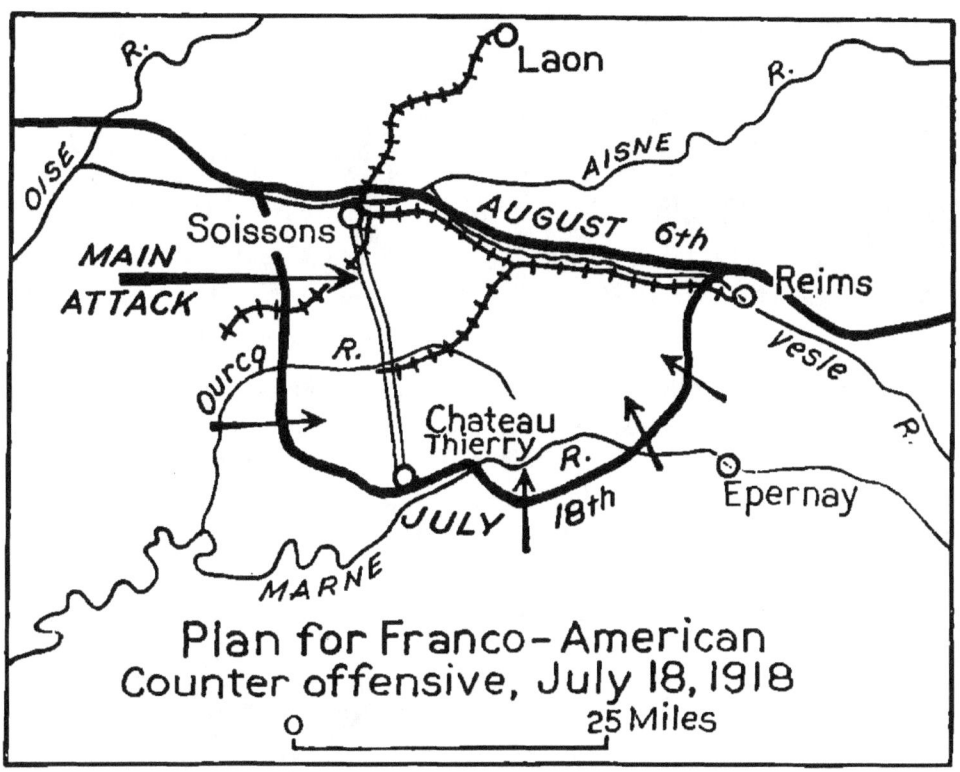

tive strength of these divisions was such that the troops of this corps were four-fifths American.

On the remainder of the front, the 3d Division was holding a sector east of Château-Thierry, parts of each brigade of the 4th were in line with a French corps, the 26th was in line west of Château-Thierry, and the 28th was in support, all under control of the French Sixth Army.

The necessary concentration of troops was carried out with the utmost secrecy, the 1st and 2d Divisions going into line only at the last minute. Some units of the 2d Division were forced to march all night, and then double-time over muddy roads in the dark in order to jump off with the barrage. The assault waves went over the top in the early morning and took the Germans completely by surprise.

The 1st and 2d Divisions, with the 1st Moroccan Division between them, advanced with characteristic dash and vigor. They quickly pierced the hostile front lines, overran the forward artillery positions, and took many prisoners. By 8 a. m. they were in possession of ground which practically assured the success of the whole battle.

To the right, elements of the 4th Division, attacking as a part of two French divisions in the Sixth Army, advanced vigorously and by nightfall had progressed about 2 miles. Still farther south the 26th Division captured the villages of **Belleau** and **Torcy**.

2D DIVISION TROOPS MOVING FORWARD, JULY 18, 1918

The situation of the Germans became most precarious, the principal point of danger being the thrust of the XX Corps south of Soissons. This had already rendered the salient untenable, but it was realized by the Germans that if they should lose the hills east of the city their main lines of communication in the region would be broken and many troops would be unable to escape.

They therefore hurriedly sent reserves to the vicinity of Soissons to hold fast at that important point, while a gradual withdrawal of the other troops in the

1ST DIVISION ARTILLERY CHANGING POSITION NEAR SOISSONS, JULY 19, 1918

salient could be effected. As a direct result of the success of the 1st and 2d American Divisions and the 1st Moroccan Division on the 18th, orders for the gradual retirement of the German troops were issued that evening.

Fresh German divisions were encountered by the 1st and 2d Divisions on the 19th, but in spite of bitter opposition throughout the day both made important gains. The 2d Division was relieved from the line that night, having driven the enemy back 6 miles, captured 3,000 prisoners, and suffered almost 5,000 casualties.

On the following day, the attention of the 1st Division was particularly directed toward **Berzy-le-Sec**. This town had originally been in the sector of an adjacent French division which, after several attempts, had failed to capture it, and the task was turned over to the Americans. The fighting here was waged with the greatest fury on both sides, and the village was taken and lost several times. The 1st Division definitely captured it on the 21st, and continued across the Soissons–Château-Thierry highway and railroad, which were the objectives of the French Tenth Army. The division was relieved on the night of July 22, after having suffered a loss of over 7,500 officers and men, and having written a most brilliant page in American military history.

While the struggle around Soissons had been going on, the American troops with the French Sixth Army had also continued forward. The units of the 4th Division gained an additional 2 miles before the last of its troops were relieved on the morning of the 21st; and the 26th Division drove the Germans through the **Bois de Bouresches** and beyond, after very hard fighting. Assisted part of the time by a brigade of the 28th, it continued the pursuit until the 24th of July,

ARTILLERY HORSES ASSEMBLED NEAR FRONT LINE TO MOVE BATTERY FORWARD, JULY 20, 1918

when it reached La Croix-Rouge Farm, having made an advance of 10 miles and suffered about 5,000 casualties during the offensive.

On July 21 the 3d Division crossed the Marne River and joined the general offensive, capturing **Mont St. Père** that day and **Jaulgonne** on the following day. Steadily pressing on, it took le **Charmel** on the 25th, after a bitter contest, and on the 28th crossed the Ourcq and seized **Ronchères**. When it was withdrawn from the line on the 30th its losses, including those in the defensive along the Marne, were, all told, over 6,000 officers and men.

The 42d Division, which relieved the 26th near La Croix-Rouge Farm, succeeded in crossing the Ourcq by July 28. Just north of that river it engaged in stubborn fighting, some points changing hands as many as four times. It persistently advanced until relieved on August 3 during its pursuit of the enemy toward the Vesle. The division had a casualty list of about 5,500.

The 32d Division, coming up from Belfort, entered the line July 29, on the right of the 28th Division, which had taken over a French sector the day before. These two divisions made some gains on July 30, after which the 28th Division passed into reserve, while the 32d continued in the offensive, covering both divisional fronts.

On the following day the 32d took **Cierges,** and on August 1, after three determined attacks, captured the important position of **les Jomblets,** holding it against sustained and vicious counterattacks. On August 2, it took up the pursuit of the Germans, who were obliged to fall back to their new prepared line north of the Vesle.

42D DIVISION MARCHING TO ATTACK NEAR BOUVARDES, JULY 24, 1918
The men are in gas masks, the road having been gassed by the Germans

The 4th, which had relieved the 42d division on August 3, and the 32d were now the only American divisions in line and they pushed forward side by side. During the next few days the 32d captured **Fismes,** on the south bank of the

32D DIVISION TROOPS RESTING NEAR MONT-ST.-MARTIN

Vesle, and the two divisions and one brigade of the 3d made desperate attempts to establish bridgeheads north of the river. It became apparent, however, that the Germans were holding the Vesle in force, and the drive as a continuous operation practically came to an end on August 6.

The results of this Second Battle of the Marne were most important. The threat against Paris had been removed, the initiative had been taken from the German armies, and their morale had been badly shaken while that of the Allies had risen by leaps and bounds.

The turning point in the four years' conflict came on July 18 when the result of the counteroffensive became assured by the achievements of the 1st and 2d American Divisions and the 1st Moroccan Division. From that time on the German High Command was forced to assume a defensive rôle and fought only to avert disaster.

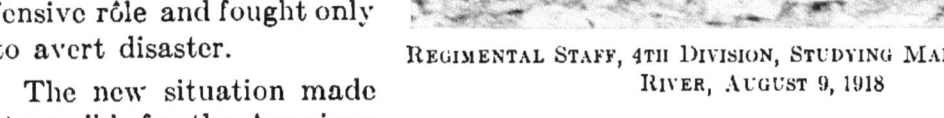

REGIMENTAL STAFF, 4TH DIVISION, STUDYING MAP NEAR VESLE RIVER, AUGUST 9, 1918

The new situation made it possible for the American Commander in Chief to take up again with General Foch the question of the formation of the American First Army. After several conferences an agreement was reached, and in August the assembly of divisions in the St. Mihiel region was begun.

AMERICAN UNIT ENTRAINING AT CHÂTEAU-THIERRY

In compliance with the desire of the Allied Commander in Chief to retain some American units with the Allied armies, the 28th and 77th Divisions were temporarily assigned sectors on the Vesle, while the 32d remained in the area as a reserve unit under orders of the French.

Immediately following the successful outcome of the Battle of the Marne, Allied operations were undertaken against those other portions of the front which the Germans had captured in their spring drives. The first, begun by the British on August 8 against the salient immediately west of Amiens, was highly successful and it dislodged the Germans, driving them in disorder to the rear.

Then followed the successful Oise-Aisne offensive begun by the French on August 18 north of the Vesle, in which the American 32d Division took part, operating in the Tenth Army.

This division attacked eastward during August 29, 30, and 31, captured the important position of **Juvigny** in a brilliant operation, and penetrated to a depth of 2½ miles. The division suffered heavy losses and was taken out of the line on September 1.

AMERICAN TROOPS EN ROUTE TO FRONT

The 28th and 77th Divisions, which had been on the Vesle since early in August, advanced on September 4 when the Germans began their retirement toward the Aisne. They encountered the new German line and initiated attacks against it which resulted in a number of local successes. The operations of these three divisions concluded the fighting by Americans in the Aisne-Marne region. The 28th was relieved on September 8 and the 77th on September 16, both divisions moving eastward to take part in the operations of the American First Army later in the month.

In the Marne Battle and up to the middle of September a total of 9 American divisions, the equivalent of 18 French divisions, gave indispensable aid to the Allies, suffering losses of over 30,000 men.

32D DIVISION TROOPS IN SUPPORT AT JUVIGNY

While some American units attracted particular attention due to their greater experience and the importance of the objectives captured by them, the gallant conduct of all in overcoming the persistent resistance of the enemy enhanced their reputation, especially among the French, from whom they received unstinted praise.

A TOUR OF THE AMERICAN BATTLE FIELDS IN THE AISNE-MARNE REGION

This tour as described begins and ends at Paris. It may be started, however, at any point en route, such as Château-Thierry, Fismes, or Soissons. The best idea of the American operations will be obtained if the tour is followed exactly as laid down.

The trip is a comparatively long one, but may be completed in one day if care is taken not to spend too much time at interesting points near the beginning of the tour. Lunch should be carried.

Soissons, where good hotel accommodations exist, is suggested as a stopping place for those who desire to spend more than one day in the area. From there one can conveniently reach the French battle fields along the Chemin des Dames, and those of the 32d American Division

BAND, 5TH MARINES

near Juvigny (see p. 62) and the 370th Infantry, 93d Division, near Vauxaillon (see p. 63) which are not on the described route.

PHOSPHORUS BOMB EXPLODING

EN ROUTE PARIS TO AISNE-MARNE AMERICAN CEMETERY NEAR BELLEAU

Leave by Pantin Gate, taking National Highway (N-3) toward Claye. *Through the suburbs of Paris, N-3 is indicated as rue de Paris.*

On passing through Livry, 12 kilometers from Pantin Gate, keep to right at road fork, following street-car tracks.

Monument to Marshal Gallieni
Erected by city of Paris

Claye, the next town, was the point nearest Paris reached by German patrols in 1914.

Keep on N–3 through Claye to Meaux. At kilometer post 37.5, between Claye and Meaux, is a monument to Marshal Gallieni, Military Governor of Paris in 1914.

Meaux was near the battle lines for several days during the First Battle of the Marne, in September, 1914. An interesting old cathedral is passed in town.

Keep on N–3 through Meaux, to la Ferté-sous-Jouarre.

On the left, at the entrance to this town, is a British monument to the Expeditionary Force of 1914. In this region the British struck back at the Germans after their memorable retreat from Mons.

Headquarters of the American First Army was organized here on August 10, 1918.

At first crossroad beyond British monument, turn left on rue de Condé; 600 meters farther on, turn left again, crossing Marne River, and continue on N–3 through Montreuil-aux-Lions. Note speedometer reading. Pass Paris Farm at crossroads about 4½ kilometers farther on. At the crossroads (at kilometer post 8.8) about 2 kilometers beyond Paris Farm, turn left on I. C. 32 toward Lucy-le-Bocage.

Just before arriving at Lucy-le-Bocage, at kilometer post 26, a culvert is crossed, at which medical officers of the United States Navy, attached to the Marine Brigade, 2d Division, maintained a dressing station. Many wounded were treated here and sent to the rear along the ditch to the left.

In Lucy-le-Bocage, take road along far side of church. 500 meters beyond village STOP without leaving automobile.

42D Division Troops Detraining, Trilport, East of Meaux, July, 1918

The narrative at the beginning of the chapter should be kept in mind and the map at the end consulted so that the various operations which took place in this region will be clearly understood.

The road straight ahead runs approximately north.

When the Germans broke through the Chemin des Dames front and were advancing rapidly during the last days of May, 1918, the 2d American Division, which included one brigade of Marines, was hurried to this locality. Arriving on June 1, it took up a battle position facing generally northeast, with its center resting near this point and its line extending across the main Château-Thierry–Paris highway, blocking the direct route to Paris.

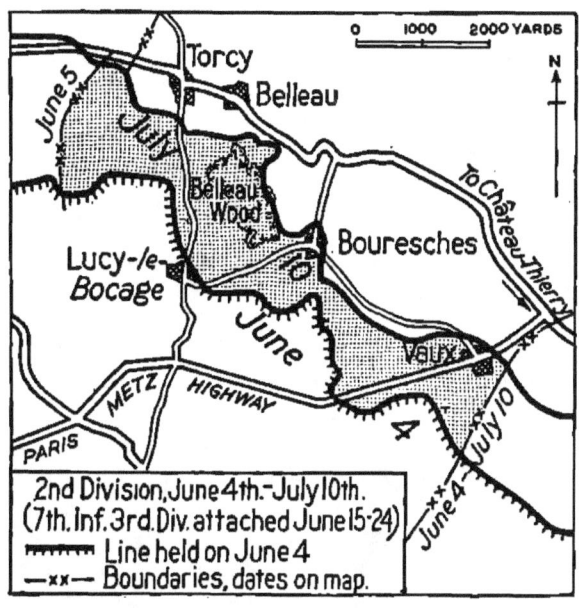

Immediately upon reaching its position, the 2d Division began digging trenches and otherwise preparing for defense, the Germans at the time being delayed by scattered French detachments about 2 miles away. The French withdrew on June 4, and that day the Germans began attacks against the American line, but were everywhere repulsed.

On June 6 the 2d Division began the series of severe local attacks which resulted in taking **Belleau Wood, Vaux,** and other important points in the German line.

The first attack against Belleau Wood, seen to the right front, was launched by the Marines from this vicinity on June 6. While advancing across the fields to the right of this road very heavy casualties were suffered.

Continue on. One kilometer beyond Lucy (at kilometer post 24.8) take road to left. 1½ kilometers farther on, on the left of the road, the wood is seen from which the 7th Infantry, 3d Division, then attached to the 2d Division, attacked to the north on June 20. It advanced parallel to this road and established its line ½ mile farther ahead.

TELEPHONE STATION, 2D DIVISION, NEAR BELLEAU WOOD

Turn right at next crossroads. This crossroads was the scene of many nocturnal clashes between American and German patrols.

Note the German cemetery on the right.

Upon entering **Aisne-Marne American Cemetery**, take road to right and STOP at top of hill beyond flagpole.

For information about this cemetery see Chapter X.

PANORAMA FROM STOP IN AISNE-MARNE AMERICAN CEMETERY

After the cemetery chapel is built, a good view of the surrounding battle fields may be had from its tower.

This point is on the most advanced line reached by the 2d Division. The series of attacks which carried that division forward to this line were invariably

(INSERT.) HUNTING LODGE IN WOOD
BELLEAU WOOD SOON AFTER ITS CAPTURE BY 2D DIVISION

accompanied by fighting of the most desperate character. The positions attacked, besides being naturally strong in themselves, were defended by an enemy whose morale had been raised to a high pitch by his previous successes of the year. **Belleau Wood**, at the edge of which the observer is standing, in particular lent itself admirably to defensive fighting on account of its rocky character and tangled undergrowth. This wood was the scene of bitter fighting, extending over a period of 21 days, and in honor of its capture by the Marine Brigade of the 2d Division the French changed its official name to the Bois de la Brigade de Marine. The 7th Infantry, 3d Division, and engineer troops of the 2d Division, acting as infantry, also assisted in the capture of part of it.

The splendid conduct of the 2d Division in taking Belleau Wood and other difficult positions along its front in spite of a casualty list of approximately 8,000 officers and men, was enthusiastically proclaimed by the French Army and people.

Face the flagpole, which is approximately north. The 2d Division was relieved here by the 26th Division on July 10, the division line at that time being about 4½ miles long, facing generally northeast, with its left flank approximately 1 mile northwest of here.

One brigade of the 26th Division, taking part in the general counteroffensive which began against the whole Marne salient, attacked from this vicinity July 18, and on that day captured **Belleau** village, seen beyond the flagpole, and **Torcy,**

PRISONERS CAPTURED AT BELLEAU WOOD

seen about ½ mile to the left of that place. It also took the hamlet of **Givry,** located just to the right of Belleau, but **Hill 193,** just beyond Givry, remained in the hands of the Germans. That hill was in the French sector, and for the next three days the hostile troops on it poured a deadly fire into the Americans near its southern base. Across the ravine to the right of Givry is **les Brusses Farm,** from which **Hill 190** slopes up gradually to the right.

On July 20 the 26th Division attacked along its entire front. Part of the attack advanced up the slopes of Hill 190, but heavy fire received from that position and Hill 193 brought it to a halt. That night the Germans withdrew to a new line, and on July 21 the 26th Division advanced eastward about 5 miles, meeting for the most part little opposition.

Face northwest. To the right of Torcy about 3 miles away is Courchamps and to the left of Torcy, about the same distance from here, is Hautevesnes, both captured by a French division in the general counteroffensive of July 18. The 8th Brigade, 4th American Division, fought as part of that French division until July 21. *See "Courchamps," page 65, for a brief description and map of the operations of this American unit.*

Belleau Wood is now owned by the Belleau Wood Memorial Association, an organization incorporated by the Congress of the United States. If time is available a walk into it is worth while, especially for those interested in the 2d Division or 7th Infantry (3d Division).

EN ROUTE AISNE-MARNE AMERICAN CEMETERY TO HILL 204

Turn right at cemetery gate. At road fork just beyond, take road to left. This road, from the point where it crosses the railroad to the top of the next hill, was in "no-man's-land" during the afternoon and evening of July 20. The Germans had dug in just to the left of it, and troops of the 26th Division were holding a line to the right.

MACHINE-GUN UNIT, 26TH DIVISION, GOING INTO ACTION NEAR BELLEAU, JULY 19, 1918

At kilometer post 21.9, by looking back a good view is obtained of the cemetery and Belleau Wood. In the valley, to the left of them, is **Bouresches,** captured by the 2d Division on June 6. The 26th Division advanced from there to this vicinity on July 20.

Near kilometer post 22.3, la Gonétrie Farm, captured by the 26th Division after hard fighting on July 20, is seen to the right.

The village of Vaux lies a short distance to the right of this road, but is not visible from it. On July 1 a terrific bombardment was placed on the town, after which the infantry and engineers of the 2d Division, in a brilliantly executed attack, captured the town with but few losses to themselves.

Cross highway (at kilometer post 25.8), taking road straight ahead. STOP at end of road at site selected for American monument on Hill 204.

Information concerning this monument is given in Chapter XI.

AMERICAN BATTERY NEAR VAUX, JULY, 1918

The large town, a mile away, lying on both sides of the Marne River, is **Château-Thierry,** and the direction to its church is east. Just beyond the church are the tree-covered ruins of the old château which gave the town its name.

During the critical days of late May and early June, 1918, when the German troops were advancing rapidly in this direction, the 3d Division was hurriedly moved up to the vicinity of Château-Thierry from its training area to the southeast.

The 7th Machine Gun Battalion of that division arrived on May 31, and took up a position along the south bank of the river to defend the bridges of Château-

Thierry which can be seen from here. A few men of this unit were sent to assist French detachments fighting north of the river. Some of them were still on that side when the main stone bridge was blown up on the night of June 1 to prevent the Germans from crossing. These men gallantly fought their way to the upper bridge where they and their French comrades, after a hand-to-hand conflict with German infantry, succeeded in recrossing the river.

The 7th and other machine-gun battalions of the 3d Division, assisted by French troops, repulsed with great losses several German attempts to cross the river.

On June 6 and 7 a French colonial division with the 30th Infantry (3d Division) attached, starting about 1½ miles south of this point, launched a series of attacks against **Hill 204,** and succeeded in reaching a line running through the woods due west from this point. The 4th Infantry of that division held part of this position for a few days later in June.

During the early part of July, elements of the 111th and 112th Infantry, 28th Division, assisted French units in local attacks which gained some ground on the east and west slopes of this hill.

As the result of the American and French attacks beginning July 18

MAIN BRIDGE AT CHÂTEAU-THIERRY, BLOWN UP TO PREVENT GERMANS FROM CROSSING
(INSERT.) MACHINE GUN, 3D DIVISION, IN POSITION AT CHÂTEAU-THIERRY, JUNE 1, 1918

against the west face of the Marne salient, the Germans withdrew from Hill 204 and Château-Thierry during the night of July 20–21.

The Marne valley, beyond Château-Thierry, part of which can be seen from here, was the scene of hard fighting by the 3d Division in July, 1918.

EN ROUTE HILL 204 TO MEZY

Return to main highway and turn right, continuing into Château-Thierry. On the left, just before reaching the bridge in Château-Thierry, there is the building of a Methodist institution, established by Americans as a war memorial, and a monument erected by the 3d American Division. The building contains a small museum of war relics.

Cross river and continue straight ahead to circular plaza; there take N–3, to left. For the next 8 kilometers the route follows along the south bank of the Marne, held by the 3d Division during part of June and July, 1918.

About 5 kilometers from Château-Thierry, Fossoy is seen to the left. This village was approximately the right (west) limit of the powerful German offensive of July 15.

A short distance farther on, at kilometer post 25.4, la Bretonnerie Farm and le Rû Chailly Farm may be seen in the valley ½ mile to the left (north) of the road. On the morning of July 15 troops of the 7th, and machine gunners of the 30th Infantry, 3d Division, at those points fought to the last man. Small groups of Germans then penetrated a short distance to the right (south) of this road opposite kilometer post 25.4, where they were either killed or captured by American troops.

In Crézancy, about 30 meters beyond kilometer post 27, turn left on G. C. 4. One kilometer farther on STOP at crossroads.

The road runs north for the next 400 yards. The village 800 yards away in that direction is **Mézy.** In the little valley ¾ mile to the right (east) of this observation point is **Surmelin Creek,** and on its other side, opposite this point, is the village of **Moulins.**

GERMAN SHELLS EXPLODING BESIDE AMERICAN OBSERVATION BALLOON NEAR CHÂTEAU-THIERRY

At the beginning of the German attack of July 15, their last great offensive of the war, the 3d Division held this side of the river from the ridge beyond Moulins to Château-Thierry. The 38th Infantry was to the right of Mézy, the 30th Infantry from Mézy to Rû Chailly Farm, and the 7th and 4th Infantry, in that order, farther on to the west.

Having learned that the long-expected offensive would begin shortly after midnight, the Allied and American artillery created great confusion in the German masses forming up for the attack, when at 11.45 p. m., July 14, every gun on

GERMAN ANTIBALLOON GUN IN ACTION. © G

the range of hills to the south blazed forth in a well-directed fire. At exactly 12.10 a. m. the German bombardment began, and about 2 a. m. the sudden increase of machine-gun and rifle fire along the river indicated that the Germans were launching their attack. A German regiment, trying to cross the river near Mézy, was badly cut up by the American artillery fire, and the hostile troops who reached the southern bank east of that town were forced back into the river. A few German units who crossed west of Mézy came up this hill about 10 a. m. in the face of rifle and machine-gun fire from Americans in the woods to the south. Nearly all who reached there were killed or captured, and later a few surrendered in this immediate vicinity.

During the 15th the Germans advanced in the French sector on the right of the 3d Division. This exposed the right of the American line on Moulins Ridge, and detachments there had to withstand several attacks from the east during

3D DIVISION TROOPS ENTRUCKING NEAR MOULINS

that day. On the 16th these detachments, being almost cut off from their neighboring units, were withdrawn to a line which had been established farther to the south.

At midnight July 15–16 the front line of the 3d Division ran generally east and west about 600 yards south of this point. The 111th Infantry, 28th Division, on July 16 relieved the 30th Infantry along this line and the following

GERMAN INFANTRY REGIMENT ON THE MARCH. © G

day reestablished the front along the river bank west of Mézy without much opposition.

By July 17 the German offensive had been definitely stopped on the whole front, and the next day the French and Americans began their great counteroffensive south of Soissons. As a result, the German High Command promptly ordered a withdrawal from the southern part of the salient, which began after dark on July 19. On July 21 the 4th Infantry crossed the river near Château-Thierry on footbridges built by the engineers of the division and occupied Mont St. Père, seen on the hillside ½ mile to the left of Mézy, in order to protect the crossing of the remainder of the division.

EN ROUTE MEZY TO HILL 192 NEAR COURMONT

Continue through Mézy. A few riflemen in position under the bridge seen over the railway tracks 100 yards west of the station in Mézy held out until late in the afternoon on July 15 and did deadly execution against Germans attempting to cross the tracks in their vicinity.

In the quarry, seen on the left of the road after passing the railway, a small group of Americans were engaged in the fighting during most of the first day of the attack.

PONTOON BRIDGE NEAR MÉZY BUILT BY 3D DIVISION

Upon approaching the bridge note the low ground between the river and the railway embankment. Reports of German officers indicate that their troops suffered heavy losses on these flats from the accurate rifle fire of the American troops.

During the night of July 21-22 most of the 3d Division crossed the river on temporary bridges near the present structure.

Take right-hand road after crossing bridge and keep to right, passing through Chartèves, captured by the 3d Division July 22. **One kilometer beyond Chartèves, near kilometer post 16.7,** by looking to the right across the river a view is obtained of Surmelin Creek valley. The Germans tried to advance from the river up that valley on July 15, but were unable to do so on account of the determined resistance of the Americans.

The next village is **Jaulgonne,** captured by the 3d Division July 22.

Just before entering Jaulgonne, at kilometer post 14.7, note the opposite river bank above the bridge. Two companies of the 28th Division there and two other companies a short distance farther up the river fought on July 15, while attached to the French. The Germans forced a crossing on both sides of and between these two groups and advanced past their flanks for a considerable distance, but were unable to cross the river in their immediate front. Later in the day, although cut off, elements of these companies fought their way back to the French line, which had been reestablished some distance to the rear.

Straight through Jaulgonne, keeping to left on G. C. 3. On July 22, troops of the 3d Division pushed up the ravine along this road to a point 2 miles beyond Jaulgonne, but fell back the same day. Again advancing on the 24th, they held their ground.

The next village is **le Charmel,** captured by the 3d Division on July 25, after extremely hard fighting.

STREET BARRICADE AT NORTHERN EDGE OF LE CHARMEL

Built by Germans in their retreat

LE CHARMEL CHÂTEAU

Just before reaching le Charmel, at kilometer post 11.4, take right-hand road, G. C. 14, through village. From this road fork le Charmel Château can be seen across the ravine 700 yards to the right front. This château was the scene of intense local fighting, the Germans holding it until July 27.

About 3.2 kilometers beyond le Charmel, at kilometer post 61, take G. C. 6 to left. At road intersection approximately 600 meters beyond keep straight ahead. A kilometer farther on STOP 30 meters before reaching crossroads.

To the left of this point near the top of the hill 1½ miles away are seen the large white buildings of **la Croix Blanche Farm.** The direction to that farm is west. The Ourcq River runs generally northwest in this region and passes about ½ mile northeast of here.

While some of the Germans were resisting the northward advance of the Americans and French between this point and the Marne, others were pre-

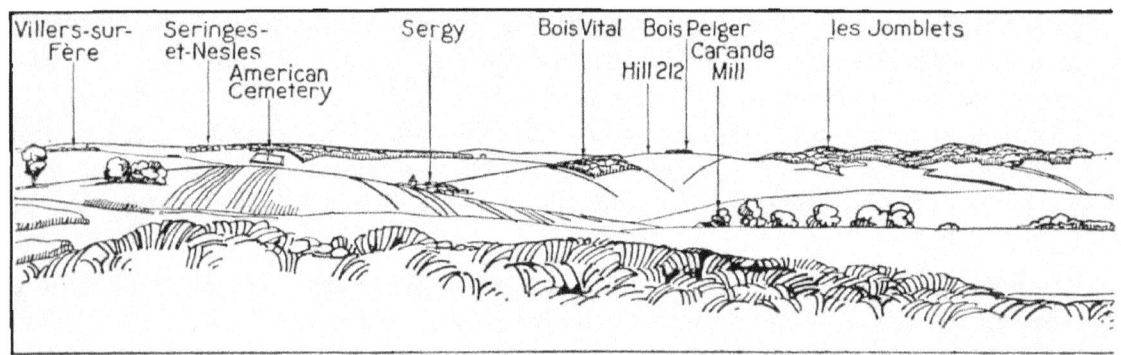

PANORAMA FROM STOP

paring a new and formidable line of defense along the hills seen on the opposite side of the Ourcq River.

That position, which was naturally strong in itself, had been well organized for defense by the time the American and French divisions arrived on this

CIERGES, FRANCE, AUGUST 3, 1918

American artillery fire concentrated here destroyed ammunition train shown in oval and prevented German narrow-gauge train shown in lower picture from being moved

side of the valley in the evening of July 27 and began a series of attacks which, in the course of the next five days, wrested it from the Germans.

If an observer had been standing at this point from July 28 to August 2, 1918, he would often have seen long, thin lines of khaki-clad American soldiers, bayonets glinting in the sunlight, advancing up the slopes seen on the other

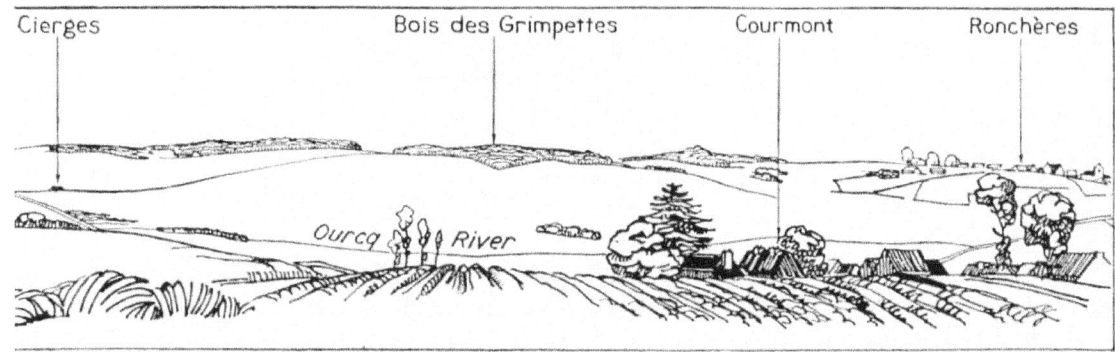

WEST OF COURMONT

side of the valley. These lines were preceded by bursts of smoke and showers of dirt as the barrage from their own artillery moved forward to prepare the way for them. Hostile fire took heavy toll from the advancing lines, and counter-attacks from the wooded heights sometimes forced the Americans back down the hills. Such setbacks, however, were but signals for new attacks, which were repeated until the entire position was finally won.

This observation point is on the line where, during the night July 27–28, the 28th Division relieved a French division which on the previous day had captured **Courmont,** the town seen 500 yards to the east.

The American divisions in line on this front on July 28 were the 3d, 28th, and 42d, in that order from right to left.

Ronchères, on the hillside a mile beyond Courmont, was captured by the 3d Division on July 28. The next day the division launched a brilliant though unsuccessful attack against the **Bois des Grimpettes,** seen on the hill a mile from here to the left of and beyond Courmont, which position had been attacked

INFANTRY IN POSITION NEAR THE OURCQ RIVER

by the 28th Division the previous day. On the night of July 29 the 3d Division, after having been continuously in line from early June and having participated creditably in three major operations, was relieved by the 32d Division.

On July 30 the 28th and 32d Divisions succeeded in taking the Bois des Grimpettes after a bitter hand-to-hand fight, and troops of the 28th Division occupied for a short time the outskirts of the village of **Cierges,** whose church tower barely shows above the hill, 500 yards to the left of the Bois des Grimpettes.

During the night July 30–31 the 32d Division took over the sector of the 28th Division, thus extending its front to the northwest as far as **Caranda Mill,** seen to the left of Cierges at the foot of this hill.

After July 30 the 32d and 42d Divisions, in line from right to left, were the American units remaining in the battle for the heights of the Ourcq.

The thin, ragged wood which covers the crest of the ridge to the right of and beyond Caranda Mill is **les Jomblets.** It lay in the German main line of defense and was an important strong point. On July 31 the 32d Division attacked, capturing Cierges and advancing its line a few hundred yards up the ridge upon which is located les Jomblets. The next day the division, after three determined attacks, captured les Jomblets and held it against several vicious counterattacks.

The village seen to the left of les Jomblets and directly to the north of here is **Sergy.** Looking northwest, between la Croix Blanche Farm and Sergy, are seen **Villers-sur-Fère,** which is on this side of the Ourcq, and **Seringes-et-Nesles,** on the other side. All of these were points in the path of the 42d Division's advance.

42D DIVISION ARTILLERY PASSING THROUGH SERGY, AUGUST 3, 1918

ROAD BEING REPAIRED BY ENGINEERS OF 26TH DIVISION

The 42d Division captured Villers-sur-Fère on the 27th, and as a result of courageous attacks gained a foothold north of the Ourcq all along its front on July 28. On the same day Sergy was entered, while ground was gained on the southwestern slope of **Hill 212,** seen to the right of the town, and on the ridge to the left of it. A German counterattack, late in the day of July 28, caused the 42d Division to withdraw from Sergy, but failed to shake the grasp of the Americans on the slopes on both sides of that town.

On July 29 two battalions of the 47th Infantry, 4th Division, were attached to the 42d Division, and with this additional strength further advances were made that day, both Sergy and Seringes-et-Nesles being captured.

The division continued to fight its way up the slopes between those two towns on July 30 and 31, and on August 1 it gained additional ground north of Sergy.

The evening of August 1 found both the 32d and 42d Divisions in secure possession of the line of crests north of the river, including Cierges, on the right, and Seringes-et-Nesles, on the left.

These successes, and those of the French farther to the west, caused the Germans to withdraw during the night of August 1–2 to their next prepared position at the Vesle River, 10 miles to the north. The pursuit, which was begun by the Americans and French on the morning of August 2, had to overcome many hostile machine-gun nests placed checkerboard fashion in the area between the Ourcq and the Vesle.

Advancing in the direction beyond les Jomblets, the 32d Division continued to the Vesle.

After pushing through the **Forêt de Nesles,** the large wooded area seen on the sky line between Sergy and Seringes-et-Nesles, the 42d was relieved by the 4th Division.

On the hillside to the right of Seringes-et-Nesles is seen the Oise-Aisne American Cemetery, which is the next stop.

4TH DIVISION TROOPS ON WAY TO FRONT, SERINGES-ET-NESLES, AUGUST 4, 1918

EN ROUTE HILL 192 TO OISE-AISNE AMERICAN CEMETERY

Continue toward Villers-sur-Fère. At kilometer post 60, 800 yards to the right on the hillside is seen the small triangular wood near which Corporal Sidney E. Manning, 167th Infantry, 42d Division, for an outstanding individual feat on July 28, won the Congressional Medal of Honor. Although severely wounded, Corporal Manning, leading 35 men, captured that wood in an attack during which he was again hit several times. He held the position against a counterattack largely because of his own accurate automatic rifle fire. He remained in charge until the position had been made secure, after which, suffering from nine wounds in all parts of the body, he dragged himself to shelter.

1½ kilometers farther on, Villers-sur-Fère is seen on the left of the road.

Cross Ourcq River, continue 300 meters and, without entering Fère-en-Tardenois, turn sharp right onto G. C. 2.

48   A TOUR OF THE AISNE-MARNE BATTLE FIELDS

The 42d Division sector is reentered at kilometer post 51. Its troops advanced on July 29 across this road from right to left.

STOP at cemetery and go to rear (north) end.

For their convenience, visitors wishing to visit a particular grave should obtain its location at the caretaker's house before entering the cemetery. For information about cemetery and the chapel to be erected at this point, see Chapter X.

Face cemetery gate, which is approximately south. The ridge beyond the caretaker's house was the scene of several assaults by troops of the 42d Division,

British Armored Motor Cars South of Villers-sur-Fère

German Dressing Station Being Used by 42d Division Soon After Its Capture

assisted by two battalions of the 4th Division, between July 28 and August 1. Attacking from the Ourcq valley to the right of and beyond that hill, the Americans gained the crest a number of times, but withdrew because of heavy fire from the Germans in the woods 1½ miles to the southeast. It was captured and held on August 2.

The little wood which lies to the right front (southwest) 400 yards beyond the cemetery is **Bois Colas,** which was almost completely destroyed by artillery fire. This wood, literally bristling with machine guns, was captured on July 29, in a brilliant attack by the 42d Division. From Bois Colas, the Americans looked out upon the Germans who held **Meurcy Farm,** seen beyond the south end of the cemetery, and the tiny **Bois Brulé,** which covered the ground where the caretaker's house now stands. After a very heavy bombardment of these places, in which smoke and thermite shells were used, troops of the 42d Division captured them on July 31.

ROOSEVELT MEMORIAL FOUNTAIN AT CHAMERY

QUENTIN ROOSEVELT'S GRAVE

The large wood to the north and northeast (rear) of the cemetery is the Forêt de Nesles through which the 42d Division advanced on August 2.

EN ROUTE OISE-AISNE AMERICAN CEMETERY TO NEAR FISMES

Continue on main road. The next village is **Nesles,** taken by the 42d Division on August 2. The ruined château seen on the left before entering it was built about 1230 A. D.

At kilometer post 55.4 is entered the sector over which the 32d Division advanced on August 2.

During an aerial combat on July 14, 1918, Lieutenant Quentin Roosevelt, son of the former President of the United States, was shot down near **Chamery.** The

CAMOUFLAGED ROAD JUST NORTH OF DRAVEGNY
Road followed on tour

Germans buried him where he fell, and marked the grave with the wheels of his plane and a rough cross bearing the inscription "Roosevelt, American Aviator." On August 2 the grave was found by advancing troops of the 32d Division, who held appropriate services and built a fence around the spot. Since that time it has been more permanently marked.

To visit the grave turn right at crossroads at kilometer post 58.4. At Chamery take first road to left (impassable in wet weather) and go 750 meters to grave. Total length of detour, 4 kilometers.

OBSERVATION BALLOON TRUCKS, COULONGES, AUGUST 4, 1918

At kilometer post 58.4, turn left on G. C. 14, passing through Coulonges and Cohan, both captured by the 32d Division on August 2.

The right boundary of the 32d Division in its advance was just to the right of this road between Coulonges and Cohan.

The next village is **Dravegny,** captured by that division the same day. **In Dravegny, turn left at church, then right at communal monument.**

After passing over the hill beyond Dravegny, the town seen across the valley to the front is **Chéry-Chartreuve.** The 4th Division, after relieving part of the 42d during the early morning of August 3 on the north edge of the Forêt de Nesles, advanced that day beyond Chéry-Chartreuve.

At communal mounment near entrance to Chéry-Chartreuve, take G. C. 21 to right. Note speedometer reading at kilometer post 9. Continue about 3 kilometers and STOP on hill overlooking valley.

AMERICAN BATTERY POSITION NEAR CHÉRY-CHARTREUVE

In the valley lies the ancient town of **Fismes,** mentioned by Julius Caesar in his Commentaries. The direction to its church is northeast. In the foreground is the valley of the tiny Ardre River, while that of the Vesle is beyond Fismes. Adjoining and slightly to the left of Fismes, but beyond the Vesle River, is **Fismette.** Both places were badly damaged by shell fire during the war.

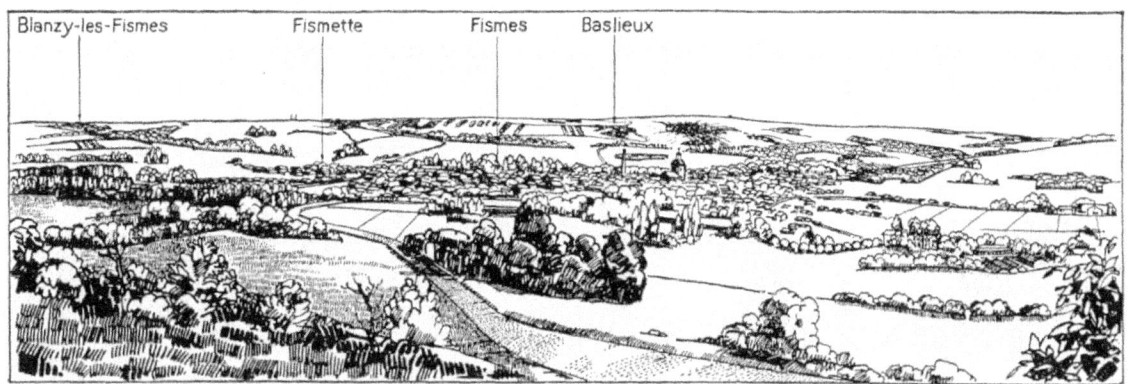

PANORAMA FROM STOP NEAR FISMES

The Germans fought desperately to hold Fismes, but the 32d Division, attacking from this hill on August 4, gained a foothold in its southern edge. Continuous house-to-house fighting took place until August 6, when the Americans completely occupied the town.

On August 6 the 6th Brigade, 3d Division, relieved a French unit along the Vesle River to the east (right) of Fismes, and remained in that sector (not visible from this point) until the night of August 10–11. On August 7, troops of this brigade attacked for the purpose of establishing a bridgehead north of the river. Some soldiers succeeded in crossing, but were withdrawn later in the day.

BRIDGE ACROSS VESLE RIVER AT FISMES

The 28th Division took over the sector of the 32d along the Vesle on August 7 and launched an unsuccessful attack upon Fismette the same day. On August 8, after a heavy bombardment, it again attacked, capturing and holding the southern and eastern portions. Bitter fighting in the streets continued until August 22, when the rest of the town was finally captured.

Five days later the Germans inclosed Fismette in a heavy barrage and attacked it in force, capturing or killing the Americans holding the place except for a few who escaped by swimming the river.

On August 13 the 77th Division, which on the previous day had relieved the 4th along the Vesle farther west, extended its front to the western (left) edge of Fismes, taking over part of the sector of the 28th. The same day the latter division extended its front about 2 miles farther east, relieving a French unit.

The French Tenth Army, to which was attached the 32d American Division, began the Oise-Aisne offensive north of Soissons on August 18 and exerted continuous pressure on the German lines in that region. As a result, on the night of September 3–4 the Germans in this vicinity withdrew from the Vesle toward the Aisne River, covering the movement with rear guards composed mostly of machine-gun units.

On September 4 the 28th and 77th Divisions started northward in pursuit, and by September 6 the 28th had pushed its front about a mile north of **Baslieux**, seen in the little ravine 3 miles away straight beyond the large chimney in Fismes.

FISMETTE, SCENE OF HARD FIGHTING BY 28TH DIVISION

There the division again faced a prepared German line. It was relieved on September 8 by a French division.

After capturing **Blanzy-lès-Fismes** and **Perles,** north of the river, seen in that order to the left of Fismette, the 77th Division's advance was stopped on September 6, south of the Aisne River, 6 miles to the north. From that day until September 16, when it was relieved by an Italian division, of which there were two serving on the Western Front, its line remained approximately in the same place.

ENGINEERS EXPLODING MINE TRAP LEFT BY GERMANS IN DUG-OUT NEAR BLANZY, SEPTEMBER 5, 1918

EN ROUTE NEAR FISMES TO NEAR BAZOCHES

Continue. Upon arriving at left (west) end of Fismes, turn left on National Highway (N-31).

The State of Pennsylvania has built a memorial bridge over the Vesle between Fismes and Fismette. To visit it, which can be done in a few minutes, turn right upon arriving at N-31, go 500 meters to open plaza, and turn left to bridge. Return to plaza and turn west (right) on N-31.

The American front line for nearly a month included the last houses on the western edge of Fismes.

Château du Diable is seen on the left 500 meters beyond the railway crossing. Troops of the 4th, 28th, 32d, and 77th Divisions, who engaged in many hot fights around that château, agree that the place was well named. It was captured on August 10 by the 28th Division.

A 4th Division monument is seen on the right, **400 meters beyond Château du Diable. Note speedometer reading.**

About a kilometer beyond the monument STOP.

From this point a good view is obtained of the sector south of the river held by the 4th and later the 77th Division.

Lying just to the left of this highway, 500 yards farther along is **la Haute Maison,** and the direction to it is west. Adjoining that village, in the valley to the left (south) of it, is **Bazoches.** Opposite Bazoches, on the hillside beyond the Vesle River is **St. Thibaut.** In the valley 1½ miles southeast of here is **Villesavoye.**

The 4th Division arrived on the hills south of the Vesle on August 4 and captured St. Thibaut and Villesavoye. On August 5 the division began attacks to establish a bridgehead on this side of

4TH DIVISION MONUMENT NEAR BAZOCHES

the river, and on that day a few troops entered Bazoches but later withdrew to the south bank. Next day part of the division forced a crossing near Villesavoye, reaching this highway about ½ mile east of here. That line was

ROLLING KITCHEN IN OPERATION SOUTH OF VESLE RIVER

maintained in spite of strong counterattacks until August 8, when it was withdrawn to the railroad embankment near the river.

From August 7 to 9 the division launched several unsuccessful attacks against Bazoches. Intense fire prevented the building of bridges, and with the exception of a few who crossed on fallen trees, the men had to swim and wade the river. Some became entangled in coils of wire which the Germans had placed in the water and were drowned.

On the morning of August 11 the Germans suffered heavy losses in an attempt to recapture St. Thibaut.

77TH DIVISION ARTILLERY ENTERING ST. THIBAUT, AUGUST, 1918

The 77th Division, on August 12, relieved the 4th, and in addition took over part of the French sector west of St. Thibaut. For the next two weeks this sector, like others along the front where troops of neither side were trying to advance, was comparatively quiet except for activities carried on at night.

During the daytime the troops on both sides of the river were forced to remain well concealed to escape the vigilance of snipers and hostile observers searching for favorable artillery targets. After nightfall, however, the hillsides swarmed with men busily strengthening their positions, while patrols from each side, trying to discover the dispositions and intentions of the other, frequently clashed along the banks of the river and engaged in small but desperate battles in the dark.

FRENCH TANK WITH AMERICAN FORCES IN THE VICINITY OF SOISSONS

On August 27, troops of the 77th Division, attacking Bazoches from the southwest, succeeded in entering the village but were forced back to their original line by a counterattack.

On September 4 the 77th Division advanced across the Vesle and over the hills to the north in pursuit of the Germans, who had withdrawn during the previous night.

Entrances to some shelters used by the Germans may be seen by descending the bank on the north side of the road.

EN ROUTE NEAR BAZOCHES TO HILL 168

Continue toward Soissons, on this highway.

Keep to right after crossing railroad tracks beyond Braine.

Soissons has held a prominent place in French military history for many centuries. A museum containing relics of the Roman epoch is located here.

The American battle fields at Juvigny and near Pinon are reached via N-37, the highway from Soissons to St. Quentin.

STREET IN SOISSONS

Upon entering Soissons keep on rue de Reims to Place de la République. Go straight through it, taking rue Thiers for one block toward St. Jean des Vignes (church with two spires). Then turn left into rue Carnot and, after crossing wide boulevard a block farther on, take first turn to right. Continue to railroad, turning sharp left across tracks and follow Paris–Maubeuge Highway (N-2). Four kilometers from the railroad crossing, a cemetery containing French, British, and German graves is seen to the right.

6 kilometers beyond Soissons, STOP at kilometer post 20.8 on Hill 168.

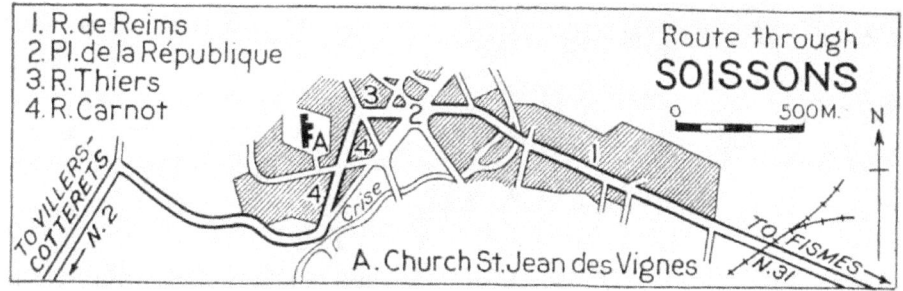

The following description may also be used from the top of the hill 400 yards to the left, which point affords a better view of the area than does this observation point. From there Berzy-le-Sec and other points to the east and south can be seen.

The tour has now entered the region in which the 1st and 2d Divisions fought during the great counteroffensive which began on July 18. The success of the whole operation depended primarily upon a rapid and deep advance in the area just south of Soissons, and the task assigned these two American divisions was therefore a most important one.

Both reached their position after a long and arduous night march in a heavy rain, over roads congested with traffic, and formed up for attack facing east, with the 2d Division on the south and the 1st French Moroccan Division between the two American divisions. Some of the units of the 2d Division reached the jump-off line barely in time to follow the rolling barrage preceding the attack.

It is difficult now to imagine these fields as the scene of the mighty battle which was fought here in July, 1918. The Germans had dug no elaborate systems

ADVANCED FIRST AID STATION, 1ST DIVISION, NEAR MISSY-AUX-BOIS, JULY 20, 1918

of trenches in this area, but every little rise in the ground had its group of individual rifle pits and nests of machine guns. The buildings of the farms and villages, largely of stone construction, afforded admirable protection for the Germans, and each constituted a strong-point which could be taken only after the most determined kind of fighting. The fields were covered with wheat, breast high, ready for the harvest. Along the farm roads and hidden by the tall grain were batteries of German artillery.

The group of buildings about a mile farther down this road is **Cravançon Farm** (Croix de Fer), and the direction to it is southwest. The village ½ mile to the west, at the head of **Missy Ravine,** is Missy-aux-Bois. On the far rim of the ravine, to the right of Missy, is **le Mont d'Arly.** The church steeple which shows above the horizon straight beyond the left of Missy is in **Dommiers.**

CAPTURED GERMAN FIELD GUN NEAR MISSY-AUX-BOIS
Gun was reversed and used against Germans until end of operation

That village, on the morning of July 18, was just within the German front line and near the southern flank of the 1st Division.

The attack started at 4.35 a. m., July 18, and the German forward positions in front of the American divisions were promptly overrun. By the time troops of the 1st Division reached Cravançon Farm and Missy Ravine, about 8 a. m., after the capture of le Mont d'Arly in a stubborn fight, the resistance had greatly increased. The ravine and village of Missy were full of hostile troops who had taken shelter from the American artillery fire. The assaulting units at once pushed on into the swampy bottom of the ravine, and while floundering across it, in some places hip deep in mire, they were fired upon point-blank by light artillery which the Germans had placed along this edge of the ravine. These guns, most of which were in the French sector to the north, destroyed a majority of the tanks which accompanied the left assault regiment of the 1st Division. After a terrible combat the Germans in the ravine were killed or captured, and the Americans emerged and overpowered the guns which had wrought so much damage.

1st Division Artillery in Position near Missy Ravine, July 18, 1918

After the front lines of the division had reached this side of the ravine it is reported that a large hostile force came out of a cave on the hillside near le Mont d'Arly and formed up to attack the American troops in rear, but were driven back into the cave by a support company of the 1st Division. Attempts to bomb them out failed, but late in the afternoon an officer came out of the cave, waving a white flag, and surrendered his entire command, consisting of 24 officers and 580 men.

During the fighting for the possession of Missy Ravine, other troops of the 1st Division captured Cravançon Farm, while the artillery placed a heavy standing barrage upon the German positions along this highway and on **Hill 168**, sloping up to the east from here. When the barrage moved forward again, the infantry continued the attack, meeting desperate resistance. The southern slope of Hill 168 was reached and held by troops in that part of the division sector. Those who advanced from Missy Ravine toward this point encountered a terrible fire from the top of the hill and from points farther north. A few Americans reached

1st Division Artillery in Position near Ploisy, July 20, 1918

the highway near here but not in sufficient numbers to hold the position. Early on the morning of July 19 another attack from the ravine reached and held this highway. At 5.30 o'clock in the afternoon the 1st Division pushed forward from this road and, supported by artillery and tanks, took all of Hill 168 from the Germans. Before nightfall the Americans advanced more than a mile farther east, capturing **Ploisy,** not visible from this point.

During the attacks upon this hill on July 19 a number of tanks were put out of action in the wheat fields to the left (east) of the highway by German shells.

58   A TOUR OF THE AISNE-MARNE BATTLE FIELDS

The 1st Division continued its attacks on July 20, and on the 21st captured Berzy-le-Sec in some extremely bitter fighting. It reached Buzancy on the latter date, cutting the Soissons—Château-Thierry highway, thereby seriously crippling the German communication system within the salient. The division, after its remarkable demonstration of fighting ability in this attack, was relieved from the line on the night of July 22–23.

Troops of 1st Division Digging in Near Chaudun

Reserves of 1st Division Going Forward

EN ROUTE HILL 168 TO NEAR BEAUREPAIRE FARM

Continue on this highway, turning left at Cravançon Farm (just before arriving at kilometer post 19), toward Chaudun.

The right boundary of the 1st Division lay 200 yards to the left of and parallel to this road. Chaudun was in the sector of the 1st Moroccan Division.

Turn sharply right at entrance to Chaudun and then straight through onto I. C. 30.

At kilometer post 3.8 **Maison Neuve Farm,** captured by the 2d Division on July 18, is passed. This farm was near the boundary between the 2d Division and the Moroccans.

STOP at kilometer post 2.5.

Beaurepaire Farm is 500 yards farther down this road. The group of buildings, a mile to the right, is **Verte-Feuille Farm,** and the direction to it is west.

Attacking from a line a mile west of Verte-Feuille Farm, the 2d Division advanced eastward, toward this vicinity.

LARGE CAVE SOUTH OF SOISSONS
Many similar caves are in this vicinity

BEAUREPAIRE FARM, JULY 19, 1918

Shortly after the attack began on the morning of July 18, French tanks which accompanied the Americans circled around Verte-Feuille Farm, and the Marines came out of the woods, overpowering the German garrison at that place after a sharp encounter.

Beaurepaire Farm, which the Germans had converted into a veritable fortress, was captured early on the morning of July 18, in a fierce hand-to-hand fight by the 3d Brigade (9th and 23d Infantry) of the 2d Division.

VERTE-FEUILLE FARM, JULY 19, 1918

Batteries of German artillery in the wheat fields around this point fired point-blank at the Americans as they advanced from the woods toward Beaurepaire Farm, and before they

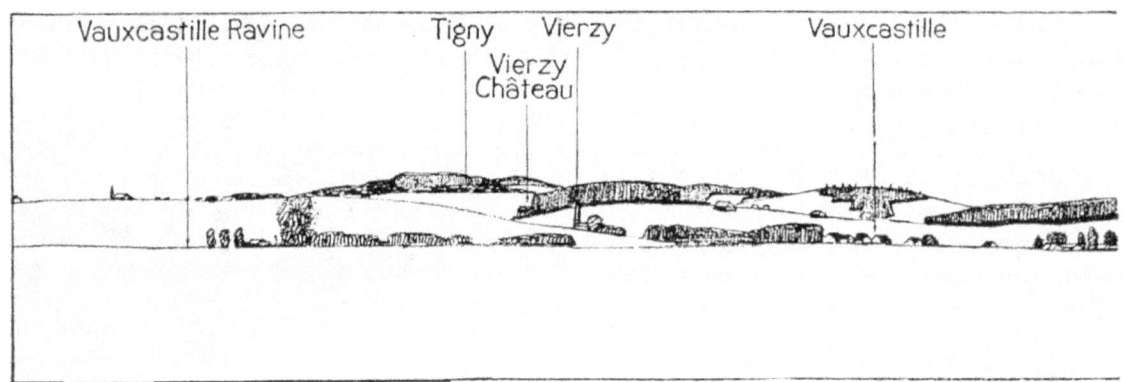

PANORAMA FROM STOP

could be silenced these guns had destroyed many of the tanks accompanying the attack.

Adding to the confusion caused by the terrific bombardments, low-flying airplanes, both Allied and German, machine-gunned and bombed the troops of their opponents.

The Americans crawled or darted through the wheat, steadily advancing against the Germans, who were often unseen until the infantry virtually stumbled on them or the rapidly moving tanks had driven them into the open.

To the southeast, a mile away is **Vauxcastille** and running toward the left from it is a deep wooded ravine. Attacking across this road in the early morning of

RAVINE AND RIDGE NEAR VIERZY, JULY, 1918

the first day of the offensive, troops of the 2d Division swarmed into that ravine, where a desperate conflict raged until about noon, when the Germans were driven beyond it. **Vierzy,** of which only a tall red chimney is visible to the left of and beyond Vauxcastille, was reached by a few Americans during the morning, but they were forced back to the ravine.

A large number of Germans who had been surrounded at Vauxcastille during the morning took refuge in the caves in that vicinity. They received a message dropped from a German airplane directing them to retire to Vierzy, and in attempting to fight their way to that place were captured.

Early in the evening the 2d Division attacked from the vicinity of Vauxcastille, and after a terrific fight in Vierzy, where a large number of Germans were made prisoners, pushed on by midnight to a line a mile beyond the latter village.

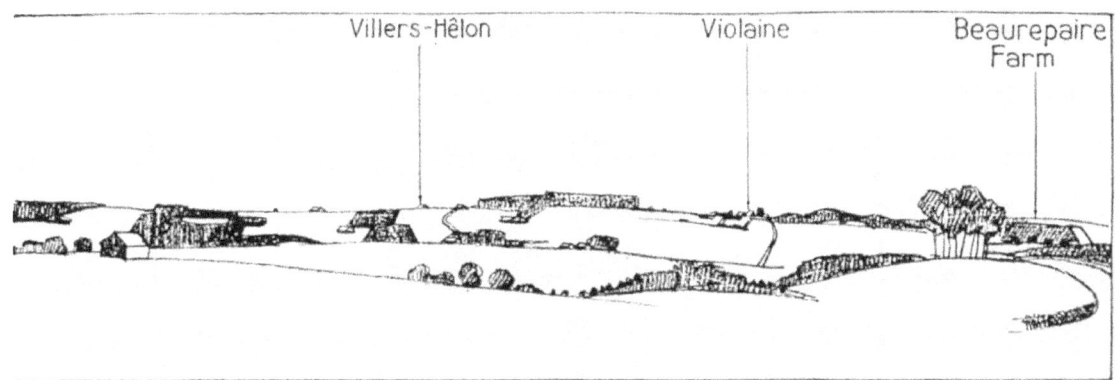

NEAR BEAUREPAIRE FARM

Spirited counterattacks were launched against the 2d Division during the early morning hours of July 19, but were unsuccessful. The Germans were steadily pushed back until by 10 a. m. the division was on a line 400 yards this side (west) of **Tigny**, which is on the hillside 4 miles from here, beyond Vierzy. The 2d Division was relieved there by a French division during the night of July 19–20 after brilliantly accomplishing its mission.

CAPTURED WEAPONS IN PUBLIC SQUARE
AT VILLERS-COTTERETS, JULY 27, 1918

EN ROUTE NEAR BEAUREPAIRE FARM TO PARIS

Those desiring to complete a loop in this area or who started the tour at a place other than Paris or Belleau should proceed to the Belleau Cemetery either by way of Vierzy, Tigny, and Château-Thierry or via Longpont and Neuilly-St. Front. Both routes are shown on the map at the end of the chapter. The route through Château-Thierry is easier to follow and will take less time. The other is slightly more pic-

turesque and goes through an area where elements of the 4th Division fought. For information concerning this fighting and certain of the villages passed through, see the list of places in this chapter.

From this point **continue on this road 2 kilometers beyond Beaurepaire Farm, turn sharply right at first road fork on to G. C. 17 and then left on Paris–Maubeuge Highway (N–2) at Verte-Feuille Farm.**

One and a half kilometers beyond Verte-Feuille Farm the National Highway (N–2) crosses, at right angles, a secondary road running through the woods, which is approximately on the jump-off line of the 2d Division on July 18.

At Villers-Cotterets, turn left immediately after crossing railroad tracks at the near end of town, and turn left again at the Place Dumas. Recross railroad tracks and continue on N–36 to La Ferté Milon and Meaux, thence via Claye to Paris.

As far as Meaux the route leads through an area which was overrun by the Germans prior to the First Battle of the Marne in September, 1914. As a result of that battle the invading forces were driven back north of Soissons.

32D DIVISION AT JUVIGNY, AUGUST 28 TO SEPTEMBER 2, 1918

The 32d Division, after its relief on the Vesle River on August 7, was assigned to the French Tenth Army, to assist in an offensive which started on August 18 and was designed to exploit the earlier gains around Soissons. It entered the line just west of **Juvigny** on August 28, and that day launched local attacks which made some gains in the face of very heavy fire.

FRENCH TANKS WITH 32D DIVISION AT JUVIGNY

The following day a general advance was begun by the whole army, but the resistance encountered was desperate in the extreme, and only minor gains were made. The numerous caves in the region provided ideal shelters for the defending troops during artillery bombardments, and the attack demonstrated that the town of Juvigny was very strongly held.

On August 30 the 32d Division, flanking the town from the south, captured it in a skillful attack, after some vicious street fighting. This success placed the Americans in a small salient protruding into the German lines.

The attacks were resumed on the 31st, during which the American artillery barrage, instead of progressing steadily on after leaving the hostile forward positions, as was customary, suddenly shifted back, this maneuver being repeated several times. The Germans who left their caves to man their trenches and machine-gun nests after the barrage first moved on were caught when it returned and suffered heavy losses.

By the end of the day the 32d Division, by hard fighting, had reached the important Soissons–St. Quentin road at a point northwest of **Terny-Sorny**. Its advance of about 3 miles into the hostile lines greatly assisted in compelling the Germans to begin their general retreat on September 3 to the new line along the Aisne.

The division passed into reserve September 2 and began preparations to move eastward to join the American First Army.

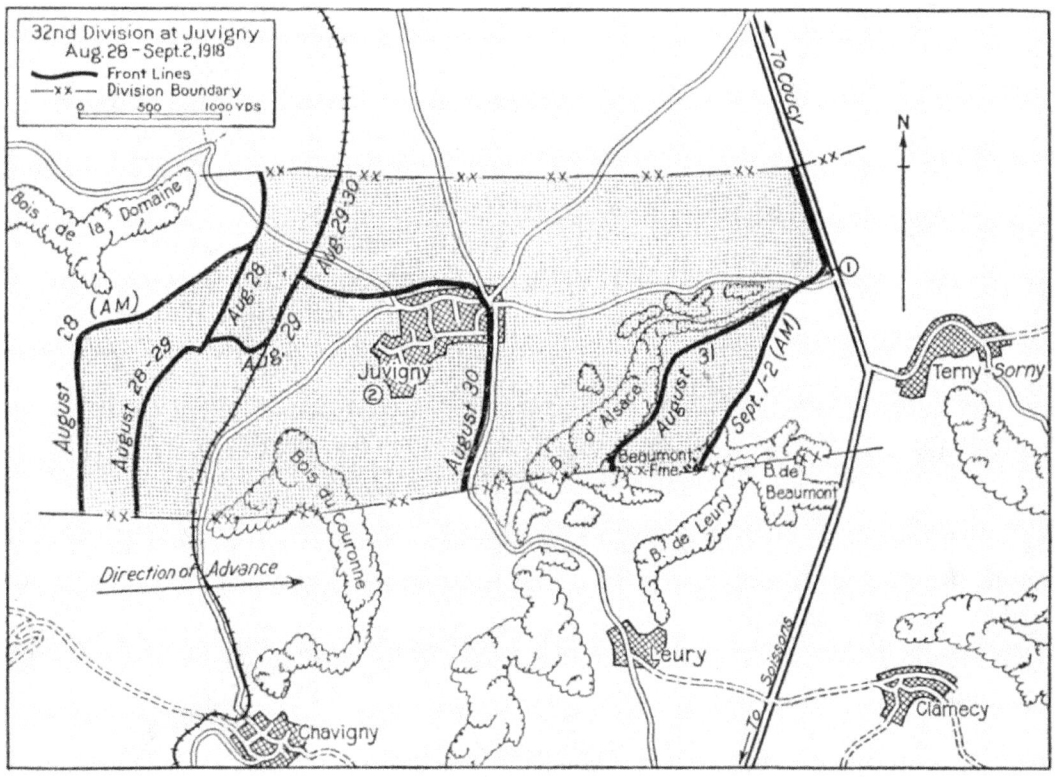

NUMBERS ON MAP INDICATE LOCATIONS OF FOLLOWING

① Ruins of Râperie (sugar beet press) destroyed during the war.
② Shelters in the rock, some now inhabited, used by the Germans during war.

THE 370TH INFANTRY, 93D DIVISION, SEPTEMBER 15 TO NOVEMBER 11, 1918

The 370th Infantry, which had served during the summer in both the St. Mihiel and Argonne regions with French units, joined the 59th French Division near Tartiers on September 15. Four of its companies assisted French troops in unsuccessful attacks against Mont des Singes between September 15 and 22, and on the 24th the regiment entered the front line as a unit, just north of **Vauxaillon**.

The 59th Division attacked September 28, and the 370th Infantry, as one of the assault units, succeeded by October 4 in advancing its lines to the south bank of the Ailette River.

The Germans began a withdrawal from this front on October 12, and the American regiment forced a crossing of the Ailette River, advancing into the

64 ADDITIONAL PLACES OF INTEREST IN AISNE-MARNE AREA

Bois de Mortier. Thereafter, acting as division reserve, it participated in the pursuit as far as **Bucy-lès-Cerny.**

The division was then relieved, only to reenter the battle at Grandlup late in October, the American regiment being placed in support near **Chantrud Farm**, northeast of Laon. There it suffered a loss of 80 men from a single shell on November 3.

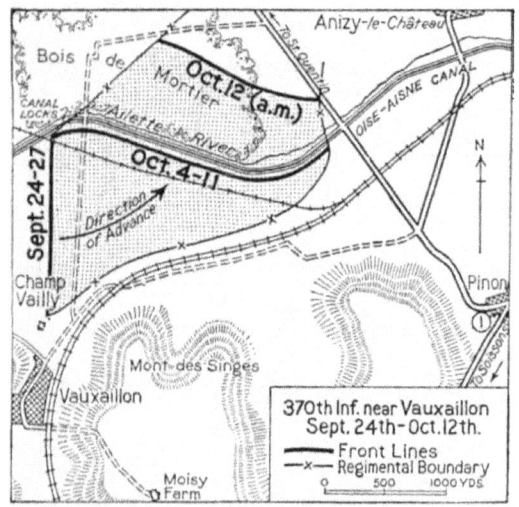

The Germans made a general retirement in early November, and the 59th Division took part in the pursuit. Although spasmodic fighting occurred, the 370th Infantry advanced mainly in march formation.

At the time of the armistice the forward battalion of the regiment was at le Gué d'Hossus, having advanced about 40 miles during the last week of the war.

① Much of Pinon is still in ruins.

PARTIAL LIST OF ADDITIONAL PLACES OF INTEREST IN THE AISNE-MARNE AREA

The following list is furnished for the convenience of the tourist who travels in the area not on the described route. The map below indicates the general location of the places mentioned.

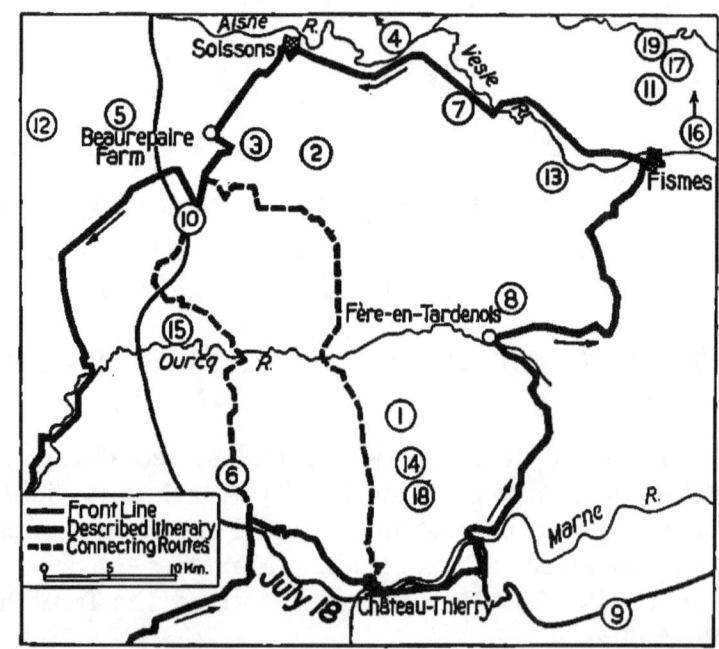

① **Brécy.** About 1¼ miles south of this town there is a platform which was the emplacement for a German "Big Bertha." It is rather difficult of access.

② **Buzancy.** This is the point near which the main Soissons–Château-Thierry highway was cut by a detachment of the 1st Division on July 21.

③ **Chazelle Ravine**, east of Chaudun, was the scene of bitter fighting by the 16th and 18th Infantry of the 1st Division on July 19.

④ **Coucy-le-Château.** See item, ②, page 203.

⑤ **Couevres-et-Valsery.** The 1st Division artillery took position in a ravine west of this town just prior to the offensive of July 18, and from that locality supported the infantry of the division during the initial stages of the attack.

ADDITIONAL PLACES OF INTEREST IN AISNE-MARNE AREA 65

⑥ **Courchamps.** The 4th Division, less the 7th Brigade and artillery, was attached to the 164th French Division in the French Sixth Army for the attack beginning July 18. Troops of the division captured the Bois de l'Orme and assisted the French in the capture of Courchamps and Hautevesnes. It was engaged in hard fighting in this vicinity until the night of July 20, making substantial gains each day. After its relief from 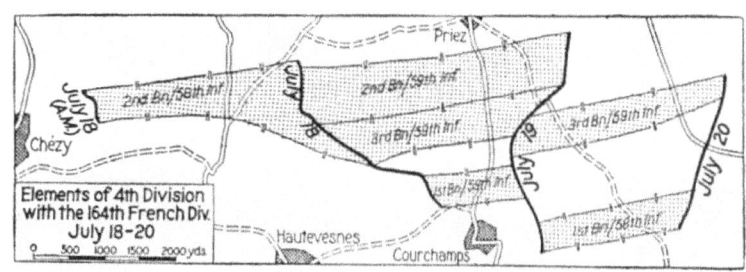 the front lines, it acted as a reserve unit until it reentered the battle north of the Ourcq River, early in August. (*See Noroy-sur-Ourcq, below.*)

⑦ **Couvrelles,** about 2 miles west of Braine, was the location of the headquarters of the 26th Division for a period in February and March, 1918. That division entered the area for training with the French, going into the front lines on the Chemin des Dames near Pinon, and remained there about six weeks.

⑧ **Fère, Castle of.** An interesting medieval castle built about 1206 A. D. is located approximately a mile northeast of Fère-en-Tardenois.

⑨ **La Chapelle-Monthodon.** In this vicinity units of the 109th Infantry, 28th Division, held trenches, and repulsed German attacks on July 15 and 16.

⑩ **Longpont.** In this town is a Cistercian abbey, built in 1226, which was badly damaged by shell fire in 1918.

⑪ **Merval** and **Serval** were captured on September 5 and 6 by the 77th Division, in its advance from the Vesle. During the following week there was considerable local fighting in the vicinity of the two villages.

⑫ **Mortefontaine.** The 1st Division assembled in the vicinity of this town just prior to deploying for the attack of July 18. It was used as a headquarters of the division just prior to the offensive.

⑬ **Mont Notre Dame.** Located here are the ruins of an old château and church. It is said that in 1650 the inhabitants of the town took refuge in the church from a Spanish invading army and were burned alive therein by the latter.

AMERICAN TROOPS EN ROUTE FROM THE FRONT LINE TO A REST CAMP

⑭ **Moucheton Castle,** 6 miles north of Château-Thierry, was used as a headquarters by Germans. Later was used for same purpose by Americans.

⑮ **Noroy-sur-Ourcq.** The 7th Brigade of the 4th Division was attached to the 33d French Division for the attack of July 18. The 39th Infantry of that brigade advanced several kilometers and captured Noroy on the first day of the offensive. The next day it continued its advance eastward from that vicinity, taking a gallant part in the fighting until relieved from the lines.

Three kilometers southeast of Noroy is a group of caves in which the Americans captured a large number of Germans. (*See Courchamps, above.*)

⑯ **Ravine Marion,** south of Glennes, was the scene of sharp fighting by the 77th Division on September 9. Southeast of here the 28th Division attacked on September 6, and made good progress in spite of strong resistance.

⑰ **Revillon.** Here occurred some severe fighting by the 308th Infantry, 77th Division, in early September.

⑱ **Trugny** and **Epieds.** In the area around these two little villages the 26th Division engaged in some desperate fighting. Four attacks were launched during July 22 and 23, and although both towns were captured they had to be given up temporarily by the Americans. When the Germans retreated on the 24th, the 56th Brigade of the 28th Division, attached to the 26th Division, followed them up through this area.

8-Inch Austrian Howitzer Left by Germans in Hasty Retreat, Epieds, July, 1918

⑲ **Villers-en-Prayères.** The 305th Infantry of the 77th Division captured this town on September 6.

CHAPTER III

THE AMERICAN ATTACK AT ST. MIHIEL, AND OPERATIONS IN THAT REGION TO THE END OF THE WAR

The St. Mihiel attack, which began on September 12, 1918, was the first operation in the World War carried out by a complete American army, under the independent control of its own Commander in Chief.

The plan to develop an army in the St. Mihiel region when sufficient troops should be available, and to reduce the salient there as a preliminary to a more decisive operation in the same vicinity, originated with American Headquarters shortly after its arrival in France. This plan was constantly kept in mind, and beginning in January, 1918, certain sectors near St. Mihiel were used to give

RESERVES MOVING FORWARD DURING THE
ST. MIHIEL OPERATION

front-line experience to our divisions and to acquaint them with the front from which they would later be called upon to attack. By the time of the operation a considerable number of our divisions had received the benefit of this service in the locality.

The succession of German drives in the spring and summer of 1918, however, had made it necessary to postpone carrying out the original plan as all available troops were urgently needed at other places on the battle front. Consequently, although there were over 1,200,000 American soldiers in France by July, the American combat units were widely distributed along the entire front from Switzerland to the North Sea, either serving with the Allied armies or undergoing training in areas behind the line.

When the reduction of the Marne salient was completed, however, General Pershing pointed out to the Allied Commander in Chief that the improved situation should now make possible the concentration of the American units, and insisted that the formation of an American army be resumed. Although the French and British authorities urged that these units be retained for service with the Allied forces, an understanding was finally reached that they should be assembled into an independent army which should occupy a sector in the region of St. Mihiel.

The Headquarters of this First Army was organized by August 10, and charged with the task of preparing detailed plans for the St. Mihiel offensive. The units that were to form that army began to concentrate late in August.

The salient at **St. Mihiel**, about 24 miles wide at its base and extending 13 miles into the Allied lines, had remained almost unchanged in shape for four years. The western face ran along the eastern heights of the Meuse. The

GERMAN TRENCH WITH SPECIAL ANTITANK RIFLE
© G

SOLDIER FIXING MINE TRIGGER IN ENTANGLEMENT
© G

southern face extended eastward across the plain of the Woëvre to the heights of the Moselle River. Over this plain are scattered patches of woods of varying sizes. The country is cut by small streams and there are several lakes and swampy areas, so that the ground becomes difficult in wet weather.

The Germans had the advantage of many excellent points of observation, including **Loupmont Ridge** and **Montsec,** looking down over the southern side of the salient. An elaborate system of wire entanglements protected their front to a depth of from 6 to 8 miles. The combined natural and artificial defenses made the position a veritable field fortress against which the French had made a number of unsuccessful attacks.

The value of the salient to the Germans lay in the fact that it interrupted traffic on the main Paris-Nancy railroad; cut the Verdun-Toul railroad; threatened the country in its vicinity, especially to the west of the Meuse; and covered the strategic center of Metz and the Briey iron basin. Its reduction was imperative before any great offensive could be launched against these two important areas or northward, between the Meuse River and the Argonne Forest, toward Sedan. As an attack just west of the Meuse River was to be undertaken by the American Army immediately after the St. Mihiel offensive, it was necessary to limit that operation merely to the reduction of the salient. The plans provided for a main drive against the southern face, a secondary blow against the

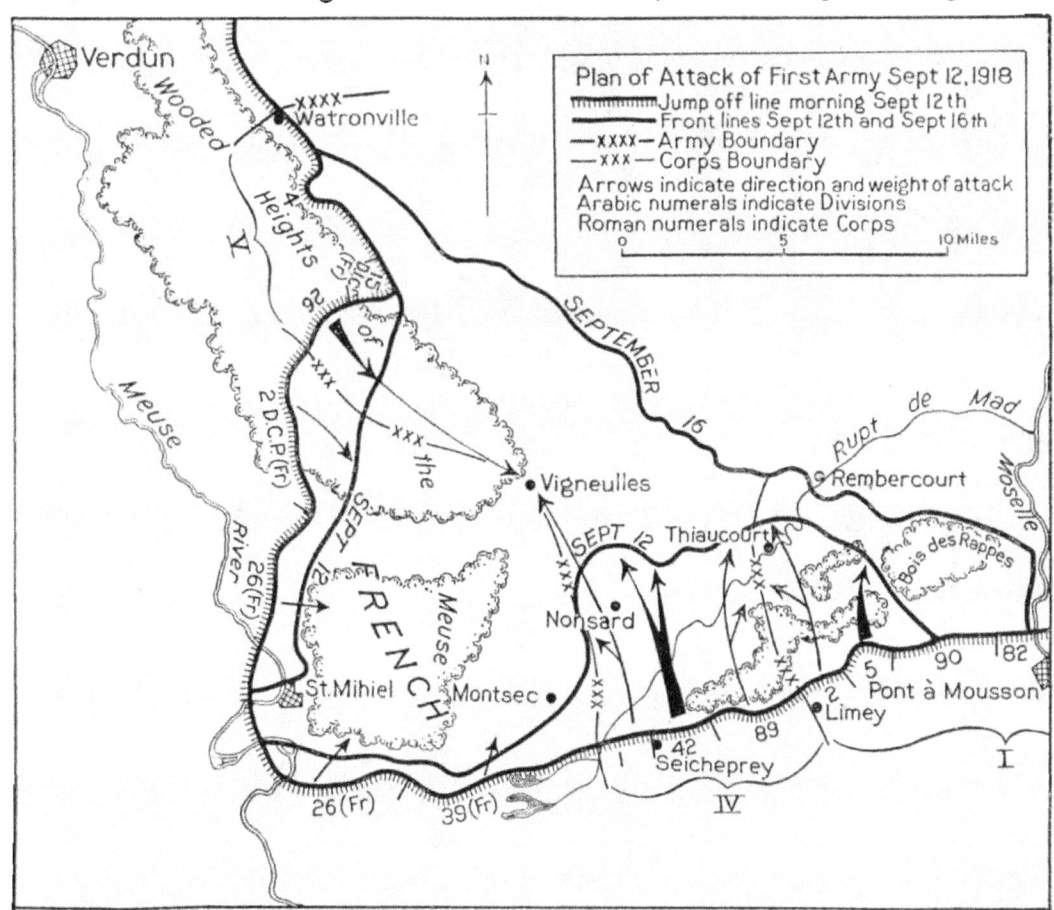

western face, with follow-up attacks and raids against the tip of the salient near St. Mihiel.

More than 550,000 Americans and about 110,000 French were involved in this offensive. The I and IV American Corps were designated to deliver the main attack. The I Corps, extending from Port-sur-Seille westward, had the 82d, 90th, 5th, and 2d Divisions in line from right to left, and the 78th in reserve. The IV Corps continued the line to the west as far as Xivray, with the 89th, 42d, and 1st Divisions in line from right to left, and the 3d in reserve.

The II French Colonial Corps, consisting of two divisions of infantry and one of dismounted cavalry, which held the line around the point of the salient, was attached to the American First Army, and was directed to exert pressure on its front and seize each foot of ground as the enemy's grasp upon it weakened from the blows which the Americans were to deliver.

The V Corps, composed of the 26th Division, the 15th French Colonial Division, and part of the 4th Division, from right to left, and the remainder of the 4th in reserve, was to make the secondary attack on and from the Meuse heights,

WRECKED BRIDGE IN ST. MIHIEL REGION
Note double line of traffic, continuous for three days after attack of September 12

south of **Haudiomont**. The Army had other divisions in reserve for use if necessary.

The additional needs of the First Army in aviation, artillery, and tanks were supplied by the Allies. By the night of September 11–12, the whole army was in position ready to attack.

"NO-MAN'S-LAND" ALONG SOUTHERN FACE OF ST. MIHIEL SALIENT

The Germans regarded the salient as in danger and suspected an attack, but information indicated that they did not believe it would be launched before the latter part of September. They had, however, actually made plans for a gradual withdrawal, but the movement was scarcely begun before the American attack burst upon them.

As an element of surprise, the artillery fire of preparation was limited to four hours, the Allied practice hitherto having been to continue it for a much longer time. The bombardment of the enemy positions began at 1 a. m. September 12 and was so intense and overpowering that the German guns could not make effective reply. At 5 a. m. the infantry of the main attack pressed forward and the advance proceeded entirely as scheduled, unchecked by the lack of tanks, only a part of which came up in time to assist the troops through the labyrinth of wire entanglements.

The plan provided that the greatest initial penetration should be made by the IV Corps and the left of the I Corps, the objective for September 12 including both **Thiaucourt** and **Nonsard**. Thiaucourt was quickly captured by the 2d Division, while the 89th, on its left, seized **Bouillonville**. By nightfall both were holding their designated objectives.

Street Scene in Village the Day After Its Capture

The 5th Division on the right of the 2d drove beyond **Viéville-en-Haye**, with its eastern flank bent back to connect with the 90th Division, which, being near the pivot of the movement, was not to make a deep advance that day.

The 42d Division on the left of the 89th captured and pressed beyond the towns of **Essey** and **Pannes** on the first day, and the 1st Division, on the left flank of the main attack, secured **Nonsard**.

On the western face the artillery preparation was continued until 8 a. m., when the infantry of the V Corps jumped off, and by midnight had captured and passed beyond **Dampierre-aux-Bois** and **Dommartin**.

While the attacks on the two faces were progressing, reports indicated that the Germans were withdrawing from the salient in front of the French troops, although raids undertaken by them on each side of the town of **St. Mihiel** had met with little success.

Army Headquarters therefore directed that detachments be rushed from the IV and V Corps during the night of September 12–13 to the region of **Vigneulles,** to connect up there and cut off the retreat of the Germans. Part of the 26th Division marched through dark forest roads directly toward the heart of the hostile position, and soon after 2 a. m. Vigneulles was in its possession. About

Supplies Going Forward and Prisoners Returning. September 12, 1918

dawn of the 13th its patrols met those of the 1st Division just northeast of that town. The salient was closed. Such German troops as had not already retired beyond that point were forced to surrender.

The occupation of the objectives was practically complete on September 13, and stabilization was begun of the new position roughly indicated by a straight

Remains of German Ammunition Train After the Attack

line joining **Haudiomont** and **Pont-à-Mousson.** Deep raids and local attacks were pushed, especially in the eastern part of the sector, until September 16, by which time the whole of the **Bois-des-Rappes** had been captured.

The entire success of this first offensive by the American Army greatly stimulated the morale of the Allies and depressed that of the Germans. Nearly 16,000 prisoners and 443 cannon had been captured, and over 200 square miles of territory, with its remaining French population, had been restored to France. The railroads in the vicinity of St. Mihiel had been freed for the use of the Allies, and the threat of the salient against surrounding territory had been removed. American staffs had shown their ability to maneuver and control large masses, and the whole Army had developed a self-confidence and sense of power essential in surmounting the more difficult tasks still ahead.

The battle was the first large Allied offensive of the year against an elaborately prepared trench system. The previous Allied successes of 1918 had been obtained against salients which had been created by the Germans in their spring and summer offensives and which were only partly organized for defense. The clean-cut victory at St. Mihiel indicated to all concerned that under conditions existing at the time in the German Armies no enemy position on the whole front was impregnable.

GERMAN BARBED WIRE IN ST. MIHIEL REGION
The large cables were charged with electricity

The ability displayed by the Americans in penetrating formidable wire entanglements so favorably impressed the French High Command that selected groups of officers and enlisted men were sent from neighboring French armies to view these obstacles through which the American soldier had made his way. French comments at the time characterized the conduct of the American divisions in this battle as "magnificent."

The transfer of American units to their next great battle field, between the Meuse River and the Argonne Forest, was begun even before the completion of the St. Mihiel Battle, and by the 20th of September only the 26th, 42d, 78th, 89th, and 90th Divisions were left on that front.

MAJ. GEN. ROBERT L. BULLARD

These divisions, and those which entered the line from time to time as relieving units, continued to strengthen the position and conducted local attacks to secure points of vantage. Artillery bombardments by both sides were of frequent occurrence.

On October 12, Major General Robert L. Bullard, the Commanding General of the newly organized American Second Army, took command of the front between **Fresnes-en-Woëvre** and **Port-sur-Seille**, then held by the 7th, 37th, 79th, 92d, and two French divisions. At that time the offensive of the First Army in the Meuse-Argonne had been in progress for over two weeks, and the situation there demanded that every American division be used to the limit of its endurance.

The Second Army assumed for the time being the rôle of holding the front principally with tired divisions while they rested and prepared for another entry into the Meuse-Argonne Battle. Active patrolling and raiding were continued, however, and the artillery carefully registered on targets in anticipation of a possible major offensive to be undertaken later.

Early in November it became evident that the Allied and American attacks, covering almost the entire front from the Meuse to the North Sea, were producing great disorganization within the German armies, and on November 5 the American Commander in Chief ordered the Second Army to begin advancing its lines in preparation for an offensive in the direction of **Briey**. The Army planned to launch these attacks on November 10, but on the evening of November 9 a message was transmitted

42D DIVISION TROOPS IN THE FRONT LINE, SEPTEMBER 16, 1918

from Marshal Foch directing that vigorous pressure be immediately applied along the whole front.

The 7th, 28th, 33d, and 92d Divisions, then on the Second Army front, began at once the attacks already planned. The scarcity of troops prohibited strong concentrations, but in spite of stubborn resistance maintained to the bitter end, the Army made considerable advance, recovering a total of about 25 square miles of territory.

The Allied Commander in Chief in the mean time had decided upon an offensive east of the Moselle, and requested the assistance of six American divisions.

EFFECT OF ARTILLERY FIRE ON GERMAN SHELTER

General Pershing had long favored such an attack and promptly designated the 3d, 4th, 28th, 29th, 35th, and 36th Divisions for the task, with the stipulation that these units should operate directly under the Second Army during the offensive.

The plans prepared by that army as a result of these instructions provided for a powerful drive in a northeasterly direction from the vicinity of **Port-sur-Seille,** east of the Moselle River. The date for the commencement of the combined offensive was fixed by the French High Command as November 14, and the American divisions directed to take part in it were already in movement toward the new area when the armistice was signed.

7TH DIVISION SOLDIERS CHEERING NEWS OF ARMISTICE

A TOUR OF THE ST. MIHIEL BATTLE FIELDS

This tour covers a distance of 108 miles, and may be completed in about eight hours, including stops at the more interesting places. The map at the end of the chapter should be consulted in following the tour.

It is suggested that lunch be carried.

EN ROUTE VERDUN TO CÔTE DE SENOUX

Leave Verdun via rue de l'Hôtel-de-Ville, rue St. Sauveur, rue and gate of St. Victor, and keep on Metz highway (N-3) after leaving gate.

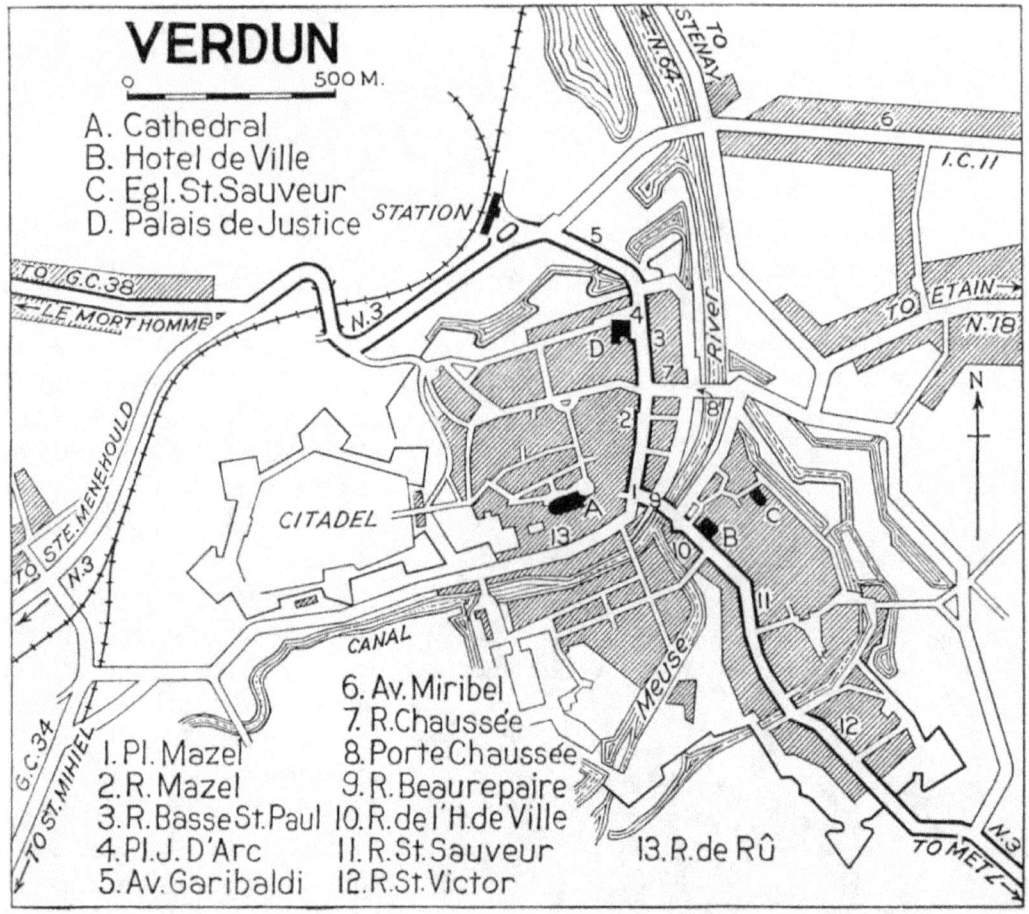

Upon passing kilometer post 39, to the right front in the valley on this side of the Meuse River is seen the village of **Haudainville** where a large American field hospital was located during the latter part of the war. On the hill overlooking the town can be seen Fort d'Haudainville, originally constructed as part of the defenses of Verdun.

At kilometer post 44.5, Fort du Rozellier, one in the ring of defenses erected around Verdun years before the outbreak of the war, is seen 200 yards off to the left of the road.

500 meters beyond Fort du Rozellier, at kilometer post 45.2, leave Metz highway (N-3) and take road to right (I. C. S.-3). This is the **Grande**

Tranchée de Calonne, a road said to have been built by direction of M. de Calonne, the Minister of Finance during the reign of Louis XVI, to give access to his château situated southeast of Verdun. During the war, this road was of great importance as an avenue of supply to the French, and subsequently to American troops fighting along this side of the St. Mihiel salient.

In the early spring of 1918 the 2d Division served for about two months along the western face of the salient.

At the beginning of the St. Mihiel offensive on September 12, 1918, the artillery and reserves of the V American Corps were grouped on either side of this road from the point where it enters the woods to the Côte de Senoux. This corps at the time was composed of the following divisions from north to south: 4th American Division, 15th French Colonial Division, and 26th American Division.

MANEUVERING BALLOON NEAR HAUDAINVILLE

At the road forks at kilometer post 7 keep on right-hand road (I. C. S.–3). About 2 kilometers farther on at point where the Grande Tranchée de Calonne crosses the Mouilly-les-Eparges road (V. O. 4) note speedometer reading. Continue on same road 400 meters where is seen a monument, located in the former second-line trenches, to Lieutenant Robert Guillie, a French officer.

GERMAN TRENCHES AT CÔTE DE SENOUX

Continue 400 meters farther and STOP on Côte de Senoux. The French front-line trenches, running almost at right angles to the road, rested at this point for nearly four years. The German trenches facing them were about 100 yards ahead, the intervening ground being "no-man's-land."

On September 8, 1918, the 26th Division took over from the French a front about 2½ miles long extending to the right and left across this road. At that time the destruction here was appalling. The continued shelling by both sides had practically destroyed every tree of the former dense growth and the ground was a maze of shell holes and shell-torn trenches, interspaced by acres of barbed-wire entanglements.

On the morning of September 12 the 26th Division attacked down this road, in conjunction with the main attack on the southern face of the St. Mihiel salient.

At this point the route enters the area captured by the American First Army in the St. Mihiel offensive, and the plan for the attack, given in the narrative at the beginning of this chapter, should be kept in mind in making the tour through the battle field.

FIELD GUN GOING INTO POSITION

ANTIAIRCRAFT MACHINE GUN MOVING TO FRONT

EN ROUTE CÔTE DE SENOUX TO HATTONCHATEL

Continue along Grande Tranchée de Calonne.

The battle front is marked by the absence of large trees for more than a kilometer behind the front lines. Other evidences of the war have disappeared to a large extent as the barbed wire has been salvaged and the young vegetation conceals the torn-up condition of the ground. The trenches are rapidly filling in and the entrances to most of the dugouts have been demolished to prevent accidents to people who might try to enter them.

4 kilometers from Côte de Senoux the front line reached by the 26th Division at nightfall of September 12 is crossed. It was from this vicinity that the 51st Brigade of that division, reinforced by some artillery and additional machine guns, began the march that night to Vigneulles in order to connect with the 1st Division, which was approaching from the southeast. With the 2d Battalion of the 102d Infantry forming the advance guard, this was the road they followed in their daring march through country occupied by the

NARROW-GAUGE RAILROAD NEAR CÔTE DE SENOUX

Germans. Fortunately, little resistance other than occasional bursts of machine-gun fire was met, because the Germans were considerably demoralized, mainly as a result of the large advance made by the Army on the south side of the salient. The march, nevertheless, was difficult as the Germans had felled many trees across the road, and the possibility of disaster was always imminent. During the advance small detachments of soldiers were left at every road or trail leading to the right (south), and in that way a "fence" was formed which effectively trapped the Germans who had not already escaped to the other side of the road.

GERMAN RAILWAY NEAR CHAILLON
Cut is made in solid rock

The troops emerged from the forest before daylight, and found the landscape dotted with burning buildings and stores set on fire by the retreating Germans, who attempted to destroy all that could not be taken with them.

Hattonchâtel was occupied by troops of the 26th Division soon after 2 a. m., September 13.

Continue through Hattonchâtel to eastern end of main street. STOP at château and walk 50 yards to edge of bluff.

Spread out in panorama to the front is the **Woëvre Plain.** The village nearest Hattonchâtel, close in at the foot of the slope to the east, is **Hattonville** and beyond it, situated in an opening in the wood about 3 miles away, is **St. Benoît,** captured by the 42d Division on September 13. Turning to the south, the most

GERMAN PLANE SHOT DOWN

prominent feature of the landscape is the isolated hill **Montsec**, which was within the German defensive position. The 1st Division on the first day of the attack pushed well into the large wooded area seen to the left of Montsec. It was from those woods that the division began its advance, during the night of September 12, toward Hattonville, near which its patrols and those of the 26th Division met about dawn September 13, thus closing the salient.

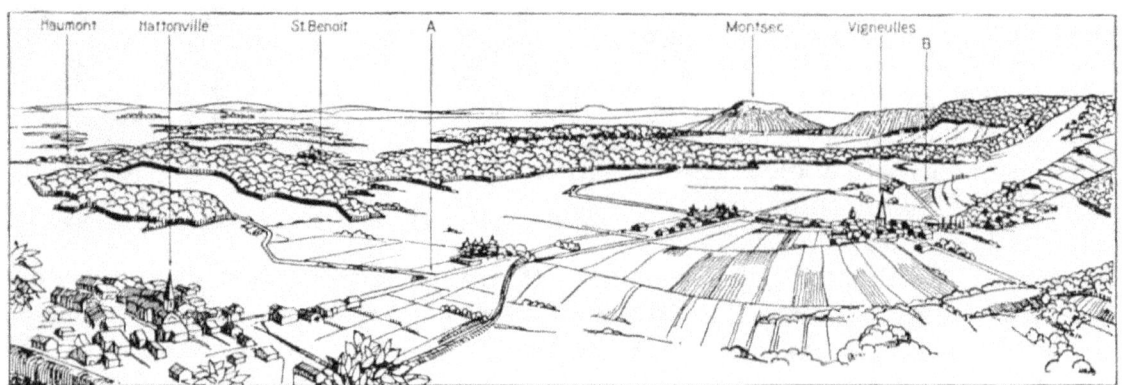

PANORAMA LOOKING SOUTH FROM STOP AT HATTONCHÂTEL
A—Approximate point where patrols of the 1st and 26th Divisions met on the morning of September 13.
B—Road to St. Mihiel

By midday of September 13 the 1st Division had reached a line which extended from Hattonville to a point on the plain about 2 miles to the east. Shortly thereafter, the 39th French Division, which had been following up the enemy retreat from the southwest, arrived and relieved the 1st Division in the front line.

1ST DIVISION MONUMENT NEAR VIGNEULLES

About a mile south of Hattonchâtel lies **Vigneulles** where the 26th Division captured a large number of prisoners, including a regimental band, early on the morning of September 13. There, also, a large amount of German supplies was captured, including a quantity of beer and rations. This was a welcome prize to the tired and hungry doughboys of the 1st and 26th Divisions, who shared it at breakfast.

Various units of the 26th Division arrived along the heights to the northwest of Hattonchâtel during the day of September 13, and established the line as far as Thillot (2½ miles to the northwest), where they connected with the 15th French Colonial Division.

On September 14 three French divisions advanced from this vicinity to a line farther out in the plain to the northeast, joining up with the American divisions on either side.

At the foot of the heights in this vicinity the Germans had established a large number of supply depots, one of which was located at Hattonville. Supplies from these depots were delivered to convenient spots close in rear of the front line by means of motor trucks and a vast system of narrow-gauge railways which had been constructed by them.

EN ROUTE HATTONCHATEL TO MONTSEC (VIA ST. MIHIEL)

Return to western edge of Hattonchâtel and take road to left down hill to Vigneulles.

A German cemetery is seen to the left ½ kilometer from Hattonchâtel.

VIGNEULLES SOON AFTER ITS CAPTURE

CHANGING GERMAN NAME OF STREET IN TOWN

Upon entering Vigneulles keep straight ahead. Turn right on main street, then turn left immediately, taking G. C. (D) 10. Follow 500 meters beyond town and take G. C. 9 to the right.

Just after leaving the road fork there is passed through an area in which one of the large German depots and railheads was located. Supplies were delivered to these depots on standard gauge railroads from points farther to the rear.

Creüe was entered very early on September 13 by patrols of the 26th Division. The town was occupied later the same day by French troops.

Straight through Creüe and Chaillon.

At kilometer post 9.5 beyond Chaillon, cross the road (I. C. 62) and continue along G. C. 9.

GERMAN POWER PLANT NEAR CHAILLON
Destroyed by them

Near the left of the road opposite **kilometer post 5.6** are two monuments, all that remain of a former German cemetery, the bodies having been removed by the French after the war to another burial place.

From kilometer post 2, Fort du Camp des Romains is seen on top of the hill to the left front about 2 miles away. Built by the French about 1879 upon the site of an old Roman camp, this is one of two forts constructed in the immediate vicinity of St. Mihiel. It was captured by the Germans in 1914 to insure their hold upon that town, and was retained by them until the American attack of September 12, 1918, caused them to abandon it.

Continue down the hill ½ kilometer. Look to the right across the Meuse River, and note the nearest village, **Chauvoncourt,** captured by the Germans in 1914 and held by them as a bridgehead across the river. On the hill to the right of and beyond Chauvoncourt is **Fort des Paroches,** the other fort in the neighborhood of St. Mihiel. It was held by the French throughout the course of the war.

St. Mihiel, captured by the Germans on September 24, 1914, gave the salient its name. Two or three thousand French

MONUMENTS IN GERMAN WAR-TIME CEMETERY
NEAR CHAILLON

civilians were held in the town by them during the war, and for that reason it was never heavily bombarded by the Allied artillery and airplanes.

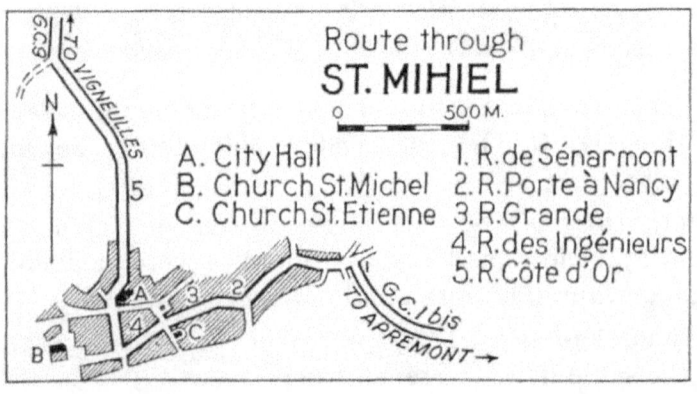

During the offensive of September 12, 1918, St. Mihiel itself was not attacked, but was in effect surrounded by the penetrations to the east and north. It was occupied on September 13 by the 26th French Division, and on the same day was visited by General Pershing with General Pétain and by the Secretary of War, Newton D. Baker.

Very shortly after the capture of the town the President of the French Republic sent a message to our Government, in which he expressed the deep gratitude of the French nation for the deliverance of St. Mihiel from the German armies.

Among the points of interest in this town are the churches of St. Etienne and St. Mihiel, and the seven great rocks just north of it on the road to Verdun, which are visited by many pilgrims.

Pass through St. Mihiel via rue Côte d'Or, turning left on rue des Ingénieurs and following G. C. 1 bis through rue de Sénarmont toward Apremont.

St. Mihiel Soon After Its Capture

Public Square

The wooded area lying to the right (south) of the road opposite **kilometer post 38** is the **Bois d'Ailly**, where extremely hard fighting occurred in April, 1915, when the Germans tried to advance toward the south.

On the right edge of the road about 2 kilometers farther on is seen a German dressing station with the name **"Verbandplatz"** over the entrance. This example of field engineering is well worth a visit. It is being preserved by the French Government as a "vestige de guerre classé" (classified relic of the war). The German front-line trenches lay about ¾ mile to the south (right) of this point, and ran approximately parallel to the road.

Continue about a kilometer to the point where road crosses I. C. S.-3. To the right front from the crossroads is the **Bois Brûlé**, the scene of particu-

German Concrete Shelter East of St. Mihiel

larly hard fighting in 1915. It was there, during that fighting, that Captain Péricard of the 95th French Regiment, seeing only dead and wounded men around him, uttered the famous cry, "Debout les morts" (Stand up ye dead).

There are some very interesting French and German trenches and field works in Bois Brûlé which are being preserved as "vestiges de guerre classés." **To visit a group of them turn right on I. C. S.-3 and go about 300 meters,** where some deep German concrete shelters are seen on both sides of the road. **Go 200 meters farther along I. C. S.-3,** passing another "vestige de guerre classé" on the left, to the German front-line trenches, constructed of reinforced concrete. Here the German line faced south (away from the crossroads just left), and ran at right angles to this road. The remains of the French front-line trenches are visible about 100 yards away.

WAR-TIME VIEW NEAR APREMONT
Tour goes over road shown

Return to crossroads and continue toward Apremont along G. C. (D) 1, which follows the German second-line trenches, an occasional trace of which may be seen near the road, as may certain field works, some of which are being preserved by the French Government.

Opposite kilometer post 42.8, along the walls of the quarry to the right of the road the Germans built a veritable village in the cliff. Tunnels led to deep underground compartments which were used for billeting troops and for field dressing stations.

The monument to the 28th United States Engineers seen at this point was built by that regiment while billeted here after the reduction of the salient and **has** no connection with the military operations.

Continue 1 kilometer to Apremont, which was just within the German lines and was completely demolished by French and American artillery fire.

At church in Apremont, take G. C. 1 bis to left, and 300 meters beyond village take G. C. 10 bis to left. Continue 400 meters and take the right-hand road (I. C. 19) to Loupmont.

Loupmont Ridge, which rises from the left of the road opposite the village of Loupmont, served the Germans as an excellent observation point.

After passing Loupmont, to the left front is seen

PRISONERS NEAR MONTSEC, SEPTEMBER 12, 1918

Montsec, which is the site selected for the monument, the design for which is shown on page 259, to be built by the American Government to commemorate the American operations in this region. From it is obtained a splendid view of the battle field. A road is being built which begins at the cemetery on this side of the hill and leads to the summit. Until that road is completed, **leave the car at the church in the village of Montsec and proceed on foot to crest.** *The walk is not an easy one.*

CHURCH AT MONTSEC

STOP. Montsec, which afforded ideal observation facilities to the Germans, was, in addition, a particularly strong point in their defenses. The direction to Hattonchâtel, seen about 7 miles away on the bluff jutting out from the Heights of the Meuse, is due north. The southeastern slope of this hill was heavily entrenched and wired, and the northwestern side contained many tunnels to underground billets for troops. Observation posts were located on its crest from which the fire of German guns, located in the woods hereabouts, was directed upon the French and Americans to the south and southeast. The remains of a number of these observation posts can still be seen.

Face south. About 2 miles away are two large ponds, the nearest of which,

SHELTER NORTH OF MONTSEC

the Etang de Vargévaux, lay on the front line, the trenches extending to the west (right) and east (left) of it. About 15 miles to the southeast of this point, and invisible from here, lies the city of Toul, which gave to this sector of the front the name by which it was popularly known.

The road which runs from the village of Montsec toward the southeast leads directly to **Richecourt**, about 2 miles away, which was on the German first line.

WAR-TIME VIEW FROM TOP OF MONTSEC
Arrows indicate successive barriers of wire

To the right of Richecourt are seen, close together, the villages of **Xivray** and **Marvoisin**, the former on the right. These villages lay just within the French and American lines, and the boundary between the 1st Division and the 39th French Division on September 12 ran between them. This boundary marked the left flank of the attack against the southern face of the salient. The front line before the battle ran generally eastward from Xivray to **Seicheprey**, which was in the sector of the 42d Division. The latter village lies about 3 miles from here, directly beyond Richecourt.

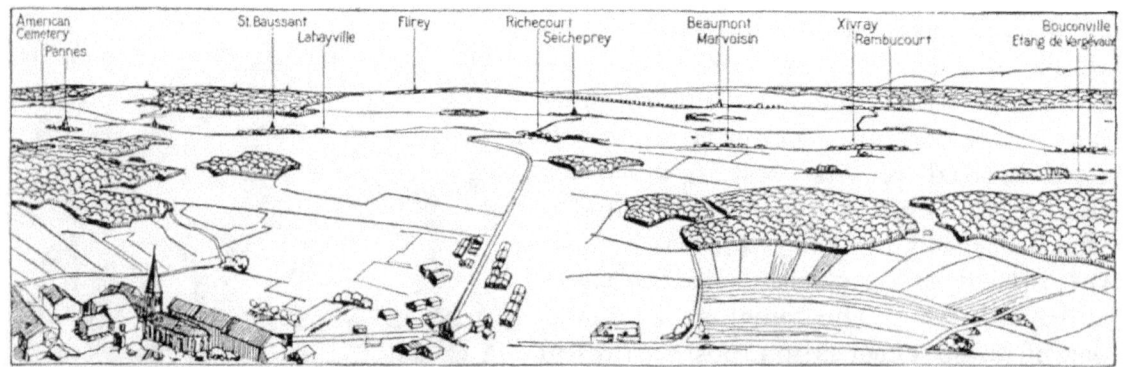

PANORAMA LOOKING SOUTHEAST FROM MONTSEC

The line continued to the east, passing near **Flirey**, which was in the sector of the 89th Division, and **Limey**, in the sector of the 2d Division. These towns, whose church spires are visible from here, are shown on the sketch on the next page, and will be passed through on the itinerary.

Beyond Seicheprey is the ridge, marked by the thin line of trees on its crest, which formed the main defensive line of the French and Americans on the southern face of the salient. The front line trenches of that position lay in the plain along the north (near) slope of that ridge.

If the Germans on Montsec had been able to see through the darkness, they would have observed, for some weeks before the attack, a scene of intense activity behind the American lines.

REMAINS OF A GERMAN TRENCH SOUTHWEST OF MONTSEC

Every night the roads were crowded with traffic, moving without lights, as the vast quantities of artillery, ammunition, and supplies necessary for the attack were brought forward. Road material and bridge equipment were hauled toward the front and placed in readiness to rebuild roads for artillery and supply trains across the riddled trench systems, while the troops who were to make the advance marched into the area. Everything brought up was carefully hidden or camouflaged, and each day when daylight came the Germans looked out upon the same lifeless landscape they had observed the evening before. Special care was taken to keep unchanged the daily routine of the sector and, therefore, when the attack came it was a tactical surprise.

At 1 o'clock on the morning of September 12 the countryside south of this point was dotted with flashes from nearly 3,000 guns of all calibers which commenced their bombardment of the hostile battery positions, observation posts, communication centers, trenches, and other vital points, and continued without ceasing until the infantry attack had proceeded beyond range.

Shortly before 5 o'clock in the morning, at which time the infantry jumped off, a smoke screen was placed around Montsec to prevent the observers on it from seeing the attack of the 1st, 42d, 89th, 2d, and 5th Divisions as they advanced northward from the ridge seen beyond Seicheprey. The Germans were forced to evacuate Montsec at once, and the 39th French Division occupied it, without opposition, on September 13.

GERMAN COMMUNICATING TRENCH NEAR MONTSEC

Face toward Hattonchâtel. To the east and northeast (right and right front) of this point, spread out as a huge relief map before the observer, is the ground over which the American attack swept on September 12 and 13.

The nearest village to the northeast is **Nonsard,** captured by the 1st Division on the first day of the offensive. Beyond Nonsard about a mile is the tiny hamlet of **Lamarche-en-Woëvre,** captured by the 42d Division on the 13th, and a little farther on is **Beney.** Beyond Beney is **Xammes,** a point near the final line reached during the offensive by the Americans. To the right of Xammes may be seen the church tower in Thiaucourt, which town was captured by the 2d

A ROAD IN REAR OF THE AMERICAN FRONT LINE, SEPTEMBER 13, 1918

Division. On the hillside to the left of Thiaucourt the **St. Mihiel American Cemetery** is visible on a clear day. It may be recognized by the two administration buildings and the white flagpole. Many other villages which are visible from the crest of Montsec may be identified by reference to the sketch given at the bottom of the preceding page.

The map illustrating the St. Mihiel operation, at the back of the book, plainly shows all localities captured by any particular division.

EN ROUTE MONTSEC TO SEICHEPREY

Leave Montsec from southeast, taking road to Richecourt, which, being virtually on the German front line, was completely destroyed.

ENGINEERS ENTERING NONSARD

Straight through Richecourt, crossing the Rupt de Mad on the opposite edge of town. This small stream offered great difficulties to the tanks and transportation of the American First Army until its destroyed bridges were replaced with temporary structures by the engineers.

Continue across the road G. C. 33 and up the hill.

The site of the German front-line trenches is passed 300 meters from the cross-roads, and 200 meters farther on the route crosses the site of the trenches from which the 1st Division began its attack.

One kilometer from Richecourt, the new railway which will be the main line from Paris to Metz, is crossed.

BRIDGE BUILT BY ENGINEERS OVER RUPT DE MAD

The next village is **Seicheprey,** the scene of a German raid against troops of the 26th Division, which was holding a sector here, in April, 1918. The American front line lay about ¾ mile to the north of Seicheprey, and just north of the **Bois de Remières,** seen about a mile directly to the left (east) of this road. On

April 20 the Germans placed around that wood and the village of Seicheprey a very heavy "box barrage" which isolated the area from any assistance from friendly troops. Screened by a dense fog, about a thousand picked German

RUINS OF RICHECOURT

assault troops quickly overran the American first-line trenches and entered Seicheprey in the early morning, where they destroyed the dugouts, first-aid station, and kitchen, capturing the American battalion headquarters. Soon

SEARCHING PRISONERS DURING ST. MIHIEL OPERATION

thereafter the Germans withdrew from Seicheprey to the American front-line trenches, where they remained most of the day, retiring to their own trenches shortly before an American counterattack was launched to drive them out.

Near the church in Seicheprey is a memorial fountain erected by the people of the State of Connecticut to commemorate the service of the 102d Infantry.

Continue through Seicheprey, keeping to right, to road junction near southern edge of town.

VIEWS AT SEICHEPREY DURING THE WAR

FLARE USED TO CALL FOR ARTILLERY BARRAGE AT NIGHT

FOUNTAIN AT SEICHEPREY

Note the speedometer reading. **Take left-hand road to Flirey marked V. O. 4. Follow it about 700 meters and STOP.**

From this point, looking back toward Montsec, the strength of the German position is readily appreciated. Beyond the woods to the right of Montsec, Hattonchâtel is seen on the bluff about 9 miles away.

Look to the right oblique (45°) from Montsec. Along this line, the nearest village, about 1½ miles away, is **St. Baussant,** and the direction to it is almost due north. The large wooded area seen immediately to the east (right) of St. Baussant is composed of the **Bois de la Sonnard** and the **Bois de Mort Mare,** the latter being on the right (east). The German front line ran along the southern (near) edges of those woods and along the high ground just beyond the Bois de Remières, the little wood 500 yards away in the foreground. The American front faced the German trenches at distances varying from 100 to several hundred yards.

The American trenches in this vicinity were held at various times prior to September 12 by the 1st, 26th, 82d, and 89th Divisions.

The 42d Division attacked on a front extending from Seicheprey to a point about 2 miles to the east, and during the first day advanced northward about 4½

GERMAN TANK MINES

TANK CROSSING TRENCH IN
ST. MIHIEL OFFENSIVE

miles. During the early stages of the attack, very stiff resistance, mostly from machine guns, was met at St. Baussant and in the Bois de la Sonnard.

On the right of the 42d, the 89th Division jumped off and quickly captured the Bois de Mort Mare and advanced 5 miles.

It may be noted from this point that the French and Americans who held the line along this face of the St. Mihiel salient were not entirely lacking in points from which to observe behind the German lines.

Observation from points such as this was supplemented by the important reconnaissance work carried on by the Air Service. Reconnoitering airplanes flew over the salient, taking photographs of selected places in the hostile defenses. These photographs, when compared with others previously taken of the same place, showed changes which had occurred. Some distance in rear of the forward trenches and at intervals along the whole front were stationed captive

A TOUR OF THE ST. MIHIEL BATTLE FIELDS

("sausage") balloons, from which the occupants, through powerful glasses, studied the hostile positions. The balloon observer, his helpers on the ground, and the supporting antiaircraft artillery had to keep a watchful eye out for German aviators, because a successful airplane attack on the inflammable bag invariably produced an explosion from which the observer could not escape unless he had previously leaped overboard.

EN ROUTE SEICHEPREY TO HILL 335.9

Continue 1½ kilometers, passing through the western end of Bois du Jury to main highway (N-58). Turn left toward Flirey. The remains of French and American front-line trenches can be seen along the hillside to the left. Upon entering **Flirey**, the site of the railway bridge, destroyed by the French during the war, is passed.

Flirey is familiar to many Americans, as several divisions served in this vicinity at various times. The front line lay about 800 yards to the north (left) of the town.

In the town, opposite the church, is a monument erected by the people of Lorraine to the American divisions that served in the region.

Straight through Flirey, keeping on N-58. As will be noted after passing the crossroad, D-3, Flirey has been rebuilt on a new site. The ruins of the old village, on both sides of the road, are seen beyond the new town.

At kilometer post 14.9, to the left about ¾ mile away, are visible the remains of the opposing trenches which paralleled this road. It was from this vicinity that the 89th Division attacked on the morning of September 12.

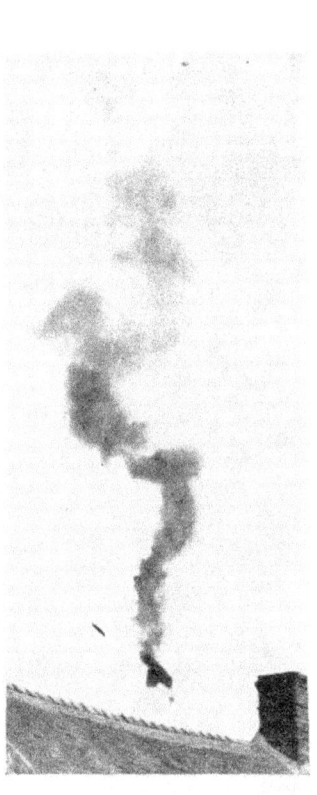

AMERICAN OBSERVERS JUMPING FROM BALLOON, AND SAME BALLOON SHOT DOWN BY GERMAN AVIATOR

DAMAGE DONE BY ONE SHELL

AIR PHOTOGRAPH OF BRIDGE NEAR FLIREY
Front lines are near top of picture. Note communicating trenches
(INSERT.) 89TH DIVISION P. C. NEAR FLIREY, SEPTEMBER 14, 1918

About 4 kilometers east of Flirey is entered **Limey,** a village lying just behind the American front line, in the sector of the 2d Division.

Straight through Limey almost to its eastern end, and there leave N–58, turning sharply left on the second-class road to Remenauville. Note speedometer reading at this point.

Ansoncourt Farm, which has been reconstructed, is seen straight to the front upon passing the last houses in Limey. The sector of the 2d Division extended from that farm to a point a mile to the east (right).

It was just this side of Ansoncourt Farm that Second Lieutenant J. Hunter Wickersham, of the 353d Infantry, 89th Division, won (posthumously) the Congressional

WAR-TIME VIEW OF FLIREY
(INSERT.) MONUMENT AT FLIREY MENTIONING AMERICAN UNITS

Medal of Honor. Severely wounded in four places by a high-explosive shell, his right arm disabled, he declined aid for himself until he had dressed the wounds of his orderly. Then leading his men forward again, he continued fighting, using his pistol with his left hand, until, exhausted from loss of blood, he fell and died.

1 kilometer from Limey a 2d Division marker, in the form of a bowlder, is passed, and 500 meters farther up the hill the front-line trenches, from which the 2d Division began its attack, are crossed. The German front-line trenches lay 200 yards beyond.

2 kilometers from Limey the ruins of the village of Remenauville are passed.

The 9th and 23d Infantry of the 2d Division, attacking from the trenches which passed 250 yards south of **Remenauville,** quickly overran the hostile lines in this vicinity, and, after crushing stiff resistance in the **Bois du Four** and **Bois la Haie l'Evêque** just to the north (left), by nightfall had made an advance of about 5 miles.

The left of the 5th Division's front, on the morning of September 12 joined the right of the 2d Division, 500 yards southeast of Remenauville, and its right lay about a mile to the east.

REMENAUVILLE, OCTOBER, 1918

ANTIAIRCRAFT GUN IN ACTION

At the crossroads halfway down the hill at the far end of the site of Remenauville take the main road to the right.

The road passes through "no-man's-land" for 800 yards, and then crosses the Franco-American trenches near the top of the hill. As is the case in nearly every other battle area, all barbed wire, wood, steel, and iron have been salvaged and only the crumbling ruins of the trenches remain.

At the road junction 1.8 kilometers from (east of) the site of Remenauville there once stood **Regniéville-en-Haye,** a village just within the French and American lines. It was totally demolished during the war, and, like Remenauville, was never rebuilt. Only a portion of the church remains standing. Prac tically all of the other villages along the St. Mihiel front, such as Apremont, Richecourt, and Seicheprey, were destroyed; but as has been noticed in passing, these have been substantially rebuilt.

Regniéville-en-Haye was almost in the center of the sector of the 5th Division on September 12, the front line passing about 300 yards north (left) of the road junction.

REGNIÉVILLE DURING WAR

REGNIÉVILLE CHURCH IN 1927

Turn right on D-15. At the road intersection there is located a 5th Division marker and one to indicate the limit of the German advance. The remains of Regniéville church are passed on left of road.

About 1 kilometer beyond the site of Regniéville-en-Haye, STOP on Hill 335.9.

The village with the tall church spire 1 kilometer farther down this road is the new town of **Fey-en-Haye** and the direction to it is southeast. The old town of Fey-en-Haye, which lay within the American front line, was not rebuilt. The ruins of it can be seen, however, about a mile to the east.

The jump-off line of the 90th Division ran eastward from this point through the large woods, of which the tops of the trees can be seen beyond Fey-en-Haye. During the attack the division made steady progress, and in the course of four days had pushed the Germans back upon Prény, 5 miles to the north.

GERMAN ANTITANK GUN. © G

Face northwest. The village to the left with the tall church spire, about 3 miles away, beyond the tip of the little pine forest, is Limey. The wood seen

1½ miles away, directly in front, is the Bois du Four. To the right of it is another wooded area, beyond which is seen the church spire in Viéville-en-Haye. The 5th Division, whose sector extended westward from the point on which the observer is standing, advanced through those woods and beyond Viéville-en-Haye on the first day of the offensive.

The remains of the trenches from which the 5th Division began its attack on September 12 are seen along the hill to the north and northwest.

Due north is seen the southern part of the dense **Forêt des Venchères** in which the 90th Division had hard fighting.

EN ROUTE HILL 335.9 TO 2 KILOMETERS NORTH OF PONT-A-MOUSSON

Continue on, turning left 1.7 kilometers beyond Fey-en-Haye on N-58.

Bois le Prêtre, visible on the left after passing Fey-en-Haye, is a famous wood of the World War. The Germans established themselves there in September,

Engineer Troops at Fey-en-Haye, September, 1918

1914, and from October 1, 1914, until May, 1915, the wood was the scene of almost continuous struggles, at the end of which time much of it was in the hands of the French. During the fierce fighting for the possession of Bois le Prêtre the French lost more than 100,000 men and the Germans lost heavily.

When the front stabilized in the woods, the opposing lines, in some places, were only 20 yards apart, each supported by a wide zone of deep trenches, bristling with machine guns in concrete emplacements, and the whole strengthened by numerous bands of barbed wire.

St. Pierre Auberge, located at the junction of **D-15** and **N-58**, was used by both French and Americans as a dressing station during the war.

At kilometer post 3, a French military cemetery is seen on the left. Straight ahead **Mousson Hill,** upon which is located the village of Mousson, can be seen. That hill served as an excellent observation post for the units which held this sector. Note on the hill the walls of the ruined castle built about the eleventh century by the Dukes of Bar, and the church tower with the statue of Joan of Arc.

Straight through the village of Montauville.

Pont-à-Mousson was captured by the Germans in August, 1914. It was retaken by French troops the following month, and thereafter remained in their possession. The town, being near the front line, was heavily shelled by the Germans.

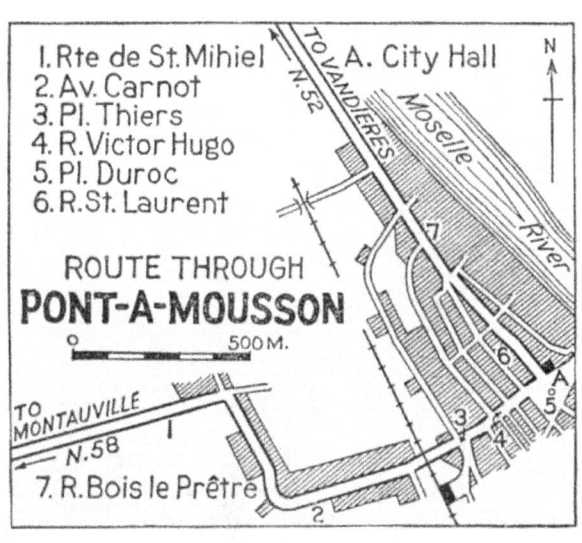

The churches of St. Laurent and St. Martin in this town are places of interest. In the war of 1870, part of the German armies crossed the Moselle here before the battles of Gravelotte and St. Privat, and the German General Headquarters was located in the town for a few days during the westward march of their armies in the same year.

The 1st and 2d Divisions held sectors in this vicinity for a short time in August, 1918.

Upon entering Pont-à-Mousson, keep right on Avenue President Carnot, and follow it across railroad tracks, entering rue Victor Hugo. Turn left at Place Duroc (plaza) into rue St. Laurent and rue Bois le Prêtre, which continues as the highway N–52.

At first railway crossing after leaving Pont-à-Mousson, note speedometer reading. Proceed approximately 600 meters and STOP near kilometer post 83.4 at corner of garden wall.

PONT-À-MOUSSON, OCTOBER, 1918

Looking straight ahead on this road the direction is approximately north. The wood, of which the edge is visible on the slope 1,000 yards to the left, is Bois le Prêtre. The high hill to the left of this road, and a mile to the north, is **Hill 324,** on which is located Vandières Signal. Lying in the ravine on this side of it is **Norroy.** The river to the right is the Moselle, and beyond it, north (left) of Mousson Hill, is **Xon Hill.**

During the attack the 82d Division was on the extreme right of the American First Army. Its right connected with a French division near Port-sur-Seille, about 5 miles east of here. Its front extended westward from that point, crossing Xon Hill near its crest, and ran close to the northern outskirts of Pont-à-Mousson. Just this side of the river it started at the railway embankment, crossed the road at this point, and continued to the left to the edge of Bois le Prêtre, where it joined the right of the 90th Division. The portion of the 82d Division's line lying west of the Moselle River was held by the 328th Infantry.

The German front line crossed this road about 400 yards farther north.

According to the initial plans for the attack, no immediate advance was to be made on the front of the 82d Division and the right half of the front of the 90th Division. Because of the success of the first day's action, how-

(INSERT) BARBED WIRE
GERMAN FRONT LINE TRENCH IN BOIS LE PRÊTRE
Note permanence of construction

ever, the right of the 90th Division and the 328th Infantry (82d Division) were ordered to attack northward on the morning of September 13. They advanced in some hard fighting that day to a line just this side of the crest of Hill 324. The 90th Division continued its advance on September 14 and 15. On the latter date the 328th Infantry attacked again, advancing its line about ¾ mile to the northern slope of Hill 324.

During these attacks the infantry received extremely heavy fire from hostile batteries located in the woods on the hills east of the river.

It was on the northern slope of Hill 324 that Lieutenant Colonel Emory J. Pike, 82d Division, won (posthumously) the Congressional Medal of Honor. Going beyond the call of his own duties as division machine-gun officer, he volunteered his assistance and reorganized advanced infantry units under terrific bombardment. Although severely wounded while going to the aid of an injured soldier in the outpost line, he nevertheless continued in command, encouraging everyone with his cheerful spirit of confidence while holding the position until it was prepared for defense. From his wounds he later died.

On October 9 the 92d Division took over from a French division the sector just east of the Moselle and held it until the end of the war. On October 26 this sector was changed to include a small part of the line this side of the river.

EN ROUTE 2 KILOMETERS NORTH OF PONT-A-MOUSSON TO AMERICAN MILITARY CEMETERY AT THIAUCOURT

Continue 3 kilometers along N-52 to Vandières.

(*NOTE.—About 1 kilometer from the last stop is a narrow and hilly road branching off to the left which passes through Norroy and over the western slope of Hill 324. It connects up with the described route at Villers-sous-Prény, and offers excellent views of this region, including the Moselle Valley. It is not recommended on account of its condition.*)

From kilometer post 82, Norroy can be seen up the ravine to the left, and beyond it on the hill are the Norroy quarries, which were a well organized

92D DIVISION SOLDIERS STRINGING WIRE

German stronghold, captured by the 90th Division and the 328th Infantry, 82d Division, on September 13, after very hard fighting.

Vandières was never actually occupied by American troops because of the severe shelling from across the river. The Germans were driven from the town on September 18 by an advance of the 90th Division, and from that date on Vandières was controlled by American troops who were on the high ridge immediately to the north and between the canal and the river to the southeast of the town.

After passing the bridge over the little creek in Vandières, turn left on I. C. 13.

At kilometer post 11 the north end of the Norroy quarries can be seen to the left front on the hill about a mile away. On this side of the hill were many German shelters for troops and posts of command.

At kilometer post 10, look to the right rear and note Hill 327 about a mile away, captured by the 90th Division on September 15. The front stabilized on that hill, and later troops of the 7th and 92d Divisions held the line there until the armistice. On the hill immediately to the right of this road is the dense **Bois des Rappes** captured by the 90th Division on September 15.

Continue on, passing through Villers-sous-Prény. The 90th Division advanced across this road from left to right. The valley through which the road runs came to be known to the 90th Division, and subsequently to the 7th and 92d Divisions, as the "Valley of Death," because of the heavy shelling it received almost continuously from the German batteries on the hills beyond the Moselle River.

The next village is **Vilcey-sur-Trey**, captured by the 90th Division on September 13. The front line on that day crossed the road 200 yards on this side of the village and extended along the edges of the woods to the right and left front.

RATION PARTY GOING FORWARD

90TH DIVISION DETACHMENT COMING OUT OF LINE NEAR VILCEY-SUR-TREY, SEPTEMBER 13, 1918

Bear right in Vilcey-sur-Trey, keeping on I. C. 13.

The road continues up the ravine, passing through the **Forêt des Venchères**. This wood was a German rest camp before the St. Mihiel operation, and in it were located many shacks and shelters for billeting troops. Traces of these may be seen on the left of this road, about 200 yards before it leaves the wood.

At kilometer post 3, the sector of the 5th Division is entered. To the left front is seen the **Bois St. Claude**, from which troops of the 5th Division emerged during the afternoon of September 12 and attacked toward the north across the road.

Straight through Viéville-en-Haye, captured by the 5th Division on September 12.

There is a large German concrete dugout on the right of the road 200 yards beyond the village.

At kilometer post 0.7, the sector of the 2d Division is entered, the right boundary of which crossed this road and passed along the right (east) edge of the **Bois d'Heiche** seen to the right.

At the crossroads 700 meters beyond kilometer post 0.7 a German machine-gun emplacement (pill box) may be seen 400 yards to the left.

Turn right on D-15.

The road passes along the west edge of Bois d'Heiche in which troops of the 2d Division captured a large number of German prisoners and a German canteen with all its stock. On the left is the **Bois du Beau Vallon,** captured by troops of the 2d and 89th Divisions.

AMERICAN P. C. IN GERMAN DUGOUT
VIÉVILLE-EN-HAYE, SEPTEMBER 16, 1918

WAITING FOR BARRAGE TO LIFT

On the left of the road in the horseshoe bend, about 1½ kilometers from the last turn, are some deep German shelters.

After completing the horseshoe bend, turn left at kilometer post 9, on the road which goes straight to Thiaucourt.

On the right, 1 kilometer farther on, is a **German cemetery** which contains about 32,000 graves.

The next town is **Thiaucourt,** captured by the 2d Division on September 12. After its capture the town received heavy and regular shelling by the Germans and was badly damaged. Before the reduction of the salient it was a very important point in the German supply system.

Thiaucourt is familiar to troops of the 7th, 28th, 37th, 78th, and 89th Divisions, who occupied the line about 2½ miles north of the town at various times after September 16.

Near the church is a monument erected by the people of Thiaucourt to commemorate the deliverance of the town by American troops.

AMERICAN ANTIAIRCRAFT MACHINE GUN

Near western (opposite) end of Thiaucourt take G. C. 7 to left. One kilometer beyond the town enter St. Mihiel American Cemetery and STOP near south end.

5TH DIVISION MONUMENT

The direction toward the cemetery gate is north. **Face the south.** To the southwest Montsec is visible on the sky line. To the south, about 3 miles away, is the northern edge of the Bois de Mort Mare. Slightly to the left of the Bois de Mort Mare, about 2 miles away, is the Bois du Beau Vallon, and to the southeast beyond Thiaucourt, about the same distance away, is Bois d'Heiche.

Face north. The town seen beyond the cemetery gate, about 1½ miles away, is **Xammes**, captured by troops of the 2d and 89th Divisions. The front line stabilized a mile north of Xammes on September 14, where it remained, with only minor changes, until the time of the armistice.

This cemetery rests on ground captured by the 89th Division on September 12. In fact, the front line of the 89th Division at the end of the first day's fighting passed over the ground where the northwest corner of this cemetery now lies, the enemy being in trenches behind bands of barbed wire just beyond the location of the cemetery gate. The Germans were pushed back more than a mile to the north of this line the following day.

For information about this cemetery and the chapel to be erected in it, see Chapter X.

THIAUCOURT BEING SHELLED BY THE GERMANS, SEPTEMBER 12, 1918

STREET IN THIAUCOURT AFTER BOMBARDMENT

EN ROUTE ST. MIHIEL AMERICAN CEMETERY (NEAR THIAUCOURT) TO HILL 221

Turn left at cemetery gate. The next village is **Beney**, captured by the 89th Division on September 13.

Straight through Beney, leaving village on G. C. (D)–7. At the road intersection on the northwestern (opposite) end of Beney the zone of the 42d Division is entered.

To the left front is seen the Bois de Beney, at the edge of which the Germans maintained a captive balloon for observation purposes. A large supply depot was located near the northern edge of the woods on a temporary railway which had been built through this area.

89TH DIVISION BATTALION HEADQUARTERS, NEAR BENEY, SEPTEMBER 16

The next village is **St. Benoît,** captured by the 42d Division on September 13, after which the headquarters of the division was located in the ruined château seen on the right upon leaving the village.

From kilometer post 20 is seen to the right front the **Bois de la Grande Souche** which was the scene of fighting between troops of the 42d Division and the Germans from September 13 until September 19, when the Americans finally occupied all of it.

A number of American artillery positions were located in the woods to the left after this front became stabilized.

Captured Donkeys Carrying Water

American Trenches near Beney, September, 1918

American Officers at German Canteen

Near kilometer post 18 is passed Hassavant Farm, where the Germans offered stubborn resistance to the troops of the 42d Division on September 13.

At this point, looking across the clearing to the right front, can be seen a swampy wooded area in which the front stabilized on September 16, on a line approximately a mile to the right (northeast) of this road. On November 10 the 28th Division attacked from that line, pushing the front, during the next two days, about a mile farther out in the swamp.

A tip of the pond called the Etang de Lachaussée lies on the near edge of the woods.

The little wood near the right side of the road about 3 kilometers beyond Hassavant Farm is called **le Rebois**. In the attacks of the American Second Army just preceding the armistice the boundary between the zones of the 28th and 33d Divisions ran at right angles to this road and passed along the northwestern edge of the woods. The front line rested, from September 14 to November 9, on the northern corner of that wood and paralleled this road for the next 3 kilometers.

ROAD WORK

Straight through Woël. At 1.6 kilometers from Woël, STOP on Hill 221.

The village 700 yards farther down the road to the northwest is Doncourt, captured by the 2d French Dismounted Cavalry Division on September 14. Across the plain, about 11 miles due south from here, Montsec can be seen. About 4 miles away, looking to the right of Montsec, is Hattonchâtel, on the prominent bluff which juts out from the neighboring heights.

The building about a mile away to the west (left front) is **la Dame Farm**. The first spur of the heights visible to the right of it is near **les Eparges** and was the scene of particularly hard fighting between the French and Germans from February to April, 1915.

Face northeast. The church spire showing about 2½ miles away is in **Jonville**, through which ran the Hindenburg line, and which was in German possession at the end of the war.

When the front stabilized at the end of the St. Mihiel offensive, the line in this vicinity rested about 400 yards northeast of this observation point, passed around the far edge of Doncourt to la Dame Farm, and thence generally to the northwest.

RUINED CHURCHES IN ST. MIHIEL AREA

The 79th Division relieved the 26th along the front northwest of Doncourt on October 8, and held that sector until October 26, when it was in turn relieved by the 33d Division.

Divisional Ration Dump in St. Mihiel Area

On November 10 the 33d Division, on a front of about 7 miles, launched an attack toward the northeast, in conjunction with similar attacks by the 28th and 81st Divisions, on its right and left, respectively. These attacks were made

On Front of 81st Division, November, 1918

in compliance with Marshal Foch's urgent instructions that the enemy be pushed all along the line, and resulted in the capture of the series of small woods seen on this side of Jonville, extending to the right and left of the town.

EN ROUTE HILL 221 TO HAUDIOMONT

Straight through Doncourt.

The next village is **St. Hilaire,** captured by the 15th French Colonial Division on September 14. On account of the flooded condition of the ground, and the

CROSSROADS AT ST. HILAIRE

fact that it made a sharp salient in the line, it was abandoned the following day by the 26th Division, which had relieved the French. The front line was withdrawn about a mile to the southwest, where it remained until November 10, when St. Hilaire was again captured by the 33d Division and held until the armistice.

MARCHÉVILLE DURING THE WAR
155-MM. GUN GOING INTO POSITION, SEPTEMBER 13, 1918

Straight through St. Hilaire.

The route then passes through **Marchéville,** where the 33d Division and the Germans were fighting when hostilities ended on November 11.

The next town is **Fresnes-en-Woëvre,** captured by the 4th Division on September 14. The front line rested near the northern edge of that town until the morning of November 11, when troops of the 33d Division pushed it about ¾ mile farther to the northeast.

Straight through Fresnes-en-Woëvre.

A point on the road about 500 meters beyond Fresnes-en-Woëvre (**kilometer post 2**) marks the boundary between the American First and Second Armies, and also the boundary between the 33d and 81st Divisions at the end of the war.

As **Manheulles** is entered, a 4th Division monument is passed. That division captured the village on September 14, after which the front lines ran just north of the town until the early morning of November 11, when the 81st Division advanced about 800 yards into the plain to the right.

During the time it was held by the Americans, Manheulles was subjected to frequent and intense bombardments from hostile artillery. A sector in this vicinity was held for a time by the 35th Division.

TROOPS OF 81ST DIVISION AT MANHEULLES, NOVEMBER 10, 1918

Straight through Manheulles, leaving village on N-3.

Haudiomont was on the front line on September 12, 1918, and was the point at which the attack on the west face of the St. Mihiel salient pivoted. The 81st Division attacked from the vicinity of Haudiomont on the morning of November 11 and pressed forward into the Bois de Manheulles, seen toward the northeast (right).

Straight through Haudiomont to kilometer post 49.4 and STOP.

The places just passed through can be seen, as well as a considerable portion of the Woëvre Plain. It was from the foot of these heights that the 4th Division, pivoting at about this point, attacked on September 14, after the 26th Division and the 15th French Colonial Division had reached the plain. The right of its line advanced to Manheulles and Fresnes-en-Woëvre.

Continue straight to Verdun.

ADDITIONAL PLACES OF INTEREST IN THE ST. MIHIEL AREA

The following list is furnished for the convenience of the tourist who travels in the area not on the described route. The map on this page indicates the general location of the places mentioned.

① **Abaucourt.**—Taken by 81st Division on November 10. Just north of this town ran the Michel I position, commonly known as the "Hindenburg line," which was a defensive position 2 to 5 kilometers deep, consisting of an elaborate series of trenches with continuous belts of wire.

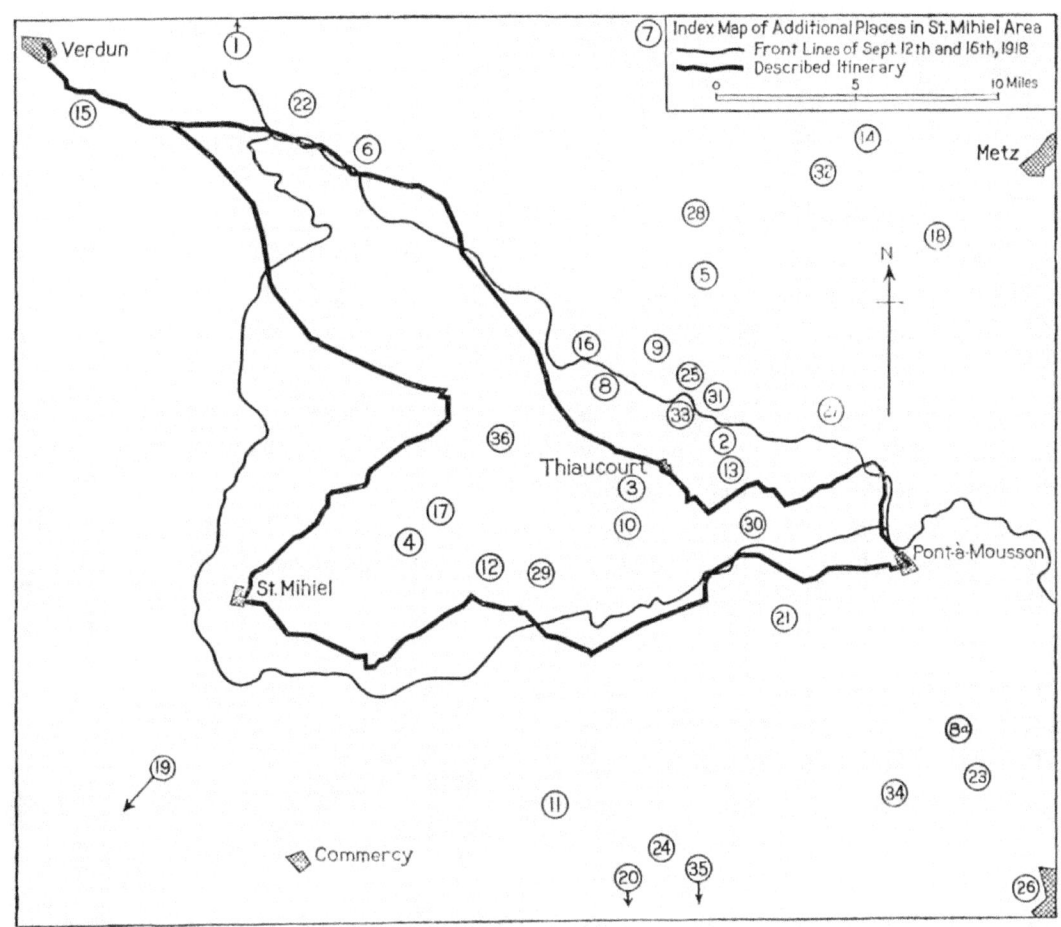

② **Bonvaux, Bois de.**—A counterattack by units of the 31st and 123d German Divisions was launched from this wood in the evening of September 12 against the 5th Division, which had advanced by that time about 4 miles from its jump-off line. The counterattack was repulsed.

③ **Bouillonville.**—Sergeant Harry J. Adams, of the 89th Division, won the Distinguished Service Cross in this town, for an act of great coolness and daring. Discovering a group of Germans in a building, he promptly fired his remaining pistol bullets through the door and demanded the instant surrender of the occupants. Some 300 Germans emerged, and Sergeant Adams, although alone and armed only with an empty pistol, made prisoners of them all.

111

④ **Buxières.**—Various German establishments were situated in the wooded ravines northwest of the town. These included a hospital camp, large dressing station, and an engineer supply dump.

⑤ **Chambley.**—Site of an important German munition depot.

ALLIED PRISONERS RETURNED TO AMERICAN LINES. ABOUCOURT, NOVEMBER 13, 1918

⑥ **Château d'Aulnois.**—Captured by 33d Division on November 11; was raided several times by various American units before that time.

⑦ **Conflans-en-Jarnisy.**—Headquarters of German Army Detachment holding St. Mihiel salient.

⑧ **Dampvitoux, Bois de.**—In this vicinity the Germans had an important aviation field and a group of barracks.

⑧ᵃ **Dieulouard.**—In northern outskirts of town is a large concrete emplacement for a heavy railroad gun.

⑨ **Dommartin-la-Chaussée.**—Location of large German supply depot which was connected by narrow-gauge railway lines with Chambley and German front-line positions on south face of salient.

⑩ **Euvezin.**—A German artillery camp was located in the ravine south of this town before the St. Mihiel offensive. It was used as a command post by the 89th American Division on September 14 and by the 37th Division later on.

⑪ **Forêt de la Reine.**—The 42d Division assembled in this forest preparatory to taking part in the St. Mihiel Battle.

⑫ **Gargantua, Bois de.**—A number of German shelters were located in this wood and on the northern slopes of Montsec and Loupmont Ridge.

⑬ **Gérard, Bois.**—The 5th Division advanced through Bois Gérard on September 12, but a powerful German counterattack, launched the next day, pushed the Americans a few hundred yards back into the wood. By midnight of the 14th, however, the 5th Division had driven the Germans from the wood and reoccupied all of it.

CHÂTEAU D'AULNOIS, NOVEMBER, 1918

⑭ **Gravelotte.**—Scene of an important battle in the War of 1870.

⑮ **Haudainville.**—Command post of 4th Division during St. Mihiel Battle.

⑯ **Haumont-les-Lachaussée.**—This village and woods southwest of it were scenes at various times of frequent small conflicts between 42d, 89th, 37th, and 28th Divisions and the Germans.

⑰ **Heudicourt.**—A small detachment of cavalry, attached to the 1st Division, while reconnoitering from Nonsard toward Heudicourt on the afternoon of September 12, encountered the enemy in force and was obliged to fall back. An important German supply depot was located here before the offensive.

⑱ **Jouy aux Arches.**—At this point there are still standing several arches of an aqueduct built by the Romans to bring water from west of Ars across the Moselle to Metz.

GERMAN DUMMY TANKS NEAR BUXIÈRES

⑲ **Ligny-en-Barrois.**—Location of First Army Headquarters during St. Mihiel offensive.

⑳ **Lucey.**—Headquarters of 89th Division for a time.

㉑ **Mamey.**—Headquarters of 90th Division during St. Mihiel Battle.

㉒ **Manheulles, Bois de.**—A battalion of the 81st Division attacked through this wood on November 9, but later in the day was ordered withdrawn. One of its companies failed to retire with the remainder of the battalion and the next morning was subjected to an attack by a hostile machine-gun battalion, only 40 of the Americans escaping.

㉓ **Marbache.**—Headquarters of 82d Division during St. Mihiel Battle and of 92d Division in November.

42D DIVISION PATROL NEAR HAUMONT

㉔ **Menil-la-Tour.**—Headquarters of 1st Division in January and of IV Corps during part of September, 1918.

㉕ **Mon Plaisir Farm.**—A strongly organized outpost of the Hindenburg line. Fire from here was largely responsible for checking the further advance of the Marines (2d Division) on September 15. This farm was repeatedly attacked and raided by all American divisions that served in the sector after the Battle of St. Mihiel. It was in possession of the Germans at the time of the armistice.

㉖ **Nancy.**—It is stated that the Kaiser came from Metz to view the German attacks north of Nancy at the beginning of the World War, expecting to make a triumphal entry into the city. Although it was shelled, all attempts to capture it were repulsed.

㉗ **Prény.**—Interesting ruins of an ancient stronghold.

㉘ **Puxieux.**—Near-by was an important German aviation field and large munitions depot.

Mon Plaisir Farm

㉙ **Quart de Reserve.**—The 1st Division encountered here many machine-gun nests during its advance of September 12, but captured the wood in a determined attack.

㉚ **Rappe, Bois de la.**—Location of important German camp.

Off Duty

㉛ **Rembercourt.**—This village was within the Hindenburg line and was held continuously by the Germans until the armistice.

㉜ **Rezonville.**—Scene of desperate battle in war of 1870. This battle and that of Gravelotte prevented Marshal Bazaine from retreating and forced his army into Metz, where it later surrendered.

㉝ **Rupt, Bois du.**—From this wood, and from Charey and Mon Plaisir Farm, a great volume of artillery and small-arms fire was directed against the 9th and 23d Infantry Regiments (2d Division) who had advanced on the afternoon of September 12 to a line just south of Jaulny. Hostile counterattacks launched from this vicinity broke up under fire of the Americans. A few members of the 2d Division pushed on into Jaulny during the day, but were soon driven out, and continuous fighting occurred in the area during the next few days.

㉞ **Saizerais.**—Location of headquarters of I Corps on August 30, 1918.

㉟ **Toul.**—Location of Headquarters of American Second Army; also of Headquarters of 42d Division while concentrating for the St. Mihiel offensive.

㊱ **Vigneulles, Bois de.**—This was a very dense wood through which elements of the 1st Division forced their way on the night of September 12–13 to the road leading east from Vigneulles and captured many Germans who were trying to escape from the salient.

CHAPTER IV

THE MEUSE-ARGONNE OPERATIONS OF THE AMERICAN FIRST ARMY

The plans of the Allied Commander in Chief for a convergent movement against the German forces were definitely made known to the Commanders of the Allied and American armies early in September. Under these plans the American Army was to advance northward between the Meuse River and the Argonne Forest, supported on its left by the French Fourth Army west of the Argonne. Northeast of Paris the center of the French armies was to throw the Germans back from the Aisne, while farther north the British were to continue operations in the direction of Cambrai and St. Quentin.

DIRECT HIT ON ALLIED TANK © G

The available German reserves had been continuously diminished by the Allied and American drives which began with the Franco-American counter-offensive south of Soissons on July 18, while the forces opposed to the Central Powers had been increasing rapidly on account of the arrival of American troops. By September the combined Allied and American armies were strong enough to attack at several points simultaneously. Faced by the threat of this, it became expedient for the Germans to keep their reserves more evenly distributed along the front; should they be compelled to concentrate to protect a particular sector, they would risk having to withdraw elsewhere, or suffer their lines to be broken.

The significance of the American Army's part in the general plan lay in the fact that it was directed against the most vital point in the German system of communications.

Within the German lines were two important railways which ran northwestward from the area around Metz and roughly paralleled the battle front. These railroads were practically the Germans' only lateral communications between their forces east and west of the Meuse, and were therefore essential to their supply system and for the transfer of troops back and forth along the front.

115

Northwest of Mézières these railways were rather widely separated and were at a considerable distance from the front lines, but in the vicinity of Sedan and to the southeast they ran through a narrow strip of territory which lay within 35 miles of the forward positions.

To the north of Sedan, as far as Liège, the country, including the Ardennes Forest, was of a difficult character, and no important east and west railways had been built through it.

The network of railways which radiated to the west and southwest from Liège passed through a restricted zone near that place, which was bounded by the rough terrain on the south and neutral Holland on the north. These railroads were the principal lines of supply and evacuation for the German troops along the front northwest of Reims.

Road Scene at Esnes During Meuse-Argonne Operation

It was apparent that an Allied attack in the vicinity of the Meuse River which penetrated far enough to gain control of the lateral railways behind the enemy's front would divide his armies. Once this was accomplished he would be unable to maintain his forces in France and Belgium because communications between the two wings would be practically impossible except by the circuitous route through the Rhine Valley and Liège.

Furthermore, the capture or defeat of his main armies would be practically certain, because under the stress of the powerful attacks which the Allies were able to deliver, he could scarcely effect an orderly withdrawal through the bottle neck at Liège. It was evident, therefore, that in the sector covering the communications near Sedan, the German forces could least afford to lose ground. The German High Command clearly appreciated this and had made elaborate preparations to prevent any Allied advance on that front.

Throughout the Western Front the Germans had constructed several successive defensive lines, one behind the other. West and northwest of the Champagne region, where loss of ground would have no decisive effect on the situation, these different positions were separated by relatively large distances. South of Sedan, between the Meuse and the Argonne Forest, however, where the important railways lay comparatively close to the battle front, the second and third defensive lines had been constructed very close to the forward positions, and formed a practically continuous zone of trenches and barbed wire about 15 miles in depth.

The nature of this region was such as to provide a series of strong defensive positions. The heights along the Meuse were not only strong defensively but furnished splendid sites from which the country to the east and west could be covered by artillery fire. The woods and under brush of the broken hills of the

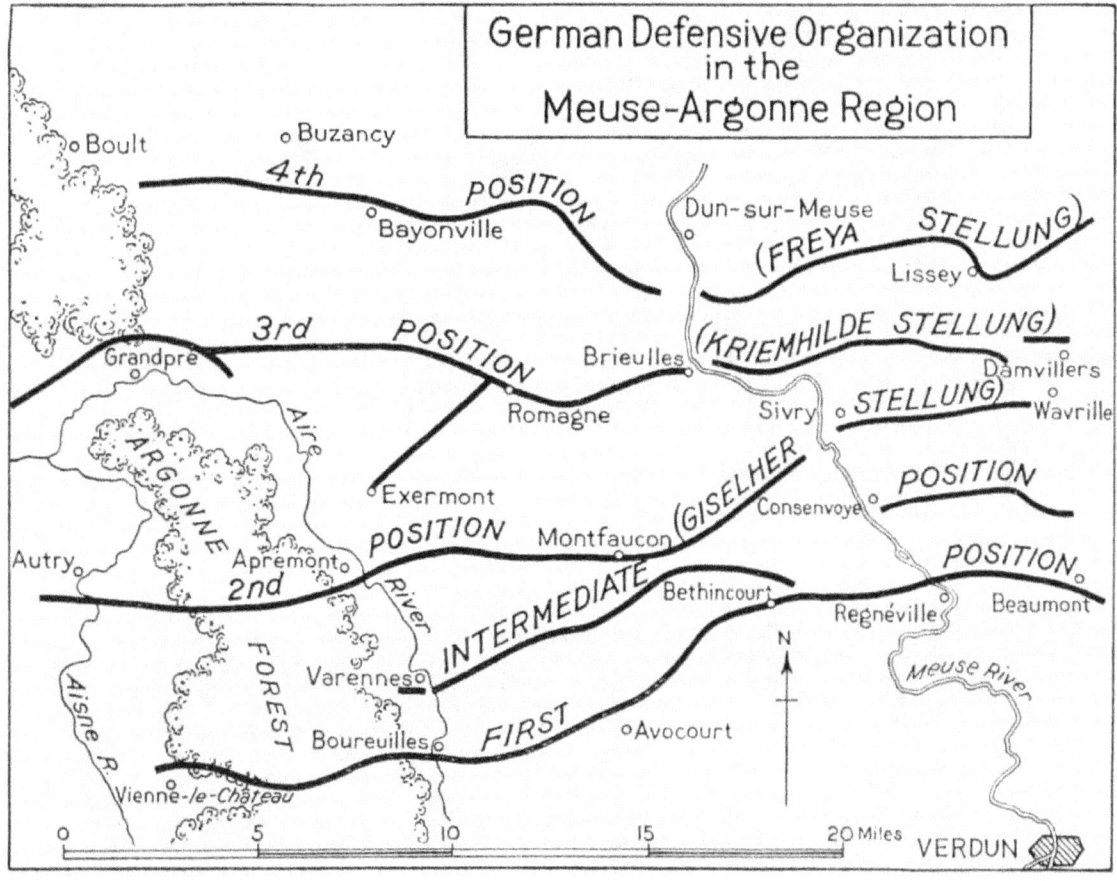

Argonne Forest had been organized into an almost impregnable position by the addition of machine guns, artillery, trenches, and obstacles of all kinds. Between these two areas lay the dominating heights of Montfaucon which afforded the Germans perfect observation, and whose inherent strength had been greatly augmented by elaborate fortifications. Furthermore, the numerous east and west ridges in this area lent themselves admirably to the construction of excellent defensive lines which connected up the heights of the Meuse and the Argonne Forest.

118 AMERICAN OPERATIONS IN THE MEUSE-ARGONNE REGION

While the difficulties to be encountered in an offensive toward Sedan were clearly appreciated by the Allied High Command, yet the decisive results to be gained by a successful attack made it well worth the effort and cost entailed.

This was the task assigned to the Americans in the proposed convergent offensive, and the whole army felt that it had been given the place of honor.

GERMAN MACHINE GUN GOING INTO POSITION. OCTOBER, 1918. © G

When the decision was made the American Army Headquarters was busily engaged in preparations for the St. Mihiel attack scheduled for September 12, and some of the divisions designated for that operation would necessarily have to be used in the drive west of the Meuse which was to take place only two weeks later.

This greater operation, to be effective, could not be delayed; accordingly the assembly of the divisions that were not to be engaged in the St. Mihiel operation was immediately begun and detailed plans for the larger battle at once prepared.

CUISY DURING THE MEUSE-ARGONNE OPERATION

The concentration of men and material was made entirely under cover of darkness, all movements being suspended and troops kept in concealment during daylight hours. At night the roads leading into the area were the scenes of great activity as the soldiers and their artillery, ammunition, and supplies moved steadily forward. The French remained in the front lines until the last minute on part of the front of the American First Army, to prevent the Germans being warned of the impending offensive. Under the circumstances the relief of the

French and their replacement by Americans was an intricate and arduous task. The accomplishment of the whole movement of concentration was in itself a tribute to the ability of the American Army, and to the skill of the staffs.

Finally, on the night of September 25–26 the First Army stood on its new front ready for the momentous battle that was to begin at dawn the next day, the units being in position as shown on the sketch on this page.

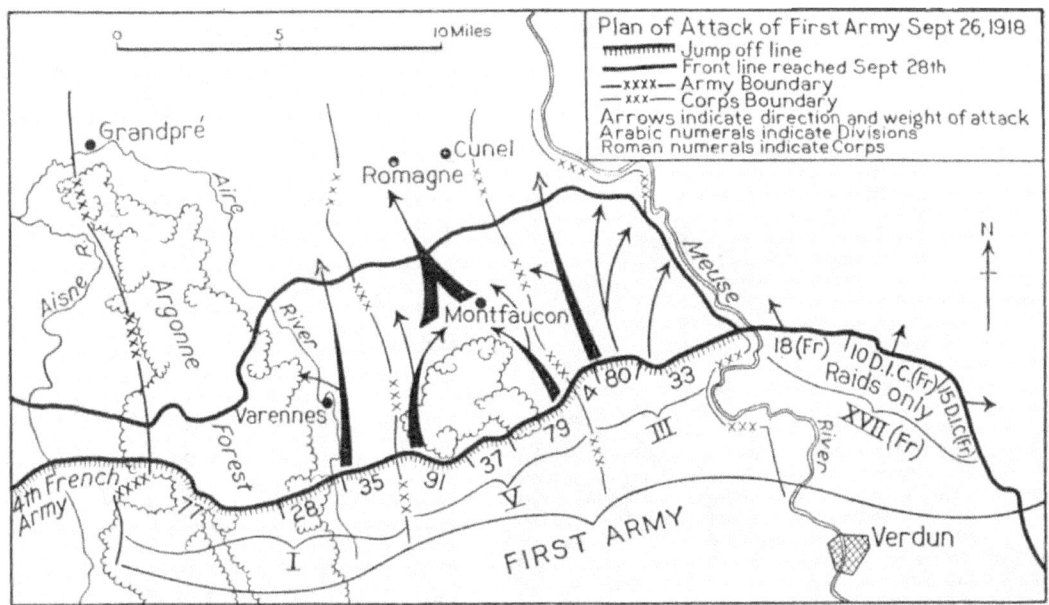

The general plans provided first for an advance of 10 miles to break through the enemy's first, second, and third positions, to be followed by a further penetration of about the same distance toward Buzancy to outflank his defenses along the Aisne in front of the French Fourth Army, and open the way toward Sedan and Mézières.

GERMAN ARTILLERY WITH MIXED TEAMS, 1918. ©G

The difficulty of capturing Montfaucon was fully considered, and it was decided to drive deep salients into the German lines on each side of that stronghold and, by threatening its rear, force the retirement of the garrison, thus enabling the divisions in front to carry it without serious opposition.

The III Corps was directed to hold the west bank of the Meuse as the movement progressed, and so protect the right flank of the army.

The Argonne Forest, on the left, was to be taken through the combined action of the Americans on the east and the French on the west. The 77th Division and a part of the 28th Division were designated to cover the front of the forest. A brigade, under French command, composed of one American and one French regiment was charged with keeping contact between the flanks of the American and the French Fourth armies.

The whole Meuse-Argonne operation may be divided into two parts, the first from September 26 to October 31, during which the army fought its way to the last of the enemy's lines of defense, and the second, from November 1 to the armistice, when he was forced into the open, driven across the Meuse, and his main lateral line of communication severed.

GERMAN OBSERVATION POST AT MONTFAUCON

A graphic representation of the succeeding operations is given in the map at the end of the chapter. It should be consulted in connection with the following narrative.

The artillery preparation for the initial attack began at 2.30 a. m. September 26. Two thousand seven hundred guns kept up an intense bombardment until 5.30 a. m., when the assaulting infantry went over the top, protected by a rolling barrage which preceded it into the hostile positions. The deep ravines, networks of wire, dense woods, and myriads of shell craters, as well as very inclement weather conditions, presented great difficulties, but, except in front of Montfaucon, the progress made that day was entirely satisfactory.

TYPE OF GROUND CAPTURED BY AMERICAN ARMY, SEPTEMBER, 1918

In the III Corps, on the right, the 33d Division captured **Bois de Forges** and wheeled toward the east along the bluffs of the Meuse, and the 80th advanced beyond **Dannevoux**. The 4th pushed vigorously forward and at nightfall found its left beyond **Montfaucon,** and about 3 miles in front of the division on that flank. In the center the V Corps did not succeed in taking Montfaucon that day, the 79th being unable to carry its defenses, and the 37th Division, on its left, could not advance beyond the hill. The 91st reached a position south of Epinonville.

The I Corps, on the army's left, made excellent progress. The 35th Division took the heights at **Vauquois** and **Very,** and the 28th, attacking along the eastern bluffs of the Argonne, passed **Varennes.** The 77th Division, within the forest, advanced about 1 mile.

The American Army had under its control over 800 airplanes, which kept down the German aircraft during the initial stages of the battle, and also rendered valuable service in bombing sensitive points and in securing information.

PLANES READY TO START ON PATROL DUTY

The army keenly felt the need of tanks, which in the first few days of the offensive were reduced in numbers from 189 to a total of 18.

On the second day the 79th Division carried Montfaucon, and by September 28th was beyond **Nantillois**, while the 37th had reached a line near the southern outskirts of **Cierges.** The center of the army had now caught up with the flanks, but the Germans' brief stand at Montfaucon had enabled them to reinforce their already strong positions south of **Cunel** and **Romagne**.

RUINS OF ESNES

While the attack on the first day had surprised the Germans, and important gains had been realized, the fighting all along the front from that time on was of the most desperate character. Every foot of ground was stubbornly contested, and the hostile troops took advantage of every available spot from which to pour enfilading and cross fire into the advancing troops.

At the end of the first four days the army had penetrated 7 miles into the strongest enemy position on the Western Front. The Germans quickly began drawing reinforcements from other sectors to strengthen their forces in the Meuse-Argonne region, in a frantic attempt to stop the progress of the Americans.

The 35th, 37th, and 79th Divisions were relieved by the 1st, 32d, and 3d, respectively, completing the relief by October 1. The 91st Division was with-

RESULTS OF TRAFFIC ON AVOCOURT-MALANCOURT ROAD BUILT OVER "NO-MAN'S-LAND"

drawn to corps reserve, and the 92d was placed at the disposal of the XXXVIII French Corps, just west of the Argonne.

The few roads leading to the front across "no-man's-land" had been almost entirely obliterated during the four years of German occupation, and the area was literally torn to pieces by shell fire. The wet weather during the attack further increased the problem of building and improving roads and railroads near the former front lines, which the limited number of engineer troops overcame only after great efforts.

OBSERVATION POST, MONTFAUCON

In the German defensive system facing the American Army on the morning of October 1, three of the most important positions from east to west were the **Cunel Heights,** the southern heights of **Bois de Romagne,** and the eastern edge of the Argonne Forest near **Châtel Chéhéry** and **Cornay.** In the next attack, the III and V Corps were to assault the Cunel Heights and the southern heights of Romagne, while the I Corps was to neutralize the hostile fire from the Argonne Forest and assist the V Corps by capturing the western end of the heights of the Bois de Romagne.

The offensive was resumed on October 4. The resistance encountered was desperate in the extreme. Not all the assigned objectives were taken, but important gains were made southeast of **Cunel** and immediately east of the Aire River. To exploit the latter gain, however, it became necessary to make a flank attack upon the heights of the Argonne near Cornay, from which the fire of

GERMAN CAVALRY REGIMENT ON WESTERN FRONT, 1918. © G

increasingly large concentrations of hostile artillery was hampering the American operations.

Early on the morning of the 7th, an assault was made by the 82d and a brigade of the 28th Division against Châtel Chéhéry and Cornay on the left and rear of the German position in the Argonne. At the same time the 77th and the other brigade of the 28th pressed forward from the south. The flank attack, although attended by very vicious fighting, was completely successful.

The advance was continued on the 8th with further valuable gains. As a result the Germans were forced to retire from the Argonne, and that menace to the left of the army was removed. This retirement freed the heroic survivors of the so-called "Lost Battalion." *See Chapter V.*

The success in the Argonne Forest on October 7 was followed on October 8 by an attack east of the Meuse. This attack was made by the French XVII Corps of the American First

AN AMERICAN DIVISIONAL HEADQUARTERS AT BRAS

Army, which was composed of two French divisions reinforced by the 29th and 33d American Divisions, making it two-thirds American in strength. It cleared the enemy from the heights opposite the III Corps, thus eliminating the serious flanking fire which had been bothering the right of that unit, and captured approximately 3,000 prisoners. This advance created a strong additional threat against the enemy's main lateral line of communication,

To reap the advantage of the two successful attacks on the flanks, the center of the army resumed the offensive on October 9. On that date, important positions in the Kriemhilde-Stellung, the name given to the Hindenburg line in this region, were gained. The incessant attacks of the III and V Corps drove the Germans back upon the Kriemhilde-Stellung all along the Army front, and by the 11th the III Corps had broken through that line and gained a foothold in the **Bois de Forêt**. On the same day, the 82d Division of the I Corps seized a valuable part of the same line east of **St. Juvin**. These operations involved fighting of the most vicious sort throughout the front, some points changing hands several times in a single day.

CAPTIVE BALLOON ON FIRE

The French Fourth Army, assisted at a critical period by the 2d and 36th American Divisions (*see Chapter V*), had gained the southern bank of the Aire River and the west bank of the Aisne as far north as **Vouziers**.

Plans were prepared for a new general assault to take place on the 15th, but upon the request of the French Fourth Army, which was to attack simultaneously in an attempt to outflank the German troops in the forest on our left, the date was changed to October 14th.

The III Corps, with the 4th, 3d, and 5th Divisions in line from right to left, and the V Corps with the 32d and 42d in the same order, were to drive salients through the Kriemhilde-Stellung along the flanks of the Bois de Romagne and the Bois de Bantheville. They were then to clean out the woods between the salients and continue the advance northward.

INFANTRY ADVANCING IN SUPPORT NEAR ROMAGNE

The I Corps, in which were the 82d and 77th Divisions, was to hold off the enemy on the west, and to protect the left of the V Corps. The Germans opposed a violent resistance to these attacks, and only small gains were made on the 14th, the most important being the capture of **Côte Dame Marie** by the 32d Division.

The attacks were continued on the 15th and 16th, the principal results being the capture of **Côte de Chatillon** and the ridge between St. Juvin and St. Georges. Although the attacking troops at almost all other points were held practically to a standstill, the penetration made by the V Corps was in a vital point and opened the way for further advances.

While this intense fighting was in progress, Marshal Foch requested two American divisions to assist the French Sixth Army near Ypres, and the 37th and 91st were sent to that region, where they materially assisted in the Allied advances in Belgium. *See Chapter VI.*

On October 12 the American Second Army was formed in the Woëvre, and after the reassignment of the American sector between the two armies, the front of the First extended from Fresnes-en-Woëvre to the western edge of the Argonne, a distance of about 47 miles. The XVII French Corps, and the III, V, and I American Corps remained in line from right to left.

AMERICAN INFANTRY IN ACTION IN THE ARGONNE FOREST

General Pershing relinquished command of the First Army on October 16, and from that time on became Commander of the group of armies, in addition to his duties as American Commander in Chief.

In his report, covering the period of the Argonne Battle from its beginning to October 16, he paid a glowing tribute to the enlisted men and junior officers of the A. E. F. He said in part: "Attended by cold and inclement weather and fought largely by partially trained troops, the battle was prosecuted with an aggressive and heroic spirit of courage and fortitude which demanded eventual success despite all obstacles. The morale of the American soldier during this most trying period was superb. Physically strong and virile, naturally courageous and aggressive, inspired by unselfish and idealistic motives, he guaranteed the victory and drove a veteran enemy from his last ditch. Too much credit can not be given him; his patriotism, courage, and fortitude were beyond praise.

BUZANCY AFTER ITS CAPTURE

"Upon the young commanders of platoons, companies, and battalions fell the heaviest burden. They not only suffered all the danger and rigors of the fight but carried the responsibility of caring for and directing their men, often newly arrived and not fully trained . . . quick to learn, they soon developed on the field into skillful leaders."

Major General Hunter Liggett, who assumed command of the First Army on October 16, was directed to make preparations for a general attack, the date for which was tentatively set as October 28. Local operations were undertaken by the different units on the front in order to secure good jump-off lines for the approaching offensive.

By the 22d of the month the III and V Corps had secured the **Bois de Forêt** and **Bois des Rappes** and had pushed to the northern and western limits of the **Bois de Bantheville**. The troops east of the Meuse gave the enemy no rest and continued to advance against fresh German divisions.

During the same period the I Corps, on the left, cleared out the woods near **Grandpré** in severe fighting, the 78th Division attacking almost continuously for 10 days. By October 27 sufficient progress had been made on this flank to enable the right of the French Fourth Army to advance. The activity of our left

ENGINEERS WORKING NEAR BARRICOURT
NOTE CONDITION OF ROAD

MAJ. GEN. HUNTER LIGGETT

corps had a material effect on the success of the final offensive, as it drew the hostile strength away from the center of the First Army where the main attack was to be delivered.

A number of front-line divisions were relieved during this period in order to give them time for needed rest and recuperation.

The American Army for the first time was enabled to prepare for an offensive under normal conditions. It was already on the front over which it was to attack, the majority of the Allied artillery and aviation units had been replaced by Americans, and supplies and ammunition were at hand in ample quantities. In addition, the weather fortunately took a turn for the better and this greatly relieved the hardships and suffering of the troops.

Upon the request of the French the date of the attack was postponed until November 1, on which date the divisions of the First Army were in line as shown on the accompanying sketch.

The general plan contemplated a deep penetration in the center to secure the **Heights of Barricourt,** followed by a drive on the left to connect with the French near **Boult-aux-Bois.** The capture of Barricourt Heights would compel a German

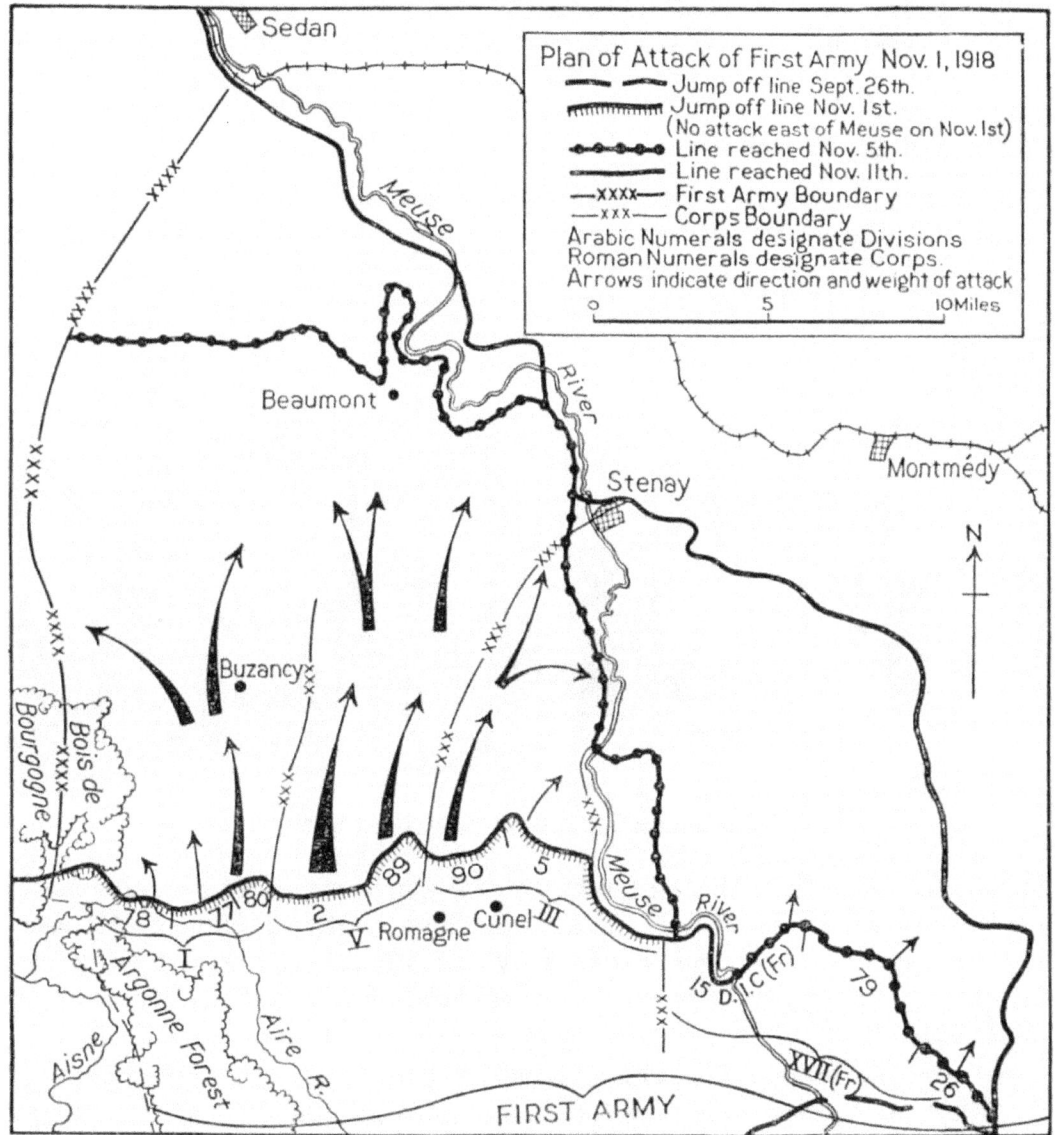

retirement to the east of the Meuse, so the III Corps, while assisting the main attack in the center, was directed to be prepared to force a crossing of the river.

The attack started on November 1, and on that day the III and V Corps broke through the hostile defensive system and artillery positions, and reached practically all their objectives. The blow was so heavy that the Germans could not organize a serious counterattack and shortly began to retire across the Meuse at **Dun-sur-Meuse and Stenay.**

Beginning on November 1 the western boundary of the army was altered several times by the Allied High Command, and as a result the general direction of the Army's advance was gradually changed from north to northeast toward **Montmédy** and **Carignan**.

The whole line was attacked with renewed vigor on the 2d and 3d, and continuous headway was made.

The Germans were in full retreat by the 4th, and the pursuit was so vigorous during the next few days that they were given no time to rest and reorganize. On the night of November 6–7, troops of the I Corps reached the heights overlooking **Sedan**. The Allied High Command then placed that city within the boundaries of the French Fourth Army.

The changes in boundary had served to narrow the front of the I Corps, and some of the divisions were gradually withdrawn to the south in preparation for an attack eastward from Dun-sur-Meuse.

VILLE-DEVANT-CHAUMONT, NOVEMBER 1, 1918

The actual crossing of the Meuse by the III Corps was begun on November 4, when the 5th Division established a bridgehead south of Dun-sur-Meuse. It continued these attacks, and, assisted by the troops on the east bank of the river, had by November 10 secured an excellent line of departure for an advance toward Montmédy.

The American Commander in Chief issued instructions on November 5 directing both American Armies to prepare for an advance in the direction of Briey and Longwy, but this occasioned no material change in the plans which had already been prepared by the First Army.

Late on November 9 Marshal Foch gave orders to all armies, directing that attacks be initiated and sustained along the whole front in order to take advantage of the demoralization of the German forces. He stressed the importance of pushing the enemy without respite to prevent him from collecting and reorganizing his troops. The First Army executed these attacks on November 10 and 11 by making advances along its entire front.

On the morning of the 11th word was received and sent to our troops as quickly as possible that the armistice had been signed, and that hostilities should cease at 11 a. m.

Thus ended the greatest battle of American history.

The First Army, which reached a strength in early October of about 900,000 Americans, reinforced by more than 100,000 French, was approximately ten times the size of the army which General Grant led through Virginia in 1864.

Its total losses from all causes were 117,000, but it had captured 26,000 prisoners and inflicted approximately 100,000 other casualties on the enemy.

EXTRACT FROM GERMAN PROPAGANDA DROPPED BEHIND AMERICAN LINES

ALLIED PROPAGANDA BEING FLOATED TO GERMAN LINES

Between September 26 and November 11 the French, British, and Belgians in the west and north gradually increased the vigor and strength of their attacks and made enormous inroads into the hostile positions.

Damaging as were these drives to the German cause, and valuable as they were in the Allied plan for victory, such was the importance to the enemy of retaining intact his defenses south of Sedan, in order to protect his lateral railroads, that he brought reserves from almost every sector on the Western Front to throw into the path of the American advance.

Even the last desperate scheme of the Germans to withdraw their armies from France and Belgium toward their own frontier, in the hope that there they could defy indefinitely the forces of America and the Allies, depended for its successful execution on the safety of these railways.

IMPROMPTU SERVICE AT EXERMONT SOON AFTER ITS CAPTURE

When the American Army, in spite of increasing reinforcements and against a well-nigh impregnable defensive system, had driven forward to a position dominating the German communications near Sedan, the termination of the war in 1918 was assured.

A VISIT TO THE MEUSE-ARGONNE BATTLE FIELDS

The visit to the Meuse-Argonne battle fields is divided into two tours, each requiring a day. The first, which is the shorter and more interesting, goes through that part of the area which was fought over from September 26, 1918, to November 1, 1918, and should be followed in case but one day is spent in the region. The second covers principally that part in which the fighting occurred from November 1, 1918, to the date of the armistice. The first day's tour begins at Verdun; the second at the American Cemetery near Romagne.

MONUMENT NEAR STATION IN VERDUN

FIRST DAY'S TOUR

The described route is about 85 miles long, and may be completed in approximately 7½ hours. *Before starting trip see page 271.*

The narrative at the beginning of this chapter should be kept in mind, and the map at the end of it should be consulted while following the tour. It is suggested that lunch be carried.

EN ROUTE VERDUN TO LE MORT HOMME

Leave Verdun via Avenue Garibaldi. (*See map p. 76.*) At monument in front of railway station, turn left on N-3 and note speedometer reading. One kilometer from monument, shortly after crossing bridge over railway, take G. C. 38 to right. For the

UNITED STATES NAVAL GUN NEAR CHARNY

next 15 kilometers the route closely follows the railroad, which is kept on the right.

About 8 kilometers from Verdun, at road fork at entrance to Charny, keep to left. During the latter part of the war, 14-inch Naval guns on railway mounts, manned by personnel of the United States Navy, fired from a position near **Charny.**

About 14 kilometers from Verdun at road fork near Chattancourt-Cumières railway station, keep straight ahead on I. C. 23.

A kilometer farther on is the ruined village of **Cumières**, now marked by a monument. During the fall of 1918 the main road which the tour has been following was an important avenue of supply for the American First Army.

FRENCH MONUMENT ON LE MORT HOMME

Take left-hand road 500 meters beyond Cumières monument. About 2 kilometers beyond Cumières, and 100 yards to left of road, is seen a tunnel entrance, marked by a sign. This tunnel, which was a very long one, was constructed and used by the Germans. From tunnel entrance, a path leads to other underground shelters used during the war, and to monuments on le Mort Homme.

About 500 meters beyond tunnel entrance STOP at top of ridge.

This point is on the northern slopes of le **Mort Homme** (Dead Man Hill). The direction to the monuments on the hill to the left is approximately south. **Hill 304** is seen 2 miles away to the west, and **Côte de l'Oie** extends toward the east from here.

Face north. The jump-off line of the American First Army on September 26 ran approximately west from the Meuse River to the western edge of the Argonne Forest. On this part of the front it lay along the northern side of Côte de l'Oie

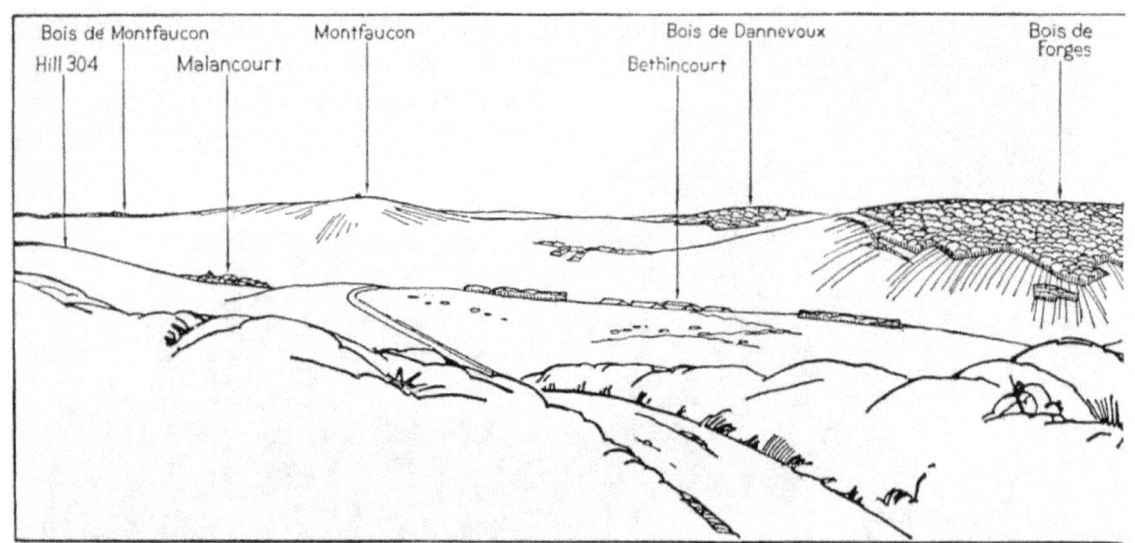

PANORAMA FROM

and passed just this side of **Béthincourt,** of which the tops of the houses can be seen to the northwest at the base of this hill. From Béthincourt it ran southwest, passing between Hill 304 and **Malancourt,** the village seen in the valley 3 miles west of this observation point.

In the middle of September, 1918, the 33d and 79th American Divisions took over from the French this front from the Meuse to Avocourt, a village lying 3 miles west of Hill 304. The 371st and 372d United States Infantry, 93d Division, serving in a French division, had held part of this sector for a considerable period prior to that time.

AMERICAN TROOPS IN LINE ON WEST BANK OF MEUSE RIVER NEAR FORGES

On September 23 the 79th Division was taken out of line, and the 33d, with some attached troops, took over its sector and held both divisional fronts, behind which other American units concentrated for the great offensive.

This point lay in the sector of the III Corps, which had the 33d, 80th, and 4th Divisions, from right to left, in line for the attack. The 79th Division, in the V Corps, was next in line, **Montfaucon,** the high hill on the sky line northwest of here, being in its zone of advance.

The German lines in this region were extremely formidable, having been strengthened to the highest degree during the terrible fighting on this front in 1916–17. The successive lines were on a series of ridges, one behind the other, and the German artillery had the advantage of splendid observation points, chief of which was Montfaucon.

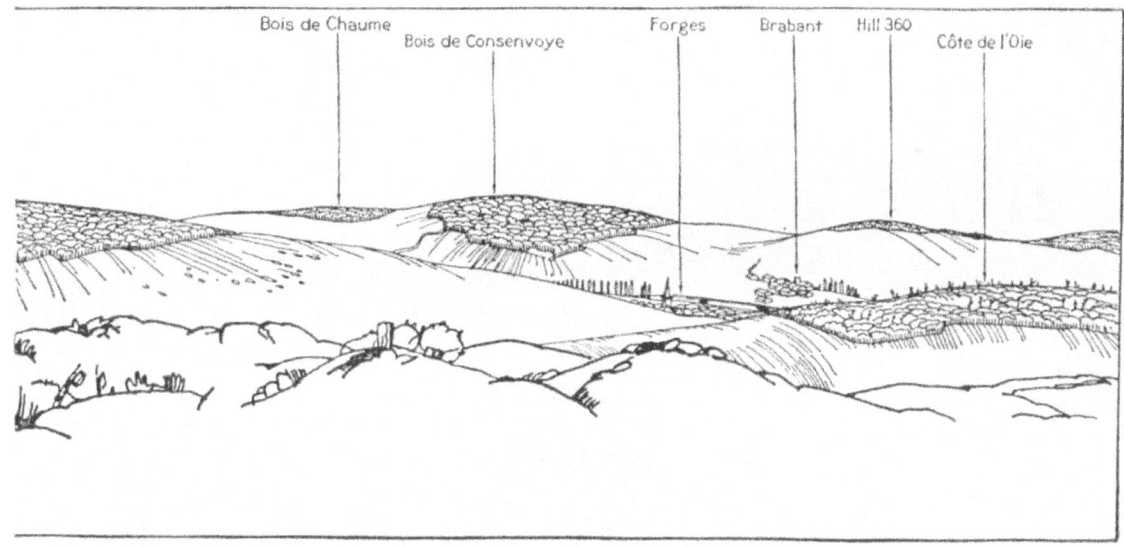

LE MORT HOMME

Supported by tremendous artillery fire, the divisions of the III Corps broke through these strong positions to a depth of 4½ miles on the first day of the attack. The 33d Division, after quickly capturing the **Bois de Forges,** the large wood seen 2 miles to the north, wheeled to the right and faced the river as a protection to the right flank of the advancing forces. The 80th Division drove ahead several miles, and that night captured the **Bois de Dannevoux,** the wood seen on the sky line to the right of and beyond Béthincourt. The 4th Division, passing this side of Montfaucon, made a rapid advance. Much of the ground gained by it will be viewed from the next stop.

Face northeast. The tops of the houses of the village of **Forges** can be seen 2 miles away, beyond which, on the opposite side of the Meuse River, is **Brabant-sur-Meuse.** The German line on that side of the river, extending eastward from

AMERICAN AIRPLANES

the vicinity of Brabant, was not attacked on September 26, although it was planned to undertake that operation within a short time.

As the attack on this side of the river progressed, the artillery fire from the wooded heights beyond it partially enfiladed the lines and became very troublesome. Preparations for the attack against those heights were consequently pushed, and on October 8 the XVII French Corps of the American First Army, composed of the 29th and 33d American Divisions and the 18th and 26th French Divisions, advanced in that area. The 29th and 33d Divisions drove forward on either side of Brabant, the latter crossing the river to take part in the operation.

GERMAN GUN DESTROYED BY AMERICAN AVIATOR

In three days the 33d Division had captured the **Bois de Chaume,** seen on the crest beyond the right corner of the Bois de Forges, and the 29th Division had captured the **Bois de Consenvoye,** seen on top of the ridge to the left of and beyond Brabant. Farther east the two French divisions of that corps made some advances. These successes relieved the situation on the right flank of the troops west of the Meuse.

The 26th and 79th Divisions, which had replaced the 29th and 33d Divisions, operated east of the Meuse during the last days of the war, pushing the Germans off the Meuse plateau, toward the northeast. That area will be visited later in the tour.

On le Mort Homme and the surrounding hills there occurred some of the most desperate fighting of the war. The Germans captured them in bitter and costly struggles in 1916, only to lose them when the French launched a local offensive here in August of the following year.

EN ROUTE LE MORT HOMME TO MONTFAUCON

Continue. Turn left after crossing creek at Béthincourt.

On September 26 the swampy parts of **Forges Creek** valley were crossed on footbridges which were carried from the American trenches and laid end to end across the mud. Later the engineers accomplished the colossal task of building roads and bridges for the artillery and supply trains across these shell-torn swamps.

At church in Malancourt keep to right. Two kilometers beyond Malancourt, on right of road, is **Hill 308,** on which are seen some remains of a strong German position known as the Ouvrage du Demon. That strong-point seriously impeded units of the 79th Division until captured on the morning of September 27.

HAUCOURT, IN NOVEMBER, 1918

DROPPING MESSAGE TO 5TH DIVISION AT FAYAL FARM
(INSERT.) WHITE PANELS DISPLAYED AS SIGNALS

Continue to ruins of church at Montfaucon and STOP.

On top of Montfaucon, just west of church, is the site selected for the monument, described in Chapter XI, which will be erected by the American Government to commemorate the entire Meuse-Argonne Battle. After monument is built the tourist should climb to its observation tower and read the following narrative from that point.

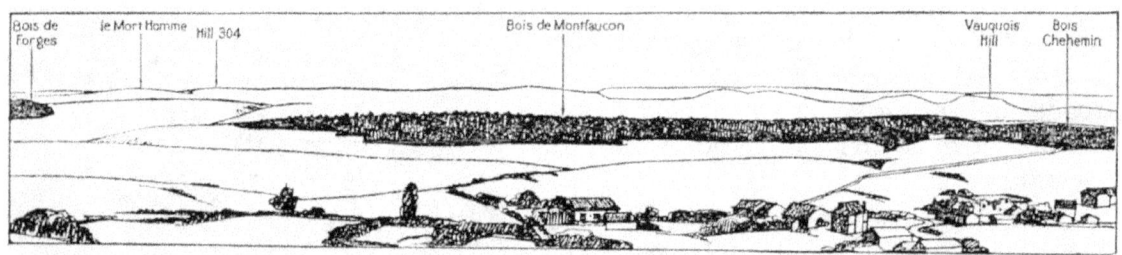

PANORAMA FROM MONTFAUCON, LOOKING SOUTH

Walk down toward Malancourt about 50 yards to a point of good observation on south side of hill. The Bois de Montfaucon is seen to right of road to Malancourt, and the direction to its nearest edge is approximately south.

Montfaucon was an extremely important point in the German scheme of defense on account of its dominating character and the facilities it afforded for observation. Several zones of deep trenches defended it on the south, east, and

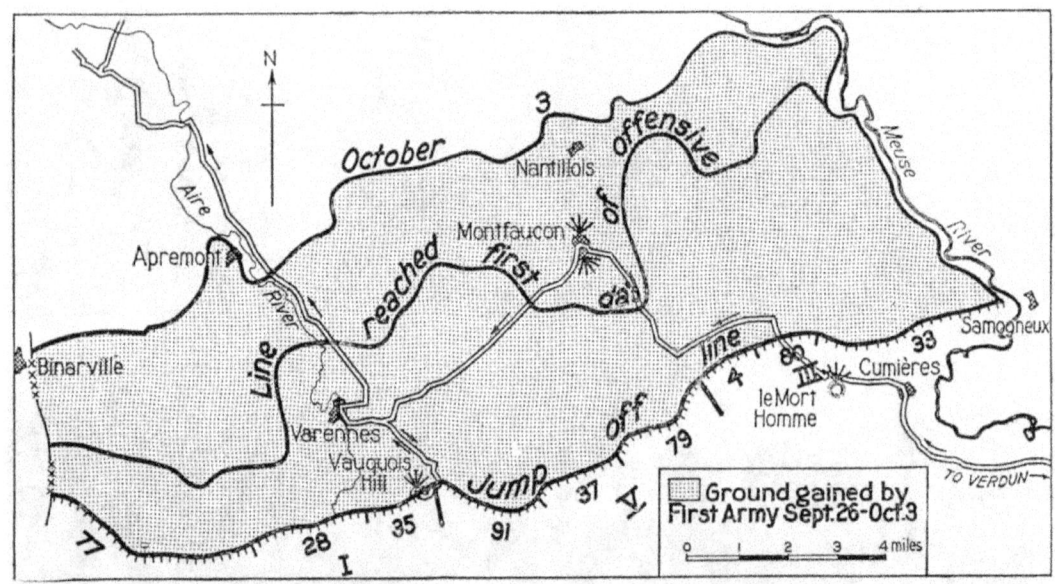

THE FIRST THREE STOPS IN THE TOUR, SHOWN BY FAN-SHAPED SYMBOLS ON THE SKETCH, DEAL PRINCIPALLY WITH OPERATIONS IN THE SHADED AREA
Arabic numerals indicate divisions. Roman numerals indicate corps.

west sides, and the hill itself was highly organized with trenches, concrete machine-gun emplacements, shelters, and observation posts. The natural strength of the hill is obvious from here. It lay in the zone of the 79th Division, but the plans of the Army contemplated its capture by making deep advances on its right and left, thus forcing its evacuation.

Before the offensive the American front line, lying just south of the Bois de Montfaucon, passed westward over the southern slopes of **Vauquois Hill**, the bare, oval-shaped hill seen 6 miles to the southwest.

The V Corps, composed of the 79th, 37th, and 91st Divisions in line from east to west, attacked northward from that line.

On the morning of September 26 a dense fog, combined with an artillery smoke screen, covered the First Army front, shielding the Americans from hostile view, but making it difficult for them to keep direction in the tangled woods and

VIEW OF MONTFAUCON TAKEN DURING THE WAR

(A) Site of memorial to be constructed by the American Government. (B) German observation post used by Crown Prince

(INSERT.) MONTFAUCON CHURCH OF THE PRESENT TIME

myriads of trenches. German machine-gun fire raked the valleys and the exposed slopes, taking a heavy toll from the attacking troops until the "pill boxes" were discovered and destroyed.

After struggling through the German defenses in the **Bois de Montfaucon** the 37th and 79th Divisions arrived in the afternoon on the near edge of that wood. Re-forming there, a regiment of the 79th Division, supported by a few tanks, launched an attack upon Montfaucon about 6.30 p. m. This attack progressed approximately ½ mile before it was stopped by machine-gun fire from Montfaucon and by heavy artillery fire which destroyed some of the tanks and forced the regiment to fall back to the edge of the wood.

By the end of the day, troops of the 37th Division, 2 miles to the west, were in the German trenches near **Ivoiry.** Farther west the 91st Division had passed those trenches and was at the foot of the hill on which **Epinonville** is situated.

Move in automobile, toward Nantillois, to opposite side of hill near kilometer post 3. The church spire of **Nantillois** shows above the rim of the valley about 2 miles to the north.

PANORAMA FROM MONT

The 4th Division, in a smashing drive, by noon of the first day captured Hill 295, 1½ miles northeast of Montfaucon, and part of the **Bois de Septsarges,** beyond it. Three vicious counterattacks failed to drive the division back.

The attacks against and on both sides of Montfaucon were renewed on September 27.

Troops of the 4th Division entered Nantillois, but were unable to hold it. The deep penetration made by the III Corps to the northeast of this hill, however, and the continued pressure of the 37th and 91st Divisions on the west, greatly aided the advance of the 79th Division in front of it. The latter made slow but continuous progress against heavy machine-gun fire, and, encircling the position, captured it about noon.

GERMAN SHELLS EXPLODING NEAR MONTFAUCON

A patrol of the 37th Division, which attacked Montfaucon from the west, did good work against machine guns on that side.

The Germans, having been driven from their successive lines south of and on either side of Montfaucon, occupied the powerful **Kriemhilde (Hindenburg) line,** which ran approximately east and west across the front of the American

First Army, passing about 4 miles north of here. The right-hand end of the high, wooded ridge 6 miles to the northwest is the **Côte Dame Marie.** It was one of the strongest positions in that line and afforded excellent observation over the advancing American troops. The rolling, hilly terrain for about 2 miles south of the German line was a highly organized outpost zone in which there were thousands of machine guns in skillfully located positions, supported by a great amount

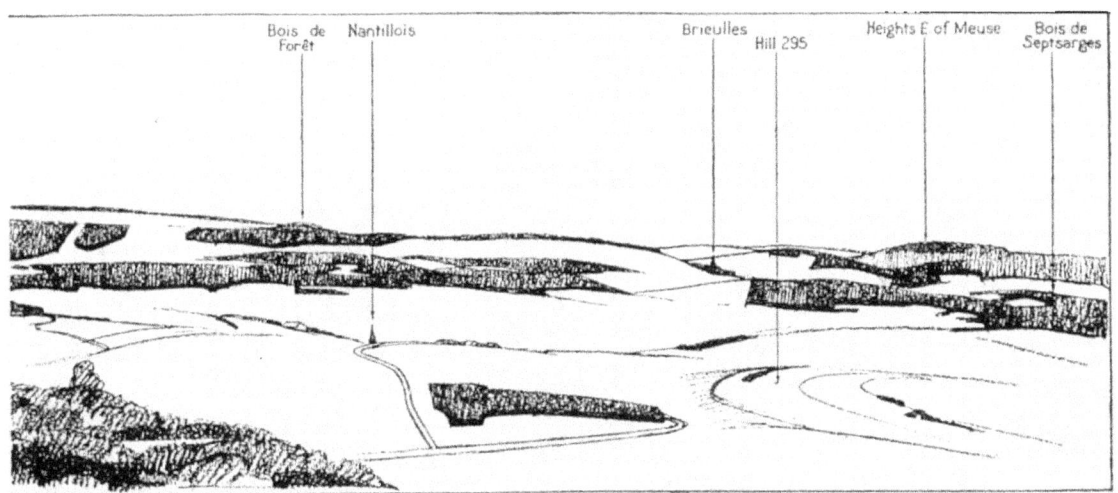

FAUCON, LOOKING NORTH

of artillery. It was through that zone that the First Army doggedly fought its way in the days following the capture of Montfaucon, and some of the hardest American fighting of the war occurred there.

Near the horizon to the west is the **Argonne Forest,** in which lay the left flank of the First Army.

On this hill are many relics of the war, including remains of machine-gun posts, concrete shelters, and the like. A walk over the area will be interesting to the visitor.

EN ROUTE MONTFAUCON TO VAUQUOIS HILL

Retrace road over Montfaucon.

About 200 meters from kilometer post 3, to right of road, is seen a Y. M. C. A. plaque which marks the former location of a house in which was built a strong concrete

TEMPORARY AMERICAN CEMETERY

tower fitted with a large periscope. It is said that the German Crown Prince, from that observatory, watched the German troops battle for Hill 304 and le Mort Homme in 1916. The periscope is now in the Military Academy Museum at West Point, N. Y.

Leave hill from southwest side. Pass through new village of Montfaucon on G. C. 19, toward Cheppy.

The American advance was from left to right across this road. About 2½ kilometers from Montfaucon, just before entering **Bois Chehemin,** the line reached by the 37th Division on the night of September 26 is crossed. That division and the 91st had severe fighting in capturing this wood that afternoon.

STREET IN CHEPPY. OCTOBER, 1918

Upon emerging from Bois Chehemin the **Bois de Cheppy** is seen a mile to the left front. That wood was quickly overrun by the 91st Division, which immediately afterwards met very strong resistance from the hostile troops on this ridge.

At la **Neuve Grange Farm**, seen on this side of the Bois de Cheppy. First Sergeant Chester H. West, of the 363d Infantry, 91st Division, won the Congressional Medal of Honor for charging and capturing, single handed, a strong machine-gun nest.

The next town is **Cheppy**, captured by the 35th Division on September 26. **Do not enter town, but keep to left to monument** erected by the State of Missouri to commemorate the 35th Division.

About 300 meters beyond monument turn sharply left on G. C. 38 and continue toward Vauquois Hill. At kilometer post 12.1 take road V. O. 3 to right.

MISSOURI MONUMENT NEAR CHEPPY

MONUMENT AT VAUQUOIS

STOP at church in Vauquois and follow path 300 yards along a communication trench to crest. The best view is obtained from the rim of the crater opposite (north of) the French monument now situated there. The direction from the monument to the church in **Vauquois** is south.

This hill was of great military importance because it dominated the surrounding country, especially the valleys to the east and west. During the war it was the scene of mining operations on a large scale, and the top, together with the old village of Vauquois which covered it, was literally blown away by French and German mines. Before the Americans arrived on this front the opposing lines faced each other on opposite sides of the mine craters, the French being on the side where the monument is located.

Vauquois was one of the strong points in front of the First Army jump-off line, which ran across the southern part of it and through the Argonne Forest to the west. The I Corps, with the 35th, 28th, and 77th Divisions in line from east to west, attacked from this part of the front. The 35th Division, which advanced in this vicinity, planned to isolate the hill by pushing through the hostile defenses on either side.

DESTROYED BRIDGE AT BOUREUILLES
Picture taken September 26, 1918

About five hours before the attack the American trenches near the crest were abandoned and the whole position was heavily bombarded. A few minutes before the assault, two infantry companies stationed themselves near the southern base of the hill, close behind the curtain of bursting shells, and waited for the fire to lift. Other troops of the 35th Division, screened by smoke with which the artillery blinded the German observers, crashed through the wire and trenches in the valleys to the east and west. When the German troops in this locality emerged from their shelters after the barrage moved on, they were killed or captured by men of the two companies who reached here almost as soon as the artillery fire had lifted.

TEMPORARY REPAIRS TO BRIDGE AT BOUREUILLES
Picture taken September 28, 1918

The zone of the 28th Division lay just the other side of the Aire River, seen to the west of here, and included the near edge of the wooded heights of the Argonne Forest. Southwest of here is **Boureuilles**, near the German front line, captured by that division on September 26. The French in 1914 had blown a number of huge craters in the road south of that town, and these occasioned considerable

A HEADQUARTERS OF THE 35TH DIVISION NEAR VAUQUOIS, SEPTEMBER 26, 1918

delay in moving heavy artillery and supplies forward until the engineers succeeded in making temporary routes around them and building bridges over them.

The 77th Division, which was the left flank unit of the I Corps and of the First Army and whose sector lay entirely within the Argonne Forest, advanced on the other side of the 28th, going forward about a mile on September 26.

PENNSYLVANIA MEMORIAL AT VARENNES

To the east, north, and northwest is seen part of the terrain passed over by the 37th, 91st, 35th, and 28th Divisions. *Consult map at end of chapter.*

By walking down the path on the north side of the hill the entrances to several German tunnels may be seen.

EN ROUTE VAUQUOIS HILL TO NEAR FARM DES GRANGES

Retrace route on G. C. 38.

At kilometer post 11 the scene of the heroic exploits of Private Nels Wold, 138th Infantry, 35th Division, is seen to the east on the slope beyond the creek. Assisted by one other soldier, he silenced several machine-gun nests and captured 11 prisoners. He then gallantly risked his life to aid a comrade, after which he was himself killed when he attempted to capture a fifth machine-gun nest. He was posthumously awarded the Congressional Medal of Honor for these outstanding deeds of valor.

At road fork near Missouri Monument (at kilometer post 9.9) keep on left hand road to Varennes.

That part of **Varennes** this side of the river was captured by the 35th Division on September 26 and the other part by the 28th Division the same day.

AMERICAN ARTILLERY NEAR VARENNES

28TH DIVISION TROOPS IN VARENNES, SEPTEMBER 26, 1918

While fleeing from Paris during the French Revolution, King Louis XVI and Marie Antoinette were arrested in Varennes.

Turn left at ruined church and keep to left after crossing river, proceeding to

AMERICAN BATTERY IN ACTION NEAR BAULNY

west edge of Varennes to monument built by the State of Pennsylvania to commemorate the fighting of all Pennsylvania troops in the war. *See page 183 concerning "Champ Mahaut," which may be conveniently visited from this point.*

Return through Varennes, cross river, and continue straight ahead to road fork near cemetery, turning left on N–46.

Opposite kilometer post 2, beyond river, is seen Montblainville, captured by the 28th Division on September 27.

A kilometer farther on, on the hill to the right of the road, is **Baulny**, taken by the 35th Division on September 27. From the road near Baulny there is seen to the left front beyond the river the village of **Apremont**, captured by the 28th

P. C. BRIGADE AT APREMONT

Division the following day. The wooded ridge on the skyline, seen about a mile to the left of Apremont, is **le Chêne Tondu**, a particularly strong German position in the Argonne Forest. Troops of the 28th Division gained a foothold on its southern slopes on September 28, but in spite of repeated daily attacks were not able to take and hold its crest until several days later.

Farm des Granges is passed on the left about 3 kilometers beyond Baulny. 400 meters beyond Farm des Granges, STOP near far end of large gravel pit, which lies to right of road.

The bank near the edge of the pit is a better observation point than the road.

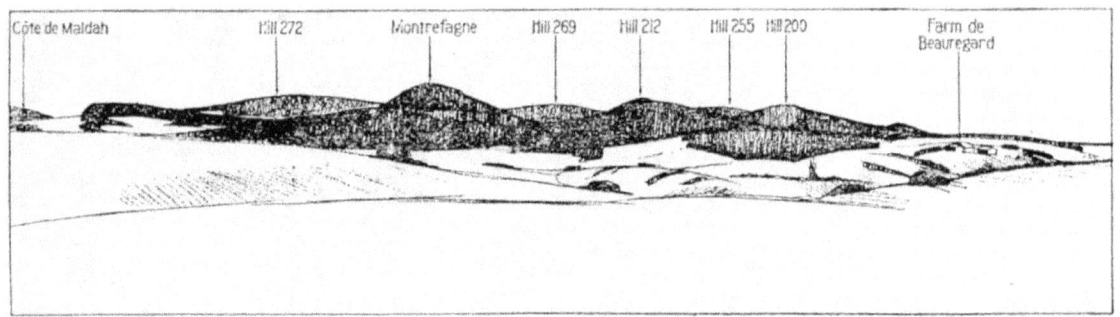

PANORAMA LOOKING NORTHEAST FROM STOP NEAR FARM DES GRANGES

Toward Farm des Granges this road runs approximately south. The large wooded area to the southeast is **Montrebeau Wood**. On the hillside a mile east of this point is the **Farm de Beauregard**. The high, round, wooded hill ½ mile to the left of Farm de Beauregard, and about a mile from here, is **Montrefagne**.

Montrebeau Wood was captured by the 35th Division on September 28. On the following day, attacking from the north edge of that wood under extremely

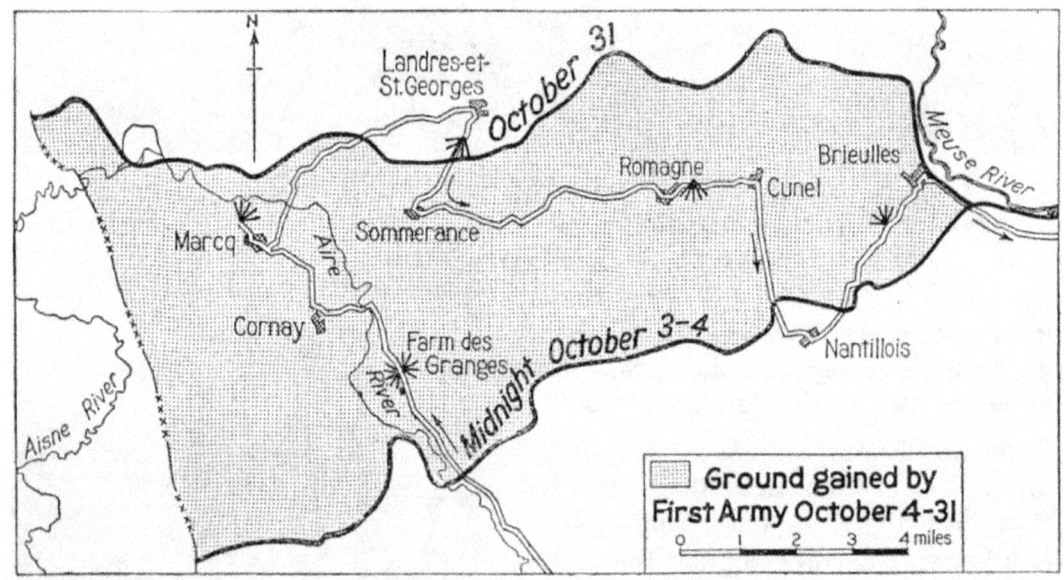

STOPS SHOWN BY SYMBOLS ON SKETCH DEAL PRINCIPALLY WITH OPERATIONS IN SHADED AREA

heavy fire, its troops succeeded in occupying Farm de Beauregard and the southern slope of Montrefagne, as well as **Exermont**, which, invisible from here, lies in the valley near Farm de Beauregard. A counterattack, supported by German batteries beyond the river, forced the 35th Division back to the ridge north of Baulny, where it was later relieved by the 1st Division.

On October 4 the 1st Division attacked northward from that line, while on its left a brigade of the 28th drove forward from just north of Apremont. The road through this point was the boundary line between those units in that attack.

Supported by tanks and a concentrated artillery fire upon all known strongpoints, the 1st Division captured Montrebeau Wood, Exermont, Farm des Granges, and Farm de Beauregard, after which it attacked Montrefagne, but was unable to take and hold that position until the following morning. The fighting in this vicinity was intense, involving many hand-to-hand combats during which the Germans fought bravely, often to the last man, before giving up a position.

DANGEROUS CORNER IN EXERMONT, OCTOBER 7, 1918

The attack of the 28th Division was also successful. In a vigorous advance it pushed forward past this point and gained a line along the river northwest of here.

Face west. The village straight to the west, across the Aire River, is **Châtel Chéhéry,** and **Hill 244** rises above it. The high, round peak immediately to the right of it is **Hill 223.** The low, flat-topped knoll near the river, to the right of Hill 223, is **Hill 180,** to the right of and beyond which is **Cornay.**

After the attacks of the 1st and 28th Divisions on October 4 and 5, the Germans continued to hold the high ground southwest of the river from Apremont north-

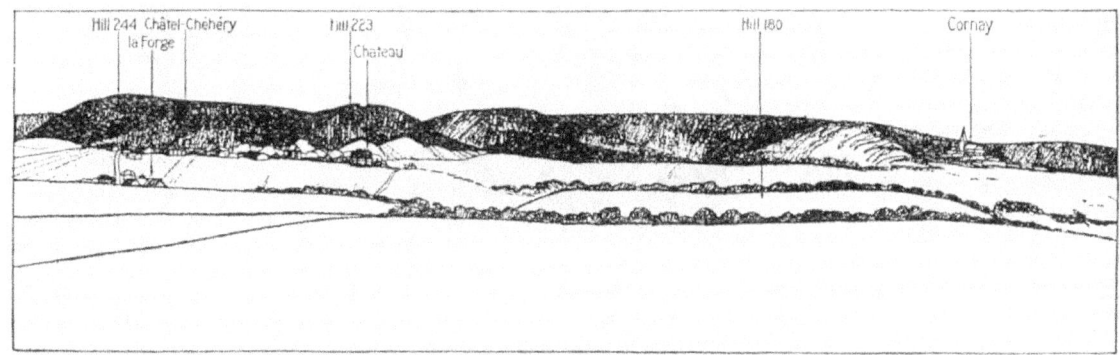

PANORAMA LOOKING WEST FROM STOP NEAR FARM DES GRANGES

westward, from which they could fire with artillery directly along the lines of the American units on this side of the river.

For the purpose of exploiting the gains of the 1st and 28th Divisions, and to stop this artillery fire, it was decided to launch an attack from this vicinity straight at the German positions near Châtel Chéhéry and Cornay. An attack in that direction would threaten the flank and rear of the hostile forces in the Argonne, and if successful would force a withdrawal from the forest. On the morning of October 7 the 82d Division, which entered the lines the night before, attacked westward from this road with a brigade of the 28th on its left. The boundary line between them passed near Châtel Chéhéry, while the right of the 82d Division was directed toward Cornay. This daring attack was remarkably successful in spite of desperate resistance, the 28th Division capturing Hill 244 and Châtel Chéhéry, and the 82d Division taking Hill 223 and Hill 180. As a result, the Germans in the Argonne Forest began a retirement during October 7 to a line extending southwest from Cornay. While the attack was progressing the 77th Division advanced from the south and effected the rescue of the survivors of the "Lost Battalion." See Chapter V.

During the early morning of October 8 a patrol of the 328th Infantry, 82d Division, in the ravine just beyond Hill 223, discovered a considerable force of

ARTILLERYMEN IN GAS MASKS

1ST DIVISION TROOPS ON HILL 240, NORTH OF EXERMONT

Germans. The patrol furiously attacked the enemy and after it had suffered heavy casualties, Corporal Alvin C. York took charge. Fearlessly leading seven men, he charged with great daring a machine-gun nest which was pouring deadly and incessant fire upon his platoon. In this heroic feat the machine-gun nest was taken and 132 prisoners were captured, largely because of Corporal York's extraordinary coolness and daring. He was awarded the Congressional Medal of Honor for this action.

On October 8 the 28th and 82d Divisions reached, and held against vicious counterattacks, a road and railway at the top of the ridge beyond Hill 223, which were the only important north and south communications available to the Germans in the Argonne Forest.

The 82d Division took over the front of the 28th on the night of October 8, and in the next two days pushed the retreating Germans from the wooded heights to the northwest, while the 77th Division, on its left, advanced rapidly through the forest.

Face northeast. The first round, densely wooded peak immediately to the right of Montrefagne and about 1½ miles farther away is **Hill 269.** In early October that hill was the scene of hard fighting by the 1st and 32d Divisions, which were assisted part of the time by units of the 91st Division.

EN ROUTE NEAR FARM DES GRANGES TO NEAR MARCQ

Continue along N–46. From bottom of hill, up valley to right, is seen Exermont, around which the fighting was particularly severe.

Sergeant Michael B. Ellis, 28th Infantry, 1st Division, was awarded a Congressional Medal of Honor for outstanding heroism displayed during the fighting on the slopes north of Exermont October 4 and 5. Constantly in front of his own lines, he, single-handed, captured machine-gun nests one after the other, and brought in over 45 prisoners.

CAPTURED GERMAN SHELLS

The next town is **Fléville**, captured by the 1st Division on October 10. **Take first road to left in Fléville and continue across Aire River, on I. C. 4; 600 meters**

GERMAN MACHINE GUN EMPLACEMENT

FLÉVILLE, OCTOBER 12, 1918

beyond railroad, at road fork near entrance to Cornay, take right-hand road toward Marcq.

Troops of the 82d Division entered **Cornay** on October 8, but were withdrawn late in the afternoon. On October 9, after a hard fight, they drove the Germans from the town and bluff above it. Later in the day the Germans recaptured

Cornay and surrounded a small force of Americans who fought desperately from house to house until they were killed or captured.

Marcq, which lay on the boundary line between the 77th and 82d Divisions, was captured on October 10 by troops from both those units.

Straight through Marcq and STOP at old quarry, 500 meters beyond.

The direction to the church steeple in Marcq is southeast. The Kriemhilde (Hindenburg) line, whose general location was pointed out at the Montfaucon stop, passed through **St. Juvin,** the town seen a mile northeast of here on the other side of the Aire River. This line, a continuous defensive position extending

GERMAN MACHINE GUN AND OBSERVATION POST NEAR GRANDPRÉ
Picture illustrates tangled character of Argonne Forest

along the entire front, was located so as to take full advantage of the natural defensive strength of the various geographical features. It was prepared by the Germans with the idea that it could not be broken and consisted of a series of well-constructed trenches, concrete emplacements and shelters, protected with continuous bands of wire; all arranged and organized in accordance with the highest art of defensive warfare perfected during four years of intensive fighting. When American troops arrived in this vicinity they were faced with the task of storming that formidable position.

Martincourt Farm is about a mile from here, in the woods to the left of Marcq. The town a mile down this road to the northwest is **Chevières,** a mile beyond which, on the other side of the Aire, is **Grandpré.**

Note that the Aire River changes direction southeast of St. Juvin, and north of here runs approximately west.

The 77th and 82d Divisions reached the southern bank of the river in this vicinity on the afternoon of October 10. The 77th was between Marcq and a point 1½ miles south of Grandpré, where its left connected with the French Fourth Army. The 82d Division lay east of Marcq, its line crossing the river southeast of Martincourt Farm and extending about 1 mile eastward from that point.

On the morning of October 11 the 82d Division attacked northward all along its front. One of its regiments advanced from the vicinity of Marcq against St. Juvin, but after crossing the river the regiment was too depleted to take its objective. The troops who attacked in the eastern part of the sector captured part of the ridge which runs eastward from St. Juvin. On October 14 the 77th Division extended its lines, taking over that part of the 82d Division sector in which St. Juvin is located.

The First Army made a general attack on the 14th. The 82d Division, in a vigorous assault, broke through the Kriemhilde line northeast of St. Juvin, thereby greatly weakening the hold of the Germans on the town.

The 77th Division was unable to cross the river that day south of St. Juvin, but some of its troops later in the day crossed near Martincourt Farm into the 82d Division sector and attacked the town from the southeast, capturing

GROUND ADVANCED OVER BY 78TH DIVISION NEAR BOIS DE BOURGOGNE

AMERICAN TANKS IN ARGONNE FOREST

it and the southern part of **Hill 182.** West of here other elements of the same division crossed the river and reached the buildings known as **La Lairesse,** seen a mile to the north, and held on until the next day when they were withdrawn.

The troops on the left of the 77th Division crossed the river late on October 15 and, attacking early the next morning, gained a foothold in the houses in the southern part of Grandpré.

The 78th Division relieved the 77th during the morning of October 16, and attacked on the front west of Hill 182, while the 82d Division launched an attack east of that hill, the combined effort forcing the Germans from its northern slopes.

Pushing on via the valley of the **Agron**, seen just to the left of Hill 182, troops of the 82d Division reached **Champigneulle**, seen about 2 miles north of here, but later retired to Hill 182. The 78th Division gained the high ground immediately to the west of the Agron River, and on the following day captured the southern part of the **Bois des Loges,** the large wooded area on the sky line to the left of Champigneulle.

CHAMPIGNEULLE AFTER ITS CAPTURE BY 77TH DIVISION
Note destruction caused by American artillery fire

Bois de Loges was a very strong position in the Kriemhilde line, and fairly bristled with machine guns. Many German batteries in that wood, and in the **Bois de Bourgogne,** the large wooded area on the sky line just to the right of Grandpré, kept up an incessant fire upon the Americans.

Bellejoyeuse Farm is seen on the edge of Bois de Bourgogne, ½ mile to the right of Grandpré. The left elements of the 78th Division reached the foot of the slopes below the farm during October 18 and 19.

After many attempts to complete the capture of the Bois des Loges and the Bellejoyeuse Farm ridge, troops of the 78th Division were withdrawn on October 20 to a line which ran roughly eastward from the southern part of Grandpré.

The high ridge north of Grandpré terminates at that town in a steep bluff, on which the Germans occupied a walled citadel of great strength. The 78th Division fought hard for the complete possession of Grandpré until October 23, when the walls of the citadel were scaled and it was taken in a hand-to-hand fight.

Beyond (west of) Bellejoyeuse Farm the same division drove forward into the Bois de Bourgogne for more than a mile north of the river, but the Germans held on to the territory in the immediate vicinity of that farm until after the close of the month.

RATION DUMP AT CHARPENTRY

The general offensive was resumed on November 1. The story of the First Army attack on this date is told in considerable detail in the general narrative. The I Corps order of battle for the attack was the 80th, 77th, and 78th Divisions from east to west, the first two units taking over the sector of the 82d the night before.

The 77th and 78th Divisions met strong resistance, the 77th gaining some ground on the ridge to the right of Champigneulle, while the 78th Division captured Bellejoyeuse Farm and part of the Bois des Loges.

CAPTURED MACHINE GUN ON CITADEL AT GRANDPRÉ

Due to a deep advance by the American forces farther east, the Germans withdrew most of their troops on this part of the front during the night of November 1-2, leaving behind machine-gun units to delay the pursuit. On the following day the 77th Division overcame the resistance around Champigneulle and advanced about 5 miles. The 78th Division cleaned out the remaining machine-gun nests in the Bois des Loges, and pushed on 4 miles beyond. On the morning of November 3 it connected up with the French Fourth Army at **Boult-aux-Bois,** 8 miles northwest of here.

The 80th Division sector will be viewed later in the tour.

The described route from here to the Meuse River crosses the Kriemhilde line several times. Its location will be pointed out at stops.

EN ROUTE NEAR MARCQ TO NEAR LANDRES-ET-ST. GEORGES

Retrace route. At far edge of Marcq turn left toward St. Juvin. About 1 kilometer from Marcq the road crosses a railroad along which the front line of the 82d Division lay from October 11 to 13. A large German supply depot was located near this point, and another was just west (left) of St. Juvin, the two being connected by a narrow-gauge railway, which has been removed.

Continue through St. Juvin to church, note speedometer reading, and take right-hand road to St. Georges.

Three kilometers from the church the road crosses **Hill 216.** The Kriemhilde line, which ran over it in an east and west direction, is still marked by concrete shelters, one of which, level with the ground, can be seen on each side of the road about 50 yards away.

The hill was captured on October 16 by the 82d Division, which then held the former German line in this vicinity until the end of the month. The 80th Division attacked northward from this line on November 1. At the beginning of that attack some of the Germans, in order to escape the American barrage, crawled forward close to the jump-off line of that division; but after the artillery fire had moved on, they were quickly mopped up by the attacking troops.

SIGNAL CORPS PHOTOGRAPHER AT ST. JUVIN

(LOWER.) MACHINE-GUN UNIT IN POSITION, ST. JUVIN, NOVEMBER 1, 1918

Straight through St. Georges, taken by troops of the 2d and 80th Divisions on November 1, **toward Landres-et-St. Georges,** captured by the 2d Division the same day.

Take first road to right in Landres-et-St. Georges; 800 meters farther on STOP at 2d Division bowlder.

The direction down the road is approximately southwest. The large sparsely wooded hill about a mile away to the east is the **Côte de Chatillon,** and to the right of and beyond it is seen **Hill 288.** In this vicinity the Kriemhilde line passed across the ridge on which the observer is standing, thence along the southwestern slopes of the Côte de Chatillon, and over Hill 288. The latter hill is the western end of a ridge which was one of the strongest and best organized points in this German line, and which included Côte Dame Marie.

Face southwest. A mile and a half away the church steeple showing above the horizon is in **Sommerance**. The twin hills seen to the left of it form the **Côte de Maldah**. The high wooded hill beyond the left end of Côte de Maldah is **Hill 272** and to the left of the latter point, rising abruptly, is **Hill 263**.

GERMAN PLANE BROUGHT DOWN, OCTOBER 4, 1918

These hills were prominent features in the outpost system protecting this part of the Kriemhilde line. The 1st Division captured them October 9 and 10 in a series of beautifully executed attacks. All the available artillery fire in the 1st Division was concentrated upon each hill individually, while the infantry pushed close up, ready to assault. Upon signal, the artillery would quickly shift to a new target while the infantry charged the hill, occupying it before the remaining Germans could offer serious resistance.

On October 10 the front line of the 1st Division included Sommerance, the Côte de Maldah, and the near edge of the Bois de Romagne, seen about 1 mile southeast of here. Its sector west of the Côte de Maldah was taken over by the 82d Division on October 10, and the remainder was taken over by the 42d Division the next day. On the 13th the 42d Division extended its line toward the east taking over that part of the front facing Hill 288.

TANK AND SUPPLY WAGON BLOWN UP BY GERMAN ROAD MINE

In the general attack of October 14 the 42d Division captured Hill 288 about noon, at the same time that Côte Dame Marie, beyond, was taken by the 32d Division. In repeated attacks that day, however, the 42d Division was unable to advance up the southwest slope of the Côte de Chatillon. In this part of its sector the ridge on which the observer is standing was reached on both sides of the road during the assault, but the troops were forced to retire soon thereafter a short distance to the south.

On October 15 the 42d Division renewed the attack all along its front. The crest of this ridge was again reached, but the gains were not held and the front lines stabilized temporarily along the little valley 600 yards south of here.

In the eastern part of the sector, the Côte de Chatillon was not taken on October 15, but by evening elements of the division had broken into the German defensive system on the southern slopes of the hill. It was captured on October 16 in a severe hand-to-hand struggle, after which no more attacks were launched by the 42d Division, which was relieved from the line on November 1.

The large forest immediately to the left of and beyond the Côte de Chatillon is the **Bois de Bantheville,** the southern half of which was captured by the 32d Division prior to October 19. The 89th Division, having relieved the 32d, completed its capture on October 22.

(Insert) Soldier Stringing a Telephone Line
Testing Line at Sommerance, November 2, 1918

Early on the morning of November 1 the 2d Division passed through the front lines of the 42d Division and attacked toward the north. The infantry jumped off from Côte de Chatillon, and the Marines from a point just south of this ridge. Supported by a heavy artillery fire the 2d Division quickly overran the strong German positions here and by nightfall had advanced more than 6 miles to the north of this point.

EN ROUTE NEAR LANDRES-ET-ST. GEORGES TO MEUSE-ARGONNE AMERICAN CEMETERY

Continue to church in Sommerance, turn right, then left toward Romagne.

Sommerance was captured by the 82d Division on October 11. The partly destroyed church was used as an American dressing station.

After passing Côte de Maldah on the right of the road 1 kilometer beyond Sommerance, the route enters the Bois de Romagne.

About 1½ kilometers farther on the road passes over the northern slope of Hill 288 and across a deep trench of the Kriemhilde line, the remains of which are visible on both sides of the road.

On this hill and on others in the vicinity were concrete emplacements for artillery and machine guns from which the Germans placed a heavy fire upon the 181st Brigade, 91st Division, when it reached the woods at the foot of the hill after hard fighting on October 9 and 10.

About a kilometer after leaving the woods on Hill 288 can be seen, on the ridge 2 miles to the front, the **Bois des Rappes,** captured by the 5th Division in the latter part of October. To the left of it, and 2 miles farther away, is the high, wooded ridge captured by the 90th Division in the general offensive beginning November 1.

Romagne was taken by the 32d Division on the morning of October 14, and a large supply depot located there fell into the hands of the Americans. Just beyond the communal cemetery at the entrance to the town a German military cemetery may be seen.

Take left-hand road at church in Romagne and keep to left. Beyond town, enter Meuse-Argonne American Cemetery and STOP at caretaker's house on hill to left.

For information about this cemetery and the chapel to be erected in it, see Chapter X.

The direction to the flagpole is south. The village a mile to the east is **Cunel**. The wood on the sky line to the right of and beyond the east gate of the cemetery is the **Bois de Cunel**. The valley in which Romagne is situated is that of the **Andon River**.

The high wooded ridge to the southwest, beyond Romagne, is **Côte Dame Marie**. From that position the Kriemhilde line passed along the southern side of the ridge beyond the flagpole, and thence toward the east, on this side of the Bois de Cunel.

Between October 4 and 9 the 3d and 32d Divisions, in line in that order from east to west, broke through the outlying defenses of the Kriemhilde position in some bitter fighting. In their

ROMAGNE CHURCH SET ON FIRE BY ARTILLERY BOMBARDMENT, OCTOBER 29, 1918

attacks during the next four days, troops of both divisions, on a number of occasions, reached the valley running through the cemetery but were unable to remain there because of the heavy fire from this ridge. During this period the 32d Division launched several unsuccessful attacks on Côte Dame Marie.

The 3d Division completed the capture of the Bois de Cunel on October 10 and the next day, after a hard fight, gained the crest of the ridge on this side of the wood, which position it held in the face of repeated determined counterattacks by the Germans.

In order to take part in the general attack of October 14, mentioned at other stops, the 5th Division took over that portion of the 3d Division sector lying this side of Cunel. On October 14 it attacked from the ridge beyond the cemetery, and in severe fighting drove the Germans from the one on which the observer is now standing. On that date Côte Dame Marie was captured by the 32d Division

AMERICAN CEMETERY AT ROMAGNE, MAY, 1919

in a brilliant maneuver. After breaking the German line at the near end of that hill, the Americans poured through the gap and attacked it in the flank and rear, capturing or killing nearly all its garrison.

On the slopes southwest of Cunel, during the fighting on October 11, Private John L. Barkley, of the 4th Infantry, 3d Division, placed a captured machine gun in a disabled tank which was well in front of the nearest American troops, hid in the tank until a German counterattacking line was abreast of him, and turned the machine gun upon it, totally disorganizing the German force. After hitting the tank with an artillery shell the Germans attacked again, but once more were driven back by machine-gun fire from Private Barkley, who had stuck with his improvised pill box. For this act of coolness and daring he was awarded the Congressional Medal of Honor.

AMERICAN 340-MM. GUN

EN ROUTE MEUSE-ARGONNE AMERICAN CEMETERY TO HILL 263 NEAR BRIEULLES

Leave cemetery by east gate to Cunel. Cunel was the center of hard fighting between October 10 and 14. Troops of the 3d, 5th, and 80th Divisions, operating near here, were subjected to heavy fire from the **Bois de la Pultière**, on the hill to the left (north). The town was captured on October 14 by the 5th Division, which also, with troops of the 3d, captured the Bois de la Pultière the same day.

Turn right at church in Cunel; 200 meters beyond take right-hand road (G. C. 15) toward Nantillois. The hillside seen 200 yards to the left of road at this point was the scene of the heroic exploits on October 12 of Lieutenant Samuel Woodfill, 60th Infantry, 5th Division, who was selected by General Pershing as the outstanding hero of the American Expeditionary Forces and was awarded the Congressional Medal of Honor. Lieutenant Woodfill was leading his company on a reconnaissance toward Cunel when it encountered heavy machine-gun fire.

"Fox Holes" Between Nantillois and Cunel

Followed at some distance by two soldiers he immediately went out ahead of his first line toward a machine-gun nest and worked his way around its flank. Four of the enemy emerged, three of whom were shot by Lieutenant Woodfill, and the fourth, an officer, was subdued in a hand-to-hand struggle. The company thereupon continued to advance until another machine-gun nest was encountered. Lieutenant Woodfill rushed ahead of his company in the face of heavy fire from the nest, and when several of the enemy appeared he shot them, capturing three other members of the crew and silencing the gun. A few minutes later this officer, for the third time, demonstrated conspicuous daring by charging another machine-gun position and, using in turn a rifle, a revolver, and finally a pick, killed seven of the enemy.

La Madeleine Farm

At kilometer post 10 is seen 300 yards to the left of the road a little wood, where troops of the 80th Division, during the night of October 9–10, captured a German battalion headquarters. The large wood to the right is the Bois de Cunel, from which the road emerges at **Farm de la Madeleine. STOP at kilometer post 9 without leaving automobile.**

This farm was the scene of some desperate fighting during September and October. It had previously been used by the Germans as a hospital, but the buildings and all the grounds near them were carefully prepared for defense. Elements of the 4th and 79th Divisions approached this vicinity on September

28 and 29, and a few supporting tanks reached the farm, but all of them were driven back a mile to the south. The farm was finally captured on October 9 by units of the 3d Division.

The wood which lies 500 yards to the left front (southeast) from here is the **Bois des Ogons.** Troops of the 79th Division advanced through it on September 28, but were forced back by counterattacks. The following day elements of both the 4th and 79th Divisions reached it but were also forced to fall back. It was attacked again on October 4 by the 80th Division, which fought almost continuously for its possession from then until October 9, when all of it was finally taken.

Six hundred yards to the right front from here is the wooded **Hill 250,** another strong German position, which was reached by the 79th Division on September 28 and again the following day, but each time was abandoned because of heavy artillery fire. It was captured by the 3d Division after a hard fight on the night of October 5–6.

Proceed. In the attacks over the ground lying to the right of the road between Madeleine Farm and the next town, **Nantillois,** many tanks were used.

AMERICAN OBSERVER JUMPING FROM CAPTIVE BALLOON
(INSERT.) AIRPLANE BROUGHT DOWN BY MACHINE GUN WHILE ATTACKING AN AMERICAN BALLOON

In the vicinity of kilometer post 7.2, Hill 274 is crossed. It was captured by the 4th and 79th Divisions on September 28, but the next day the 79th Division which was holding the hill withdrew its lines about ½ mile to the south because of their exposed position and the intense shell fire on and around this hill.

To the right front from Hill 274 is seen the **Bois de Beuge,** a particularly strong German position, which was captured on September 28 by the 79th and 37th Divisions, the latter taking the west end of it.

In the attack of October 4, the road we are on was the boundary line between the 3d and 80th Divisions. The 3d jumped off from the near edge of the Bois de Beuge, and the 80th from southeast of the crest of Hill 274.

At road fork at kilometer post 6.7, note Montfaucon, 2 miles to the right.

Nantillois was entered by troops of the 4th Division, who attacked it from the east early on the morning of September 27, but the Americans were compelled

NANTILLOIS BEING SHELLED BY THE GERMANS

to retire from the town. It was attacked without success that afternoon by troops of the 79th Division, but on September 28 it was taken and held by them. It was quite a road center and on that account was subjected to particularly heavy shelling by the German artillery after its capture.

Turn left in Nantillois at communal monument, taking I. C. 64 toward Brieulles-sur-Meuse.

Near kilometer post 2, on the left, is **Etanche Mill**, and to the right is the **Bois de Brieulles,** both scenes of hard fighting by the 4th Division between September 27 and 29. On the latter date a battalion of the 80th Division, attached to the 4th, assisted in the capture of the northern edge of the Bois de Brieulles.

PENNSYLVANIA MONUMENT AT NANTILLOIS

About 2 kilometers beyond Etanche Mill, STOP at monument on Hill 263. The town a mile farther down this road is **Brieulles-sur-Meuse** and the direction to it is northeast. The valley beyond it is that of the Meuse River. The **Bois de Forêt** is on **Martinvaux Ridge** which rises to the left of Brieulles. The road which runs along the foot of Martinvaux Ridge disappears from view between the **Bois de Peut de Faux** on the north and the **Bois de Fays** on the south side of it.

The Kriemhilde line running from Cunel, 2 miles west of here, passed through the Bois de Peut de Faux and along Martinvaux Ridge to Brieulles. This section of the line was covered by the fire of many German guns on each side of the Meuse River.

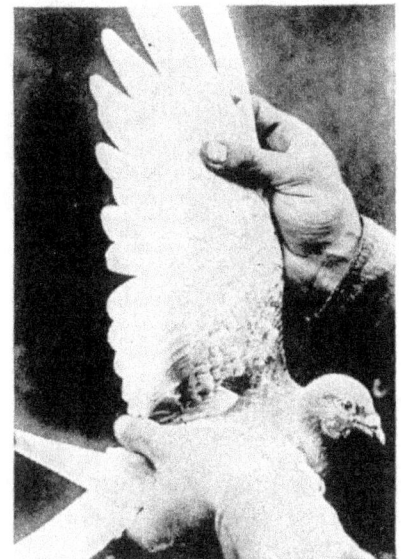

PIGEON USED TO CARRY MESSAGES

When the III Corps reached a position facing these defenses, that part of its line opposite Martinvaux Ridge was allowed to stabilize, and it was planned to effect the capture of that strong-point by attacking through the Bois de Fays and the Bois de Peut de Faux, after which an advance through the Bois de Forêt would completely outflank the ridge.

On October 4 the 4th Division, after previous attempts on September 28 and 29 had been unsuccessful, captured the Bois de Fays, and on October 10, with the assistance of a battalion and a machine-gun company from the 33d Division, captured the Bois de Peut de Faux.

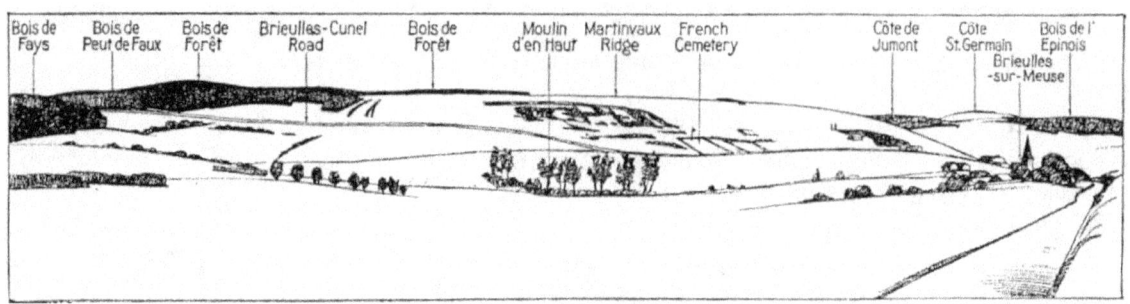

PANORAMA LOOKING NORTH FROM STOP NEAR BRIEULLES

On October 11 the western part of the Bois de Forêt was taken, where part of the 4th Division was relieved two days later by the 3d Division, the rest of it being relieved by the night of October 18.

The Germans had a very strong position known as the Trench de Teton on the crest of this hill, 500 yards east of this point. It was attacked several times by troops of the 4th, 33d, and 80th Divisions from September 28 until it was finally occupied on October 10. After that date, the Germans abandoned

AMERICAN PONTOON BRIDGE EAST OF BRIEULLES

Brieulles, it being dominated by the fire of American machine guns located on this hill.

The 3d Division, after advancing through some strong positions immediately west of the Bois de Forêt, completed the capture of that wood on October 22, finally forcing the Germans to evacuate Martinvaux Ridge.

The 5th Division relieved the 3d during the night of October 26–27 and took part in the offensive of November 1, swinging toward the Meuse River. In the face of strong resistance and many difficulties, it effected a crossing in force over that obstacle near Brieulles by November 5, and pushed the Germans back from the opposite bank. The detailed story of that operation is told in the second day's itinerary.

EN ROUTE HILL 263 TO NEAR MOLLEVILLE FARM

Continue toward Brieulles. A French military cemetery is seen to the left.

Turn right in Brieulles, taking I. C. 49. At kilometer post 5, about ½ kilometer beyond Brieulles, the **Bois de Chatillon,** captured early on November 5 by the 5th Division, is seen across the river.

At kilometer post 4 the **Bois de la Côte Lemont** is passed on the right. That wood was captured after hard fighting on September 27 and 28 by the 80th Division, which established its front line along this road. The line stabilized here and was held subsequently by the 33d Division. The troops holding it were frequently shelled by German guns on the hills across the river.

33D DIVISION TROOPS AT DRILLANCOURT

Keep straight ahead at Vilosnes railway station. At kilometer post 11.6, near concrete bridge, STOP without leaving automobile.

Across the river is **Sivry-sur-Meuse.** Two miles straight beyond Sivry rises the bald top of **la Borne de Cornouiller,** called by the soldiers "Corn Willy Hill." It was the scene of bitter fighting by the 79th Division, which took it on November 4. A violent counterattack launched a few minutes later was beaten off, but the Americans suffered severely. Later in the day, the Germans placed a heavy artillery concentration on the hill and attacked again, capturing the crest and 25 Americans, the only survivors of the garrison. A hastily reorganized battalion of the 79th Division renewed the assaults late in the day, gaining the southern (right) half of the hill. On the morning of November 5, three battalions, after a hard fight, again drove the Germans back and held the position in spite of terrific artillery fire and repeated counterattacks.

The **Bois de Chaume** captured by the 33d Division on October 10, covers the hill a mile to the right (southeast) of Sivry. Troops of that division, on October 9, reached the ridge straight beyond Sivry but were forced later that day to withdraw because of German counterattacks on their right flank and rear. During this withdrawal about 100 men were cut off and surrounded on the northern edge of the wood. They held out and were rescued the following morning when the advancing troops of the 33d Division reached them.

Proceed. About a kilometer farther on, up a valley to the right, is seen **Dannevoux,** captured by the 80th Division during the night of September 26–27.

PRACTICING FOR AN OFFENSIVE

Between this road and Dannevoux, the **Americans** captured an enormous depot containing valuable military supplies.

The little rise which the road crosses just after passing Dannevoux marks the boundary between the 80th and 33d Divisions. The front line of the 33d Division faced the river and lay practically along this road from this point for about 3 miles to the southeast, from September 26 until October 9. Near here, on October 7, a French airplane was shot down, landing in the flats on the German side of the river. Corporal Ralyn Hill, 129th Infantry, 33d Division, ran across a foot-

AMERICAN SUPPLY DUMP DURING MEUSE-ARGONNE OPERATION

bridge in the face of heavy fire and carried the wounded aviator to the American lines. For his gallant exploit he was awarded the Congressional Medal of Honor.

Turn left at Consenvoye railway station and cross river. After the capture of **Consenvoye** this road, an important avenue of communication for the 33d Division, was under direct observation from German positions on the high ridge 4 miles to the left, and was therefore elaborately camouflaged along that side.

During the early morning of October 8, engineers of the 33d Division, in spite of hostile artillery fire, built a bridge near Consenvoye on which part of the division crossed to join in the attack of that date east of the river.

The Germans were driven from Consenvoye in a sharp fight about noon October 8.

Straight through Consenvoye on G. C. 19 toward Etraye. At kilometer post 19, 500 meters beyond Consenvoye, is a large German bomb-proof shelter on the left of the road.

At kilometer post 17.5, by looking back, a good view is obtained of the ground beyond the river over which the III Corps of the American First Army advanced on September 26. Montfaucon is visible on the sky line about 7½ miles to the west.

At the entrance to the **Bois de Consenvoye,** near kilometer post 16, the Germans built a massive reinforced concrete post on each side of the road. These were so equipped that heavy chains could be suspended between them to check an advance by tanks along the road.

STOP near entrance to clearing at kilometer post 15.

The woods in this vicinity had been skillfully prepared for defense by the Germans with trenches, concrete emplacements, wire, and other obstacles, as well as by machine-gun nests and observation posts built in many of the trees.

In the ravine 500 yards to the right front (southeast) is **Molleville Farm.** The wooded peak straight beyond it, and about 2 miles from here, is **Hill 360,** which was a very strong German position.

AMERICAN TROOPS NEAR MOLLEVILLE FARM

When the heights east of the Meuse were attacked on October 8, troops of the 29th Division drove northward from a jump-off line about 3 miles south of this point. By October 10 they had advanced to a line along the southern and southwestern edges of this clearing, and in a hard fight had captured **Richene Hill,** located in the woods ½ mile west of here.

On October 12 a regiment of the 29th Division, in conjunction with an attack by troops of the 18th French Division, captured the western (right) end of Hill 360.

From October 11 to 15 the 29th Division engaged in severe fighting around Molleville Farm, finally establishing the line on this side of the clearing on the latter date. Attacks on the following day pushed forward, in spite of great opposition, ½ mile into the **Bois de la Grande Montagne,** to the left (north) of this road.

About the middle of October the 26th Division took over a sector immediately to the east of the 29th Division. Attacking northeastward on October 23, the 26th and 29th Divisions reached a line in the woods about a mile east of this point, where the 29th was relieved by the 79th Division on October 30.

Observation Turrets at Douaumont

In a general advance toward the northeast on November 8, by the 26th and 79th Divisions, Hill 360 was captured by the former unit.

On the sky line beyond the right of Hill 360 can be seen the hill upon which Fort Douaumont is situated.

EN ROUTE NEAR MOLLEVILLE FARM TO VERDUN

Continue on this road.

Just before leaving the clearing the remains of some trenches may be seen on the right, and about 2 kilometers farther on are some German shelters on each side of the road.

Road Through Bois d'Etraye, November 10, 1918
Route passes over this road

Straight through Etraye, captured by the 79th Division on November 8.

At road fork about 2 kilometers farther on, near which there are some German concrete shelters, **turn sharp right onto G. C. D. 5.**

A kilometer beyond the road fork **Wavrille** is passed on the right of the road. It was captured by the 79th Division on November 9, after which that division pushed across the little stream to the left; and at the hour of the armistice was fighting on the near slopes of the bald, shell-scarred hills 1½ miles to left of road.

At kilometer post 30.3, leave G. C. D. 5 and turn sharp right onto G. C. D. 6 to Ville-devant-Chaumont. Just before turning onto G. C. D. 6, the Côte de

MAIN STREET, VILLE-DEVANT-CHAUMONT, NOVEMBER, 1918

Romagne can be seen about a mile to the left front, upon whose near slope part of the 79th Division line rested at the armistice.

Straight through Ville-devant-Chaumont, which lay near the boundary between the 26th and 79th Divisions, and was captured on November 10 by troops of both. **300 meters beyond the village** a German cemetery is passed.

DIVISION P. C. AT VACHERAUVILLE, OCTOBER 31, 1918

Just beyond Ville-devant-Chaumont the route passes between the **Bois le Comte** and **Bois de Ville,** which were captured by the 26th Division on November 9 and 10. The advance was across this road from right to left.

Just beyond road junction 3 kilometers from Ville-devant-Chaumont is a French monument. After leaving the wood near that point, there is seen a mile to the left front the site, marked by a monument, of the village of **Beaumont,** completely destroyed in 1916. The front line of the 26th Division lay a mile east of Beaumont at the end of the war.

Continue into Vacherauville, turn left onto N-64, and continue through Bras into Verdun.

The route leading east from Bras, shown in broken red lines on the map at the end of the chapter, is a tour of the French forts near Verdun. It will take the visitor to the Trench of Bayonets, Fort Douaumont, and other places of interest.

35TH DIVISION TROOPS NORTHEAST OF VERDUN, OCTOBER 29, 1918

The town of **Verdun** was severely damaged during the terrific French fighting in the vicinity as the result of German bombardments with artillery and airplane bombs.

GATE AT VERDUN

Points of interest in Verdun are the underground part of the citadel; the cathedral and house of the bishop; and the Hôtel de Ville. The citadel is located on the western edge of the town. Its underground compartments served to house various French headquarters and thousands of reserves during the great battles near here in 1916–17. In the house of the bishop, which adjoins the cathedral, on rue de la Belle Vierge, there is a museum containing battle-field relics, as well as ancient relics of Verdun. The cathedral and cloister, badly damaged during the war, are objects of interest. In a room in the Hôtel de Ville, located on rue de l'Hôtel de Ville, are stored the many beautiful tokens of esteem given to the town by various nations in appreciation of its heroic defense in 1916.

SECOND DAY'S TOUR

The American Military Cemetery at Romagne, where this route starts, may be reached from Verdun in about 1½ hours by following the first day's tour as far as Montfaucon, thence proceeding to the cemetery via Nantillois and Cunel. If the cemetery has been visited previously, this tour should be started at Cunel.

The tour itself is about 95 miles long, ending in Verdun, and may be completed in approximately 8½ hours, allowing a reasonable time for stops.

Lunch may be obtained at Sedan, although time will be saved if it is carried.

See page 247 for information about the cemetery, and page 155 for description of the fighting in the immediate vicinity.

EN ROUTE MEUSE-ARGONNE AMERICAN CEMETERY TO NORTH OF CUNEL

Leave the cemetery by east gate. Turn left at church in Cunel on G. C. 15, bearing left on main road at end of village.

On the right, immediately after leaving Cunel, is the **Bois de la Pultière**, which was captured by the 3d and 5th Divisions in hard fighting on October 14 and 15. It contained many machine-gun nests which dominated the area around Cunel.

About 1½ kilometers beyond Cunel STOP at kilometer post 12.6.

GERMAN "KRIEMHILDE" LINE, BOIS DE BANTHEVILLE

The wood 100 yards to the right is the **Bois des Rappes**, where the 5th Division was engaged in almost continuous fighting for nine days in the middle of October. The Germans had prepared it for defense with many trenches, machine-gun nests, and quantities of wire, and the whole position was supported by artillery fire from the hills beyond the valley to the north (left of wood). Parts of it changed hands a number of times, until October 21, when the wood was definitely taken and held by the Americans.

The following day the 90th Division relieved the 5th on the north edge of the Bois des Rappes and immediately west thereof, coming into the line on the right of the 89th Division.

The village a mile farther down this road in the Andon River valley is **Bourrut,** and the direction to it is northwest. The **Bois de Bantheville** covers part of the sky line to the west.

As a preliminary to the general offensive of November 1, the 89th Division completed, on October 22, the conquest of the Bois de Bantheville, which had been partly accomplished by the 32d Division prior to its relief on October 20. The 90th Division attacked in conjunction with the 89th on October 23, and reached a line on the slopes seen just beyond Bourrut on the other side of the Andon River. From that date until the end of the month the 90th engaged in some severe local fighting, and made slight gains to the northwest up those slopes.

Straight beyond Bourrut is **Grand Carré Farm,** and the wooded ridge on the sky line to its right and some distance farther away is the **Heights of Barricourt.**

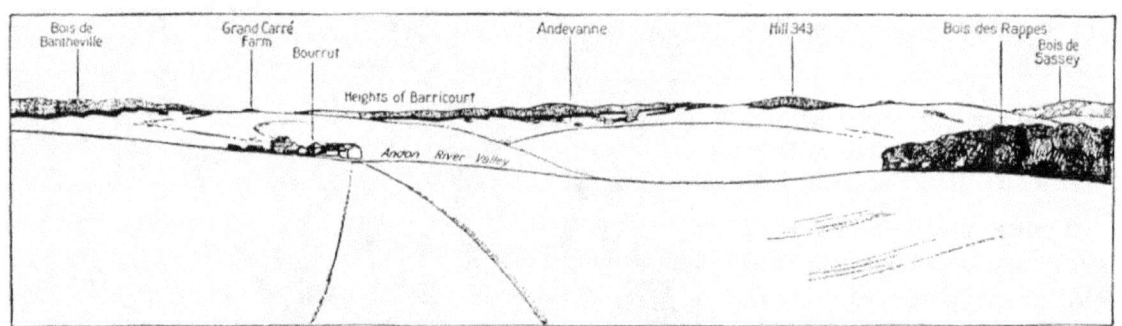

PANORAMA LOOKING NORTH FROM STOP NEAR CUNEL

The village to the right of Grand Carré Farm and about 2½ miles from here is **Andevanne;** and to its right, on the sky line, is the wooded **Hill 343.** Part of the wood on the horizon beyond the Bois des Rappes is the **Bois de Sassey.**

The strong Freya line, the last organized German position in front of the American First Army, in this region lay along the Heights of Barricourt, passed through Andevanne, thence across Hill 343 toward the east through the Bois de Sassey.

The First Army had prepared carefully for its next general offensive. The main attack was to be launched in the center by the V Corps, with the 89th and 2d Divisions from right to left as assault units, with the intention of capturing the Heights of Barricourt and thus forcing a German retirement across the Meuse. The III Corps, on the right, with the 5th and 90th Divisions in line, was to assist in the main attack, and be ready to force a crossing over the river. On the left, the I Corps, with the 80th, 77th, and 78th Divisions in the front line, was to begin a drive directly toward Boult-aux-Bois immediately after the hostile line was broken in the center. The activity of the I Corps during late October west of St. Juvin (visited in the first day's tour), had served to draw the Germans' attention to that part of the front, and this contributed materially to the success of the final offensive.

SECOND DAY'S TOUR OF THE MEUSE-ARGONNE BATTLE FIELDS

After a tremendous artillery bombardment lasting for two hours, the attack, with the immediate objective of breaking the Freya line, was launched early in the morning of November 1. The 89th Division captured the Heights of Barricourt, while the 90th took the wooded ridge north of Andevanne. The fighting on Barricourt Heights and just north of Andevanne was severe, involving many hand-to-hand combats with Germans in strong-points in the thick woods. Hill 343 held out until the next day, when it was overrun by the 90th Division in a hard struggle. On that hill, the Americans captured a battery of 77-millimeter guns and two larger pieces of artillery, with a large quantity of ammunition. These guns were then turned about and used against the Germans until the ammunition was exhausted.

The 5th Division on the far (eastern) side of the Bois des Rappes attacked toward the northeast, passing on this side of the Bois de Sassey. In its advance

1ST DIVISION TROOPS AT BANTHEVILLE, NOVEMBER 12, 1918

it swung toward the Meuse River, over which it effected a crossing in force on the night of November 4–5.

EN ROUTE NORTH OF CUNEL TO HILL 242

Continue toward Bourrut.

A 5th Division marker, on the line of relief of that division on October 22, is passed farther down this hill.

Just before reaching the bridge over the Andon River, **Aincreville**, captured by the 5th Division on October 30, can be seen 1½ miles to the right. To the left is **Bantheville**, one of the points captured by the 90th Division in its attack of October 23.

At far end of Bourrut keep to left on main road.

While on outpost duty on the hill to the right of the road (opposite kilometer post 15), it is reported that a 90th Division soldier, of Italian descent, left the American lines and charged a machine-gun nest manned by six Germans. He killed three of them and made prisoners of the others, marching them back nearly six miles to division headquarters, where, in broken English, he insisted upon telling the Division Commander about it.

The northern end of the Bois de Bantheville (on the left) was shelled almost continuously with high explosives and mustard gas by the Germans after its capture by American troops.

ROAD BETWEEN BANTHEVILLE AND RÉMONVILLE, NOVEMBER, 1918
Road is passed over on tour

The road fork at kilometer post **16.8** marked the boundary between the 89th and 90th Divisions at the jump-off on November 1. **At this road fork take right-hand road to Rémonville.**

In the woods opposite kilometer post 17, on the morning of November 1, Lieutenant Harold A. Furlong, of the 89th Division, finding his company held up

RELOADING ARTILLERY AMMUNITION, RÉMONVILLE, NOVEMBER 3, 1918

by machine-gun fire, moved out alone and worked his way into the German lines. He attacked in succession four separate machine-gun nests and put all of them out of action, securing 20 prisoners, whom he brought back into our lines. For his daring exploit he was awarded the Congressional Medal of Honor.

Descending the hill about 2 kilometers farther on, the **Bois de Barricourt** is seen to the right front, and Rémonville in the valley below.

In Rémonville, keep to left on road toward Bayonville.

The sector of the 2d Division is entered 500 meters beyond Rémonville.

RÉMONVILLE SOON AFTER ITS CAPTURE BY THE 89TH DIVISION

The next village is **Bayonville et Chénnery,** captured by the 2d Division on November 1. **Take street to right at entrance to village and then straight through.**

A German cemetery is passed just before entering **Buzancy,** captured by the 80th Division on November 2. The area around it at the time of the American advance was very swampy as the result of floods, and the only roads available for the use of the 77th and 80th Divisions passed through the town. The Germans shelled the crossroads in it continuously for several days, rendering the moving of troops and supplies forward a dangerous undertaking.

GERMAN WARNING AGAINST AIRPLANES AT BAYONVILLE

At entrance to Buzancy, keep to right at monument and take street to left after passing church.

While going through town, note how the garden walls and buildings on the right (north) side of the streets are marked by American rifle and machine-gun bullets.

Pass through Bar. ½ kilometer farther on, opposite village cemetery of Harricourt, take I. C. 6 to right. 1 kilometer farther on STOP on Hill 242.

The direction back to Bar, the nearest village, is south. To the left of it is **Buzancy.** The wide, marshy valley in which these villages are situated contains the **Bar River.** A mile and a half beyond and just to the left of Buzancy is **Hill 289.** On the sky line beyond are the wooded Heights of Barricourt.

The Freya line eastward from the Barricourt Heights was pointed out at the last stop. That line extended westward across Hill 289 and thence along the low ridge seen running toward the southwest immediately beyond the valley.

At Bar, November 4, 1918. Engineer Soldier Having Fun with Advancing Infantry Over Name of the Town

Infantry at Buzancy, November 3, 1918

On November 1 the right elements of the 80th Division captured Hill 289, while the 2d Division, on its right, broke through the Freya position and reached **Hill 313,** seen a mile to the left (northeast) of Hill 289. These successes forced the Germans to withdraw to a new line which lay to the north (left) of Hill 313 and ran across the hill on which the observer is standing.

On November 3 this line was attacked all along this part of the front, and in spite of great resistance the Germans were driven a considerable distance to the rear. That night part of the 2d Division began a bold and rapid advance, the details of which will be explained later on as the tour follows the road taken by the advancing units.

Face west. The village on the sky line to the west is **Belleville-sur-Bar.** To its left the **Bois de Bourgogne** is seen on the horizon. This wood was on the left (west) boundary of the First Army.

TROOPS PASSING AROUND BRIDGE BEING REPAIRED, WEST OF BAR, NOVEMBER 3, 1918

From their jump-off line near St. Juvin, about 7 miles south of here, the 80th, 77th, and 78th Divisions, in a splendid attack, had advanced north of this point by November 3, passing between Hill 289 and the Bois de Bourgogne.

On the hillside, a mile to the left of Belleville-sur-Bar, is **Boult-aux-Bois,** where, on the morning of November 3, the 78th Division joined with troops of

AMERICAN AND FRENCH SOLDIERS AFTER MEETING AT BOULT-AUX-BOIS

the French Fourth Army who had advanced on the far (west) side of the Bois de Bourgogne, thus pinching out that strong defensive feature.

EN ROUTE HILL 242 TO NEAR MOULINS

Continue on I. C. 6. The road for some distance passes over ground gained by the 80th Division on November 3 and 4.

At road fork about 5 kilometers beyond, keep to right to Vaux-en-Dieulet which lies at the foot of the hill. Pass to left of church and keep to right beyond town.

At first crossroads, about 2 kilometers beyond Vaux-en-Dieulet, take left-hand road Ardennes I. C. No. 4. Brief STOP suggested.

For the next 6 kilometers beyond this crossroads, the tour follows the route of a daring march by the 2d Division. By dark on November 3 the front line of the division was just south of this crossroads. In order to take advantage of the disorganized state of the German forces on this part of the front, who were withdrawing, the 9th and 23d Infantry of that division were ordered to begin a vigorous advance during that night. After a sharp fight in breaking through the German infantry line, the two regiments, marching in column, continued along this road, pushing aside all resistance in their path. The night was extremely dark, and the marching troops passed unmolested through the German artillery positions where guns were still firing on the lines to the south.

GERMAN HOWITZER CAPTURED BY 80TH DIVISION, VAUX, ARDENNES, NOVEMBER 5, 1918.

Note speedometer reading and continue on this road.

About 5 kilometers from last crossroads **la Tuilerie Farm** is seen to the right of the road. Emerging from the woods before daylight, November 4, the troops of the 2d Division surprised and captured several officers near that farm and continued about a kilometer farther, where they deployed on the hill, forming a line which crossed this road near the present site of the 2d Division bowlder.

GERMAN OFFICER PRISONERS CAPTURED BY 2D DIVISION

The seizure of this hill by the Americans created considerable confusion among the Germans, since it was one of the points in a new defensive line which they had expected to occupy and hold.

It is rather a coincidence that the route taken by the 2d Division was the same as that used by the Germans on August 30, 1870, when they surprised and defeated the French who were in camp near Beaumont.

Various German monuments on the hills around the town commemorate their soldiers killed in that battle.

Continue into Beaumont, which was captured by joint attacks of the 2d and 80th Divisions on November 5. **Pass in front of church and continue straight ahead on I. C. 30. Note speedometer reading.**

At midnight November 5–6 the front line of the 80th Division lay generally along this road, but at daylight next morning when the 1st Division moved to the front to relieve the 80th, the line had been pushed a mile farther on to the northeast (right).

From a point about 5 kilometers beyond Beaumont there is seen on the sky line, straight down this road, the high hill at **Stonne,** captured by the 77th Division on November 5

(INSERT.) DESTRUCTION CAUSED BY DIRECT HIT OF ARTILLERY SHELL
AMERICAN ANTIAIRCRAFT MACHINE GUN IN POSITION AT RAUCOURT

About 6½ kilometers beyond Beaumont turn right onto I. C. 6. A kilometer farther on is passed **la Besace,** captured by the 77th Division on November 5.

Continue through Raucourt. The little valley which this road follows formed the boundary between the 42d and 77th Divisions, the former being to the left (west), while they advanced on November 6 to the Meuse River.

Straight through Haraucourt and Angecourt, keeping railway on left. Turn left just beyond church in Remilly. After reaching the hills overlooking the Meuse River about 5 miles southeast of Remilly, the 1st Division moved to the northwest across the zones of the 77th and 42d Divisions with a view to assisting in the capture of Sedan.

About 2½ kilometers beyond Remilly, STOP without leaving automobile. The bridge on which the Metz–Sedan–Mézières railway crosses the Meuse River is seen to the right. This railway, one of the objectives of the American First Army, was reached during the night of November 6–7.

The village straight ahead is **Pont Maugis** and to the right of it about 2½ miles away is **Sedan.**

The 16th Infantry, 1st Division, attacked a strong German position on the hills overlooking Pont Maugis during the night of November 6–7, and after a sharp fight in the darkness dislodged the Germans and drove them to the north.

Pont Maugis marked the official left flank of the First Army at the time of the armistice, the 77th Division holding a line on this side of the river running toward the southeast approximately 7 miles.

On the morning of November 7 troops of the 1st and 42d Divisions captured the high hill seen just beyond Pont Maugis, and their fire from it dominated Sedan.

The French desired, evidently for sentimental reasons, to be the first to enter Sedan; and early on the morning of November 8 Marshal Foch ordered the American line on the hills overlooking that city to be turned over to French troops. The efforts of the American First Army were then turned toward forcing the Germans back from the east side of the Meuse and driving them across their border east of Luxembourg.

AMERICANS ADVANCING THROUGH THELONNE (NEAR PONT MAUGIS) UNDER MACHINE-GUN FIRE

Continue. About 1½ kilometers beyond Pont Maugis a 1st Division monument is passed on the left.

Straight through Wadelincourt to Sedan, which is important in French history as the place where the Army of Napoleon III surrendered to the Germans in 1870.

Turn right at railway station in Sedan and continue straight ahead across river to Place de Nassau via Avenue Philippoteaux. At that point, turn right on rue Vuidel Bizot and continue straight ahead through Balan, keeping on National Highway (N–64) thereafter.

On the left, at the entrance to **Bazeilles,** the next town, there is an interesting museum of the War of 1870 (La Maison de la Dernière Cartouche). A short distance to the right of the road is an ossuary containing the remains of those killed in battles near here in 1870.

Keep on N-64 through Bazeilles.

To the right, across the Meuse River, can be seen the line of hills extending to the southeast on which the front line of the 77th Division rested at the end of the war.

Turn sharply right in Douzy, pass in front of church, and cross Chiers River.

RAILWAY STATION AT SEDAN

The 77th Division maintained for a short time a small force in the flats on this side of the Meuse River, opposite **Villers-devant-Mouzon,** which is seen to the right from kilometer post 7.

At **Mouzon, keep to left on N-64.** At kilometer post 1.7, approximately 2 kilometers beyond Mouzon, is a bowlder monument which marks the left of the 2d Division at the armistice.

STOP 2 kilometers farther on, just after emerging from woods, at V Corps monument.

The village in the valley about a mile farther down this road is **Moulins,** and the direction to it is approximately east. In the valley of the Meuse, 3 miles to the south, is **Pouilly.** Halfway between here and that village is **Farm St. Rémy.**

ENGINEERS, 89TH DIVISION, BUILDING BRIDGE AT POUILLY

On the evening of November 10 the 2d and 89th Divisions forced crossings under very heavy fire at the bend of the river northwest of Pouilly. The Germans on this side were heavily bombarded with machine-gun and artillery fire, while footbridges and rafts were launched, on which small detachments crossed. Having gained this side, these detachments attacked and drove back the Germans near the river, permitting more troops to cross, thus gaining a firm foothold on this bank.

Pouilly was captured before daylight, November 11, by the 89th Division, which pushed on to the north, crossing this highway about 2 miles southeast of here.

After capturing Farm St. Rémy, the 2d Division drove the Germans from this ridge and established a line on this highway. Some of its troops were also in Moulins at the time of the armistice.

Three German divisions fought desperately to maintain their hold on this highway, since it was necessary for use in withdrawing their troops from along the river farther south, there being no suitable roads through the wooded and hilly country immediately east of this point.

TANKS BESIDE MACHINE-GUN NEST WHICH THEY PUT OUT OF ACTION NOVEMBER 7, 1918

GERMAN ARTILLERY POSITION SOON AFTER ITS CAPTURE

Trees and ground torn up by American artillery fire

EN ROUTE NEAR MOULINS TO HILL 260

About 2½ kilometers beyond Moulins, to the left of the road and near it, is the Bois de Hache in which the front line of the 89th Division lay at 11 a. m., November 11.

Some of the troops of that division failed to get the message concerning the hour of the armistice, and continued fighting for a few minutes after the time fixed.

Straight through Inor, Martincourt, and Cervisy, keeping on N-64.

The **Château du Tilleuls**, on the north edge of Stenay, is reputed to have been the billet of the German Crown Prince during the Battle of Verdun in 1916.

Stenay was captured early on November 11 by the combined action of the 90th and 89th Divisions. About 200 French civilians were in the town when it was entered by the Americans.

Keep on N-64, through Stenay. The military barracks on the left of the road ½ kilometer beyond the cemetery of Stenay were damaged comparatively little during the war, and were used by the Americans after the armistice, who found there facilities for bathing, as well as shelter from the cold, rainy weather.

Straight through Mouzay. During the afternoon of November 7, five ambulances lost their way and ran into the German lines near Mouzay, where

MEUSE RIVER NEAR STENAY, NOVEMBER 11, 1918

they were captured. Observing their plight, a 90th Division company, which was near the river to the right of this road, attacked and recaptured the ambulances, loaded them up with German prisoners, and sent them on their way properly directed.

To the left, opposite kilometer post 124, is the towering hill, **Côte St. Germain,** captured by the 5th Division on November 6 and 7. To the right is **Sassey,** near which the 90th Division crossed the river to join in the offensive on this side.

The next town is **Dun-sur-Meuse,** captured after a hard fight by the 5th Division on November 5.

Straight through Dun-sur-Meuse, keeping on N-64. About 2 kilometers beyond town STOP on Hill 260, near kilometer post 117.7.

The direction back to Dun-sur-Meuse is approximately north.

BRIDGE BUILT BY AMERICANS AT STENAY

Across the river from it is **Doulcon,** lying in a peculiar geographical formation which the 5th Division called the "Punch Bowl."

When the 5th Division attacked on November 1 it swung northeastward, and by November 3 had cleared the rim of the "Punch Bowl," entered Doulcon, and reached the line of the river as far north as **Cléry-le-Petit.**

The divisional plan for forcing a crossing of the Meuse River involved the establishment of two bridgeheads, one by the 10th Brigade at **Brieulles** and one by the 9th Brigade at Cléry-le-Petit. A church tower in Brieulles can be seen above the ridge on the other side of the river, 2 miles south of here. Cléry-le-

Bridge Constructed by 5th Division Engineers, Near Dun-sur-Meuse

Petit lies about ¾ mile northwest of this point, some of its houses being visible above the little ridge on the other side of the river.

The construction of pontoon bridges was commenced at Brieulles on the night of November 2–3 and a few troops crossed the river there, but were held up at the canal. On the evening of November 4 this was crossed in the face of heavy fire and a bridgehead was established on the eastern bank opposite that place.

American Soldiers Constructing Heavy Timber Bridge, Dun-sur-Meuse

The 9th Brigade did not attempt a crossing until the afternoon of November 4, when an unsuccessful attempt was made at 4 p. m. in the vicinity of Cléry-le-Petit. During the night of November 4–5, more pontoons were brought up and the river was bridged immediately to the west of this observation point. By dawn two battalions had crossed the river and were on the swampy flats between it and the canal. The Germans damaged the bridge which had been built across the canal during the night, and the two battalions, except for small units which had gained this bank of the canal, found themselves in a difficult position on account of direct hostile fire from this hill and the **Côte de Jumont,** the hill on the right of the road between here and Dun-sur-Meuse. To relieve this situation, Captain Edward C. Allworth, of the 60th Infantry, calling upon his company to follow, plunged into the canal, swam across under a hail of bullets, and led his men in a ferocious assault against this hill, which was quickly captured, together with a large number of prisoners. This onslaught cleared the way for other troops to cross, who overran Côte de Jumont, and, pushing northward, took Dun-sur-Meuse. For his gallant work Captain Allworth was awarded the Congressional Medal of Honor.

By dark of November 5 the German troops had been driven back more than a mile from the river by the 5th Division, and by the hour of the armistice they had been forced eastward over 10 miles into the Woëvre Plain.

EN ROUTE HILL 260 TO VERDUN

Continue on N–64, straight through Liny-devant-Dun.

The 5th Division, advancing from the Meuse, reached a line along this highway on November 5.

Engineers Resting After Working Under Fire, Dun-sur-Meuse

3 kilometers beyond Liny note the 5th Division marker on the ridge (at kilometer post 113.4). A brief **STOP** is suggested here.

From this point **Vilosne-sur-Meuse** is seen in the valley to the right front, where elements of the 5th Division assisted the 15th French Colonial Division to cross the river by attacking the defending troops in rear.

Monument Over Trench of Bayonets Near Verdun

From here on, this tour has no further connection with the First Army offensive of November 1.

On the right of the road, 20 yards from and beyond this monument, is a German concrete observation post.

The bald-topped **Borne de Cornouiller** is seen on the sky line about 4 miles to the left front. The story of its capture after hard fighting on November 4 and 5 by the 79th Division is told in the first day's itinerary. To the right of that hill, on the sky line, is the **Bois de la Grande Montagne,** entered by the 29th Division on October 16, and from which the 79th Division began its attacks on November 3.

Continue on N-64.

The wood which crowns the ridge beyond Sivry-sur-Meuse, the next town, is the **Bois de Chaume,** captured by the 33d Division on October 10.

Straight through Sivry-sur-Meuse and Consenvoye on N-64. A German cemetery is passed a kilometer beyond Consenvoye.

The next town is Brabant-sur-Meuse, captured by troops of the 18th French Division in a local attack on October 5. Part of the 33d Division crossed the river at Brabant during the morning of October 8 and advanced toward Consenvoye.

Upon passing Brabant, note **Forges** across the river and **le Mort Homme** beyond it.

VIEW OF BRABANT-SUR-MEUSE, NOVEMBER 3, 1918

The boundary between the 33d and 29th Divisions for their attack of October 8 passed through Brabant. The latter division formed for attack before daylight along this road from Brabant to the southeast, and advanced over the slopes seen to the left. During the next few days the 29th Division was opposed partly by Austrian troops.

2 kilometers beyond the ruins of Samogneux the road, at kilometer post 98, begins the climb over the Côte de Talou, captured by the Germans in the Verdun operations in February, 1916, and recaptured by the French in August, 1917.

Pass through Vacherauville, completely destroyed during the war.

The route shown on the map at the end of the chapter in broken red lines, leading east from **Bras,** is the one generally followed by tourists who visit the French battle fields near **Verdun.**

Continue on N-64 through Bras into Verdun.

A few of the interesting points in the city are indicated at the end of the first day's itinerary.

ADDITIONAL PLACES OF INTEREST IN THE MEUSE-ARGONNE AREA

The following list is furnished for the convenience of the tourist who travels in the area not on the described route. The map on this page indicates the general location of the places mentioned.

① **Authe.** A large German hospital and munitions depot were located in this town prior to its capture by the 78th Division on November 3.

② **Avocourt** was just in rear of the 37th Division's jump-off line on September 26. When the 79th Division held a sector in this vicinity in the middle of September the Germans captured a few prisoners in two raids east of the village.

③ **Baâlon** was captured by the 90th Division on the morning of the armistice.

④ **Brandeville** was captured on November 8 by part of the 5th Division, assisted by a regiment of the 32d Division. The latter unit had previously engaged in hard fighting in capturing Hill 388, a mile southwest of the village.

⑤ **Champ Mahaut.** A large number of concrete shelters and dugouts, many of which still exist, were located here, and are said to have been used at one time as the headquarters of the Crown Prince of Bavaria. They were captured by the 28th and 77th Divisions in hard fighting from September 26 to 28. To reach them from Varennes go southwest 4 kilometers on road leading toward Vienne-le-Château, turn right at road fork at kilometer post 5.4, and follow poor road 600 meters.

⑥ **Chaudron Farm**, in the ravine a mile north of Baulny, was the scene of hard fighting by the 35th Division on September 27 and 29. A mounted troop of the 2d Cavalry operated near there on September 29. 1st Division patrols engaged in many fights around the farm.

183

⑦ **Clairs Chênes Wood,** northeast of Cunel, was the scene of hard fighting by the 3d Division from October 14 until it was captured on October 20. Hill 299, immediately east of the wood, was a particularly strong position which was taken by the same division on October 22.

CONCRETE DUGOUT, CHAMP MAHAUT

⑧ **Cuisy.** On September 26 a complete 77-millimeter battery, in good condition, and a considerable supply of ammunition, was captured here. It was renamed Battery Q, and was used against the Germans until the ammunition was exhausted.

⑨ **Emont, Bois,** ¾ mile south of Cierges, was captured by the 37th Division after a hard fight on September 28.

⑩ **Forêt de Dieulet** was used as a screen by the Germans to cover their withdrawal to the east bank of the Meuse, checking the advance of the 89th Division for several hours. The engineers of that division built rafts in the Forêt de Dieulet which were floated down Wame Creek to the Meuse River where they were lashed together and swung across that stream. Troops crossed on them near Pouilly on November 10.

⑪ **Forêt de Woëvre.** This forest and the heights it covers were cleared of the Germans by the 5th Division on November 9 and 10.

⑫ **Gercourt-et-Drillancourt.** The 33d and 80th Divisions captured a considerable number of pieces of German artillery, some of them of large caliber, near this village.

⑬ **Gesnes** was captured on September 29 after three fierce attacks by the 91st Division, but was abandoned that night. The Germans launched a powerful counterattack two days later which resulted in capturing an unoccupied village. It was recaptured by the 32d Division on October 9, after four days of desperate battling in the streets.

⑭ **Grurie, Bois de la.** The jump-off line of the 77th Division on September 26, 1918, passed through this wood, in which the Germans had built large groups of dugouts.

⑮ **Hill 285,** in the Argonne Forest, was on the jump-off line on September 26. It

MONUMENT ON HILL 285

was the scene of bitter fighting in 1914–15, and is marked by many deep mine craters. A French ossuary monument, which mentions the American units

ADDITIONAL PLACES OF INTEREST IN THE MEUSE-ARGONNE AREA 185

serving in the vicinity, is on the hill. To reach it from Varennes, go southwest 5 kilometers, on road leading toward Vienne-le-Château, to crossroads at kilometer post 4.7. From that point a poor road, impassable for automobiles, leads south (to left) 2½ kilometers to hill.

⑯ **Imécourt.** A battalion of the 321st Field Artillery, 80th Division, went into position in advance of the American lines about ½ mile southwest of this village on the evening of November 1. Being mistaken for Germans, the battalion was fired upon for a short time by friendly artillery.

⑰ **Jametz** was captured by the 5th Division just before the hour of the armistice. A German aviation field was located near here.

⑱ **Les Petites Armoises,** a village on the left boundary of the American First Army, was captured by the 78th Division on November 4.

FIRST ARMY HEADQUARTERS AT SOUILLY

⑲ **Marfée, Bois de la,** 5 kilometers southwest of Sedan, contained many German machine guns which were driven out by troops of the 1st and 42d Divisions on November 7.

5TH DIVISION TROOPS ON THE ARMISTICE LINE

⑳ **Montzéville** was the location of Headquarters of the American III Corps from September 29 to October 26.

㉑ **Murvaux** was captured by the 5th Division on November 6. On September 29, 1918, Lieutenant Frank Luke, jr., an American ace, after destroying three observation balloons in spite of the fact that he was being fired at by several German planes, swooped low over Murvaux, inflicting casualties on the hostile infantry. Mortally wounded, and his plane disabled, he landed near Murvaux; but fought with his pistol until he died. He was posthumously awarded the Congressional Medal of Honor.

㉒ **Neuvilly** and dugouts in that vicinity were used as headquarters by the American I Corps from September 29 to October 26.

㉓ **Peuvillers.** On November 10, troops of the 32d Division fought their way in the fog to positions about 2½ miles east of Peuvillers, but finding themselves almost surrounded, retired to the highway which passes just east of the village, where the line rested at the end of the war.

CHURCH SERVICES AT VERDUN, OCTOBER 18, 1918

㉔ **Sachet, Bois de,** a mile west of Gercourt, was captured by the 80th Division after a hard fight on September 26.

㉕ **Sivry-lès-Buzancy** was captured by the 80th Division on November 2. It is reported that while 45 American officers in an old stable were discussing plans that night for the next day's attack, a large shell came through the roof, causing some casualties among them.

㉖ **Sy.** A small patrol of the 78th Division was ambushed near this village on November 5 and practically every member was killed or captured.

㉗ **Talma and Farm de Talma** were scenes of bitter fighting by the 78th Division between October 18 and 29.

㉘ **Villemontry** was entered on November 6 by a small detachment of the 1st Division just as the last Germans were leaving. The 2d Division took over the village on the following day; and on November 10, after a hard fight, forced a crossing of the Meuse River about a mile to the southwest.

CHAPTER V

AMERICAN OPERATIONS IN THE CHAMPAGNE REGION

The operations mentioned in this chapter include the combat service of the 2d, 36th, 42d, and 93d Divisions at different points between the Argonne Forest and Reims. The account of the so-called "Lost Battalion" of the 77th Division, and that of the 368th Infantry, 92d Division, while acting as a connecting unit on the left flank of the First Army, properly belong to the story of the Meuse-Argonne Battle, but because the areas concerned are more easily reached from the Champagne they are included in this chapter.

No attempt has been made to describe in detail a complete tour because the areas of the American operations are quite widely distributed in the territory and most tourists will probably not be greatly interested in more than one or two of them.

A short account and map of each operation, with the excep-

REIMS CATHEDRAL DURING THE WAR

tion of a map for the 368th Infantry, have been given. Places that are of special interest either because of existing features or the fighting which took place at them, if not pointed out in the story of the operation, are located on these maps. By consulting them the tourist visiting the scene of any particular action will have sufficient data to plan his own route through the area.

The route indicated on the general map, between Reims and Binarville, by way of Blanc Mont, is suggested for the use of tourists who wish, while crossing

FORT DE LA POMPELLE, EAST OF REIMS

this region en route to other places, to visit in a minimum of time most of the points of interest to Americans.

That part of the route running southwestward from Binarville to Souain is given for the convenience of tourists stopping at Reims who desire to complete a loop in the area, or for those who want to visit the region near Hurlus and Tahure, which is most interesting, as little if any reconstruction work has been done there.

The roads through the French artillery training camp in this region are blocked at certain times when the artillery is firing.

188 AMERICAN OPERATIONS IN THE CHAMPAGNE REGION

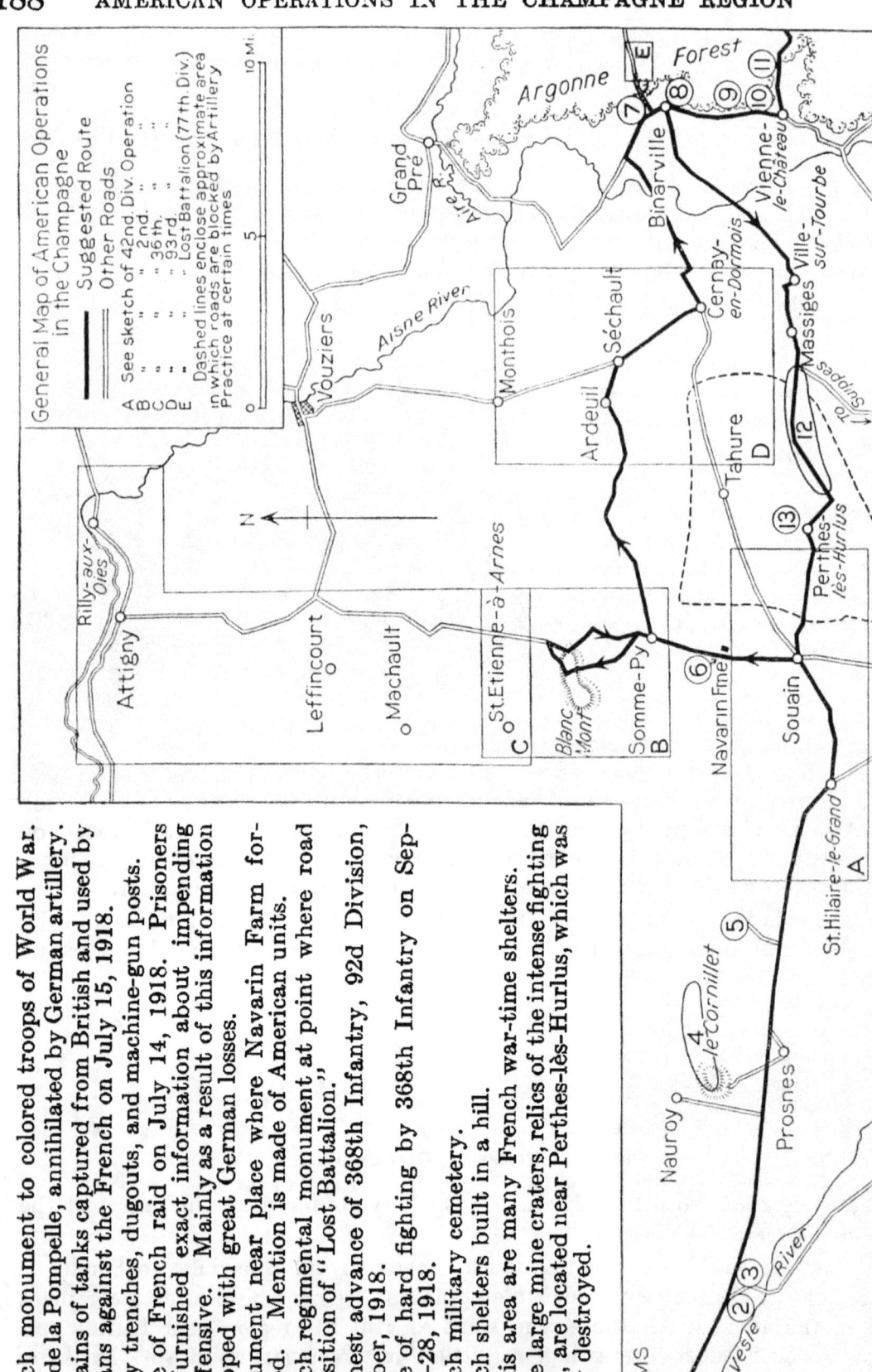

① French monument to colored troops of World War.
② Fort de la Pompelle, annihilated by German artillery.
③ Remains of tanks captured from British and used by the Germans against the French on July 15, 1918.
④ Many trenches, dugouts, and machine-gun posts.
⑤ Scene of French raid on July 14, 1918. Prisoners captured furnished exact information about impending German offensive. Mainly as a result of this information it was stopped with great German losses.
⑥ Monument near place where Navarin Farm formerly stood. Mention is made of American units.
⑦ French regimental monument at point where road leads to position of "Lost Battalion."
⑧ Farthest advance of 368th Infantry, 92d Division, in September, 1918.
⑨ Scene of hard fighting by 368th Infantry on September 27–28, 1918.
⑩ French military cemetery.
⑪ French shelters built in a hill.
⑫ In this area are many French war-time shelters.
⑬ Three large mine craters, relics of the intense fighting of 1915–16, are located near Perthes-lès-Hurlus, which was completely destroyed.

THE 42D DIVISION WITH THE FRENCH IN THE CHAMPAGNE

Following the failure of the German offensive toward **Compiègne** in June, the French secured information which indicated that an attack would soon be launched in the vicinity of **Reims**. In early July the 42d American Division was sent up to reinforce the French Fourth Army then holding the front between the Argonne Forest and Reims.

The Commander in Chief of the French Army decided to meet the expected attack by holding the first position with very few troops and making his main defense on the intermediate one some 2 or 3 kilometers in rear. All troops were put to work organizing the intermediate position and a secondary position to be used in case the intermediate one was captured.

42D DIVISION BRIGADE HEADQUARTERS NEAR SUIPPES FARM. JULY 6, 1918

The 42d Division was assigned to the XXI French Corps and given the task of organizing part of the secondary line, near **Souain** and **Jonchéry-sur-Suippes,** and, in addition, three of its battalions were placed in the intermediate position, which became the first line when the attack began. The division and all French troops on the intermediate and second positions were directed to hold their ground at "every event and at all costs." The limited number of men in the first forward areas were to retire in case of a determined attack.

GERMAN TRENCH MORTAR DETACHMENT IN THE ASSAULT, JULY 15, 1918. © G

The French Intelligence Service discovered further details of the impending attack, and was able to forecast its direction, the frontage it would cover, and the exact time it would take place.

The French had moved a great deal of artillery into the sector, and during the night preceding the attack placed an intense bombardment on the German assembly points. The execution was such that 2 German divisions had to be replaced before the assaulting troops started.

The Germans had likewise concentrated a great mass of artillery for the battle, and on the night of July 14 put down upon the French and American positions a tremendous volume of gas and high-explosive shells. While there were many casualties, the effect was very much less than in the previous German offensives, as a portion of this bombardment was on the first position from which the French had been withdrawn a few minutes before it started.

GERMAN TROOPS ATTACKING VILLAGE BEHIND SMOKE SCREEN, JULY 15, 1918. © G

The assault began early on July 15 on a wide front extending to the east and west of the city of Reims. The Germans had named this drive the "peace offensive," in the conviction that the shock of the heavy onslaught would be irresistible.

On the front of the XXI French Corps, the Germans, finding the French first line evacuated and suffering heavily from hostile artillery fire while in it, approached the intermediate position, where the French and Americans were waiting. They repeatedly attacked during the first day, but were everywhere repulsed with terrible losses, except at one or two points, from which they were promptly driven by counterattacks.

42D DIVISION TROOPS NEAR SECOND LINE IN CHAMPAGNE

The Germans continued their effort on some parts of the front until July 17, but they made no gains of importance except in the sector of the French Fifth Army southwest of Reims, where they advanced a short distance in the direction of **Epernay,** and pushed several divisions across the Marne River.

Although this powerful and ambitious drive was made in a desperate effort to win the war, it lacked the quality of surprise which had characterized the German attacks of March, April, and May. The Allies not only avoided exposing their men to much of the crushing effects of the hostile preliminary artillery bombardment, but fought the battle on ground of their own choosing, inflicting a serious repulse on the Germans.

The 42d Division suffered about 1,600 casualties and was enthusiastically commended by General Gouraud, commanding the French Fourth Army, for its gallant conduct in the defense. It was withdrawn from the line on July 18 and started westward to take part in the Franco-American offensive against the Marne salient which was begun on that date.

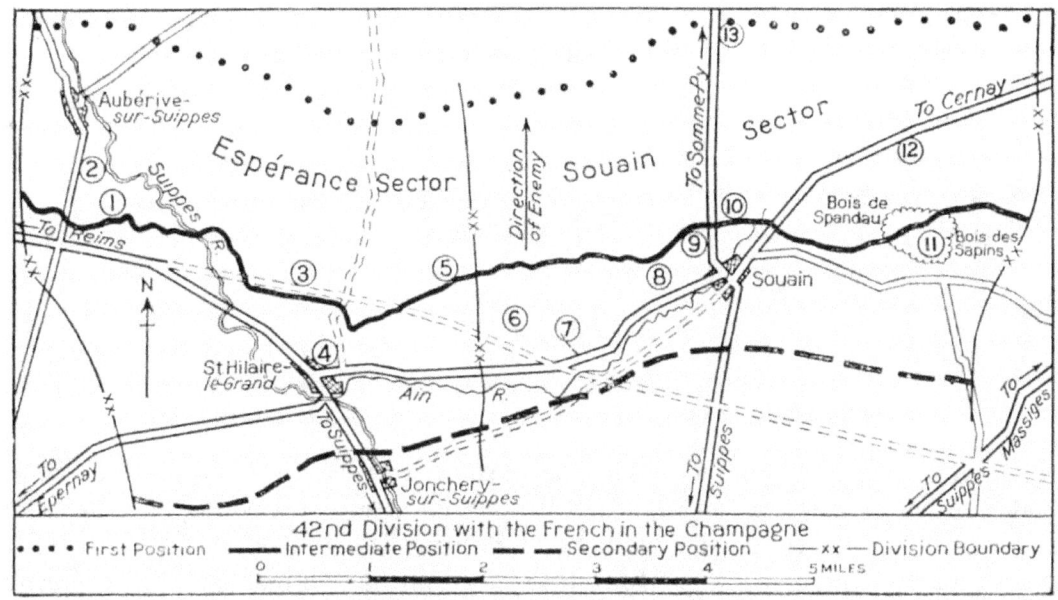

NUMBERS ON MAP INDICATE LOCATIONS OF FOLLOWING

① Companies F and G, 165th Infantry, held in this vicinity about 800 yards of trenches, no traces of which remain, repelling all attacks made on them. Company H of the same regiment was in support just to the south.

② Monument to a French infantry regiment.

③ Location of trenches where sector about 400 yards long was held by Company E, 165th Infantry. Just east of this point Company K of the 166th was in line. All German attacks against them failed.

④ French machine-gun emplacement.

⑤ Site of trenches held by Companies I and L, 166th Infantry, which the Germans attacked unsuccessfully. Company M was in a support trench south of the old Roman road shown by dotted lines on map.

⑥ French monument.

⑦ Interesting French monument and cemetery.

⑧ Mine crater at the site of the Moulin de Souain, destroyed in 1915.

⑨ Cemetery containing 22,000 French and 13,000 German graves.

⑩ Position held by Companies E and F, 167th Infantry. The Germans effected a slight penetration here but were driven out in a hand-to-hand fight.

⑪ Companies E and F, 168th Infantry, and G and H, 167th Infantry, were in support and took part in some fighting near this point.

⑫ Monument to French Foreign Legion erected by an American. The road to the east leads to Tahure, which was completely obliterated.

⑬ Marker indicating German front line. It was presented by a citizen of Minneapolis, and bears the inscription "151st Minnesota Field Artillery."

THE 2D AND 36TH DIVISIONS IN THE CHAMPAGNE

The French Fourth Army, holding the front between the Argonne Forest and Reims, was directed by the Allied Commander in Chief to advance on September 26, in conjunction with the American drive, beginning the same day, between the Meuse River and the Argonne. The French requested the use of two American divisions to assist them in this attack, and the American Commander in Chief detailed the 2d and 36th Divisions for the purpose.

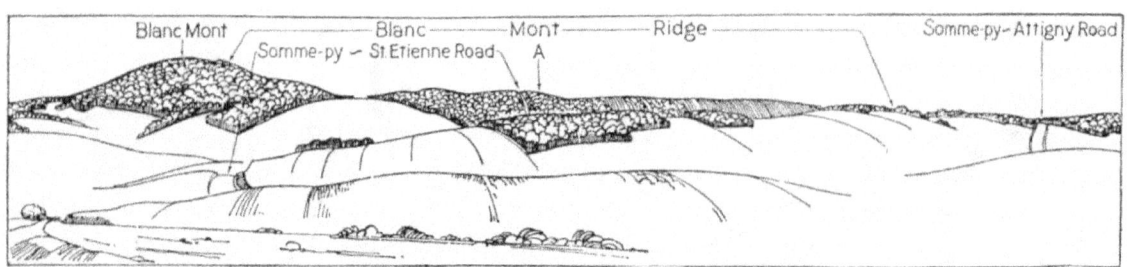

BLANC MONT RIDGE FROM NORTH OF SOMME-PY
A. Site of monument to be erected by the United States Government.

The XXI French Corps, attacking as part of the Fourth Army, had advanced about 3 miles by September 30, when it was definitely stopped by the desperate resistance encountered in the vicinity of **Somme-Py,** south of the Blanc Mont–Medeah Farm Ridge. **Blanc Mont** was the dominating feature of the German defensive position, which was located on the last natural defense line south of the Aisne River. This position had been strengthened with an elaborate system of trenches and wire and many machine guns and other weapons.

SCENE ON BLANC MONT CAPTURED BY 2D DIVISION

The capture of this ridge was essential to the further progress of the Fourth French Army, and on the night of October 1 the 2d Division went into the line to undertake the task. Prior to the time set for the army attack on October 3 the division, with characteristic energy, captured certain sections of hostile trenches necessary to provide a suitable jump-off line.

The division formed up to attack with the 3d Brigade (9th and 23d Infantry) on the right and the 4th Brigade (5th and 6th Marines) on the left.

Promptly at 5.50 a. m., October 3, the troops began the advance. In a little over two hours the crest of Blanc Mont was firmly in their grasp and the division was considerably ahead of those on its flanks. The French division on the left was unable to make any progress against the western end of Blanc Mont Ridge, which remained in the possession of the Germans. This enabled them to keep up a deadly fire against the left of the 2d Division, and the Marine brigade was compelled to deploy part of its forces facing to the west to cover that flank.

The 3d Brigade drove forward again in the afternoon, reaching a point about 2 kilometers from St. Etienne-à-Arnes, and, being temporarily unsupported on its flanks, had to beat off several vicious counterattacks against them.

GERMAN MACHINE-GUN EMPLACEMENT ON BLANC MONT RIDGE

The next day the Marine brigade pushed its front lines abreast of the 3d Brigade, while some of its troops continued to hold off the Germans on the left where the French still found it impossible to advance. The fighting was bitter and continuous through the 5th, when the enemy was cleared from the western end of the ridge by the Marines. This enabled the French units on that flank to come up, and the whole line moved forward again on the 6th.

The 71st Brigade of the 36th Division went into the line to assist the 2d Division, and on the 8th the attacks were renewed. **St. Etienne-à-Arnes** was captured that day, and some particularly heavy counterattacks were repulsed.

GERMAN PLANE SHOT DOWN BY AMERICAN ANTIAIRCRAFT GUN

The 2d Division by this time had broken into the German lines to a depth of about 4 miles, and had captured approximately 2,300 prisoners and the vitally important ridge of Blanc Mont. Its great initial success had assisted materially the advance of the French divisions on its flanks, and thus precipitated the retreat of the Germans to the Aisne. For this brilliant exploit it was commended in the highest terms by the French Army and Corps Commanders.

194 AMERICAN OPERATIONS IN THE CHAMPAGNE REGION

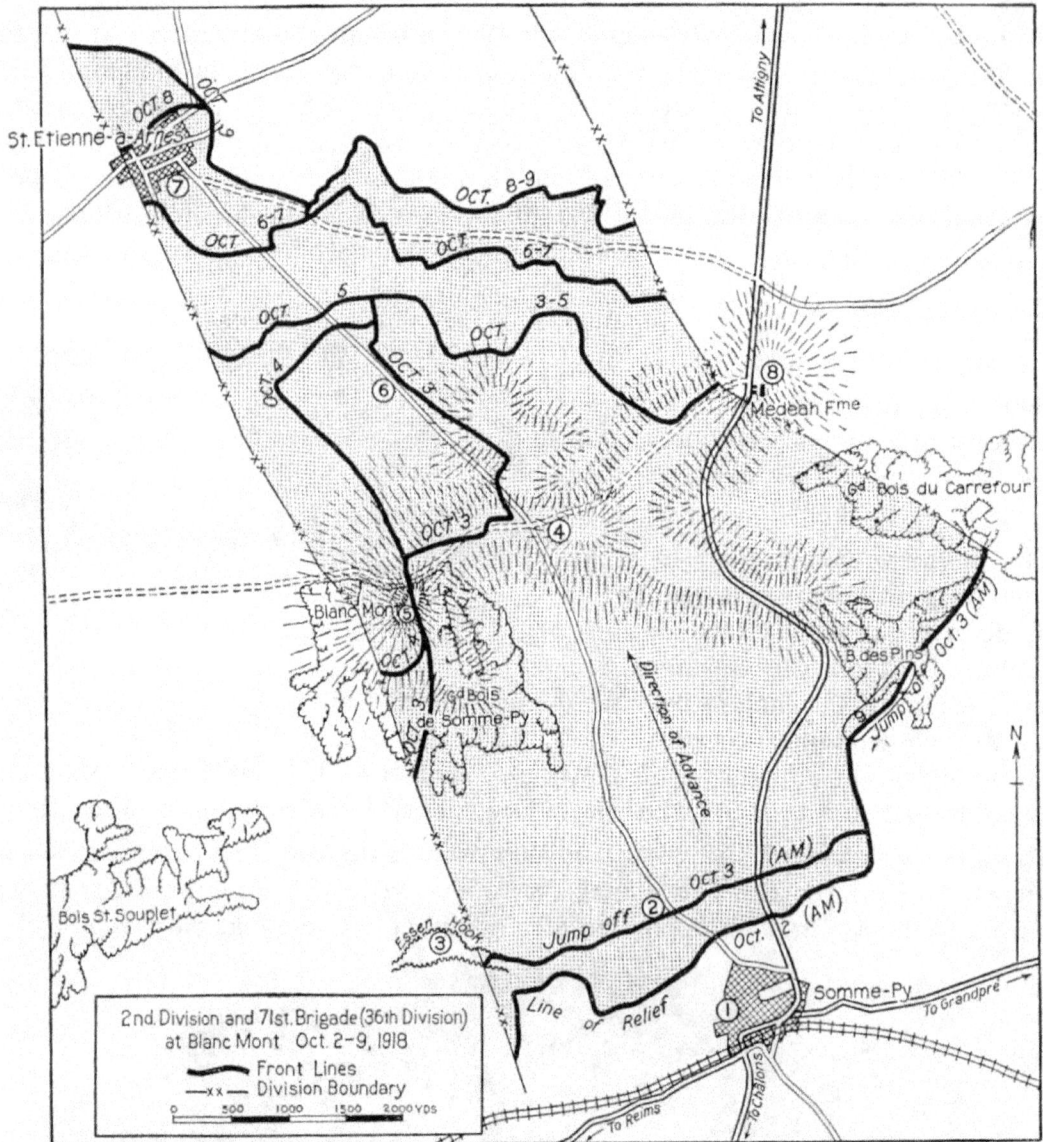

NUMBERS ON MAP INDICATE LOCATIONS OF FOLLOWING

① Somme-Py.—Beneath the ruined church, German shelters used during the war are being preserved. The town hall has been reconstructed from funds raised by American women, and contains the names of those Americans who died in the fighting which drove the Germans from the vicinity.

② Second Division marker.

③ Site of Essen Hook, a formidable German strong-point, and the scene of bitter fighting. *Not easily visited.*

④ Site of monument to be erected on Blanc Mont Ridge by the United States Government to the American troops who fought in the Champagne. The ridge contains many traces of the war, including trenches, underground shelters, and a power station.

⑤ Location of a German concrete machine-gun post which seriously interfered with the advance of the 2d Division until captured on October 5.

⑥ Second Division marker.

⑦ St. Etienne was cleared of Germans on October 8 by the 142d Infantry, 36th Division, assisted by a battalion of Marines. Near the town are located a 2d Division marker and a German cemetery. A series of hostile machine-gun nests just south of the town caused many casualties among the attacking American troops. No traces of these works now exist.

⑧ Site of Medeah Farm, of which nothing remains. The 9th and 23d Infantry, 2d Division, holding a line running northwest from this point, gallantly repulsed a heavy counterattack on the morning of October 4.

⑨ Traces of trenches at this point from which the 2d Division jumped off on October 3 may be seen from road just west of it.

The 2d Division, except for its artillery and engineers, which continued on with the relieving division, was relieved after dark on October 9 by the 36th Division.

The 36th Division, which was entering the front line for the first time, took immediate advantage of the favorable conditions created by the successful attack of the 2d Division, and after some hard fighting beyond St. Etienne-à-Arnes on the 10th, pushed the Germans north of **Machault** on the 11th. Its vigorous advance, in conjunction with the French, was continued on the 12th and 13th until it reached the Aisne.

During the next few days it extended its flanks to take over sectors from French units leaving the line. On the 23d it assumed control of the front facing the loop of the Aisne in which is located **Rilly-aux-Oies**. At that point enemy forces had remained south of the river, and had organized a strong position across the base of the loop, which a French division had assaulted unsuccessfully on October 16.

Monument in German Cemetery Near St. Etienne

At 4.30 in the afternoon of October 27 the right brigade of the division attacked in order to drive the Germans north of **Forest Farm**, promptly secured its objectives, and organized them for defense. The operations of the division, which were begun at St. Etienne-à-Arnes, about 12 miles to the south, were terminated on October 27, and on that date the division passed into reserve.

This was the only operation in which the 36th Division participated, since just as it was again preparing to enter the battle line with the American Second Army, about 10 days later, the armistice was signed.

French Monument Near Navarin Farm
See page 188

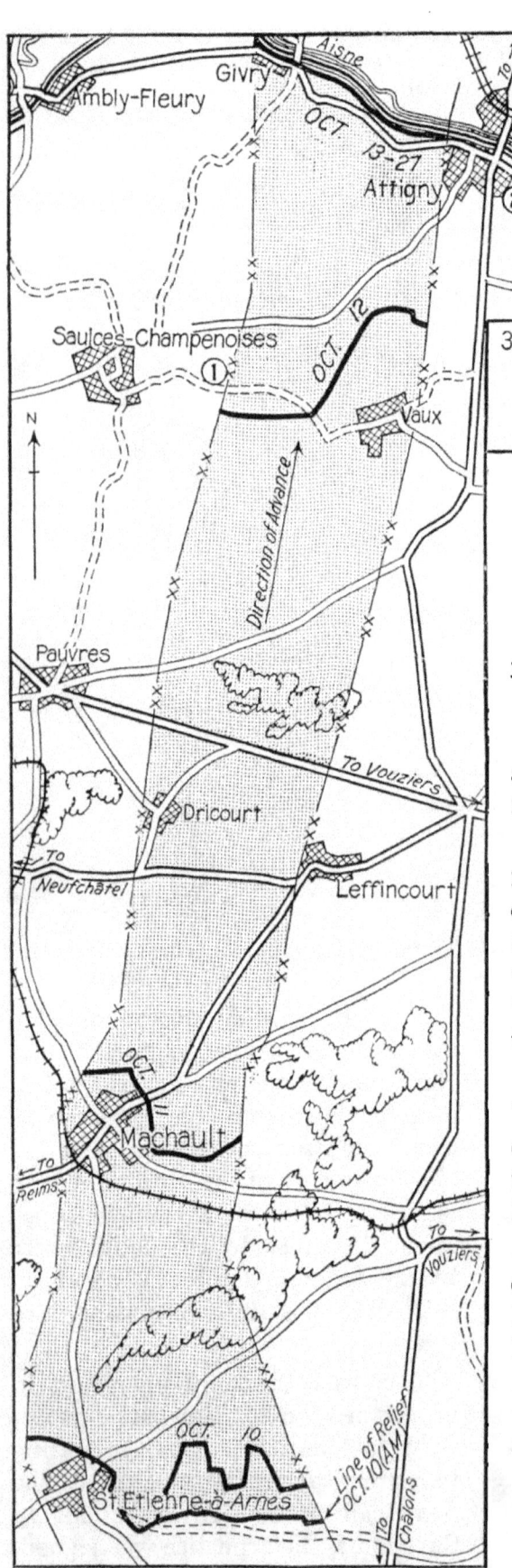

NUMBERS ON MAP INDICATE LOCATIONS OF FOLLOWING

① An excellent view of Attigny and the valley of the Aisne River may be obtained from this point.

② The 36th Division held the river bank in front of and to the east of Attigny from October 14 to October 27, on which date the division was relieved from the line. The church at Attigny is in ruins as the result of artillery fire.

③ This point, on the edge of Voncq, affords the best general view of the area in which the attack of the 36th Division against Forest Farm occurred.

On October 21–22 the western end of the front line of the 36th Division was just east of Ambly-Fleury.

369TH, 371ST, AND 372D INFANTRY (93D DIVISION) WITH FRENCH IN THE CHAMPAGNE

When the French Fourth Army advanced northward in the Champagne on September 26 three regiments of the 93d American Division were included as

TROOPS OF 369TH REGIMENT, 93D DIVISION, IN THE FRONT LINE TRENCHES

units in the French divisions of the IX Corps, which was directed to attack from a position a few miles west of the Argonne Forest.

The 369th Infantry had entered this general area on April 16, 1918, and was in support when the attack of September 26 started, attached to the 161st French Division. It entered a gap in the line during the first day and took the town of **Ripont**, capturing a number of prisoners and several pieces of artillery. It continued forward during the 27th and the 28th, gaining a foothold on **Bellevue Signal Ridge**.

On the 28th the 371st and the 372d Infantry entered the lines as part of the 157th French Division and attacked at once, advancing about 1 kilometer. The 372d made an unsuccessful attack against Séchault from the west on the 29th, its units became intermingled, and it was withdrawn for reorganization.

MONUMENT TO 371ST INFANTRY NEAR ARDEUIL

MONUMENT TO 372D INFANTRY SOUTH OF MONTHOIS

On the 29th the 369th Infantry captured **Séchault**, while the 371st took **Ardeuil** and **Montfauxelles**. On the 30th, the 369th again made a small advance and was relieved from the line that evening, after having suffered heavy casualties. On the same date the 371st captured **Trières Farm**.

On October 1 the 372d relieved the 371st and advanced to a point a few hundred yards south of **Monthois** where it was subjected to enfilading fire from the high ground to the southwest of that town. It held this position until the night of the 6th. A few days later all three of the regiments, having won the praise of the French authorities for their conduct in the attack, entrained with their French divisions for the Vosges.

During these operations, the other infantry regiment (370th) of the 93d Division was with a French division northeast of Soissons.

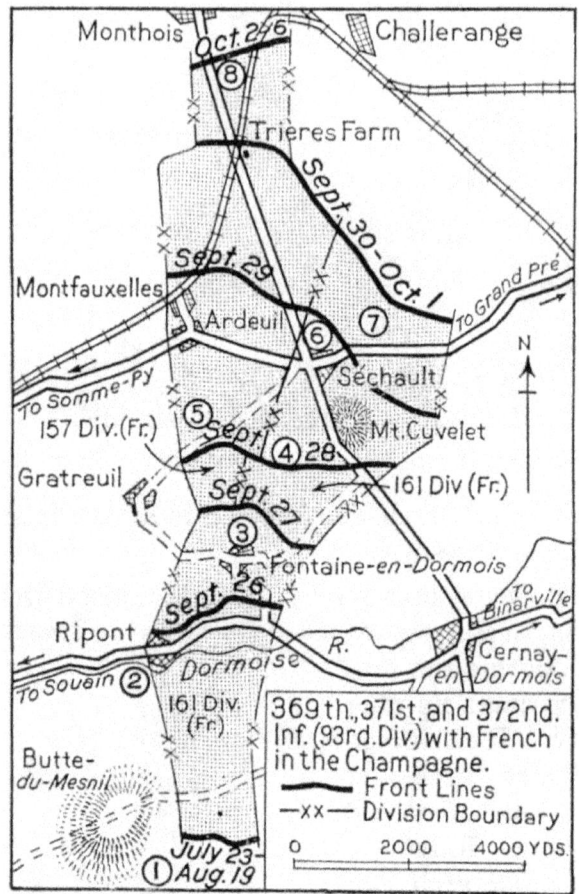

NUMBERS ON MAP INDICATE LOCATIONS OF FOLLOWING

① The 369th Infantry held a section of trenches along the line indicated from July 23 to August 19.

② The town of Ripont, captured by the 369th Infantry, has disappeared completely, and a monument to its war dead now marks its location.

③ A German concrete machine-gun post can still be seen in Fontaine, which town was captured by the 369th Infantry on September 27.

④ Bellevue Signal Ridge. Traces of a German camp now remain on its crest, which was the scene of hard fighting by the 369th Infantry and French troops.

⑤ Monument to 371st Infantry.

⑥ The town of Séchault was captured by the 369th Infantry.

⑦ German cemetery.

⑧ 372d Infantry monument.

THE LOST BATTALION OF THE 77TH DIVISION

On October 2 the 77th Division, attacking northward in the Argonne Forest, encountered heavy resistance and made little progress except in the sector of the 308th Infantry. Six companies of that regiment and parts of two companies of the 306th Machine Gun Battalion penetrated the enemy's lines by following a small valley and established themselves on the north slope of the ravine to the east of **Charlevaux Mill**. Communication was maintained with the troops in rear throughout

FRENCH MONUMENT, NORTH OF BINARVILLE
Road to right leads to scene of "Lost Battalion"

the day, and late in the evening one company of the 307th Infantry succeeded in advancing to them.

The Germans, however, pushed troops between the main body of the division and these companies, with the result that by noon of October 3 they were completely surrounded.

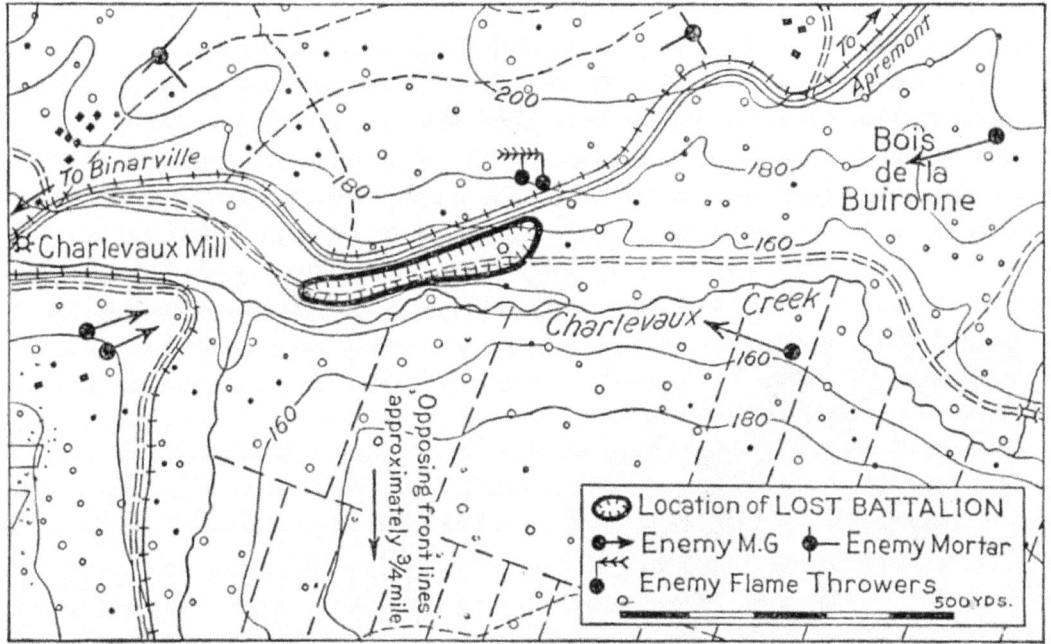

This little force, holding a position about a mile in advance of the divisional front lines, was subjected to repeated assaults and exposed to incessant machine-gun and minenwerfer fire from all sides. Food was exhausted on the second day,

SCENE OF "LOST BATTALION"
Battalion occupied slope below road

water could be procured only with difficulty from the muddy creek, which was exposed to hostile fire, and suffering from hunger and thirst became more and more acute. Ammunition soon became scarce and the Americans were forced to salvage German rifles and ammunition from the dead near-by.

The Air Service did not succeed in its attempts to drop food, medical supplies, and ammunition in the position, and the efforts of the 77th Division to push forward to relieve the detachment were also unsuccessful.

Finally, on October 7, the 28th and 82d Divisions launched a flank attack from the east against the hostile position in the Argonne Forest and at the same time the 77th renewed its attacks from the south.

The flanking movement was completely successful, and that evening the troops advancing from the south rescued the "Lost Battalion," which had that afternoon beaten off the last and fiercest of the hostile attacks made against it.

When relieved on the night of October 7, after having been cut off for five days and nights, only about 194 men of the original 600 who entered the position were able to walk out of it.

In the year 1927 the individual rifle pits used by the men of this battalion could be seen by climbing a short distance down the steep slope south of the road.

GAS MASK DRILL

368TH INFANTRY (92D DIVISION) ON THE LEFT OF FIRST ARMY, SEPTEMBER 26 TO SEPTEMBER 30

The connecting force between the French Fourth Army in the Champagne and the American First Army on September 26 was composed of the 368th Infantry, 92d Division, and the 11th Regiment of Cuirassiers-à-pied (French), and operated under the direction of the XXXVIII French Corps.

These units went into line on September 25, and part of the 368th Infantry advanced about 2 kilometers on the morning of the 26th but retired to its jump-off position the same day.

On the 27th the composite force, reinforced by 2 companies of the 351st Machine Gun Battalion, 92d Division, advanced again, and continued forward on the 28th.

The American First Army placed the remainder of the 92d Division, less the 183d Brigade, at the disposal of the XXXVIII French Corps on September 29. The 368th remained in line and spent the day chiefly in reorganizing its units. On the 30th a French regiment was directed to capture **Binarville,** and part of the 368th assisted in the attack. The town was entered, but the volume of hostile fire forced the French and Americans to withdraw to a line several hundred yards to the south. During the night of September 30 the American regiment was relieved from the front line, passing into reserve with other units of the 92d Division.

The division was returned to the control of the American First Army on October 3.

CHAPTER VI

AMERICAN OPERATIONS NORTH OF PARIS

This chapter gives brief accounts of all American operations on that part of the battle front in the general region north of Paris. These include descriptions of fighting by the 1st, 27th, 30th, 33d, 37th, 80th, and 91st Divisions and the 6th and 11th Engineers.

No attempt has been made to describe in detail a complete itinerary because most of the different areas of American operations are long distances apart and the average tourist will not be interested in all of them.

The general map shown on the next page gives a route

RAMPARTS AT COUCY-LE-CHÂTEAU

which is recommended for those who desire to make an extended automobile tour over the territory of these operations. Starting from Paris, this route can be completely covered in about 4 days, allowing plenty of time in each American area. By using this map other routes can also be planned which will take the tourist only to those areas in which he is particularly interested.

In addition to the description of each operation, a map illustrating it has been included in most cases. Places that are of special interest, either because of existing features or the fighting which took place at them, if not pointed out in the story of the operation, are located on

GERMAN GUN NEAR CHUIGNOLLES

these maps. By consulting them, the tourist visiting the scene of any particular operation will have sufficient data to plan his own route through the area.

Many great battles in which American troops took no part were fought north of Paris. No attempt has been made to describe these battles or to point out on the way more than a few of the important memorials which have been constructed to commemorate them. Any visitor interested in these should provide himself with proper British or French guidebooks before starting on his tour.

MARSHAL FOCH'S TRAIN ARRIVING AT COMPIÈGNE
The armistice was signed on the car in the foreground

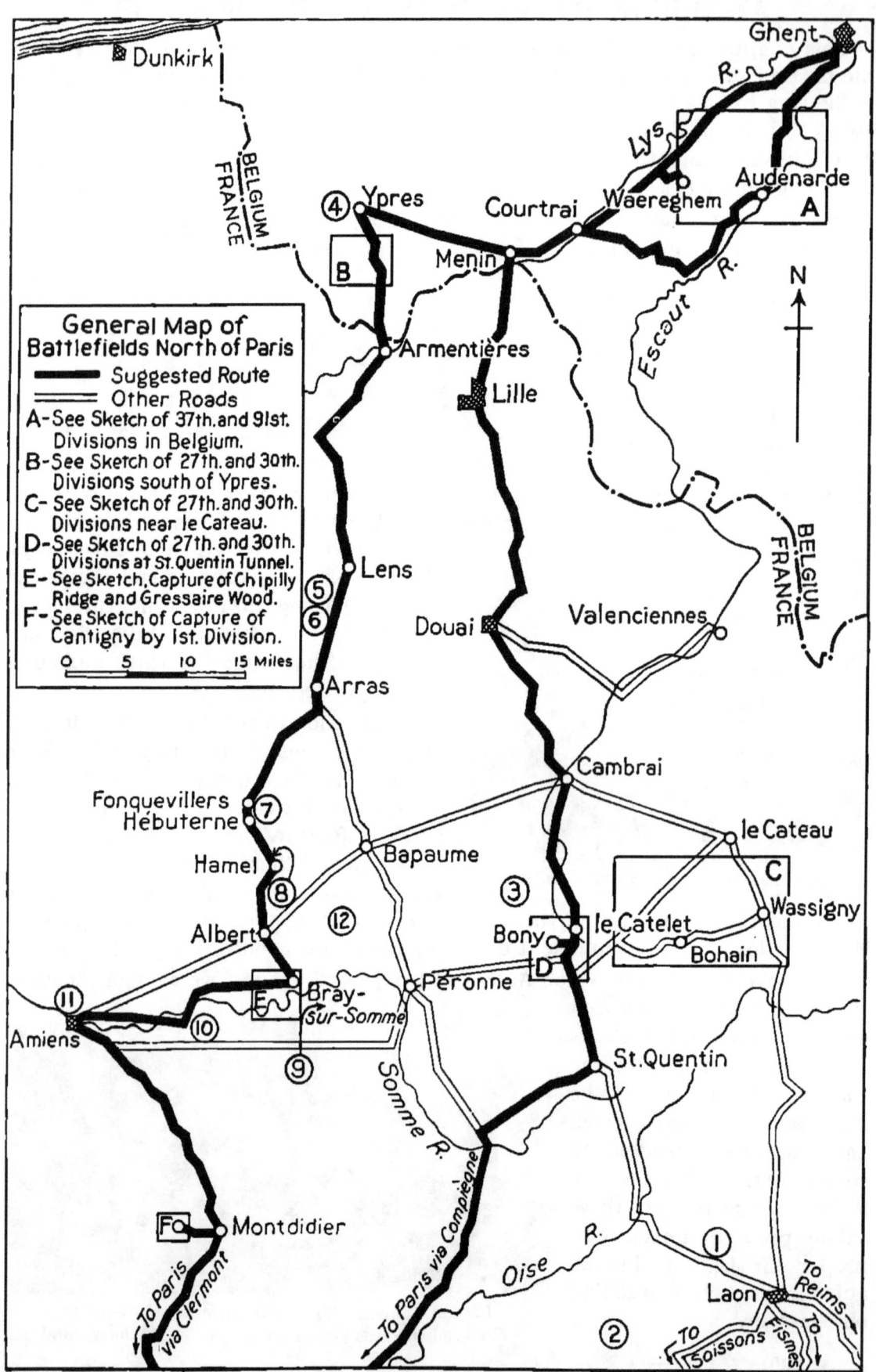

In this chapter the accounts of the different operations have been arranged in the order they are reached when following the eastern route north from Paris and the western route returning.

Excellent hotel accommodations are available in Ghent and Lille. Good accommodations may be had at Amiens, Laon, St. Quentin, Valenciennes, and Ypres. It is possible to stay overnight at Albert, Armentières, Arras, Audenarde, Bapaume, Cambrai, Courtrai, Douai, Lens, and Montdidier.

INFORMATION CONCERNING MAP ON OPPOSITE PAGE

The highway from Paris to St. Quentin passes through Compiègne, which lies outside the limits of the map. Six kilometers northeast of Compiègne and just south of the Aisne River is the place where the armistice was signed. A monument is located there, and the railway car in which the signing took place is housed in a near-by building.

NUMBERS ON MAP INDICATE LOCATIONS OF FOLLOWING

① The emplacement of the large gun (Big Bertha), which bombarded Paris in 1918, is located about 1 mile northwest of Crépy. The gun itself was removed by the Germans before the French captured the locality.

② Location of very interesting ruins of the ancient castle of Coucy-le-Château, partly destroyed by Germans during the war. One kilometer northwest of here in the woods is the concrete emplacement of a large German gun.

③ Locality near Gouzeaucourt in which members of 11th U. S. Engineers fought with the British forces in repelling the German advance near Cambrai at the end of November, 1917.

④ Ypres is located in a region which was the scene of much Allied fighting, mostly British, against the Germans. There are many interesting monuments and cemeteries in and around the town.

⑤ Site of the chapel of Notre-Dame-de-Lorette, which was obliterated during the war, and now the location of a French cemetery containing 34,000 graves and a beautiful French memorial.

⑥ A large Canadian monument is being built on the famous Vimy Ridge, about a mile west of the town of Vimy. Near the monument a portion of the original Canadian and German defensive systems has been restored. About a mile south of this monument and between Thélus and Neuville-St. Vaast is an interesting British cemetery built in a mine crater.

⑦ Vicinity in which part of 80th Division trained in line with British.

⑧ About ½ mile northwest of Hamel is the location of a Newfoundland war memorial park. The ground is being preserved in its war-time state and gives an excellent idea of the conditions under which the troops lived.

About ½ mile southeast of Hamel on the road to Thiepval is a memorial tower to the 36th British Division which contains a small museum.

⑨ About ¾ mile southeast of Chuignolles is located the emplacement and remains of a large German gun of 380 mm. caliber. It was 70 feet long, and had a range of 24 miles.

⑩ Locality in which the 6th U. S. Engineers participated in the defense of Amiens in the critical days around April 1, 1918.

⑪ In the cathedral at Amiens is a plaque commemorating the dead of the 6th Engineers who lost their lives in the defense of the town in March and April, 1918; also other plaques to British dead.

⑫ South African memorial at Delville Wood, northeast of Longueval.

THE 27TH AND 30TH DIVISIONS AT THE ST. QUENTIN TUNNEL, SEPTEMBER 24-30, 1918

The 27th and 30th Divisions, composing the II American Corps, had trained and served with the British Army through the summer of 1918, and had taken part in an operation near Ypres in the early part of September. Following that engagement they were sent southward, entering the lines as part of the British Fourth Army, north of St. Quentin.

On this section of the front the Hindenburg line followed roughly the St. Quentin Canal and made use of that obstacle as a primary feature in its defensive system. Between Le Catelet and Bellicourt the canal flows through a tunnel, which the Germans used as a huge underground shelter and storehouse. They had

ROAD NEAR GUILLEMONT FARM. © B

connected the tunnel with their positions above by means of passageways, and the outpost area west of the tunnel had been organized with trenches, obstacles, machine-gun nests, and all other elements of a modern defensive system.

ENTRANCE TO CANAL TUNNEL NEAR BELLICOURT

About the middle of September the British began to drive in these outposts in order to establish a good line of departure for a general attack to be delivered against the Hindenburg line, but in this they were only partly successful.

The II American Corps went into the line on September 24 and 25, and was designated to lead the main attack. The 30th Division, on the south, took over a sector west of **Bellicourt,** and the 27th Division, immediately on its left, went into the line in an adjoining sector just west of **Bony.**

In order to capture the remaining outpost positions before launching the general offensive, the 30th Division undertook a night operation during the evening of September 26, and the 118th Infantry making the attack succeeded in advancing its lines some 300 to 400 yards.

30TH DIVISION DIGGING IN NEAR MOLAIN

Similarly, the 106th Infantry, assisted by one battalion of the 105th, attacked on the following morning along the front of the 27th Division, with a difficult task on account of the strength of the German position. The principal strong points of this position were **The Knoll, Guillemont Farm,** and **Quennemont Farm** which were on the reverse slope of a ridge and had successfully resisted previous attacks

AMERICANS ADVANCING FOR ATTACK ON HINDENBURG LINE

Near Bellicourt, September 29, 1918. © B

by the British. Detachments of these units, however, reached the designated objective, but the comparatively few men remaining made the organization of the new line impossible. Bitter fighting by isolated groups continued throughout the day, and casualties were unusually heavy, all company officers except two being either killed or wounded. At nightfall the survivors were scattered in detachments over a front of 2 miles.

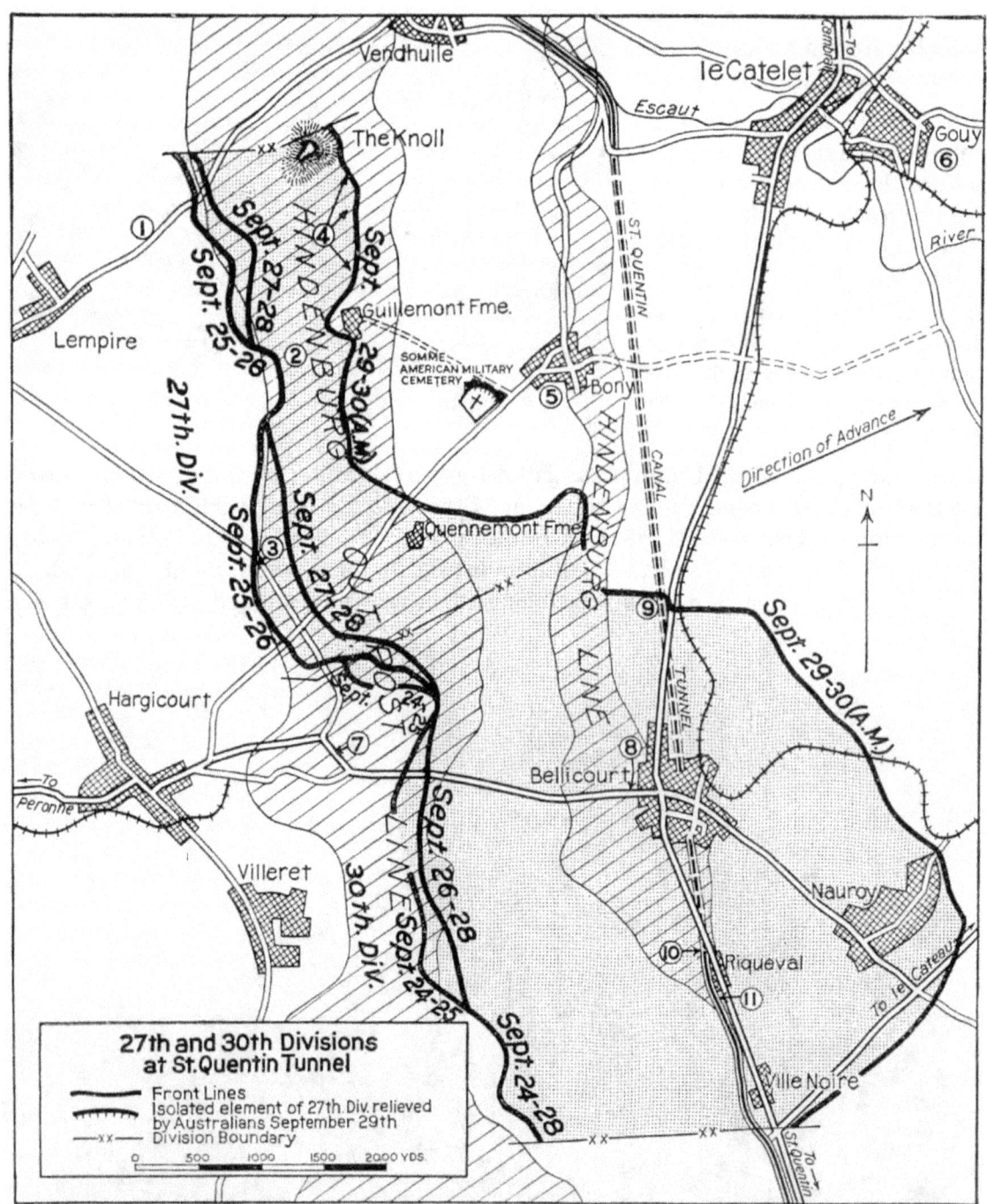

NUMBERS ON MAP INDICATE LOCATIONS OF FOLLOWING

① British cemetery.
② Monument to 27th Division erected by the engineers of that division soon after their fighting in the vicinity.
③ From this point, on the jump-off line of the 27th Division, an excellent view is obtained of the battle field.

④ Site of Willow and Knoll trenches, where heavy fighting occurred.

⑤ Monument to 27th Division erected by the engineers of that division soon after the fighting. The town hall and school (one building) at Bony was presented by friends and relations of American soldiers who fought near there.

⑥ Gouy, one of the objectives of the 27th Division on September 29, was entered on that morning by detachments of the division, which were unable to maintain themselves there on account of their exposed position.

⑦ An excellent view of the 30th Division sector is obtained from this point.

⑧ British military cemetery.

⑨ Site of monument to be erected by the American Government to commemorate the American operations with the British Army in France.

⑩ Southern entrance of canal and gate-room over the entrance. The face bears marks of machine-gun fire. Troops of the 30th Division are reported to have captured over 200 prisoners here on September 29.

⑪ Monument to 30th Division erected by the State of Tennessee.

German Prisoners Captured by 27th and 30th Divisions

After dark on September 27 the 54th Brigade took over the front line of the division preparatory to the general assault. Although orders prohibited any prior organized attack, patrols were pushed to the front to secure the line designated as the jump-off position. These efforts did not produce results, and when the larger offensive started the assaulting troops of the 27th Division were more than ½ mile behind their own barrage.

Both divisions went over the top early on the 29th. The 30th Division drove ahead through Bellicourt and in some particularly severe fighting overran in a few hours the greater portion of the Hindenburg line in its zone. Although the 27th Division met great resistance, considerable gains were made. The fight was thrown mainly on the infantry, as it was without the protection of a barrage, and had little effective help from the tanks, which were put out of action early in the fight. In spite of this, however, the troops attacked boldly and incessantly, although suffering heavy casualties.

On the afternoon of September 29, Australian divisions passed through the 27th and 30th and continued the drive. Units in which both Americans and Australians

AFTER THE BATTLE NEAR NAUROY
German prisoners in foreground. 30th Division troops on road in rear

were intermingled pushed the attacks, and by nightfall the line included **Nauroy** and ran generally northwestward from there to a point just southwest of **Vendhuile**.

The divisions were relieved early on September 30, but some elements of the 27th Division stayed in line and continued the attack with the Australians during September 30 and October 1.

MONUMENT ERECTED BY STATE OF TENNESSEE

Although the losses in this operation were heavy, one regiment of the 27th Division losing more men than any other American regiment in a single day during the war, the Hindenburg line had been broken and the way opened for further great advances.

Following this battle, the 27th and 30th Divisions received many commendations for their heroic conduct. General Pershing and Marshal Haig, as well as the Commander of the Australian Corps under whose command they had fought, were warm in their praise of the splendid fighting qualities of the Americans, and of the results they had achieved.

This battle field may be visited by taking a train to St. Quentin, and hiring an automobile there.

THE 27TH AND 30TH DIVISIONS NEAR LE CATEAU

After taking a prominent part in the attack which resulted in breaking the Hindenburg line north of St. Quentin, the II American Corps was withdrawn from the front on September 30 for a short rest, while the British continued the pressure against the retreating Germans. By October 5 they had been pushed back about 3½ miles, and that night the 30th Division again entered the lines, while the 27th remained in reserve.

On the morning of October 7 the 30th Division attacked from the vicinity of **Montbrehain** and kept up a continuous drive against the Germans until the 11th, during which time it advanced about 10 miles in some hard fighting, reaching the Selle River (also known as the Sourcelle River) in the vicinity of **St. Souplet**.

27TH DIVISION CROSSING STREAM ON TEMPORARY BRIDGE AT ST. SOUPLET, OCTOBER, 1918

The 27th Division relieved the 30th after dark on October 11, and held an extended front pending the launching of a new general attack. On the night preceding the offensive the 30th Division again came into the line, taking over part of the sector of the 27th, and the II American Corps, as part of the British Fourth Army, attacked eastward across the Selle River on the morning of the 17th. The assigned objective was the high ground lying just west of the Oise-Sambre Canal about 6,000 yards east of the jump-off line. At that time both divisions were seriously depleted in strength as a result of the severe fighting in which they had been engaged since September 25, but the assault was gallantly delivered and important advances were made.

The attacks were renewed on October 18 and 19, and, although desperate resistance was encountered, the corps made an advance of about 6,000 yards, gaining practically all its objectives by the evening of the latter date. The 30th Division was relieved from the line that night, but the 27th remained in position until the 20th, when it also was withdrawn for rest and replacements.

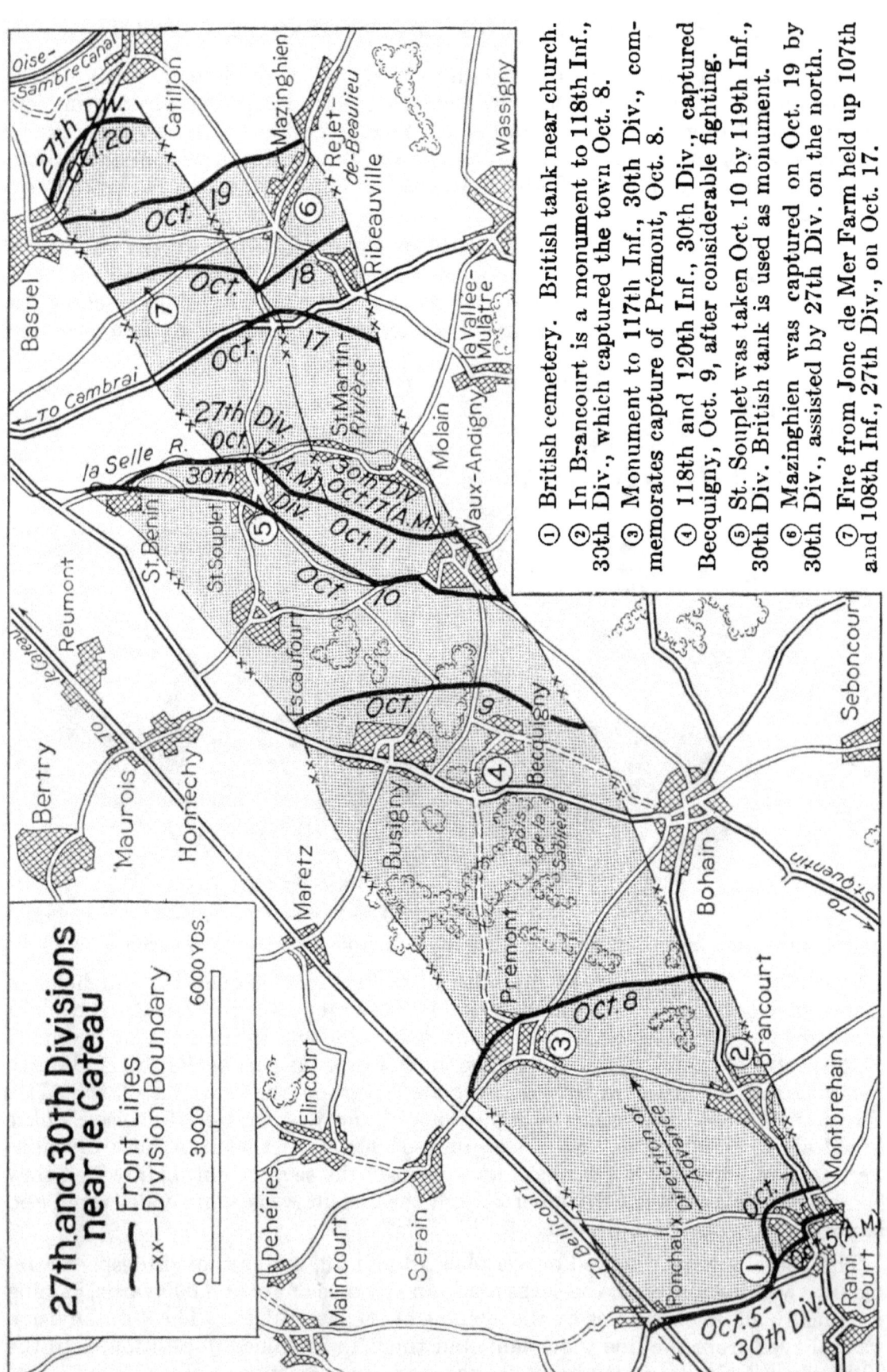

In the operations subsequent to October 7 the 30th Division captured about 2,400 prisoners, and the 27th about 1,500. This was the last battle in which these two divisions were engaged, as the armistice was signed before they could again enter the front lines.

SALVAGE DUMP OF 30TH DIVISION AT MONTBREHAIN

THE 11TH ENGINEERS

Two enlisted men of the 11th American Engineers (railway) were wounded by shell fire near the little town of **Gouzeaucourt** on September 5, 1917, while

AMERICAN TROOPS AWAITING ORDERS BEHIND FRONT LINE
Near Prémont, September, 1918. © B

their regiment was serving with the British Army in that vicinity. These were the first American soldiers in the war to be wounded while serving at the front.

When the Germans launched a surprise counteroffensive at **Cambrai** on November 30, troops of the regiment, who were working on the railroad immediately behind the lines, joined with the British and helped stop the attack, using as weapons their picks and shovels and any other equipment they could find.

This locality may be visited by taking a train to Cambrai, and hiring an automobile there.

American Engineers Repairing Blown-up Tracks near Waereghem.

THE 37TH AND 91ST DIVISIONS IN FLANDERS (BELGIUM)

In the middle of October, while the American First Army was heavily engaged in the Meuse-Argonne Battle, a request was received from the Allied Commander in Chief for two American divisions to aid in the attacks in Flanders. Urgent as

American Soldier Sightseeing in Belgium

Waereghem, Belgium, November, 1918

was his own need for troops, the American Commander in Chief nevertheless designated the 37th and 91st Divisions, which units reported within a few days to the King of the Belgians, who was commanding the group of armies in the north.

The two divisions, with a French division between them, went into the front lines a few miles west of **Audenarde** on October 30. They took part in a general attack on October 31, driving eastward toward the Escaut River, each division advancing several kilometers in the face of stiff opposition. The 91st Division, south of the 37th, was held up to some extent because of the slow progress of the French on its right, who had encountered considerable resistance.

American Transportation Near Hotel de Ville, Audenarde

When the advance was resumed on November 1, it became evident that the Germans were beginning a general retirement, and the 37th and 91st Divisions hastened forward vigorously, reaching the western bank of the Escaut River during the day. Attacks were continued on the 2d, and the 37th succeeded in effecting a crossing of the river east of **Heurne** on improvised bridges.

Bridge Built by 37th Division Near Heuvel

On November 3 the 91st Division was relieved, while the 37th continued to push troops across the river until the night of the 4th, when it was also relieved.

Both divisions reentered the line in time to attack on the morning of November 10. The 37th took over a sector a few kilometers north of the one it had previously held, and a second time forced its way across the river, while the 91st Division went into action some kilometers east of the Escaut. By this date the

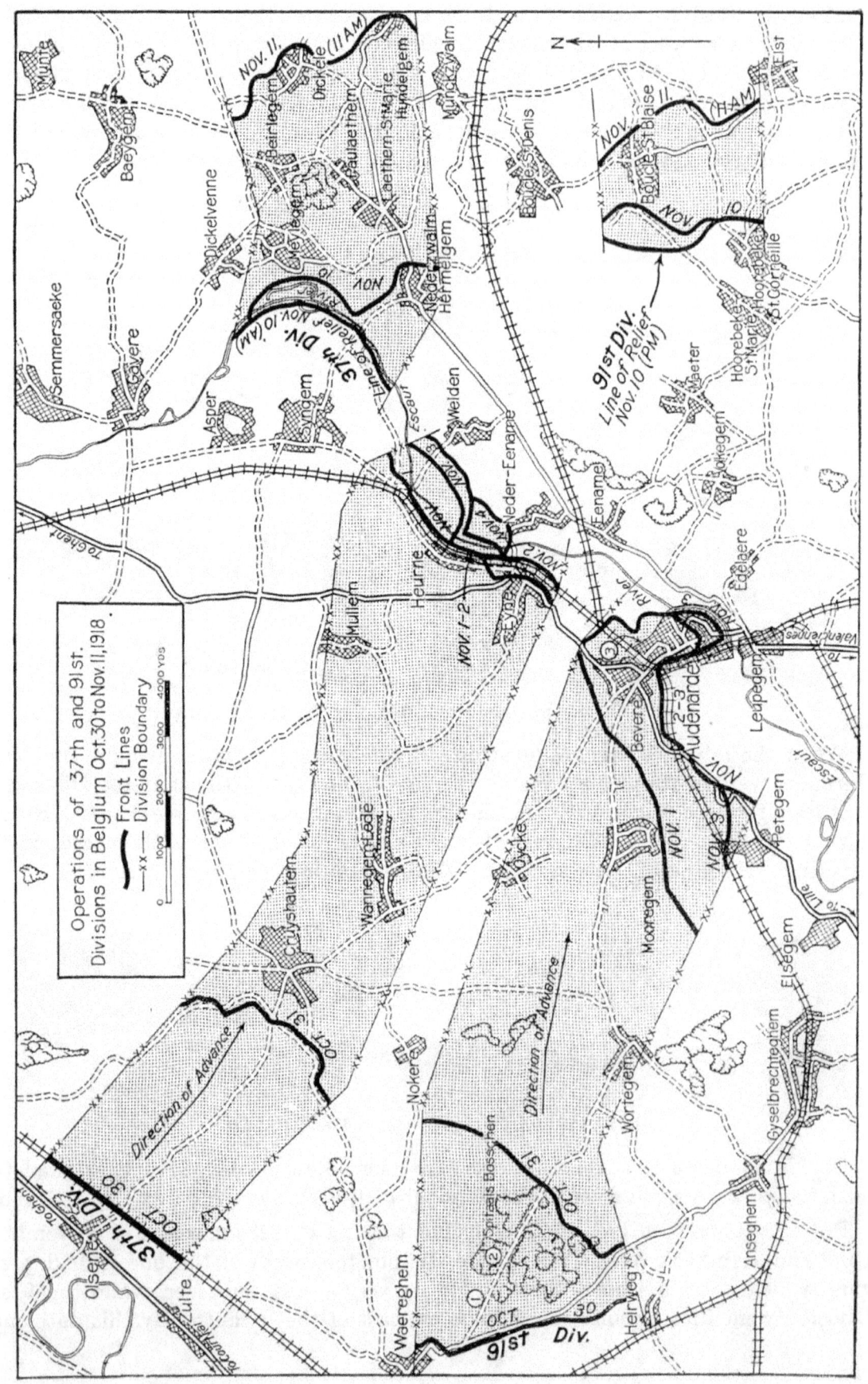

Germans were badly disorganized, and were retiring rapidly. The divisions continued their advances to the eastward until hostilities ceased at 11 a. m. on November 11.

In their operations in Flanders the two divisions had made deep penetrations into the hostile lines and each had captured many prisoners and a great amount of material.

The armistice found them occupying a line running approximately north and south about 6 miles east of Audenarde.

DUGOUT PROTECTING "TEST POINT" ON BURIED CABLE NEAR YPRES

This battle field may be visited by taking a train to Ghent, and hiring an automobile there.

NUMBERS ON MAP ON OPPOSITE PAGE INDICATE LOCATIONS OF FOLLOWING

① Flanders Field American Cemetery.

② Heavy resistance was encountered in this wood by the 91st Division on October 31, but by nightfall the Germans had been driven well to the east.

③ At the Place Tocambaro in Audenarde a monument is to be built by the American Government to commemorate the American operations in the region.

THE 27TH AND 30TH DIVISIONS SOUTH OF YPRES

These two divisions served, throughout their stay in Europe, with the British Army. During the summer of 1918 they were trained at the front by attaching small units to British organizations, and about the middle of August they assumed complete charge of adjoining divisional sectors on the line just south of Ypres.

On the 30th it was discovered that the Germans were retiring from the Lys salient and the British reoccupied Mont Kemmel. The 27th Division was directed to move forward the next day in cooperation with a like movement by the British units on its right, while the 30th Division was to advance the southern portion of its front to capture **Voormezeele,** and keep abreast of the left of the 27th.

Both divisions pushed forward to their objectives before daylight of the following day, and the 27th continued to make small gains until September 2, during which time it had captured **Vierstraat Ridge** and pressed the Germans back about a mile.

The 27th Division was relieved on the night of September 2-3 and the 30th on the night of September 3-4. Both divisions entered the line again about three weeks later north of **St. Quentin** in the fierce battles for the possession of the Hindenburg line.

This battle field may be visited by taking a train to Ypres.

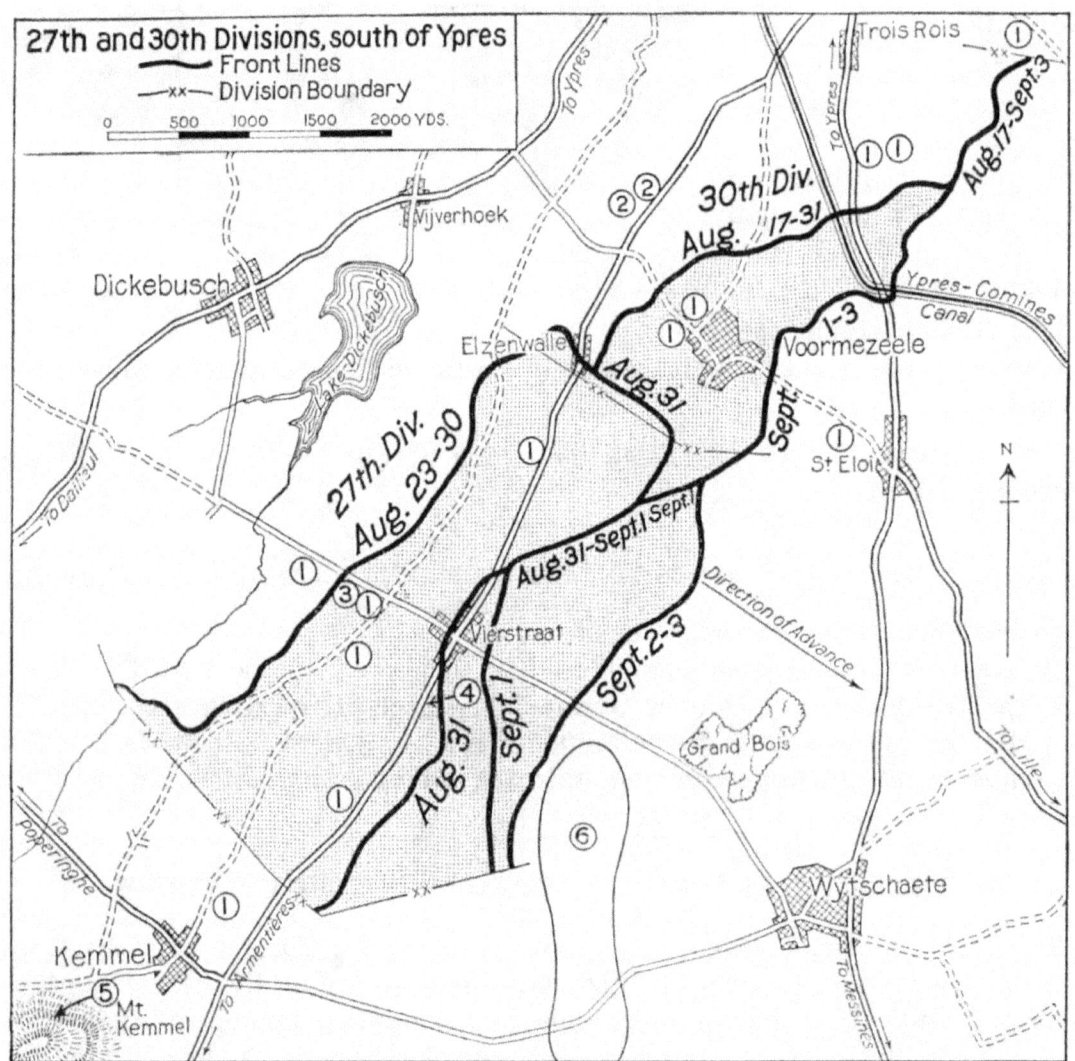

NUMBERS ON MAP INDICATE LOCATIONS OF FOLLOWING

① British military cemeteries.
② British concrete machine-gun post.
③ French military cemetery.
④ Site of monument to be erected by the United States Government to commemorate the American operations in this region during the war.
⑤ Observation tower on Mont Kemmel, giving a fine view of the region to the northeast. On the west side of the hill is a French military cemetery.
⑥ Area containing craters of mines exploded under the German lines by the British in 1917. Largest crater is about 100 yards in diameter.

80TH DIVISION WITH THE BRITISH THIRD ARMY

The 80th Division arrived for training with the British Third Army in July, and the regiments were assigned to the three corps composing that army.

During the first half of August the Germans made substantial retirements along the Third Army front, especially just north of **Albert** and in the vicinity of **Puisieux-au-Mont**. The American detachments then in line with the British followed up the retiring Germans, encountering little opposition.

The division was relieved from the British area on August 19, and entrained to join the American Army near St. Mihiel.

This locality may be visited by taking a train to Albert, and hiring an automobile there.

American Wagon Train Near Cloth Hall, Ypres

THE 33D DIVISION WITH BRITISH FOURTH ARMY. CAPTURE OF CHIPILLY RIDGE AND GRESSAIRE WOOD

The 33d Division arrived in France in the latter part of May, 1918, and joined the British Fourth Army for preliminary training in the front lines.

The 4th Australian Division, then with that army, was directed to attack on July 4 with the object of capturing the village of **Hamel**, just south of the Somme River and a few miles east of Amiens. Four companies of the 33d Division, totaling about 1,000 men, were attached to the Australians for the operation, and

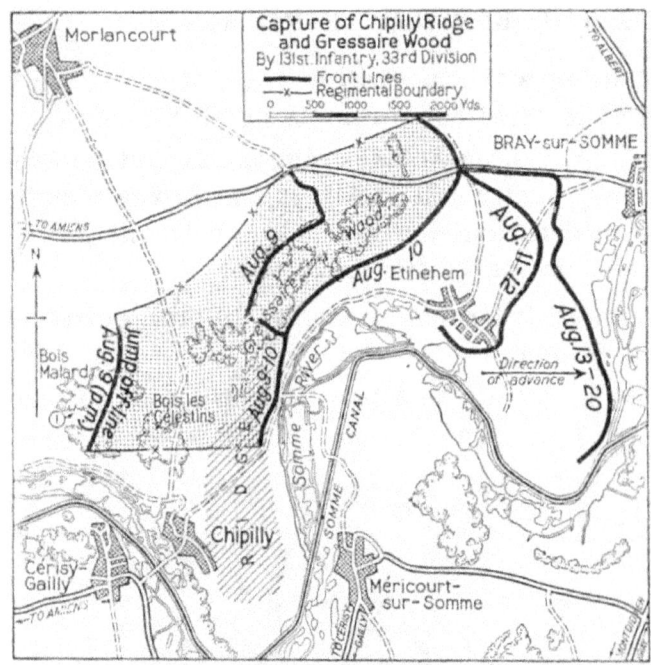

① In Bois Malard exist traces of trenches, shelters, and effects of shell fire

advancing with them promptly secured their objectives. Although but comparatively few Americans were engaged, their conduct was such as to receive high commendation from the British commanders. The four companies were withdrawn on July 5 and rejoined their division.

When the offensive against the Amiens salient was undertaken by the British and the French on August 8, one regiment (131st) of the 33d Division was placed at the disposal of the 58th British Division, and was directed to join it immediately. It moved forward and after a difficult night march took part, during the afternoon of August 9, in an assault against a particularly strong point in the German lines at **Chipilly Ridge** and **Gressaire Wood**.

The attack was made at 5.30 p. m., the American regiment double-timing part of the last 4 miles to reach its jump-off line. The assault made between two British brigades, under extemporized orders and without detailed reconnaissance, was nevertheless characterized by dash and gallantry, and by dark the troops had passed beyond the crest of Chipilly Ridge. The Americans continued the next morning, driving back the Germans on their front. The regiment stayed in the line until the night of August 19–20, taking part in local attacks and assisting in organizing the position.

During this period other units of the division were in the front lines or served

KING OF ENGLAND DECORATING MEN OF 33D DIVISION

as reserves of British divisions. The attack of August 9 and 10 again won for the troops of the 33d Division warm praise from the British commanders, and on August 12 the King of England, in person, visited the divisional headquarters to present decorations to individuals of the command.

In late August the division was relieved from duty with the British and began entraining to join the American Army near St. Mihiel.

This battle field may be visited by taking a train to Amiens and hiring an automobile there.

BRITISH, FRENCH, AND AMERICAN MILITARY POLICE. © B
Amiens, May, 1918

(INSERT.) WRECKED BRITISH AEROPLANE
AMERICAN TROOPS MARCHING TO MUSIC OF BRITISH BAND. © B

THE 6TH ENGINEERS IN THE SOMME DEFENSIVE

Early in February of 1918, parts of the 6th U. S. Engineers, 3d Division, joined the British Fifth Army to help with engineering work, as that army was busy with defensive construction on account of the probability of a German attack on its front. These engineers were working near Péronne when the German offensive of March 21 began, and were immediately ordered to the rear.

Street Scene in Amiens, April 25, 1918. © B

The German advance toward Amiens was so rapid, however, and the troops opposing it so few that as a measure almost of desperation the British assembled every available man to occupy the old French trenches, known as the Amiens defense line, which ran approximately north and south a few miles east of the town.

1st Division Attacking at Cantigny

The detachments of various classes of troops, including 3 companies of the 6th Engineers, which were hurriedly collected and put in position, were popularly known as "Carey's Forces" on account of the name of the British general who commanded them.

The 6th Engineers were holding a short section of trenches just west of **Warfusée-Abancourt** on March 28 when the Germans made a heavy attack along the front, which made no headway. Other attempts to advance were made during the next two days without success.

The American detachment was relieved from the line April 2 and stationed in support near the small town of Hamel. On June 9 it entrained for the south to join its division on the Marne.

This locality may be visited by taking a train to Amiens and hiring an automobile there.

THE 1ST DIVISION AT CANTIGNY

The American program of training troops in quiet sectors gave several of our divisions front-line experience during the winter of 1917-18, but none of them had seen service in active operations until the 1st Division entered the lines west of **Montdidier** on April 25, 1918, on a very active front.

GERMANS LEAVING DUGOUT AT CANTIGNY AFTER FLAME THROWER HAD BEEN USED IN IT

At that time the Germans were in the midst of their great spring offensives, and there were many indications that the next attack might include this place. The activity and firing on the front were so great that it was only with difficulty that any semblance of a defensive position could be organized.

The most prominent point in the German lines facing the 1st Division was the high ground on which **Cantigny** is located. Not only did it furnish excellent positions from which the Germans could observe the American sector, but it also served as a screen for hostile activities in its rear.

About the middle of May it was decided to dislodge the Germans from that point, in order to reduce the difficulties of holding the sector, and also to impede a possible offensive by them in the region.

The 28th Infantry was selected to carry out the attack, and supported by a mass of French and American artillery it jumped off on the morning of May 28 and promptly captured the town. Assisted by an intense artillery fire, the Germans made several desperate counterattacks on the position during the next two days but were compelled to accept defeat.

The capture of Cantigny, the first offensive action by an American division, was considered a brilliant exploit and was particularly gratifying to the Allies as it furnished a concrete example of the fighting qualities of the American troops, who were then beginning to arrive in France in large numbers. As this engage-

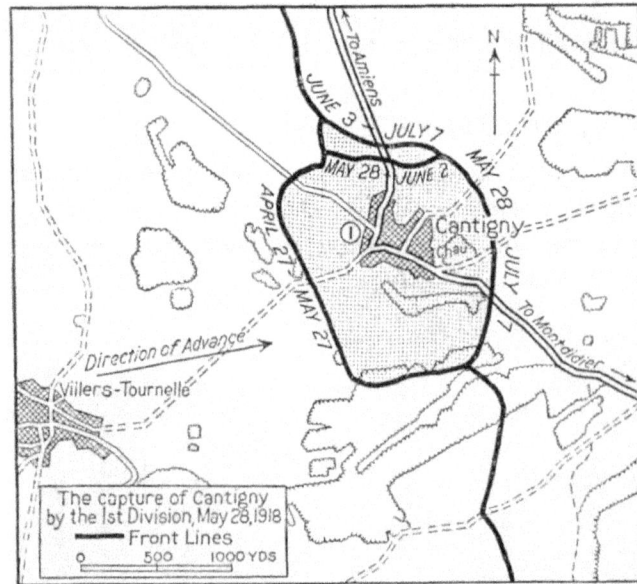

① In Cantigny, at the southwest corner of the central park area, a monument will be erected by the American Government to commemorate the capture of the town by the 1st Division. A memorial fountain built by the National Geographic Society of North America is located in the village, and southeast of town about 300 yards is a 1st Division monument of temporary construction.

ment occurred the day after the great German offensive of May 27 broke through the French lines at the Chemin des Dames, it was a very bright spot in an otherwise gloomy situation. The 1st Division on June 2 took over additional frontage in order to release French troops for use elsewhere.

CANTIGNY AFTER ITS CAPTURE, MAY 28, 1918

The division remained in line 72 days and suffered a total of about 5,000 casualties. It was relieved on July 8, and 10 days later took part in the important counteroffensive against the Marne salient.

This battle field may be visited by taking a train to Amiens and hiring an automobile there.

CHAPTER VII

SECTOR OCCUPATION BY AMERICAN DIVISIONS

The term "sector occupation" is used here to indicate the service of units in the front lines during periods in which no major operation took place in the particular sector concerned.

TYPICAL SCENE IN VOSGES MOUNTAINS

As the battle front (extending from Switzerland to the North Sea) was more than 400 miles long, it was obviously impossible for either side to obtain sufficient men and material to undertake operations on a large scale all along the entire

STREET IN BADONVILLER ON APRIL 29, 1918
Note entrances to dugouts and cellars

front. Consequently each massed its troops most heavily in those localities where there existed a strong likelihood that the other might attack or where the terrain and other factors made it appear that an offensive would obtain important results.

The region in the Vosges Mountains, north of the Swiss border, was such as to prevent the carrying on of major operations because of the difficulty of

FRONT LINE TRENCH NEAR BACCARAT

maneuvering and supplying troops during an advance. Between these mountains and the St. Mihiel salient, and south of them near Belfort, no great amount of fighting had taken place since early in the war, and consequently when our troops arrived in France the entire stretch southeastward from the salient was a quiet or inactive front held by relatively few troops. The major portion of sector occupation by American divisions occurred on this front.

Quiet sectors were in general held by partially trained troops, or by those which, having suffered heavy casualties in active operations, required time to rest and recuperate. Throughout the war there was a constant rotation of divisions between the battle sectors and the quiet ones.

American divisions used the quiet sectors for training purposes after they arrived in France. The normal procedure for divisions was first to carry out intensive

FRONT LINE TRENCH, 32D DIVISION SECTOR, ALSACE

training in rear of the front lines, then to serve in quiet sectors for a time with French or British troops, and finally to complete their training for battle in sectors of their own. This procedure was broken in emergencies, and some American divisions, such as the 3d, 36th, 79th, and 91st, went directly from training areas into battle.

AN OUTPOST NEAR BELFORT
Destroyed by German shell soon after picture was taken

Service in sector varied widely in character. On some parts of the front, particularly in the rougher stretches of the Vosges Mountains, the daily life of front-line troops was comparatively uneventful except for an occasional raid.

FRENCH MONUMENT AT BATHELÉMONT
Erected over first three Americans killed at the front

Y. M. C. A. HEADQUARTERS AT BATHELÉMONT

In other localities, where there existed the possibility of either side undertaking an offensive, the incessant efforts of each to discover the intentions of the other resulted in many raids, local attacks and frequent artillery bombardments. Service in these localities was almost as difficult as that in battle.

When an American division took over a sector the natural enthusiasm of the American soldiers, undiminished by years of war, usually produced a marked increase in the fighting in the sector. While this had no immediate effect on the general military situation, it did result in valuable experience for our divisions which later served so creditably on the Marne, at St. Mihiel, and in the Argonne.

Firing a Trench Mortar During Sector Occupation in Lorraine

The first time an American division placed its units in the battle lines was on October 21, 1917, when troops of the 1st Division went into sector, north of Lunéville, for training with the French. During that tour in the trenches the division took the first prisoner captured by our forces; it lost the first American prisoners in a German raid at **Bathelémont** on November 2; and in the same affair the first American soldiers were killed in action, 3 men losing their lives.

The 2d Division was holding a sector on the west face of the St. Mihiel salient in April, 1918, when part of its trenches were raided by German troops impersonating Allied soldiers. In spite of the confusion thus created, the troops concerned acquitted themselves with great credit and repulsed the enemy with greater losses than they themselves suffered.

2d Division Troops South of Verdun
Marching toward front to take over a sector

On April 20, 1918, the front lines of the 26th Division at **Seicheprey** were subjected to an intense bombardment and were raided in force by special German assault troops. The American losses were heavy considering the numbers engaged, but the Germans finally withdrew to their own trenches.

DELOUSING MACHINE IN OPERATION
Used to disinfect clothing of all men after a tour in the trenches

The 5th Division, on August 17, 1918, in a small but well-executed attack, captured the town of **Frapelle** and **Hill 451,** in the Vosges Mountains. It consolidated the new positions under heavy fire and held them in spite of a determined counterattack.

At **Flirey** the 89th Division, while engaged in relieving the 82d Division in August, was subjected to a heavy bombardment with gas shells and suffered a considerable number of casualties.

The front-line troops of the 42d Division, in a sector east of **Baccarat, in** May, 1918, were also gassed severely as a preliminary to a raid on their trenches.

On October 4 about 50 men of the 6th Division near **Sondernach,** east of **Gérardmer,** in the Vosges, were attacked by a raiding party of 300 Germans, equipped with machine guns and flame throwers. Although completely surrounded and greatly outnumbered, the Americans repelled the raid and captured 7 prisoners.

The 88th Division held a sector in the Vosges east of **Belfort** in October, during which period its troops in **Schonholz Woods** were subjected to two raids.

42D DIVISION TRENCH AFTER GERMAN RAID NEAR BADONVILLER, MARCH 4, 1918

NARROW GAUGE RAILWAY TRAIN BRINGING UP RATIONS NEAR MÉNIL-LA-TOUR

Many other interesting incidents took place, but the above will give an idea of the more active part of the service in "quiet" sectors.

The accompanying sketch indicates the sectors held by American divisions at various times on that part of the front between Verdun and the Swiss border. Divisions which entered the line to take part in the St. Mihiel offensive are not shown, unless they were on the front lines in the area for a considerable period prior, or subsequent, to the offensive.

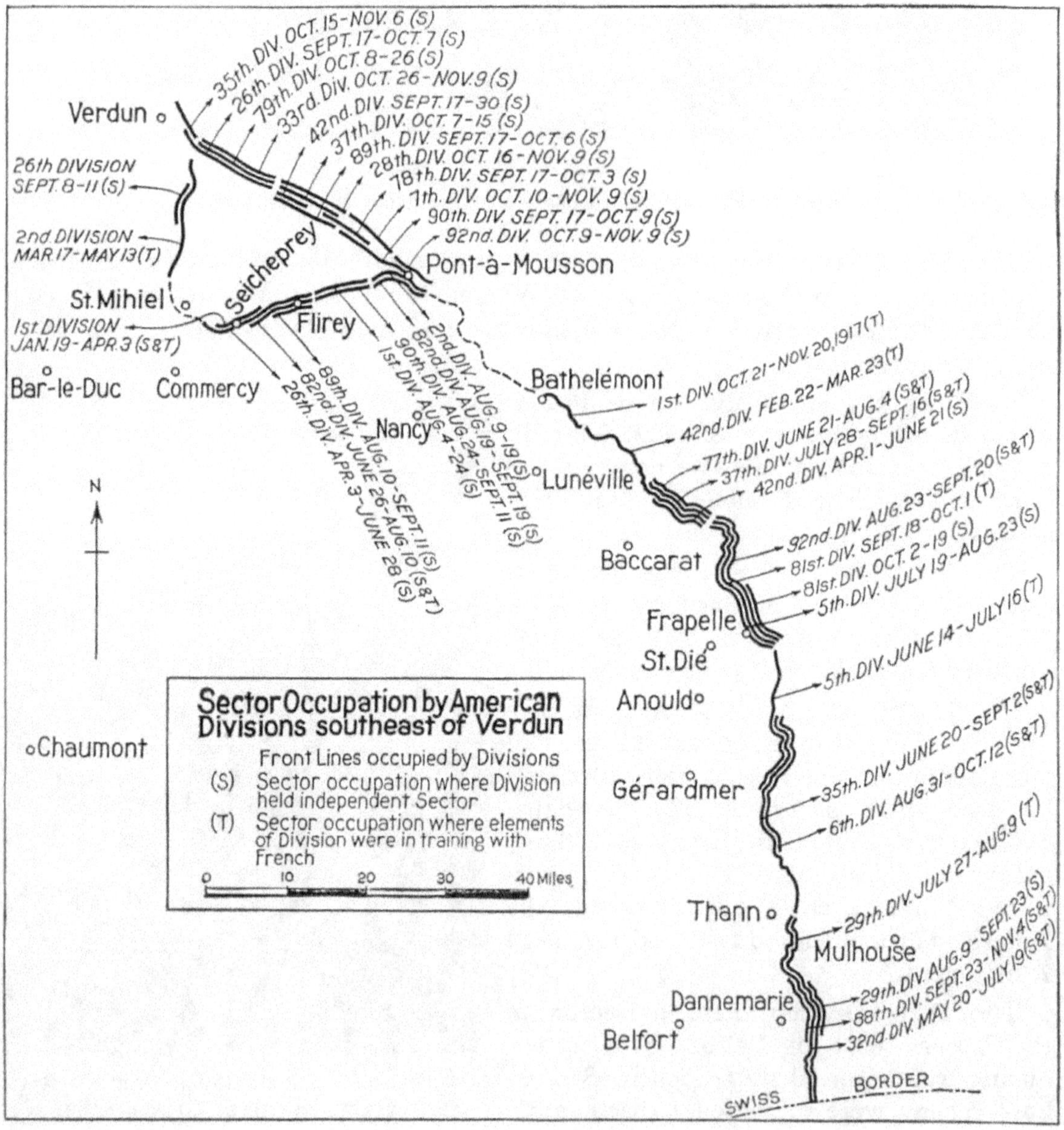

CHAPTER VIII

SERVICES OF SUPPLY

In rear of the area actually occupied by the fighting elements of a modern army, a great force is required to keep the combat units constantly in condition to engage in operations against the enemy. Replacements in men and animals, great quantities of rations, ammunition, weapons, and equipment of all kinds

AMERICAN DOCKS AT NANTES

must be received and sent to the front. To accomplish this, complete transportation facilities must be provided, and these must also be adequate to move organizations from one point to another, and to evacuate the wounded to the rear for proper medical care. In the American Expeditionary Forces these tasks, which involved the construction and operation of transportation systems, telephone and telegraph lines, hospitals, depots, docks, repair shops, and factories of various kinds, were performed by a huge organization known as the Services of Supply, or "S. O. S."

The American lines of supply and communication began within the United States and extended across the sea to France. They entered France mainly at ports along the western coast from Brest southward, as those farther north were

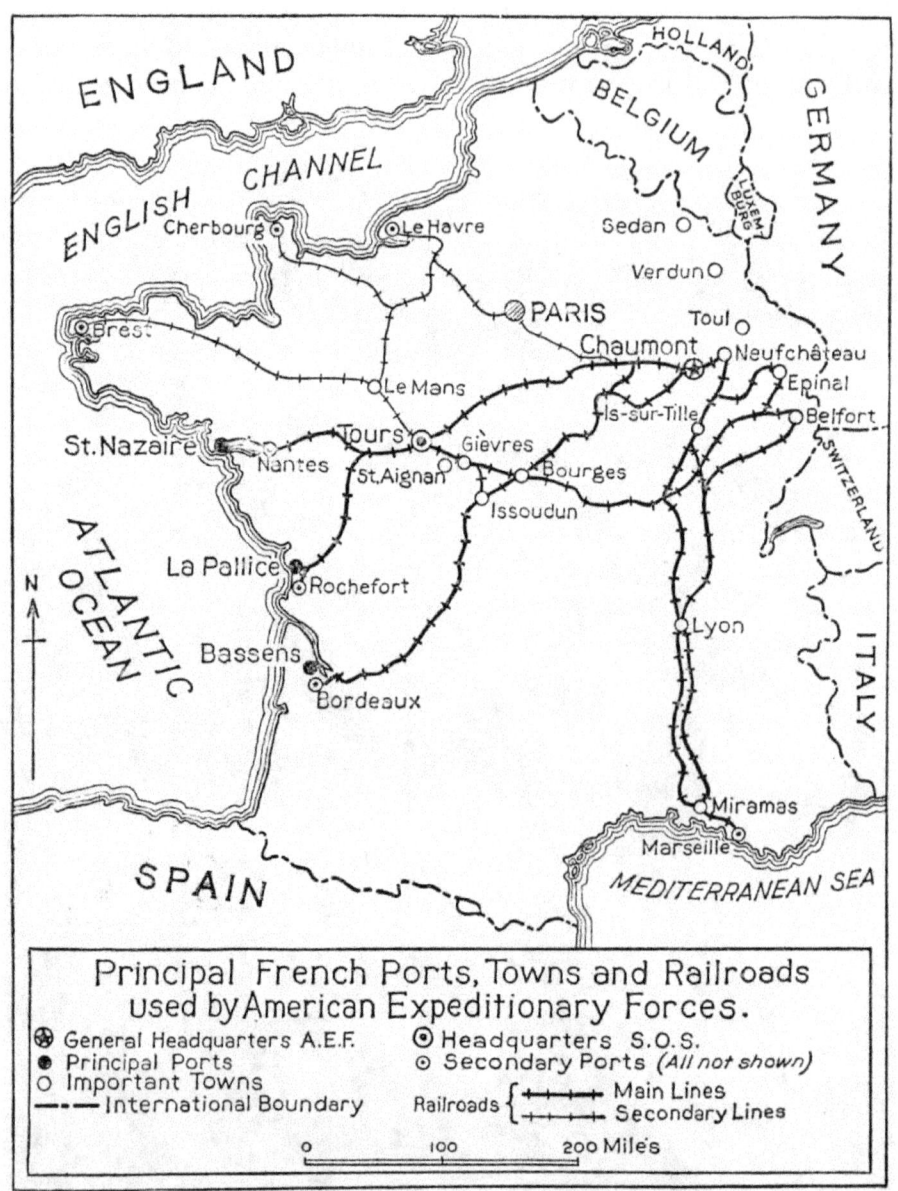

already heavily burdened with British traffic. The railway lines which ran northeastward from these ports to the main areas of American operations avoided the congested region near Paris, where the greater part of the French war factories and supply depots were located.

The scarcity of vessels made it imperative that as many articles as possible be purchased in Europe, so agencies of the Services of Supply were created for this purpose The formation of a salvage service, which collected, repaired, and reissued discarded shoes, hats, clothing, and every other article of equipment, also conserved ship tonnage and raw material and, moreover, saved many millions of dollars.

The vast area pertaining to the Services of Supply was divided for purposes of administration into base sections around the ports of debarkation, and one intermediate and one advance section located progressively nearer the front lines.

REPAIR SHOP UNDER CONSTRUCTION
Work done by American engineers

The Commanding General of the S. O. S. was responsible directly to the American Commander in Chief. He was in charge of all activities of the Services of Supply and of all personnel and material from the moment they arrived at the ports until they reached points in the forward areas designated by General Headquarters. He coordinated the work of the different branches under him, such as the quarter-

VIEW OF YARDS AT LA ROCHELLE, FRANCE
Shows 80 cars, representing one day's assembling at this American plant

master, ordnance, engineer, signal, transportation, and medical, and so planned that, as far as possible, there would be on hand at all times sufficient supplies to meet every requirement of the Army.

The construction of the many establishments necessary to the proper functioning of the supply service was chiefly performed by our engineer troops. More than 1,000 miles of standard-gauge railway tracks; many docks, including the necessary equipment for unloading ships; over 20,000,000 square feet of covered storage space; 16,000 barracks; bakeries; several enormous hospitals; refrigeration plants; and many other structures were built by the American Army in France. The base hospital at Mars consisted of 700 buildings, and covered a ground space of 33 acres. One of the refrigerating plants could store 6,500 tons of meat and produce 500 tons of ice per day; and one of the mechanical bakeries had a daily

SUPPLIES IN STORAGE AT MONTOIR

capacity of 800,000 pounds of bread. Forestry operations, which produced 200,000,000 feet of lumber and 4,000,000 railway ties, were carried on to assist in providing the materials needed in the construction program, the size of which is indicated by the examples given above.

The transportation of supplies required a great amount of equipment, and, in addition to that procured from the French, more than 1,500 locomotives and 20,000 cars were sent to France and assembled there. American railroad repair shops in France also reconditioned approximately 50,000 cars and 2,000 locomotives for the Allies.

ASSEMBLING LOCOMOTIVE AT ST. NAZAIRE AMERICAN ASSEMBLING YARDS

The supplies collected were stored at different points between the base ports and the combat area. It was inadvisable to place them too close to the front because of the enormous losses and consequent scarcity of supplies which would result if the Germans made a substantial advance. On the other hand, near the base ports they would not be readily available at the battle front and an interruption on the lines of communication might seriously embarrass the troops in contact with the enemy. Depots were therefore established in the base, intermediate, and advance sections, those in the last section containing relatively small reserves and being located as near to the combat areas as practicable. The total reserve stocks in France were, as far as possible, kept sufficient to supply the needs of the army for approximately three months, thus providing a factor of safety in case ocean traffic were interrupted. From the advance depots supplies were distributed regularly to the troops through great combination depots and railway yards known as regulating stations.

The vital importance of the work performed is indicated by the following telegram which was sent to the Commanding General of the Services of Supply by the American Commander in Chief in October, 1918, after the successful attack of the American First Army in the Meuse-Argonne region:

"I want the S. O. S. to know how much the First Army appreciated the prompt response made to every demand for men, equipment, supplies, and transportation necessary to carry out the recent operations. Hearty congratulations. The S. O. S. shares the success with it."

The Services of Supply was so planned and organized as to care for the needs of an army of 4,000,000 men, and actually supplied successfully an army of 2,000,000. By November 11, 1918, it had reached a numerical strength of 644,540 men, not including civilian employees, or about one-third of the American soldiers in Europe.

AMERICAN LUMBER MILL IN FRANCE
Over 100 of these were operated by American engineers

LOCATION OF ACTIVITIES IN THE SERVICES OF SUPPLY

The following list gives some of the places in France where establishments were created or operated by the Services of Supply. This list will give an idea of the work performed by that organization.

Aigrefeuille.—Base depot; railroad construction plant.
Aix-les-Bains.—Central point of one of principal leave areas.
Allerey.—Hospital center; storage depot; ice-making plant.
Angers.—Heavy artillery school; ordnance and salvage shops; hospital center; engineer and replacement camps; cold-storage plant.
Arnauville.—Army antiaircraft school.
Bar-sur-Aube.—Concentration camp; supply depot.
Bassens.—Large American docks; storage warehouses and cold-storage plant; ship repair shop; railroad construction center, and many other activities.
Bayonne.—Remount depot; important port for coal.
Bazoilles.—Hospital area; center for quartermaster activities; cold-storage and ice-making plants.
Beau Désert.—Hospital center; depots.
Beaune.—A university was established here by the A. E. F. after the armistice and was attended by many Americans; hospital center.
Belfort.—Motor transport unit; hospital.
Besançon.—Headquarters for forestry operations in vicinity; remount depot.

Blois.—Reclassification camp for officers; concentration point for casuals discharged from hospitals.

Bordeaux.—Headquarters of Base Section No. 2. Over 1,000,000 tons of freight were brought in through this port, and when the war ended it was rapidly becoming the principal freight port. In its vicinity were a large number of sawmills, hospitals, warehouses, etc.

Bourbonne-les-Bains.—Remount depot.

Bourges.—Central Records Office for all the personnel in the A. E. F.; railroad and ordnance shops; one of two women's camps in France; headquarters for forestry operations in this area.

Brest.—Headquarters of Base Section No. 5; principal port for embarkation and debarkation of troops. Large docks and warehouses were constructed and huge camps established in the locality.

Calais.—One of principal ports for troops that arrived via England.

Cannes.—Important town in leave area on the Riviera.

Cazaux.—Location of an aerial gunnery school.

Châteauroux.—Hospital and storage center; Air Service school; location of gas-mask factory; railroad construction center.

Châtillon-sur-Seine.—Corps and aviation schools; gasoline storage depot.

Cherbourg.—Debarkation point for troops transshipped from England.

ICE PLANT AT GIÈVRES
Third largest in world. Constructed by Americans

Clermont-Ferrand.—Artillery camp; aviation instruction center; hospital center; quartermaster depots; ordnance repair shop.

Coetquidan.—Artillery school and camp; Air Service school; veterinary hospital; ordnance repair shop.

Colombey-les-Belles.—Air Service depot for advance section.

Courcelles.—Antiaircraft machine-gun school.

Dijon.—Motor transport shops; camouflage plant; women's camp.

Donges.—Railroad construction shops.

Donjeux.—Tractor repair shops; motor transport park.

Doulaincourt.—Ordnance shops.

Epinal.—Headquarters for forestry operations; motor transport overhauling plant; railhead.

Gien.—Heavy artillery tractor school; headquarters for forestry operations.

Gièvres.—Great storage depot; largest refrigeration plant in the A. E. F.; railway construction center. More than 25,000 soldiers were on duty here.

Gondrecourt.—Location of I Corps schools.

Haussimont.—Observation school; artillery camp.

Issoudun.—Aviation instruction center in which were 12 flying fields; camp hospital; storage depot.

Is-sur-Tille.—Regulating station; ordnance shops; largest bakery in A. E. F.

Jonchery.—Railroad construction camp; storage depot.

La Corneau.—Artillery camp and school.

Langres.—Army General Staff school; hospital center.

La Pallice.—Headquarters of Base Section No. 7 for a time; port for coal and freight.

La Rochelle.—Headquarters of Base Section No. 7; port for supplies and coal; railroad repair shops.

Latrecey.—Air Service depot.

Le Blanc.—Field artillery motor tractor and ordnance school, and repair shops.

Le Havre.—Headquarters of Base Section No. 4; auxilliary port for American shipping; part of men transshipped from England landed here; storage depot.

Le Mans.—Principal area in which troops were assembled, inspected, and equipped preparatory to embarking for United States. Its maximum capacity was 250,000 men.

Les Cors.—Bomb and grenade storage depot.

Les Sables-d'Olonne.—Secondary port of entry.

Les Vals.—Chemical Warfare Service dump and camp.

SORTING SALVAGED SHOES

Liffol-le-Grand.—Regulating station; depot camp; railroad repair shop; and scene of large general activities.

Limoges.—Artillery camp; hospital center.

Lux.—Remount depot.

Marcy.—Railroad center and shops.

Mars.—Hospital center.

Marseille.—Headquarters of Base Section No. 6; due to submarine activities in the Mediterranean the port here was not used to any extent by the A. E. F. during the war, but later it became an important embarkation port for troops returning to the United States.

Mehun-sur-Yèvre.—Ordnance school; railroad construction center; location of largest ordnance repair shop in A. E. F., where rifles, cannon, and machine guns were reconditioned.

Meucon.—Large Artillery school; Air Service school.

Montierchaume.—Large storage depot.

Montlouis.—Potato-storage depot.

Montmorillon.—Artillery school.

LOADING CARS AT QUARTERMASTER DEPOT 1, NEVERS, FRANCE
Note women laborers employed for this work

Montoir.—Large docks, storage depots, and railroad yards, which formed the main terminal for the port of St. Nazaire, were constructed here.

Nantes.—Port of entry; hospital center.

Neufchâteau.—Headquarters of advance section of S. O. S.; served as a joint French and American regulating station; hospital center.

Neuvy Pailloux.—Tank center.
Nevers.—Headquarters of intermediate section of S. O. S.; important railroad and storage center.
Nice.—Principal town in the Riviera leave area.
Nogent-en-Bassigny.—Headquarters of advance section of S. O. S. was originally located here, but later moved to Neufchâteau.
Noisy-le-Sec.—Regulating station used in conjunction with French.
Orleans.—Refrigerating plant; hospital center.
Pau.—Hospital center.
Pauillac.—Naval air station; hospital center; port of entry and port of embarkation for troops returning to the United States after armistice.
Pontanézen Barracks.—Largest American camp in France; rest camp for troops arriving in and leaving France at Brest.
Pont-de-Claix.—Chemical Warfare Service training camp.
Pouilly.—Prison camp; supply depot.
Richelieu.—Camp for officer prisoners of war.
Rimaucourt.—Hospital center.
Rochefort.—Secondary debarkation port.
Romorantin.—Aviation production center.
Rouen.—Port of entry; Motor Transport Corps shops; depot camp.
St. Aignan.—Schools; replacement depot. After the war it became clearing point for returning troops.
St. Dizier.—Regulating station.
St. Loubès.—Large base depot; railway construction center.

RAILWAY YARDS AND WAREHOUSES AT ST. SULPICE
Constructed by Americans

St. Malo.—Leave center in Brittany.
St. Nazaire.—Headquarters of Base Section No. 1; principal freight port; 1,600,000 tons of freight were handled here before November 11, 1918; railroad construction center; camps.
St. Pierre-des-Corps.—Central camp for prisoners of war; supply depot; salvage plant; factories.
St. Sulpice.—Supply depot; coffee-roasting plant; railroad construction center.
Sampigny.—Large motor transport park and repair center.
Saumur.—Field artillery and aviation school.
Savenay.—Hospital center for wounded returning to the United States.
Sougé-Champ-de-Tir.—Balloon and ordnance school; artillery concentration and training camp; railroad construction center.
Tours.—Headquarters of the Services of Supply; aviation instruction center. A monument to commemorate the services of the S. O. S. will be erected here by the United States Government.
Trampot.—Convalescent camp.
Valbonne.—Infantry school for officer candidates.
Valdahon.—Large field artillery school and camp; ordnance repair shop.
Vannes.—Hospital center.
Vaucouleurs.—Storage depots.
Versailles.—Engineer training school.
Vitrey.—Trench mortar school.
Vitry-le-François.—Important railroad junction; motor transport repair center.

CHAPTER IX

OPERATIONS OF THE UNITED STATES NAVY IN THE WORLD WAR

The information given in this chapter is based on official reports of the Secretary of the Navy, dispatches from the Commander of the United States Naval Forces operating in European waters during the war, and on information furnished officially by the Secretary of the Navy.

When the United States entered the war the Allied Navies appeared to be lacking in effective means for combating the German submarines which had started

U. S. S. "GEORGE WASHINGTON," "AMERICA," AND "DE KALB" IN CONVOY, MAY 18, 1918

a campaign of unrestricted warfare two months previously; and immediate American Naval assistance to meet the crisis was extremely important.

Admiral William S. Sims, who had been appointed Commander in Chief of the United States Naval Forces operating in European waters, landed in England shortly after our entry into the war and established his headquarters at London. He was at once informed by the British authorities that if losses due to hostile submarines were not checked quickly the Allies would probably be defeated, as they were then losing about 800,000 tons of shipping a month, which was much greater than the rate of replacement.

GERMAN SUBMARINE "U-58" SURRENDERING TO UNITED STATES DESTROYERS "FANNING" AND "NICHOLSON"

The task facing the American Navy was a difficult one. It had to assist as soon as possible in counteracting the submarine menace, and, in addition, had to organize means of providing safe passage across the Atlantic for hundreds of thousands of American troops and vast quantities of supplies.

Action against submarines was initiated at once by dispatching the limited number of available destroyers to Europe. These were augmented by converted yachts, gunboats, small cruisers, and revenue cutters, and immediate steps were taken to build additional destroyers.

The first fighting unit of the American Navy to arrive in European waters was a detachment of six destroyers which, on May 4, 1917, steamed into the harbor at **Queenstown**, Ireland, where a main base was established. This force was soon increased to 34 destroyers. A main base was later established at **Brest,** and the force operating from there gradually grew in size until it approximated that at Queenstown. A third main base was established at **Gibraltar.** Secondary bases were also established along the Bay of Biscay and other portions of the European coast.

United States Destroyer at Sea

Soon after we entered the war a transport service was organized to carry American troops overseas. The few suitable vessels available were taken over by the Government at once and the German liners interned in our ports were later added to this fleet. Every effort was made

Stern of Destroyer, Showing Depth Bombs Used Against Submarines

Explosion of a 300-Pound Depth Bomb

throughout the war to obtain additional boats for this service, which carried a total of 911,000 men to Europe, or a little less than half of the number sent. Most of the remainder were transported by British ships.

To guard against submarine attack, American transports making the trip to Europe were, as far as practicable, gathered into groups and escorted through the danger zone by destroyers and other armed vessels. This method of combating the submarine menace was most successful and the results obtained were remarkable. Not

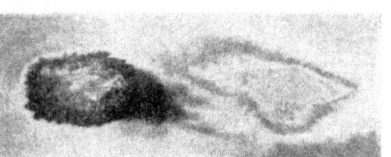
Oil Patch Indicating a "Hit" with a Depth Bomb

one Europe-bound soldier, while under the care of the American Naval vessels, lost his life from a submarine attack; and not a single vessel of the transport service was lost on the eastward voyage, although 3 ships returning to the United States were sunk out of a total of 5 torpedoed.

Nearly all the troops who crossed the Atlantic in American and French ships landed at French ports, while those going in other vessels landed in England. This necessitated the establishment of a small transport force of American ships

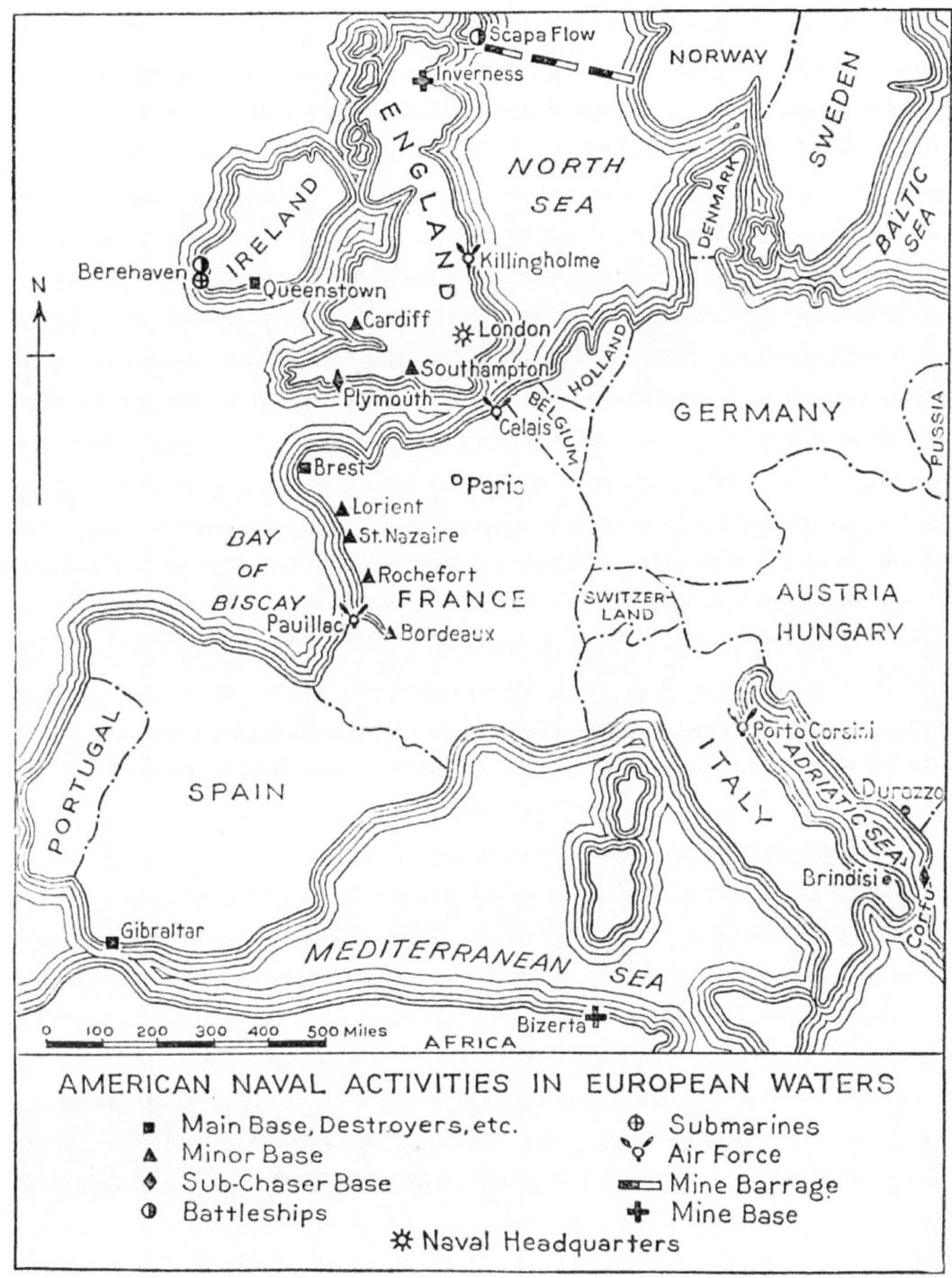

AMERICAN NAVAL ACTIVITIES IN EUROPEAN WATERS

- ■ Main Base, Destroyers, etc.
- ▲ Minor Base
- ♦ Sub-Chaser Base
- ⊙ Battleships
- ⊕ Submarines
- ⚲ Air Force
- ▬ Mine Barrage
- ✠ Mine Base
- ☀ Naval Headquarters

at **Southampton,** the chief port of reembarkation for France, in order to augment the British cross-channel service.

As the number of troops overseas increased, the task of supplying them became more difficult. This problem was met by the formation of the Naval Overseas Transportation Service, which was a force distinct and apart from other Naval activities. It developed into a fleet of more than 400 vessels, manned by approximately 4,500 officers and 29,000 men. To form this great organization it was necessary to take vessels from every available source, and included in it were ships taken over from the Shipping Board, new tonnage resulting from the intensive building program of the Emergency Fleet Corporation, and a number of boats which were brought from the Great Lakes under considerable difficulties. The convoy system was also used in so far as possible in the operation of this fleet, and the record made was exceptional.

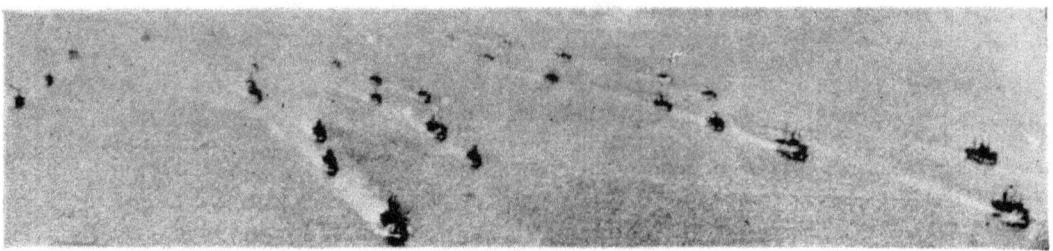

A UNITED STATES CONVOY AT SEA

As soon as the safety of the transports and supply ships had been reasonably assured, other steps were taken in offensive warfare against the submarines. This was done by the laying of "mine barrages," the employment of a hunting force of small ships, supplemented by aircraft, and the use of submarines.

Before America's entry into the war the British had considered closing the northern entrance to the North Sea by placing a mine barrage from Scotland to Norway, but had given this idea up as impracticable. Our Naval authorities felt, however, that with a new type of mine which had been developed in the United States this scheme could be undertaken successfully. In October, 1917,

TRANSPORTS EN ROUTE TO FRANCE

it was decided to make the attempt, in conjunction with the British, and the construction of mines was begun in the United States. The total length of the "mine barrage" to be put down was 230 miles, and the estimated number of mines required was about 75,000. Bases were established on the eastern coast of Scotland, necessary vessels were procured and equipped, and in June, 1918, operations began. By the time hostilities ceased the British had placed approximately 14,000 and the Americans 56,000 mines, as a result of which 12 enemy submarines are known to have been sunk or damaged.

Plans were also made for placing mine barrages in other areas, and a mine base was planned at **Bizerta**, Tunis, from where operations were to be conducted in the

UNITED STATES NAVAL VESSELS WITH CAPTIVE BALLOON IN TOW
Balloon was used in searching for German submarines

Adriatic and Ægean Seas, but the signing of the armistice halted the undertaking.

In order to establish a large and effective hunting force of surface vessels, construction was undertaken in America of several hundred boats called "submarine chasers." These were small wooden vessels, 110 feet long, powered by gasoline motors, and equipped with sound-detecting devices. A force of 235 of these vessels were sent to Europe. Most of them based at **Plymouth**, **Queenstown**, and **Corfu**, and were very effective in the protection of merchant shipping. During the period of operation of the Plymouth detachment not a single merchant vessel was lost in its area as a result of German submarine attacks. A detachment from the Corfu group sailed from **Brindisi** with the Allied fleet and participated with it in the attack on the Austrian port of **Durazzo**, being credited with destroying 2 submarines and doing especially valuable work in screening the larger vessels of the fleet.

SUBMARINE CHASERS LEAVING EUROPEAN PORT FOR CONVOY DUTY

In June, 1917, a small detachment of the Naval Air Service arrived in Europe and soon thereafter the establishment of aviation bases was begun along the French,

AMERICAN SUBMARINE CHASERS AT CORFU, GREECE

English, and Italian coasts in order to assist in the escort of shipping. At the signing of the armistice this force had developed into an organization of approximately 19,000 officers and enlisted men, operating from 27 bases.

The operations of this force against hostile craft at sea were very successful. With its growth, plans were made for offensive action against the submarines at their bases, and 8 squadrons, based near **Calais** and **Dunkirk**, bombed **Zeebruge**, Ostend, and Bruges until these ports were freed in the fall of 1918 by the combined attacks of the Allied Armies. The American Naval air units then aided the Royal Air Force in covering the advance of the northern British armies until the cessation of hostilities.

The Allied Naval authorities having decided to employ some of their own submarines as an additional means of combating similar hostile craft, two groups of American submarines were dispatched to European

UNITED STATES NAVAL AIR STATION AT L'ABER-VRACH, FINISTÈRE, FRANCE

waters. One group operated from **Ponta Delgada**, Azores, and the other from **Berehaven**, Bantry Bay, Ireland, and effectively covered these two areas.

AMERICAN SUBMARINE CREDITED WITH DESTRUCTION OF GERMAN SUBMARINE

During the early days of America's effort there appeared to be no necessity for dispatching any great portion of her battle fleet to European waters. It, therefore, except for two divisions, remained on this side of the Atlantic, where it was principally engaged in the work of training large numbers of recruits assimilated by the Navy. In December, 1917, a division of battleships reinforced the British Grand Fleet at **Scapa Flow**, after which it participated in routine work of the Grand Fleet, while in 1918 a division of 3 American battleships took station on the southwest coast of Ireland, at Berehaven, from where it was to operate against any enemy raiding cruisers that might break through the cordon drawn around the German coast.

UNITED STATES WARSHIPS WITH BRITISH NAVY AT FIRTH OF FORTH, SCOTLAND

Aside from the foregoing purely Naval operations, a brigade of Marines served as part of the 2d Division, and five 14-inch Naval guns on railroad mounts, manned by Naval personnel, operated along the battle front against distant targets. These Naval railroad batteries arrived in France during July and August, 1918. They went into action in September, 1918, and from then on continued in operation until the end of the war.

To commemorate the achievements of the Navy, six memorials will be erected in Europe by the United States Government. *Further information concerning these memorials is given in Chapter XI.*

LARGE NAVAL GUN ON AMERICAN FRONT NEAR VERDUN

PARTIAL LIST OF ADDITIONAL PLACES WHERE AMERICAN NAVAL ACTIVITIES OCCURRED IN EUROPE

Bordeaux, France.—Naval District Headquarters, located here, directed the operations of vessels engaged in convoy work and submarine hunting in this vicinity. Near the city the construction of a high-powered Naval radio station was undertaken for communication with the United States, but was not finished by the time of the armistice.

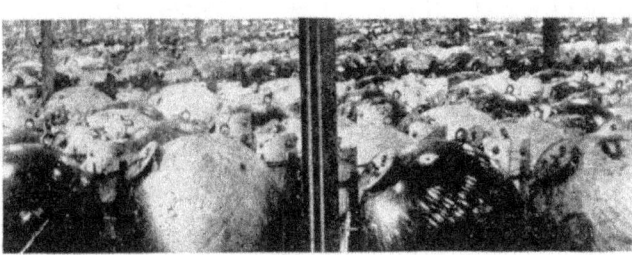

AMERICAN MINE BASE AT INVERNESS

Brest, France.—Location of American Naval Headquarters in France, and main port of debarkation for troops carried on American Naval transports. A force of over 30 destroyers and many yachts based here and operated as escorts for troops and supply convoys. During July and August, 1918, over 3,000,000 tons of shipping were convoyed in and out of French ports by vessels from this base with a loss of less than one-tenth of 1 per cent.

Cardiff, Wales.—Location of American Naval Headquarters for administration of the coal transport service, which carried coal for the Army from this port to France.

Gibraltar.—A Naval force operating from here made many attacks upon submarines, and during July and August, 1918, escorted 25 per cent of all Mediterranean convoys to French ports, as well as 70 per cent of all convoys to English ports from Gibraltar.

Inverness, Scotland.—The main base for mining operations in the North Sea was established here in the fall of 1917.

Killingholme, England.—Site of Naval air base, planes from which flew 57,000 sea-miles while escorting 6,000 vessels through the submarine zone.

Pauillac, France.—An assembly plant for all Naval planes shipped to the Continent was located here. A force of over 5,000 officers and men built and operated this plant.

United States Transport "George Washington," Battleship "Pennsylvania," and Submarine Chaser at Brest, France

Porto Corsini, Italy.—American Naval flyers from this base, which was taken over from the Italians in July, 1918, participated in raids upon the Austrian port of Pola and carried out 5,500 flights while patrolling and reconnoitering.

Queenstown, Ireland.—First American Naval base in Europe. The U. S. S. *Nicholson* and *Fanning*, based here, sank the German *U-58* and captured its crew in November, 1917. During July and August, 1918, destroyers operating chiefly from this port furnished 75 per cent of escorting vessels for approximately 2,700,000 tons of shipping into British harbors, steaming a total of 260,000 miles and accomplishing the task without the loss of a single ship.

Rochefort, France.—Eight Naval vessels, including 5 converted yachts, operated from this port and escorted a total of 182 convoys.

St. Nazaire, France.—Naval District Headquarters. First detachment of American troops landed here June 26, 1917. A force consisting principally of converted yachts was concentrated at this port for mine sweeping, submarine hunting, and convoy escorting.

CHAPTER X

AMERICAN MILITARY CEMETERIES IN EUROPE

There are eight permanent American military cemeteries in Europe. These are being developed by our Government into resting places of beauty and dignity, and no American who travels in Europe should fail to visit them.

The cemeteries are widely distributed, yet conveniently located with respect to the routes which most travelers would naturally follow. From the walls of Paris it is only 3 miles to the cemetery at Suresnes, and from London it is less than an hour by train to the one at Brookwood. The other six are scattered over the battle fields of France and Belgium, on ground where Americans fought, and are included in the tours outlined in this book. Most of them are also included in the regular battle-field tours conducted by tourist agencies. Good roads lead to all the cemeteries, and any one of them can be visited comfortably either by automobile alone or by train to the nearest large town and thence by motor.

The development of the cemeteries to their present condition has been carried out under the jurisdiction of the War Department with the advice and cooperation of the National Commission of Fine Arts. Responsibility for their future architectural improvement rests upon the American Battle Monuments Commission, which was created by Congress in 1923 for the purpose of commemorating the services of the American forces in Europe during the World War. The plans of the Commission call for the erection in each cemetery of a beautiful memorial chapel, masonry walls, and such other architectural features as are necessary to give completeness. The designs for the chapels, which will be nondenominational in character, have already been selected and are shown in this chapter. Each chapel will contain a tablet bearing the names of the American missing in the battles of the vicinity.

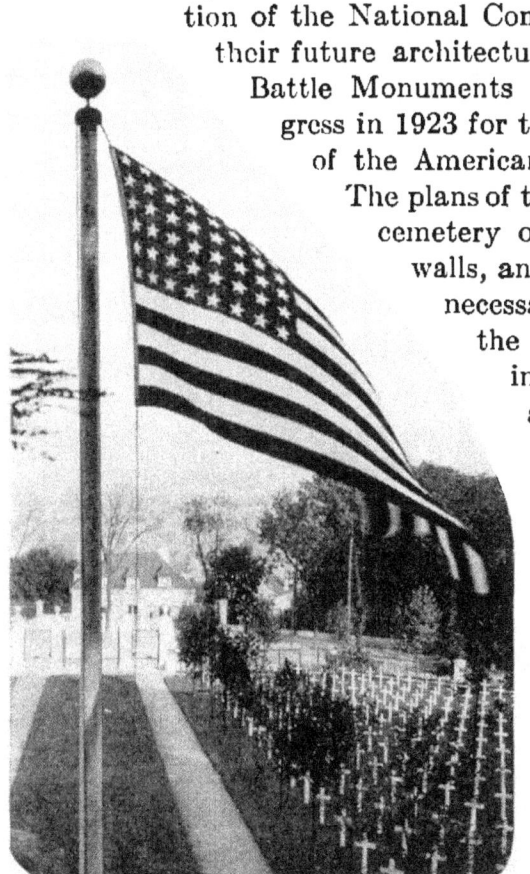

FLAG AT SURESNES CEMETERY

The cemeteries are under direct charge of the American Graves Registration Service, Quartermaster Corps, United States Army, whose offices at the present time are at 20 rue Molitor, Paris. An information bureau is maintained at that office, where data concerning American burials in Europe can be obtained. This bureau should be consulted by those who desire general information or who wish to know in which cemetery a particular grave is located.

AMERICAN MILITARY CEMETERIES

American Cemetery

The records show that 78,734 members of the American Expeditionary Forces gave their lives during the World War. At the request of relatives 46,284 of these were returned to the United States, 605 were sent to other countries, 128 were left in their original graves outside of permanent American cemeteries, and 30,592 are now buried in the cemeteries described in this chapter. Approximately 1,125 bodies have not yet been recovered.

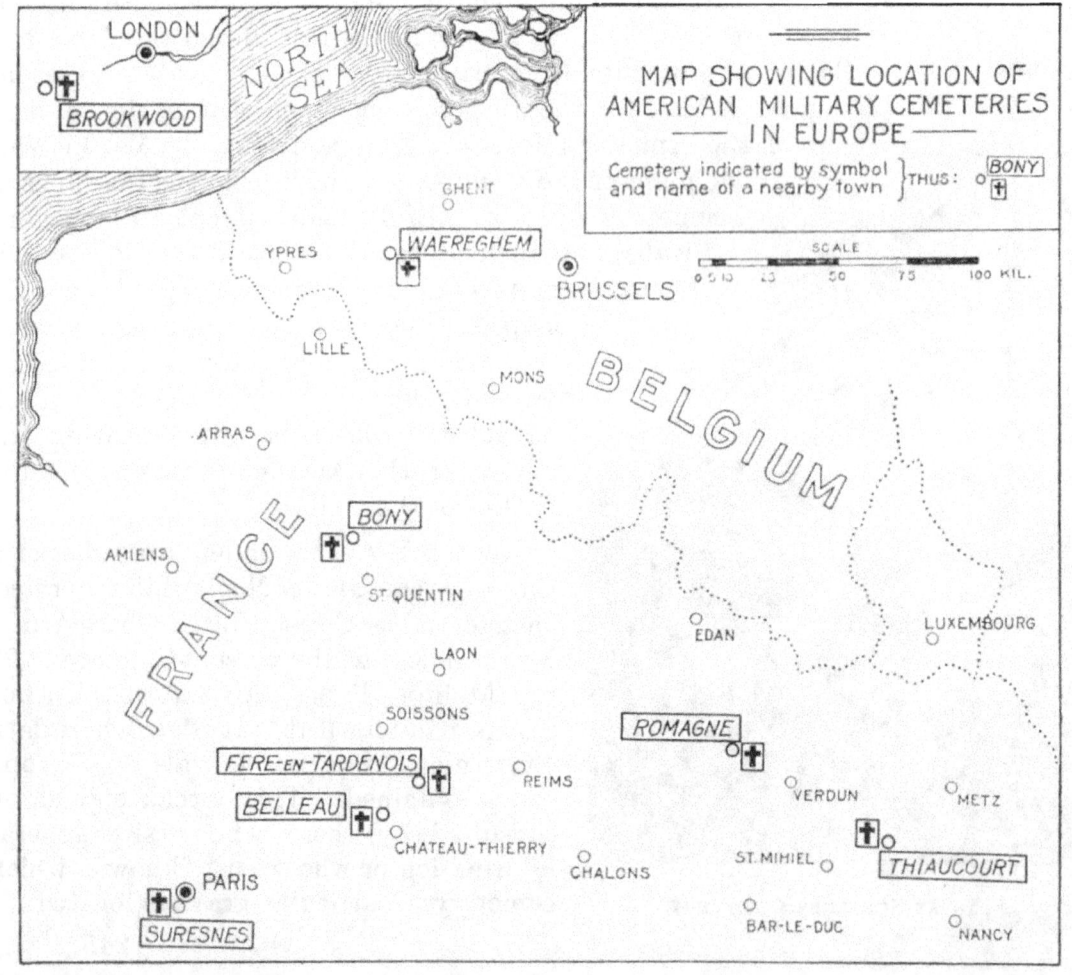

NEAR ROMAGNE, FRANCE

The work of removing bodies to their final graves from the 2,400 American burial places which existed at the time of the armistice began shortly thereafter and was completed in 1922. These removals were made in such a way that the relative sizes of the battle-field cemeteries now give a good idea of the comparative importance of each of the principal American operations with respect to the others.

Specific information concerning these cemeteries is given below. The name of a near-by town is used in each case to designate them, and the small sketches show their locations with respect to these towns.

At each cemetery is an American caretaker whose duty it is to assist visitors in locating individual graves and in obtaining other desired information.

ROMAGNE-SOUS-MONTFAUCON, FRANCE

This cemetery, officially called the **Meuse-Argonne American Cemetery**, contains 14,134 graves. The soldiers who rest here came from almost every division in the American Expeditionary Forces, most of them having given their lives in the Meuse-Argonne operation, one of the decisive battles of the war. In 1922 bodies were brought here from the area immediately west of the Argonne Forest, from the general vicinity of the Vosges Mountains, from occupied Germany, and from Archangel, Russia.

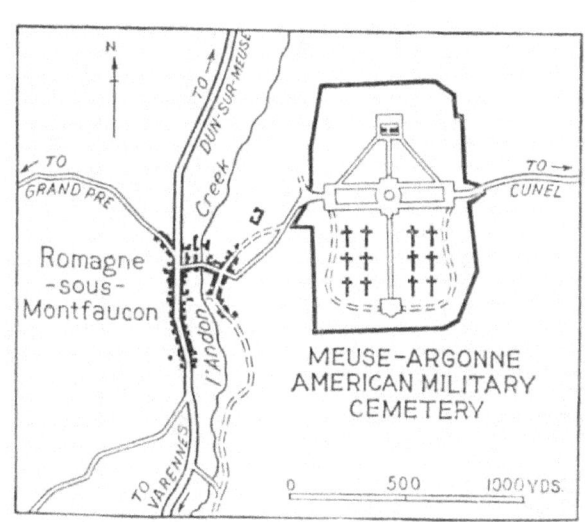

The cemetery is about 23 miles northwest of Verdun, which can be easily reached by train. Good hotel accommodations are available there, and automobiles for a visit to the cemetery can be readily obtained. A hostess house which is maintained at the cemetery can provide rooms and meals for a limited number of visitors during the summer months.

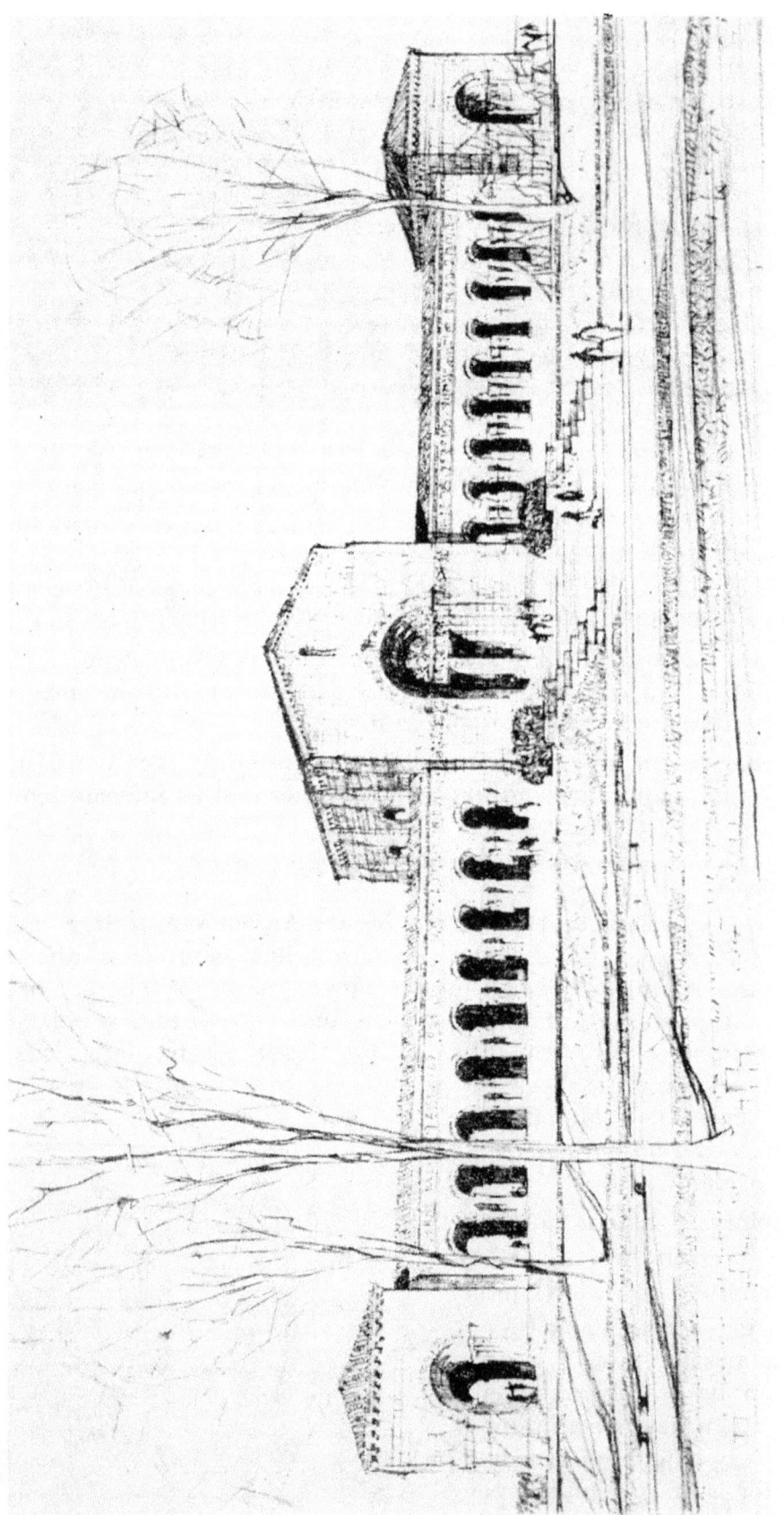

Design for Chapel at American Cemetery Near Romagne
York & Sawyer, New York, architects

AMERICAN CEMETERY NEAR THIAUCOURT, FRANCE

THIAUCOURT, FRANCE

The only American cemetery in the area of the St. Mihiel operation of the American Army is the **St. Mihiel American Cemetery** west of Thiaucourt. Here lie 4,143 soldiers, the majority of whom were members of the American divisions attacking in the great offensive action of our First Army which resulted in the reduction of the St. Mihiel salient. Others buried here were among those who died while serving in sectors in the vicinity, or who were removed to this region in 1922 from training areas to the southwest.

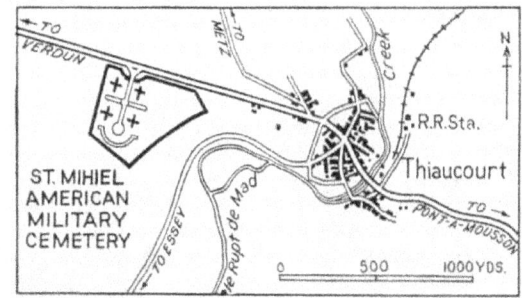

The cemetery is almost equidistant by road, about 20 miles, from Nancy, Verdun, and Metz. There is good train service to each place, and at each of them fairly good hotel accommodations are available and automobiles may be hired. In the near future a main railroad line will pass through Thiaucourt. No suitable hotel accommodations are now available there.

DESIGN FOR CHAPEL AT AMERICAN CEMETERY NEAR THIAUCOURT
Thomas Harlan Ellett, New York, architect

American Cemetery Near Fère-en-Tardenois, France

FERE-EN-TARDENOIS, FRANCE

The **Oise-Aisne American Cemetery** contains 5,962 graves. The majority of the battle dead who sleep here are from the divisions that fought in the vicinity of the Ourcq River and in the territory from there to the north as far as the Oise River. In 1922, American soldiers then buried in France in the general

Design for Chapel at American Cemetery Near Fère-en-Tardenois
Cram & Ferguson, Boston, architects

area west of the line Tours-Romorantin-Paris-LeHavre were removed to this cemetery.

It is about 18 miles by road from Château-Thierry or from Soissons to the cemetery, and slightly more from Reims. Good train service is available to

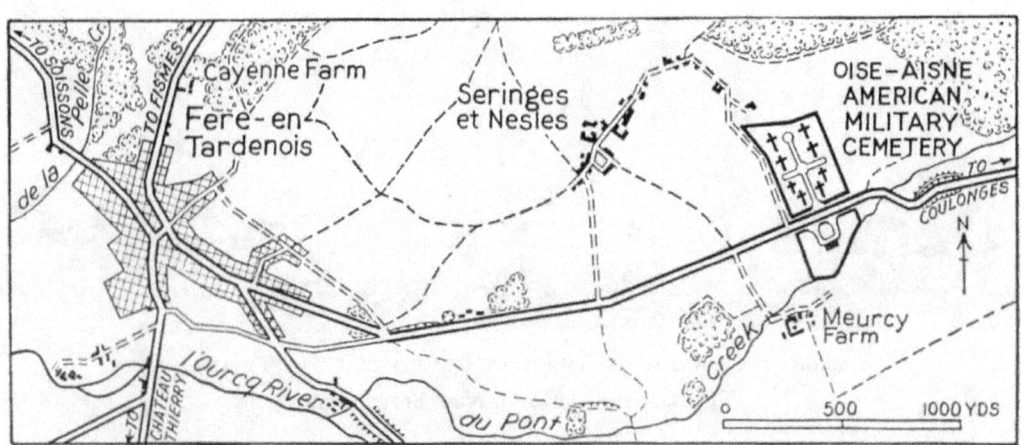

each of these places, where hotel accommodations can be obtained and automobiles hired.

BELLEAU, FRANCE

The **Aisne-Marne American Cemetery,** containing 2,212 graves, lies at the foot of the hill upon which stands Belleau Wood. The

AMERICAN CEMETERY NEAR BELLEAU, FRANCE

majority of those who died in battle and are buried here are from units that fought in the immediate vicinity and along the Marne River. A number of

DESIGN FOR CHAPEL AT AMERICAN CEMETERY NEAR BELLEAU
Cram & Ferguson, Boston, architects

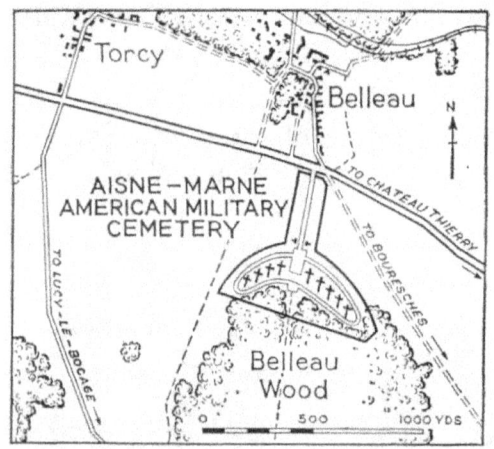

bodies were concentrated in this place in 1922 from the general vicinity of Lyon and Clermont in central France.

The cemetery is 6 miles northwest of Château-Thierry, which is on the main railroad running east from Paris. Fair hotel accommodations are available at Château-Thierry and automobiles may be hired there.

BONY, FRANCE

The **Somme American Cemetery** is the resting place of 1,830 soldiers. Members of the 27th and 30th Divisions who fell in the vicinity, as well as those of the 1st Division who gave their lives in the operations near Cantigny, and of the 33d and

AMERICAN CEMETERY NEAR BONY, FRANCE

80th Divisions who fell in the operations while serving with the British, are buried here. In addition, all other American soldiers who died on or behind the British

DESIGN FOR CHAPEL AT AMERICAN CEMETERY NEAR BONY
Mellor, Meigs & Howe, Philadelphia, architects

front in France and who were not removed to the United States in 1922 now sleep here.

The site is about 11 miles northeast of St. Quentin, which can be reached by train from Paris. Hotel accommodations are available and motor transportation may be hired there.

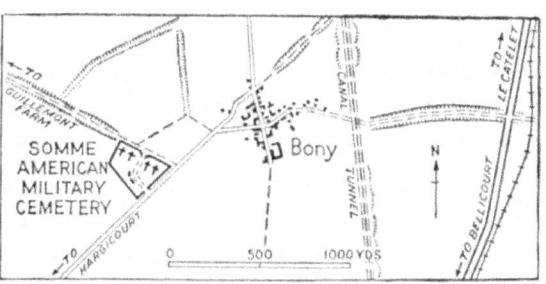

AMERICAN CEMETERY NEAR WAEREGHEM, BELGIUM

DESIGN FOR CHAPEL AT AMERICAN CEMETERY NEAR WAEREGHEM
Paul P. Cret, Philadelphia, architect

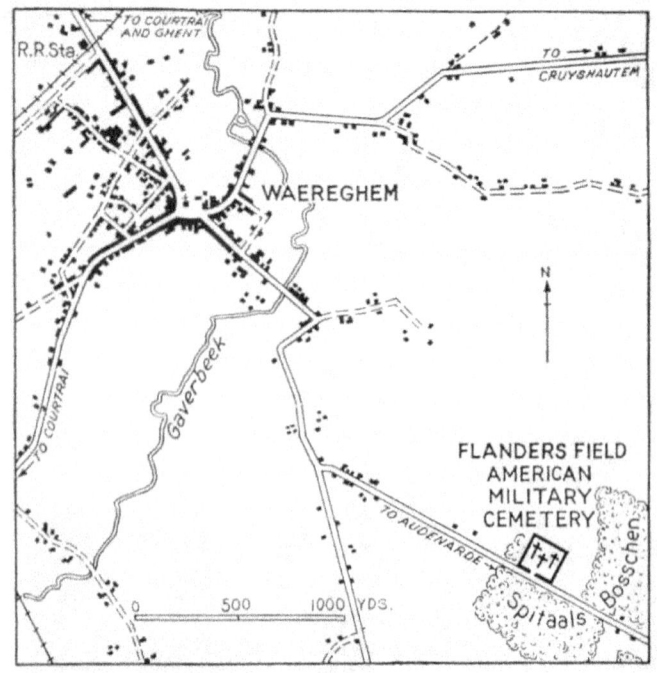

WAEREGHEM, BELGIUM

This cemetery, officially called **Flanders Field American Cemetery,** is situated about halfway between Brussels and Ypres and contains 367 graves. It is on ground captured by the 91st Division. The soldiers buried here are mainly those of the 37th and 91st Divisions who died in this part of Flanders, and of the 27th and 30th Divisions who fell near Ypres.

The cemetery is about 19 miles from Ghent, 27 miles from Lille, and 46 miles from Brussels. These places are easily reached by railroad and have good hotel accommodations. Automobiles may be hired at them.

SURESNES, FRANCE

Three miles west of the walls of Paris, on the slope of Mont Valérien, lies the **Suresnes American Cemetery.** It overlooks the capital and contains 1,507 graves.

The town of Suresnes can easily be reached from Paris by train, street car, or automobile. The cemetery is about 200 yards from the railroad station.

American Cemetery Near Suresnes, France

DESIGN FOR CHAPEL AT AMERICAN CEMETERY NEAR SURESNES
Charles A. Platt, New York, architect

BROOKWOOD, ENGLAND

The **Brookwood American Cemetery,** located about 28 miles southwest of London, contains 437 graves. It forms part of a very large and beautiful British cemetery which was established many years ago. The American section adjoins one used for British war burials which contains many of the dead from their Colonial Forces.

The American bodies buried in this cemetery were concentrated after the armistice from various places throughout England, Scotland, and Ireland, and consist of those members of the American Expeditionary Forces who lost their lives in Great Britain or its surrounding waters during the war.

AMERICAN CEMETERY NEAR BROOKWOOD, ENGLAND

DESIGN FOR CHAPEL AT AMERICAN CEMETERY NEAR BROOKWOOD
Egerton Swartwout, New York, architect

It is a pleasant drive by automobile from London to Brookwood, through an interesting part of England, and a trip to the cemetery in this way can be comfortably made in half a day. Brookwood can also be reached from London on the London & South Western Railway. The American cemetery is about 400 yards southwest of the railroad station.

REST HOUSE AT BROOKWOOD

CHAPTER XI

AMERICAN PROJECT FOR MEMORIALS IN EUROPE

The memorial project of the United States Government to commemorate the services of the American forces in Europe during the World War, with the exception of the memorial chapels referred to in the preceding chapter, is outlined here.

DESIGN FOR MEMORIAL AT MONTFAUCON, FRANCE
John Russell Pope, New York, architect

This project, which was prepared by the American Battle Monuments Commission, includes the erection of the battle-field memorials shown on the sketch on the next page, a monument to the Services of Supply, tablets to mark certain headquarters, and other memorials in recognition of the work of the Navy.

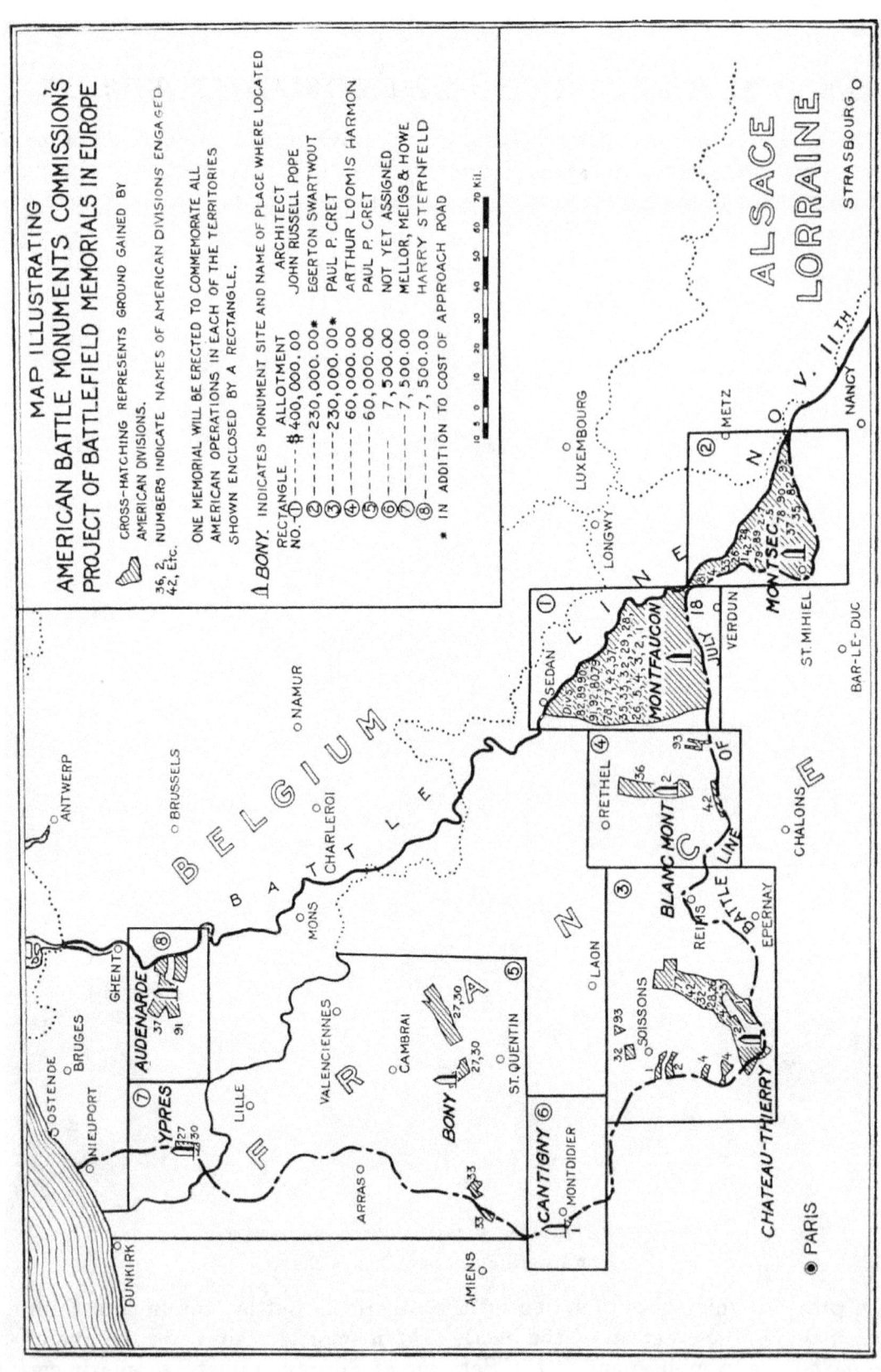

In the preparation of this project the Commission decided to construct a few imposing memorials rather than a great number of smaller ones. To be of any value a memorial must be seen. This is assured by placing it where people naturally go, or else by making the memorial of such a striking nature that people will go out of their way to see it. As the rehabilitation of the devastated regions progresses, the battle fields will lose more and more of their war-time character, and before long most of the evidences of the war will have disappeared. With this change, fewer and fewer people will visit these regions, and it is the Commission's idea that its memorials should be of an impressive character so that an effort will be made to see them.

As shown by the sketch on the opposite page, three major battlefield memorials and five minor ones are contemplated. The largest will commemorate the Meuse-Argonne offensive, the greatest battle in American history. It will stand on the ruins of the old town of **Montfaucon**, which occupied the dominating hill of that name.

The operation second in importance conducted by the American Army was the elimination of the St. Mihiel salient, which for four years had stood as a threat to the Allied lines. The monument to this battle will be on **Montsec,** an isolated hill about 400 feet high, which lay within the German lines until captured. The November 9–11 operation of the American Second Army in this region will be commemorated by the same monument.

The series of American operations in the Aisne-Marne region of France will be commemorated by a monu-

Design for Memorial on Montsec, France
Egerton Swartwout, New York, architect

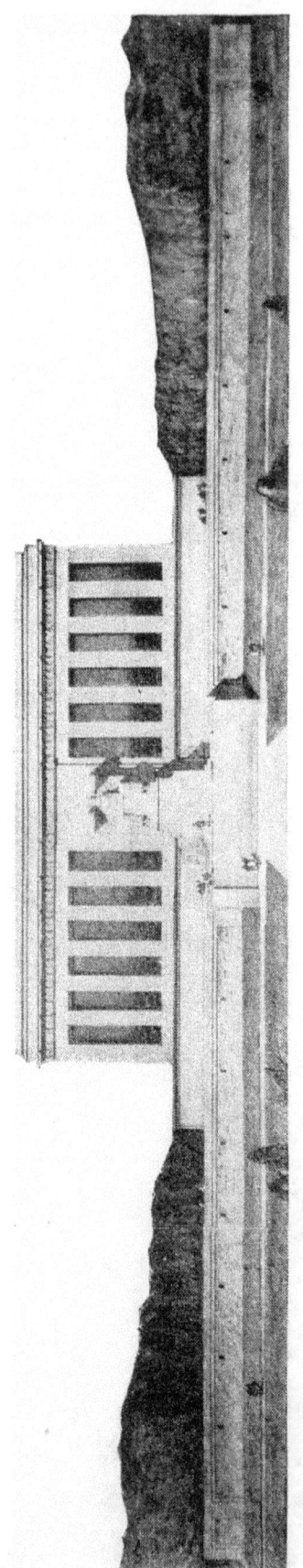

Design for Memorial Near Château-Thierry, France
Paul P. Cret, Philadelphia, architect

ment on Hill 204. This monument will stand near the village of Courteau, just west of **Château-Thierry,** on a site which affords a splendid view of Château-Thierry and the Marne Valley.

The five minor monuments mentioned above will be of modest character, conforming to the lesser importance of the operations involved. On **Blanc Mont Ridge,** in the Champagne, one will recall the services of the 2d, 36th, 42d, and 93d Divisions in that region while serving with the French.

Near **Bony** a monument will preserve the memory of the services of the American troops that fought in France with the British Army. It will occupy a site over the canal tunnel north of St. Quentin, between Bony and Bellicourt, and overlook our cemetery in that vicinity.

A monument at **Cantigny** will commemorate the capture of that town by the 1st Division in our first independent divisional operation of the war.

In the public square at **Audenarde,** Belgium, a monument will be erected to the 37th and 91st Divisions for their services in Belgium; and another, on the road between **Ypres** and Mont Kemmel, will recall the battle in which the 27th and 30th Divisions participated with the British in that vicinity.

The exact site of each of these battle-field monuments is given in the chapter of this book dealing with the operations in the region concerned.

The Services of Supply, numbering more than half a million men, contributed very materially to the final victory, and a memorial to their splendid work will be placed at **Tours.**

The General Headquarters of the American Expeditionary Forces at **Chaumont** and the headquarters of the First Army at **Souilly** will be marked with bronze tablets.

As to the Naval memorials, it is planned to erect one in **Rome** to commemorate jointly the services of our troops who fought with the Italian armies, and the services of the Navy in the Mediterranean.

Before our entrance into the war, the burden of keeping the seas open had fallen principally upon the British Navy, in which task our Navy later cooperated effectively. Therefore, one of the two principal Naval monuments will be placed in **England**.

A memorial at **Brest** will recognize the work of the Navy in convoying troops and supplies to Europe. The site selected is a splendid one on the ancient fortifications overlooking the harbor, which is so familiar to the many Americans who received their first and last impression of France at this port.

DESIGN FOR MEMORIAL NEAR BONY, FRANCE
Paul P. Cret, Philadelphia, architect

Other smaller memorials commemorating the services of the Navy will be placed at **Gibraltar**, at **Corfu,** in Greece, and at **Ponta Delgada**, in the Azores.

Designs and sites have been obtained for most of the monuments mentioned above, and unless unforeseen difficulties occur, construction work on some of them will begin in the summer of 1927.

The French and Belgian Governments have agreed to withhold their approval of memorials which Americans desire to erect in these countries until they have first been approved by the American Battle Monuments Commission. Such an arrangement was found necessary to prevent the construction in Europe of too many monuments to a particular unit and of monuments which the people of this country would not be proud to claim. The monuments to be built by the Commission will commemorate American units in a complete and equitable way; and there is no real need for others, unless they are useful in character. For this reason the Commission requires that all memorials erected by Americans in Europe shall be of a character useful to the inhabitants of the locality in which they are placed, such as bridges, fountains, or public buildings.

DESIGN FOR MONUMENT NEAR YPRES, BELGIUM
Mellor, Meigs & Howe, Philadelphia, architects

An excessive number of American monuments in these countries would be in poor taste and might create an entirely erroneous impression of our object in erecting them. It must not be forgotten that there are but few French, British, Belgian, or Italian monuments on these battle fields, and it is improbable that many will be erected. Many of the American battle fields in Europe had been courageously fought over by the Allies before we arrived, and all of them were battle fields at some time or other throughout history.

The Commission has and will exercise the greatest care to insure that all inscriptions on monuments and tablets shall be accurate. Up to the present time this has not been a simple task and has involved voluminous research. In many instances the original records of units have been found to be confusing or contradictory, owing to the circumstances under which maps were marked

DESIGN PROPOSED FOR NAVAL
MONUMENT, BREST, FRANCE
Howard Shaw Associates, Chicago,
architects

and messages written in the stress of battle. It has often taken months of research in special cases to determine which division should have been entitled to be recorded as the captors of this or that position. In every instance the Commission has written to men involved in the operations. Valuable data, which have become a part of the permanent archives, have thus been obtained from former officers and enlisted men.

CHAPTER XII

AFTER THE ARMISTICE

The armistice was signed about 5 a. m., November 11, 1918, in the Forest of Compiègne, and went into effect six hours later. One of its clauses provided for the occupation of part of Germany by American and Allied forces.

The advance to the Rhine was begun at 5.30 a. m., November 17. The American Third Army, known as the Army of Occupation, was organized for this purpose under command of Major General Joseph T. Dickman, and was composed of the 1st, 2d, 3d, 4th, 32d, and 42d Divisions, to which were added later the 5th, 89th, and 90th. The march was long and arduous, much of it accomplished

AMERICAN SOLDIERS EMBARKING AT ST. NAZAIRE

in cold and inclement weather. The participating troops had had no opportunity to rest and refit after the Argonne Battle, but the march was made smoothly and in perfect order. On December 1 the German frontier was crossed, and on December 13 the Third Army crossed the Rhine, occupying a bridgehead at Coblentz.

As soon as the armistice had been signed the American Commander in Chief undertook the task of moving our forces back to the United States with the least possible delay. An organization to carry out the intricate details connected with this work was quickly established and actual homeward shipments began in December, 1918.

Upon the cessation of hostilities practically every man of the 2,000,000 in the American Expeditionary Forces wanted to return to the United States at once; but with the limited number of ships available this was, of course, impossible. Drill and fatigue became monotonous because the incentive of training for combat had been removed. It was realized by the higher authorities that this was a most trying period for the units, and measures were undertaken to make the life of the soldiers as interesting as possible.

Men were allowed regular leaves to the various leave areas which had been established at the summer and winter resorts of southwestern Europe.

A vast school system was started throughout the A. E. F., of which many thousands of men took advantage. Wherever troops were quartered in any numbers, classes were organized and instruction given to those desiring it in practically every subject taught in the public schools of the United States, as well as in trade and business subjects. At Beaune a huge university was established for advanced instruction, where approximately 10,000 soldiers registered as students.

Horse shows were held by nearly every division, and many units organized theatrical troupes, which traveled throughout the A. E. F. giving their performances. These were encouraged and aided in every way, and contributed greatly to the pleasure of the troops.

MAJOR GENERAL
JOSEPH T. DICKMAN

The men were also encouraged to participate in sports and games, and a great athletic program was carried out which culminated in the Interallied Games held near Paris in June and July, 1919. Upon the invitation of the American Commander in Chief each Allied nation sent contestants to this meet, which from every standpoint was a remarkable success. The Pershing Stadium, where it took place, was mainly built by our military engineers with funds donated by the Y. M. C. A., who presented the structure to General Pershing. It was later presented by him to the French people for their use in the realm of sports.

AN IDLE HOUR

In the meantime the transfer of troops to the United States had been progressing rapidly. By May of 1919 all combat units, except for troops in Germany, had received their embarkation orders.

The units of the Army of Occupation were relieved as fast as practicable during the spring and summer of 1919, and the 1st Division, the last large organization to leave for home, began its movement on August 15. With the dissolution of the Third Army, American representation in the occupied territory was taken over by a small force known as the American Forces in Germany. The American flag was finally lowered on January 24, 1923, when the last of the troops in Germany entrained, and the American zone was formally turned over to the French military authorities three days later.

SHARING A MEAL

SOLDIERS ON LIGHTER EMBARKING ON LEVIATHAN AT BREST

SOLDIERS ON LEAVE AT NICE IN ESTABLISHMENT RUN BY Y. M. C. A.

TROOPS ARRIVING HOME FROM FRANCE

CHAPTER XIII

GENERAL INFORMATION

The General Headquarters of the American Expeditionary Forces was first established at Paris. It remained there until September 1, 1917, on which date it was moved to Chaumont, France, where it operated until after the armistice.

✿ ✿ ✿

The greatest number of men in the American forces overseas at any one time was 2,057,907, excluding those in the Navy. The greatest number of Marines with the A. E. F. at any one time was 21,571.

✿ ✿ ✿

	Men
The normal strength of an American division was	28,105
The approximate normal strength of a French division was	13,000
The strength of a British division at the front varied quite widely; it averaged during 1918 about	12,000
The approximate normal strength of a German division was	10,600

✿ ✿ ✿

GENERAL HEADQUARTERS OF THE A. E. F. AT CHAUMONT

In the second week of October, 1918, 29 American divisions, the equivalent of about 58 European divisions, were in action.

✿ ✿ ✿

The maximum front held at one time by the American forces was 110 miles.

✿ ✿ ✿

The greatest number of Americans landing in Europe in any one month was 306,000, in July, 1918.

✿ ✿ ✿

The **Lafayette Escadrille** was an organization composed of American volunteers who became aviators in the French Army soon after the beginning of hostilities. After the United States entered the war they were commissioned in our Army.

✿ ✿ ✿

Some units of the **American Field Service** joined the French forces as early as September, 1914. It was officially organized in April, 1915, and consisted of volunteers from this country, who served with the French Army as ambulance and truck drivers. By the time the United States entered the war it was a large organization, and in that year was, except for some of its units operating in the Balkans, incorporated into the American Army. On the special request of Marshal Joffre it was continued on duty with the French Army, where it served until the armistice.

The following table contains certain statistics concerning the American divisions which were sent to Europe:

REGULAR ARMY DIVISIONS

No. of division	Date arrived in France	Battle deaths, and died of wounds	Wounded	Location from which divisions were raised
1	June, 1917	4,996	17,324	At large.
2	Aug., 1917	5,150	18,066	At large. (Includes one brigade of Marines.)
3	Mar., 1918	3,401	12,000	At large.
4	May, 1918	2,003	9,917	Do.
5	Mar., 1918	2,120	6,996	Do.
6	May, 1918	68	318	Do.
7	Aug., 1918	287	1,422	Do.
8	Oct., 1918	--------	--------	At large. (Part arrived in France just prior to armistice.)

NATIONAL GUARD DIVISIONS

26	Sept., 1917	2,281	11,383	New England.
27	May, 1918	1,829	6,505	New York.
28	...do...	2,874	11,265	Pennsylvania.
29	June, 1918	1,053	4,517	New Jersey, Delaware, Virginia, Maryland, and District of Columbia.
30	May, 1918	1,641	6,774	Tennessee, North Carolina, South Carolina, and District of Columbia.
31	Oct., 1918	--------	--------	Georgia, Alabama, and Florida. (Became 7th Depot Division.)
32	Feb., 1918	3,028	10,233	Michigan and Wisconsin.
33	May, 1918	993	5,871	Illinois.
34	Sept., 1918	--------	--------	Nebraska, Iowa, South Dakota, and Minnesota. (Became a replacement division.)
35	May, 1918	1,298	5,998	Missouri and Kansas.
36	July, 1918	591	1,993	Texas and Oklahoma.
37	June, 1918	1,066	4,321	Ohio.
38	Oct., 1918	--------	--------	Indiana, Kentucky, and West Virginia. (Became a replacement division.)
39	Aug., 1918	--------	--------	Alabama, Mississippi, and Louisiana. (Became 5th Depot Division.)
40	...do...			California, Colorado, Utah, Arizona, and New Mexico. (Became 6th Depot Division.)
41	Dec., 1917	--------	--------	Washington, Oregon, Montana, Idaho, and Wyoming. (Became 1st Depot Division.)
42	Nov., 1917	2,810	11,873	Composite division from many States.

NATIONAL ARMY DIVISIONS

76	July, 1918	--------	--------	New England and New York. (Became 3d Depot Division.)
77	Apr., 1918	2,110	8,084	New York City.
78	June, 1918	1,530	5,614	Western New York, New Jersey, and Delaware.
79	July, 1918	1,517	5,357	Northeastern Pennsylvania, Maryland, and District of Columbia.
80	May, 1918	1,241	4,788	Virginia, West Virginia, and western Pennsylvania.
81	Aug., 1918	248	856	North Carolina, South Carolina, Florida, and Porto Rico.
82	May, 1918	1,413	6,664	Georgia, Alabama, and Tennessee.
[1] 83	June, 1918	67	257	Ohio and western Pennsylvania. (Became 2d Depot Division.)
84	Sept., 1918	--------	--------	Kentucky, Indiana, and southern Illinois. (Became a replacement division.)
[2] 85	Aug., 1918	145	281	Michigan and Wisconsin. (Became 4th Depot Division.)
86	Sept., 1918	--------	--------	Chicago and Illinois. (Became a replacement division.)
87	...do...	--------	--------	Arkansas, Louisiana, Mississippi, and Alabama. (In training at time of armistice.)
88	Aug., 1918	20	58	North Dakota, Minnesota, Iowa, and Illinois.
89	June, 1918	1,466	5,625	Kansas, Missouri, South Dakota, and Nebraska.
90	...do...	1,496	6,053	Texas and Oklahoma.
91	July, 1918	1,454	4,654	Nebraska, Montana, Wyoming, Utah, Alaska, Washington, Oregon, California, and Idaho.
92	June, 1918	182	1,465	Colored troops (various States).
93	{Dec., 1917– Apr., 1918}	591	2,943	Colored troops (various States) four infantry regiments only.
Other troops		1,073	3,139	
Total		52,942	202,614	

[1] 332d Infantry regiment of this division went to Italy in July, 1918, and saw active service.
[2] 339th Infantry regiment of this division served at Archangel, Russia, for a time during the war.

DISTINCTIVE INSIGNIA

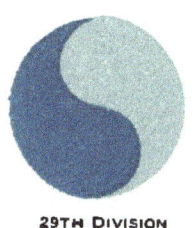    

29TH DIVISION   30TH DIVISION   32ND DIVISION   33RD DIVISION   35TH DIVISION

 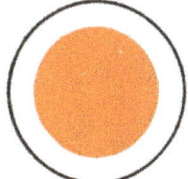   

36TH DIVISION   37TH DIVISION   41ST DIVISION   42ND DIVISION   76TH DIVISION

77TH DIVISION   78TH DIVISION   79TH DIVISION   80TH DIVISION   81ST DIVISION

82ND DIVISION   83RD DIVISION   85TH DIVISION   88TH DIVISION   89TH DIVISION

90TH DIVISION   91ST DIVISION   92ND DIVISION   93RD DIVISION

SERVICES OF SUPPLY   ADVANCE SECTION SERVICES OF SUPPLY

There was a great amount of artillery, aside from that pertaining to divisions and corps, employed by the American forces. This consisted of units of railway artillery, antiaircraft guns, and other guns of large caliber or special types. These were employed wherever the necessity for their use arose. The Coast Artillery Corps of the United States Army operated a large number of them.

✣ ✣ ✣

All tanks operated by the American Tank Corps in the war were of French and British make. Our manufacturers were just beginning to turn out these machines in quantities when the armistice was signed.

✣ ✣ ✣

The Air Service of the United States Army grew rapidly from a very small beginning. At the time of the armistice we had 45 squadrons in action, operating 740 planes, while, in addition, thousands of cadet flyers were undergoing training.

✣ ✣ ✣

The first Americans killed by the enemy after the United States entered the war were: Lieutenant W. T. Fitzsimmons, Private Oscar Tugo, Private Rudolph

LIGHT RAILWAY OPERATED BY AMERICANS, MOVING CIVILIAN PROPERTY FROM NEAR FRONT LINE

Rubino, and Private Leslie Woods, all of United States Base Hospital No. 5. These men lost their lives at 10.55 p. m., September 4, 1917, when the Germans bombed a British hospital where they were on duty near Dannes-Camiers, France.

✣ ✣ ✣

The first American soldiers killed in action were: Corporal James B. Gresham, Private Thomas F. Enright, and Private Merle D. Hay, all belonging to the 16th Infantry of the 1st Division. They lost their lives when the Germans raided the American trenches at Bathelémont on November 2, 1917.

✣ ✣ ✣

The greatest number of American soldiers in hospitals in Europe at one time was on November 7, 1918, when 190,564 men were under treatment.

✣ ✣ ✣

American infantry and engineer units which served in Europe on other than the Western Front were the 332d Infantry, in Italy, and the 339th Infantry and the 1st Battalion, 310th Engineers, at Archangel, Russia.

One of the greatest aids in keeping up the spirit and morale of the men overseas was the *Stars and Stripes*, the service newspaper of the A. E. F., written, edited,

FIRST EDITION OF "THE STARS AND STRIPES"

and published by men from the ranks. The first number was issued in Paris on February 8, 1918, and it appeared weekly thereafter until June 13, 1919. At the height of its popularity a circulation of 526,000 was attained.

Equivalent metric and English units

Units	Equivalents
1 kilometer (km.)	0.62137 mile.
1 meter (m.)	39.37 inches.
1 liter (l.)	0.2642 gallon.
1 mile (mi.)	1.6093 kilometers.
1 yard (yd.)	0.9144 meter.
1 gallon (gal.)	3.785 liters.

For the 25 months from April, 1917, to May, 1919, the war cost the United States more than $1,000,000 per hour. At the time of the armistice the cost was about $2,000,000 per hour. Pay of officers and enlisted men took only

MAIL CALL

about 13 per cent of this amount. The remainder was for supplies, munitions, transportation, etc. The total expenditure of twenty-two billions was practically equal to the entire cost of running the United States Government from 1791 to 1914, inclusive.

HELPFUL INFORMATION FOR USE ON DESCRIBED TOURS

The roads in France are numbered. National Highways are designated by the letter "N" followed by a numeral; for example, N-3 is the National Highway No. 3. Departmental roads are designated by the letters "G. C." or "G. C. D." and a number; for example G. C. 6 or G. C. D. 6. These are all good roads and rank just below the National Highways. The letters "I. C." and "V. O." indicate local roads. The main difference in all these roads is in width rather than in the character of the surface. National roads are wide, run comparatively straight, and are easy to follow, whereas local roads are narrow, very winding, and often difficult to follow.

Kilometer posts are used extensively in this book as reference points in connection with the described tours. All roads except poor ones are marked at each kilometer with a stone post. That part of the post facing the road bears a

Kilometer Posts

SIDE FACING ROAD

SIDE READ AS APPROACHED

INTERMEDIATE POST

kilometer number and the designation of the road. The sides of the posts generally bear the name of the next large village or town and the distance to it. Small posts about 8 inches high mark each tenth of a kilometer (100 meters) between successive kilometer posts, except in a few cases where intermediate markings are only at the halfway point. Roads change their kilometer post numberings at departmental boundaries.

It is suggested that a compass be carried on the tours.

To determine compass directions with round faced watch when the sun is shining, place watch flat in hand and face the sun. Point hour hand in direction you are facing. The point on the rim of the watch halfway between the end of the hour hand and the figure 12 on the dial will be the southernmost point of watch face.

AN AMERICAN HEADQUARTERS AT THE FRONT.

When facing south, the right side of a person is west and the left side east.

A simple rule for roughly converting kilometers to miles is to multiply the number of kilometers by 0.6. To change from miles to kilometers divide the number of miles by 0.6.

GLOSSARY

Each definition given below is limited in scope to the sense in which the word or expression is used in this book.

Artillery preparation.—The concentration of artillery fire placed on hostile positions to demoralize the troops therein and damage the defenses, before an infantry attack is launched against them.

Assault troops.—Those troops actually in line and delivering the attack.

Barracks.—Permanent quarters for troops.

Barrage.—A barrier formed by fire from artillery or other weapons firing from stable mounts. A "rolling barrage" is one which advances into the hostile lines immediately in front of the attacking troops and at the same rate which the infantry is expected to maintain. A "box barrage" is one which incloses, generally, three sides of a position in order to prevent access to it by all except troops of the side firing the barrage. (*See* "*Mine Barrage.*")

Near Front Line Hunting for "Cooties"

Base Hospital.—A hospital within the Services of Supply to which sick and wounded are sent from the forward areas.

Battalion (Infantry).—In the American Army about 1,000 men organized into four infantry companies.

Bridgehead.—A position covering a bridge or defile on the side toward the enemy.

Brigade (Infantry).—In the American Army two regiments and a machine-gun battalion.

Camouflage.—Means employed to screen troops and material, located in exposed areas, from hostile observation.

Captive balloons.—Balloons used for observation purposes, held by cables. Some of these, because of their shape, were called "sausage balloons."

Command post.—A point from which a commander directs the operations of his unit.

Concentration camp.—A place where troops are assembled in large numbers.

Consolidate (a position).—To prepare a captured position for defense.

Converted yachts.—Yachts taken over by the Navy and armed for use against the enemy.

Corps (Army Corps).—A force consisting of a headquarters, artillery and other services, and one or more divisions.

Counterattack.—An attack made by a force against troops which are themselves attacking, or who are holding a position recently captured from the counterattacking side.

Division.—An American division had 2 brigades of infantry and 1 brigade of artillery. It contained also engineer, machine gun, signal, medical, and transportation units.

Doughboy.—Name applied to an American infantryman.

Dressing station.—Point near front where wounds were dressed. Also known as aid station.

Drive.—A powerful attack.

Dugout.—An underground shelter.

Dump.—A point where material is stored for future use.

Emplacement.—A prepared gun position.

Enfilading fire.—Fire delivered from a position located in prolongation of an opposing line, thus striking the enemy from a direction in which he is not well protected. The effect of such fire is increased by the fact that "overs" and "shorts" fall along the hostile line and may damage the enemy as much as those which strike directly where aimed. Also known as "flanking fire."

Evacuate.—To abandon. Also, in speaking of wounded, to send them to a hospital in rear.

Exploit.—The action of an attacking force, after reaching its objective, in further demoralizing the enemy through local attacks and raids.

Field hospital.—A hospital established close to the immediate scene of action.

Field fortifications.—All shelters and obstacles constructed by a force to increase its powers of resistance.

Flame thrower.—Device for projecting a stream of flame on enemy troops.

Flank.—The right or left portions of a command or position.

French Colonial Division.—A division composed of troops from a French colony.

NAVAL STATION AT PAUILLAC, FRANCE

Front.—Zone of active operations; sometimes used to designate a particular portion of the battle lines.

Gassed.—Subjected to gas attack either from shells or gas projectors. Also to be overcome by gas.

High Command.—Directing head of a nation's forces.

Hindenburg line.—A continuous defensive position of great strength prepared by the Germans on the Western Front. It was known by various local names in different parts of the front.

Jump-off line.—The line from which the infantry attack starts.

Limited attack.—One which halts upon reaching a certain designated objective.

Local attack.—An attack by relatively small forces, confined to the immediate front of the unit making it.

Maneuver.—To perform a movement of troops in the battle area.

Mine barrage.—A line or network of sea mines to prevent the passage of ships. A mine layer is a boat equipped for placing mines, and a mine sweeper is one used in removing them from the water.

Mobilization.—The change from a peace to a war status. Generally applied to the military forces of a nation.

Morale.—The psychological condition or spirit of troops; also applies to civilian population.

Neutral.—A nation taking no part in a contest between others.

No-man's-land.—The strip of ground between opposing front lines. On the Western Front it varied in width from a few yards to several hundred.

Noncombatant.—Any person in the Army or Navy whose duties do not include fighting; also any civilian.

Objective.—The point, or result, toward which the operations of a force are directed.

Observation post.—Position from which hostile areas can be viewed.

Offensive.—An aggressive operation in large force.

Patrols.—Small detachments employed for a variety of purposes, such as raiding and reconnoitering the enemy, and protecting their own forces.

Pill box.—A slang term for concrete shelters in which machine guns were usually stationed.

Pivot of attack.—When an attacking force advances in an oblique direction into the hostile lines, the point on its flank where the lines remain practically stationary is known as the pivot, or hinge, of the attack.

Raid.—A sudden, rapid invasion of the hostile forward positions, usually carried out by a small force for the purpose of obtaining prisoners and information.

Railhead.—A point on the railway where ammunition and supplies are transferred to dumps and vehicles or delivery to the troops.

Reclassification camp.—Camp to which certain individuals are sent for examination in order to determine the duty for which they are best fitted.

Reconnaissance.—Examination of a locality or of a hostile force in order to gather information of military value.

Regiment (Infantry).—In the American Army about 103 officers and 3,650 enlisted men.

Register on targets.—The determination of firing data by actually firing on selected targets.

Regulating stations.—Vast combination supply depots and railway yards from which supplies are forwarded to troops.

Remount depot.—Replacement station for animals killed or disabled.

Salient.—A projection in a battle line.

Salvaged.—Recovered and reused.

Sausage balloon.—(*See "Captive balloons."*)

AMERICANS RECEIVING COFFEE FROM INHABITANT OF PRÉMONT SOON AFTER CAPTURING TOWN

Secondary fronts.—Any front held by troops other than the one on which it is expected to fight to a decision. From the standpoint of the Allies all fronts other than that in France and Belgium were secondary. Within the Western Front, regions such as the Vosges Mountain area were secondary as compared to the Champagne and similar localities.

Sector.—The portion of the battle lines alloted to a particular unit, and therefore designated as a regimental, battalion, or divisional sector, etc. Sometimes named for a local geographical feature.

Smoke screen.—Dense cloud of smoke placed in desired localities by means of shells, bombs, and smoke-producing apparatus.

Sortie.—A sudden offensive movement from a fortified base.

Stabilized.—The front was stabilized when the lines on each side remained relatively stationary for a period of time. This occurred when both sides in the particular area had temporarily assumed a defensive attitude.

Strategic center.—A region which because of its commanding position, or because of the lines of communication or bases of supply contained there, is of great advantage to the holder in the conduct of operations, and the loss of which would seriously cripple him.

Terrain.—The topographical character of the country, region, or tract as viewed from a military standpoint.

Western Front.—The battle front in France and Belgium extending from the North Sea to the Swiss border

Wheel.—To change direction.

Wire entanglements.—Bands of barbed wire placed in defensive positions, to impede the progress of attacking troops.

INDEX

NOTE.—Places alphabetically listed at the end of the chapter on the Services of Supply are not repeated in this index.

	Page
Abaucourt	111
Agron River	150
Ailette River	63
Aincreville	169
Air Service	269
Aire River	141
Aisne River	51
Albert	217
American Field Service	267
Amiens	18, 203, 218
Andevanne	168
Andon River	155
Angecourt	175
Anizy-le-Château	21
Ansoncourt Farm	95
Apremont	84, 143
Ardeuil	197
Argonne Forest	115, 139
Army of Occupation	263
Attigny	196
Audenarde	213
Authe	183
Avocourt	133, 183
Azores	242
Baâlon	183
Baccarat	227
Bantheville	169
Bar	172
Bar River	172
Barricourt, Heights of	127, 168
Baslieux	52
Bathelémont	226, 269
Baulny	143
Bayonneville et Chénnery	171
Bazeilles	177
Bazoches	53

	Page
Beaumont (east of Meuse)	165
Beaumont (west of Meuse)	174
Beaurepaire Farm	59
Becquigny	210
Belfort	227
Belleau	28, 37, 251
Belleau Wood	22, 35, 38
Bellejoyeuse Farm	150
Belleville-sur-Bar	173
Bellevue Signal Ridge	197
Bellicourt	205
Beney	88, 105
Berehaven	242
Berry-au-Bac	21
Berzy-le-Sec	29, 58
Besace, la	175
Béthincourt	132
Binarville	200
Bizerta	241
Blanc Mont	192
Blanzy-lès-Fismes	52
Bois d'Ailly	83
Bois de Bantheville	126, 154, 168
Bois de Barricourt	170
Bois du Beau Vallon	103
Bois de Beney	105
Bois de Beuge	158
Bois de Bonvaux	111
Bois de Bouresches	29
Bois de Brieulles	159
Bois Brulé	49
Bois Brûlé	83
Bois de Bourgogne	150, 173
Bois de Chatillon	161
Bois de Chaume	134, 161, 182
Bois Chehemin	139

275

	Page
Bois de Cheppy	140
Bois Colas	48
Bois le Comte	165
Bois de Consenvoye	134, 163
Bois de la Côte Lemont	161
Bois de Cunel	155
Bois de Dampvitoux	112
Bois de Dannevoux	134
Bois Emont	184
Bois de Fays	159
Bois de Forêt	124, 159
Bois de Forges	120, 133
Bois du Four	96
Bois de Gargantua	112
Bois Gérard	112
Bois de la Grande Montagne	164, 181
Bois de la Grande Souche	106
Bois des Grimpettes	45
Bois de la Grurie	184
Bois de Hache	178
Bois la Haie l'Evêque	96
Bois d'Heiche	103
Bois du Jury	93
Bois des Loges	150
Bois de l'Orme	65
Bois de Manheulles	113
Bois de la Marfée	185
Bois de Montfaucon	137
Bois de Mortier	64
Bois de Mort Mare	92
Bois des Ogons	158
Bois de Peut de Faux	159
Bois le Prêtre	98
Bois de la Pultière	156, 167
Bois de la Rappe	114
Bois des Rappes	126, 154, 167
Bois des Rappes (SM)	72, 102
Bois de Remières	89
Bois de Romagne	122, 153
Bois du Rupt	114
Bois de Sachet	186
Bois de Sassey	168
Bois de Septsarges	138
Bois de la Sonnard	92
Bois St. Claude	102
Bois de Vigneulles	114
Bois de Ville	165
Bony	205, 252
Bordeaux	243
Borne de Cornouiller	161, 181
Bouillonville	71, 111
Boult-aux-Bois	127, 151, 173
Bouresches	22, 38
Boureuilles	141
Bourrut	168
Brabant-sur-Meuse	134, 182
Brancourt	210
Brandeville	183
Bras	165
Brécy	64
Brest	238, 243
Bretonnerie Farm, la	40
Brieulles-sur-Meuse	159, 179
Briey	74
Brigade:	
6th	51
56th	66
71st	193
Brindisi	241
Bruges	242
Brusses Farm, les	37
Bucy-lès-Cerny	64
Buxières	112
Buzancy	64, 171
Calais	242
Cambrai	211
Cantigny	20, 221
Caranda Mill	45
Cardiff	243
Carignan	128
Cateau, le	209
Cemeteries, American:	
Aisne-Marne	251, 252
Brookwood	255, 256
Flanders Field	253, 254
Meuse-Argonne	247, 248
Oise-Aisne	250
St. Mihiel	249
Somme	252, 253
Suresnes	254, 255
Catelet, le	204
Chaillon	81
Chambley	112

INDEX

	Page
Chamery	49
Champagne	187
Champigneulle	150
Champ Mahaut	183
Chantrud Farm	64
Chapelle-Monthodon, la	65
Charlevaux Mill	198
Charmel, le	29, 43
Charny	131
Chartèves	42
Château d'Aulnois	112
Château du Diable	53
Château du Tilleuls	178
Château-Thierry	22, 26, 38, 40
Châtel-Chéhéry	122, 145
Chaudron Farm	183
Chaudun	58
Chaumont	260, 267
Chauvoncourt	82
Chazelle Ravine	64
Chemin des Dames	35
Chêne Tondu, le	143
Cheppy	140
Chéry-Chartreuve	50
Chevières	148
Chiers River	177
Chipilly Ridge	217
Chuignolles	203
Cierges	121
Cierges (Marne)	30, 45
Clairs Chênes Wood	184
Claye	34
Cléry-le-Petit	179
Coblentz	263
Cohan	50
Compiègne	189, 263
Conflans-en-Jarnisy	112
Consenvoye	162
Corfu	241
Cornay	122, 147
Côte Dame Marie	124, 139, 153
Côte de Chatillon	124, 152
Côte de Jumont	181
Côte de l'Oie	132
Côte de Maldah	153
Côte de Romagne	165
Côte de Senoux	77
Côte de Talou	182
Côte St. Germain	179
Coucy-le-Château	203
Coulonges	50
Courchamps	65
Courmont	45
Couvrelles	65
Couvres-et-Valsery	64
Cravançon Farm	56
Creüe	81
Crézancy	40
Croix Blanche Farm	43
Croix de Fer	56
Croix Rouge Farm	29
Cuisy	184
Cumières	132
Cunel	121, 155, 167
Dame Farm, la	107
Dampierre-aux-Bois	71
Dannevoux	120, 162
Dieulouard	112
Divisions:[1]	
1st	10, 15, 20, 27, 31, 55, 57, 64, 69, 80, 88, 114, 122, 145, 147, 153, 176, 221, 226, 263, 265, 269.
2d	18, 22, 31, 35, 37, 55, 59, 69, 88, 95, 99, 103, 113, 154, 171, 174, 178, 192, 226, 263
3d	22, 26, 38, 40, 43, 45, 51, 69, 75, 122, 155, 158, 160, 167, 184, 263.
4th	28, 30, 48, 50, 53, 65, 70, 75, 109, 120, 133, 138, 158, 263.
5th	69, 88, 96, 102, 112, 128, 154, 160, 167, 179, 181, 227, 263.
6th	227
7th	75, 101, 104

[1] Additional mention of division will usually be found on pages preceding and following the pages listed here.

Divisions—Continued.
    26th .... 17, 26, 29, 37, 65, 70, 78, 89, 134, 164, 226.
    27th 204, 209, 215
    28th .... 26, 29, 39, 42, 45, 51, 53, 65, 75, 104, 108, 121, 123, 142, 145.
    29th 75, 123, 134, 163, 181
    30th 204, 209, 215
    32d .... 18, 29, 32, 45, 47, 51, 62, 122, 124, 147, 155, 186, 263.
    33d 75, 109, 112, 120, 123, 133, 160, 182, 217
    35th 75, 110, 121, 141, 144
    36th 75, 192
    37th 74, 104, 112, 121, 138, 142, 183, 212
    42d 18, 26, 29, 45, 48, 69, 79, 88, 92, 105, 106, 112, 176, 185, 187, 189, 227, 263
    77th 32, 54, 65, 121, 142, 147, 150, 173, 175, 198
    78th 69, 104, 126, 150, 173, 186
    79th 74, 108, 121, 133, 135, 137, 158, 161
    80th 133, 151, 160, 171, 175, 184, 217
    81st 108, 110
    82d 69, 99, 113, 123, 145, 149, 152, 227
    88th 227
    89th 69, 88, 93, 103, 112, 169, 177, 227, 263
    90th 69, 97, 100, 102, 155, 168, 178, 263
    91st 120, 138, 140, 142, 212
    92d 75, 101, 200
Divisions, Statistics concerning 268
Divisions, Insignia of .... opposite 268
Dommartin 71
Dommartin-la-Chaussée 112
Dommiers 56
Doncourt 107
Doulcon 179
Dravegny 50
Dunkirk 242
Dun-sur-Meuse 127, 179
Durazzo 241

Engineers:
    6th 220
    11th 211
Eparges, les 107
Epernay 190
Epieds 66
Epinonville 138
Escaut River 213
Essen Hook 194
Essey 71
Etanche Mill 159
Etang de Lachaussée 107
Etraye 164
Euvezin 112
Exermont 144

Farm de Beauregarde 144
Farm des Granges 144
Fère, Castle of 65
Fère-en-Tardenois 65, 250
Ferté-sous-Jouarre, la 34
Fey-en-Haye 97
Fismes 30, 50
Fismette 50
Fléville 147
Flirey 86, 93, 227
Forest Farm 195
Forêt de Dieulet 184
Forêt de la Reine 112
Forêt de Nesles 47, 50
Forêt des Venchères 98, 102
Forêt de Woëvre 184
Forges 134
Forges Creek 135
Fort des Paroches 82
Fort de la Pompelle 188
Fort Douaumont 166
Fort du Camp des Romains 82
Fort du Rozellier 76
Fossoy 40
Frapelle 227
Fresnes-en-Woëvre 74, 109

INDEX

	Page
Gérardmer	227
Gercourt-et-Drillancourt	184
Gesnes	184
Gibraltar	238, 244
Givry	37
Gonétrie Farm	38
Gouy	207
Gouzeaucourt	203, 211
Grand Carré Farm	168
Grandpré	126, 150
Grande Tranchée de Calonne	77
Gravelotte	112
Gressaire Wood	217
Gué d' Hossus	64
Guillemont Farm	205
Hamel	217
Haraucourt	175
Harricourt	172
Hassavant Farm	106
Hattonchâtel	79
Hattonville	79
Haudainville	76, 112
Haudiomont	70, 110
Haumont-les-Lachaussée	112
Haute Maison, la	53
Hautevesnes	65
Heudicourt	113
Heurne	213
Hill:	
168	57
180	145
182	149
190	37
193	37
204	38
212	46
216	152
221	107
223	145
242	172
244	145
250	158
260	179
263	153, 159
269	147
272	153
Hill—Continued.	
274	158
285	184
288	152
289	172
295	138
304	132
308	135
313	172
324	99
327	101
335.9	97
343	168
360	163
451	227
Imécourt	185
Insignia	opposite 268
Inverness	244
Ivoiry	138
Jametz	185
Jaulgonne	22, 26, 29, 43
Jomblets, les	30, 46
Jonc de Mer Farm	210
Jonchéry-sur-Suippes	189
Jonville	107
Jouy aux Arches	113
Juvigny	32, 55, 62
Killingholme	244
Knoll, The	205
Knoll Trench	207
Lafayette Escadrille	267
Lairesse, la	149
Lamarche-en-Woëvre	88
Landres-et-St. Georges	152
Laon	64
Ligny-en-Barrois	113
Limey	86, 95
Liny-devant-Dun	181
London	237
Longpont	65
"Lost Battalion"	198
Loupmont Ridge	68, 85
Lucey	113
Lucy-le-Bocage	22, 34
Lunéville	226

	Page
Machault	195
Madeleine Farm	157
Maison Neuve Farm	59
Mamey	113
Manheulles	110
Marbache	113
Marchéville	109
Marcq	148
Marion Ravine	66
Mars	232
Martincourt Farm	148
Martinvaux Ridge	159
Marvoisin	86
Mazinghien	210
Meaux	34
Medeah Farm	195
Memorials in Europe, projected:	
Audenarde	260
Blanc Mont	260
Bony	260
Brest	261
Cantigny	260
Château-Thierry	260
Chaumont	260
Corfu	261
England	261
Gibraltar	261
Montfaucon	259
Montsec	259
Ponta Delgada	261
Rome	260
Souilly	260
Tours	260
Ypres	260
Menil-la-Tour	113
Metz	69
Meurcy Farm	49
Meuse-Argonne	131
Meuse River	169
Merval	65
Mézières	116
Mézy	40, 42
Missy-aux-Bois	56
Missy Ravine	56
Molleville Farm	163
Montblainville	143
Montbrehain	209

	Page
Mont d'Arly	56
Montdidier	221
Montfaucon	117, 119, 120, 133, 136
Montfauxelles	197
Monthois	198
Mont Kemmel	215
Montmédy	128
Mont Notre Dame	65
Mon Plaisir Farm	113
Montrebeau Wood	144
Montrefagne	144
Montsec	68, 80, 85, 88
Mont St. Père	29, 42
Montzéville	185
Mortefontaine	65
Mort Homme, le	132
Moucheton Castle	65
Moulins	40, 177
Mousson Hill	98
Mouzay	179
Mouzon	177
Murvaux	185
Nancy	113
Nantillois	121, 138, 159
Nauroy	208
Navarin Farm	188
Nesles	49
Neuve Grange Farm, la	140
Neuvilly	186
Nonsard	71, 88
Noroy-sur-Ourcq	66
Norroy	99, 101
Notre-Dame-de-Lorette	203
Oise-Sambre Canal	209
Ostend	242
Pannes	71
Paris Farm	34
Pauillac	244
Perles	52
Péronne	220
Perthes-lès-Hurlus	188
Petites Armoises, les	185
Peuvillers	186
Pinon	55

INDEX

	Page		Page
Ploisy	57	Sassey	179
Plymouth	241	Scapa Flow	242
Ponta Delgada	242	Schonholz Woods	227
Pont-à-Mousson	72, 99	Séchault	197
Pont Maugis	176	Sedan	128, 130, 176
Porto Corsini	244	Seicheprey	86, 89, 226
Port-sur-Seille	69, 74	Selle River	209
Pouilly	177	Sergy	46
Prémont	210	Seringes-et-Nesles	46
Prény	97, 114	Serval	65
Puisieux-au-Mont	217	Services of Supply	229
Puxieux	114	Sivry-lès-Buzancy	186
		Sivry-sur-Meuse	161
Quart de Reserve	114	Soissons	27, 41, 55
Queenstown	238, 241, 244	Somme-Py	192
Quennemont Farm	205	Sommerance	153
		Sondernach	227
Raucourt	175	Souain	189
Rebois, le	107	Southhampton	239
Regiments:		St. Baussant	91
332d Inf	269	St. Benoît	79, 106
339th Inf	269	St. Etienne-à-Arnes	193
368th Inf	200	St. Georges	152
369th Inf	197	St. Hilaire	109
370th Inf	63	St. Juvin	124, 148, 173
371st Inf	133, 197	St. Mihiel	67, 82, 226
372d Inf	133, 197	St. Nazaire	244
Regniéville-en-Haye	96	St. Pierre Auberge	98
Reims	189	St. Quentin	204, 219
Rembercourt	114	St. Remy Farm	177
Remenauville	95	St. Souplet	209
Remilly	175	St. Thibaut	53
Rémonville	170	Stenay	127, 178
Revillon	66	Stonne	175
Rezonville	114	Surmelin Creek	40
Richecourt	86, 89	Sy	186
Richene Hill	163		
Rilly-aux-Oies	195		
Ripont	197	Talma	186
Rochefort	244	Talma Farm	186
Romagne	121, 155, 247	Terny-Sorny	63
Ronchères	29, 45	Thiaucourt	71, 88, 103, 249
Rû Chailly Farm	40	Thillot	80
Rupt de Mad	89	Tigny	61
		Torcy	28, 37
Saizerais	114	Toul	17, 114
Samogneux	182	Trench of Bayonets	166

	Page		Page
Trières Farm	197	Villers-Cotterets	62
Trugny	66	Villers-devant-Mouzon	177
Tuilerie Farm	174	Villers-en-Prayères	66
		Villers-sous-Prény	102
Vacherauville	182	Villers-sur-Fère	46
Vandières	101	Villesavoye	53
Varennes	121, 143	Vilosnes-sur-Meuse	161, 181
Vauquois	121, 140	Vimy	203
Vauquois Hill	140	Vosges	224
Vaux	22, 35	Voormezeele	215
Vauxaillon	63	Vouzieres	124
Vauxcastille	60		
Vendhuile	208	Waereghem	254
Verdun	76, 131, 166	Warfusée-Abancourt	220
Verte-Feuille Farm	59	Wavrille	165
Very	121	Willow Trench	207
Vesle	22, 30, 47, 54	Woël	107
Vierstraat Ridge	215	Woëvre Plain	79
Vierzy	60		
Viéville-en-Haye	71, 98, 102	Xammes	88, 104
Vigneulles	72, 79	Xivray	69, 86
Vilcey-sur-Trey	102	Xon Hill	99
Ville-devant-Chaumont	165		
Villemontry	186	Ypres	204, 215
		Zeebruge	242

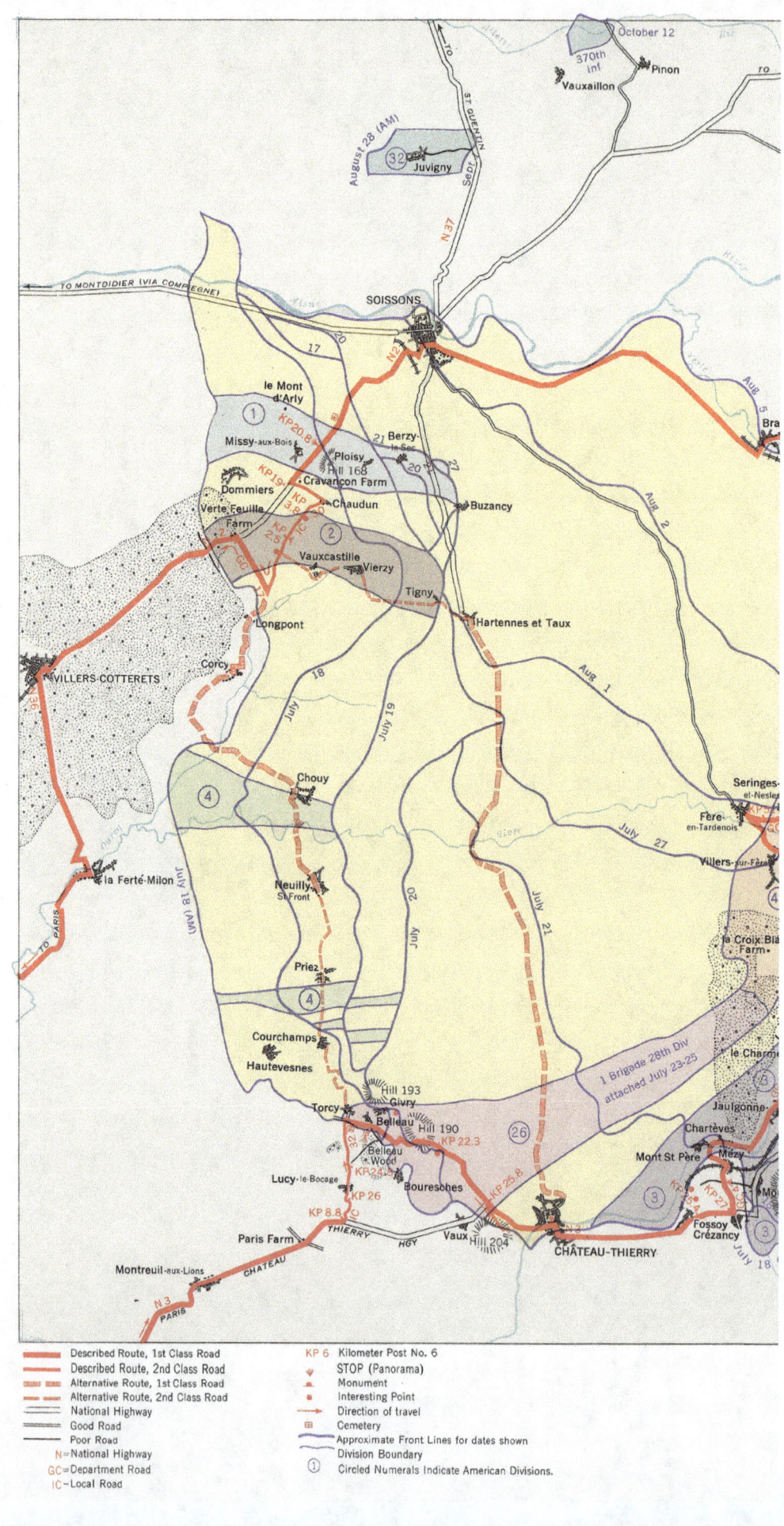

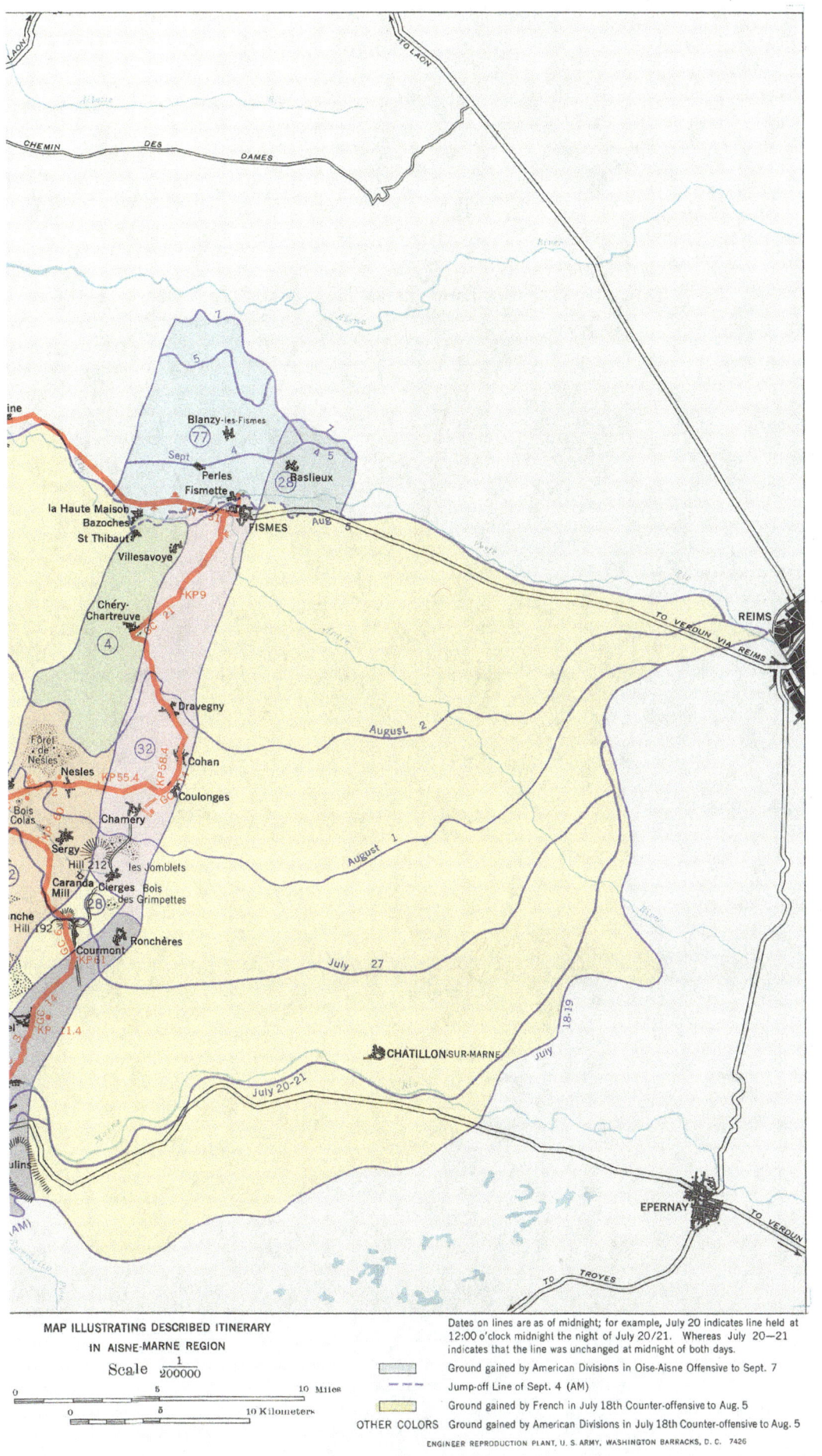

MAP ILLUSTRATING DESCRIBED ITINERARY IN AISNE-MARNE REGION

Scale $\frac{1}{200000}$

0   5   10 Miles
0   5   10 Kilometers

Dates on lines are as of midnight; for example, July 20 indicates line held at 12:00 o'clock midnight the night of July 20/21. Whereas July 20—21 indicates that the line was unchanged at midnight of both days.

- Ground gained by American Divisions in Oise-Aisne Offensive to Sept. 7
- Jump-off Line of Sept. 4 (AM)
- Ground gained by French in July 18th Counter-offensive to Aug. 5
- OTHER COLORS Ground gained by American Divisions in July 18th Counter-offensive to Aug. 5

ENGINEER REPRODUCTION PLANT, U. S. ARMY, WASHINGTON BARRACKS, D. C. 7426

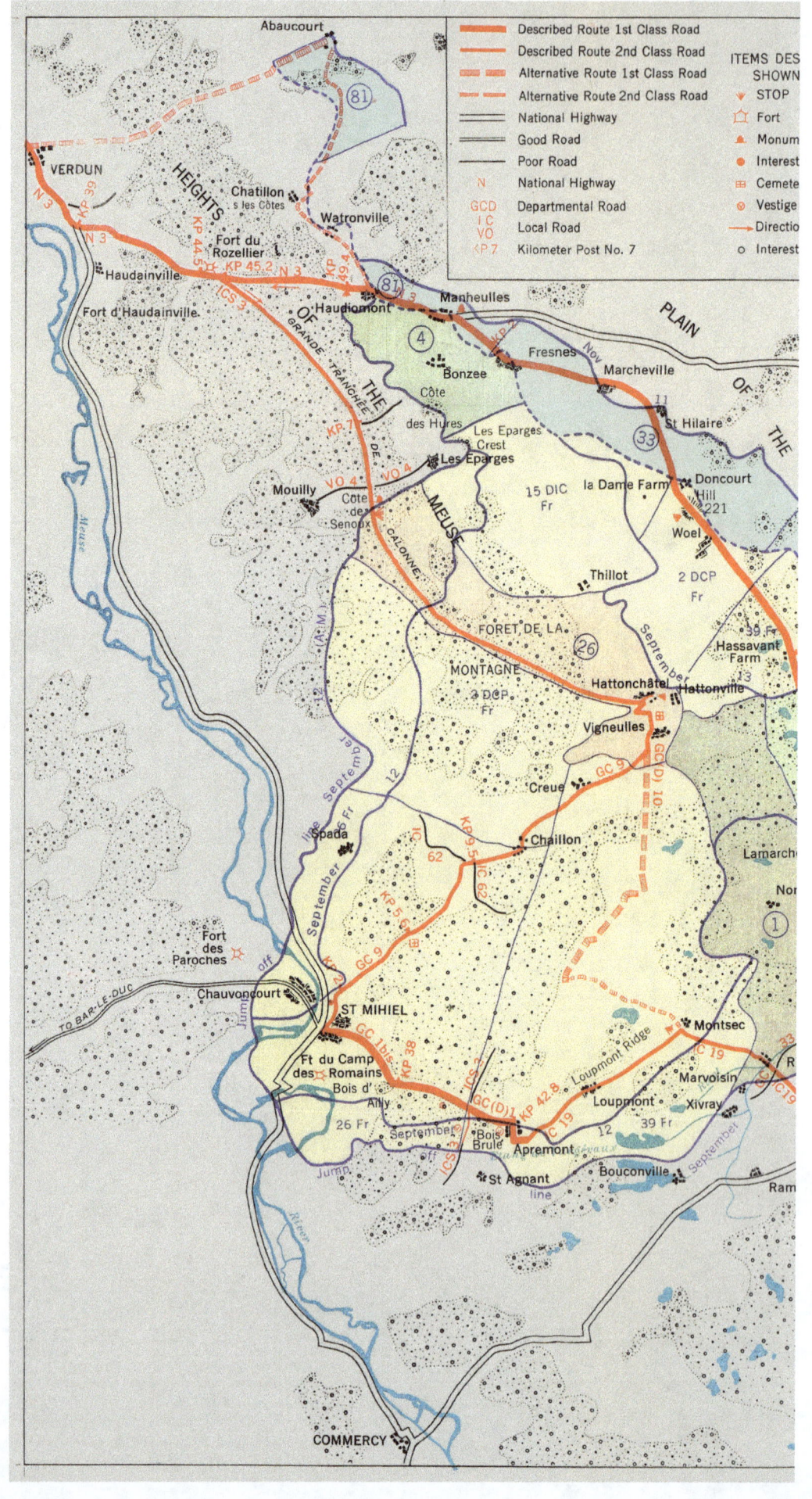

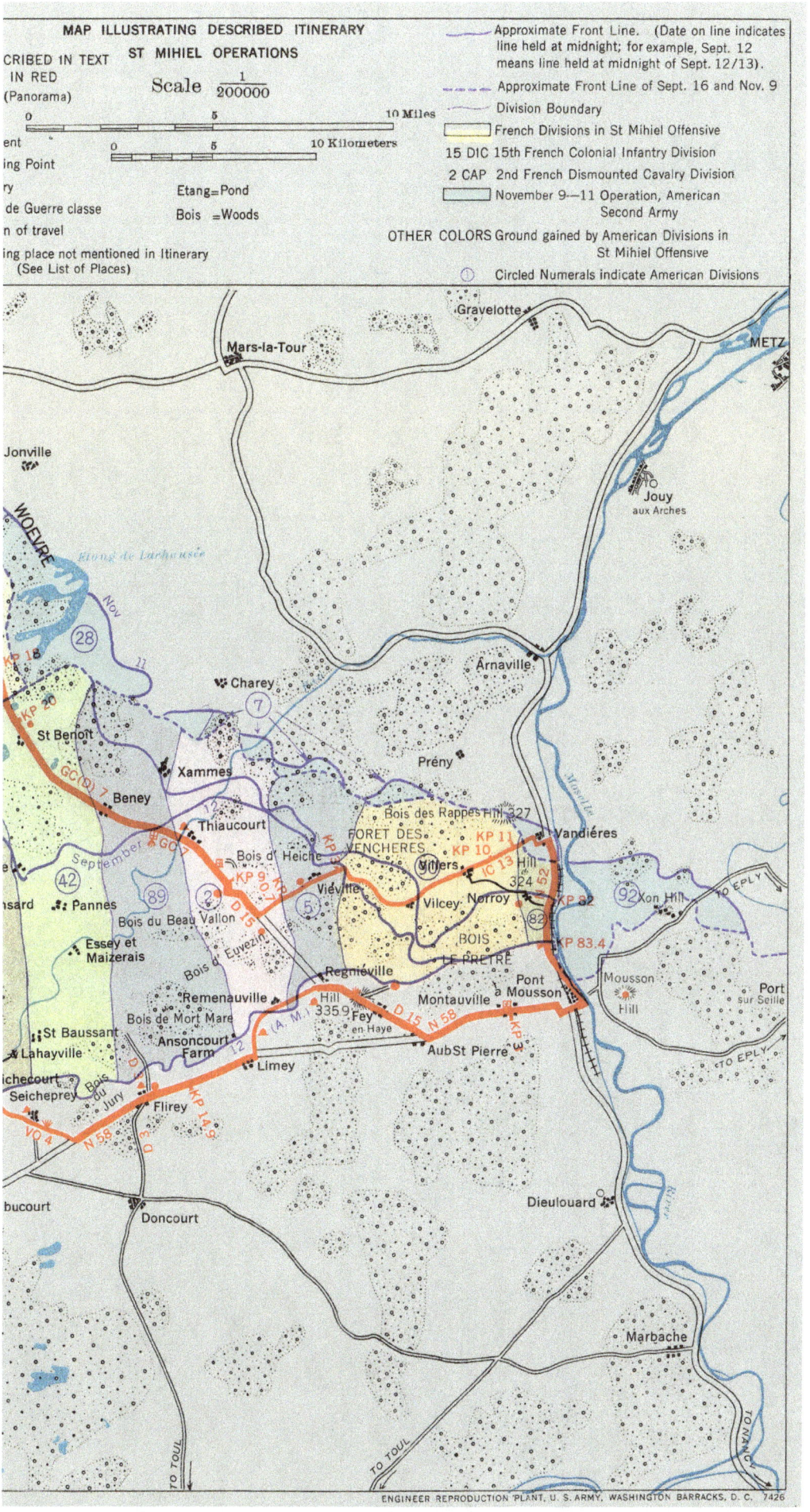

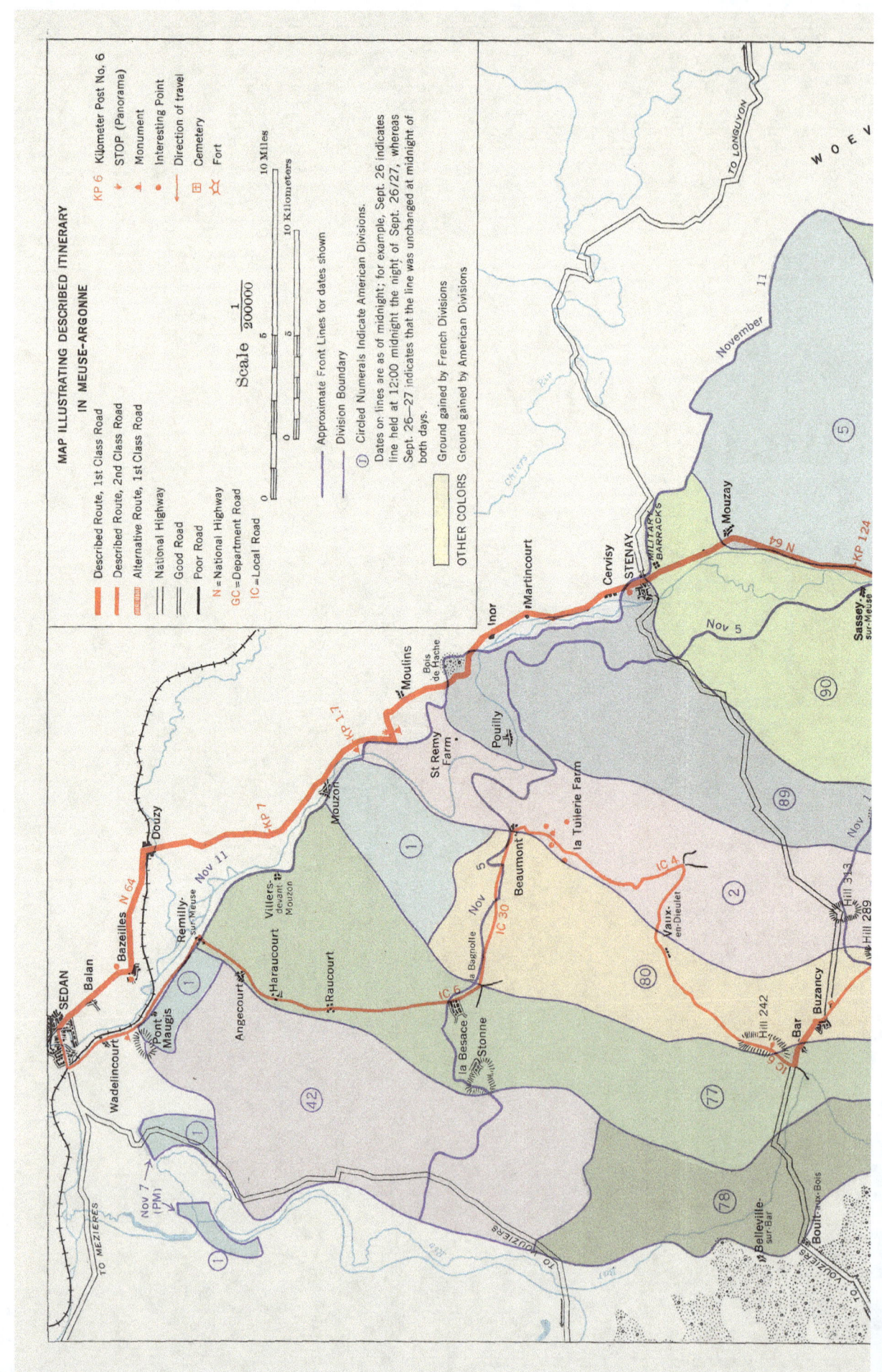

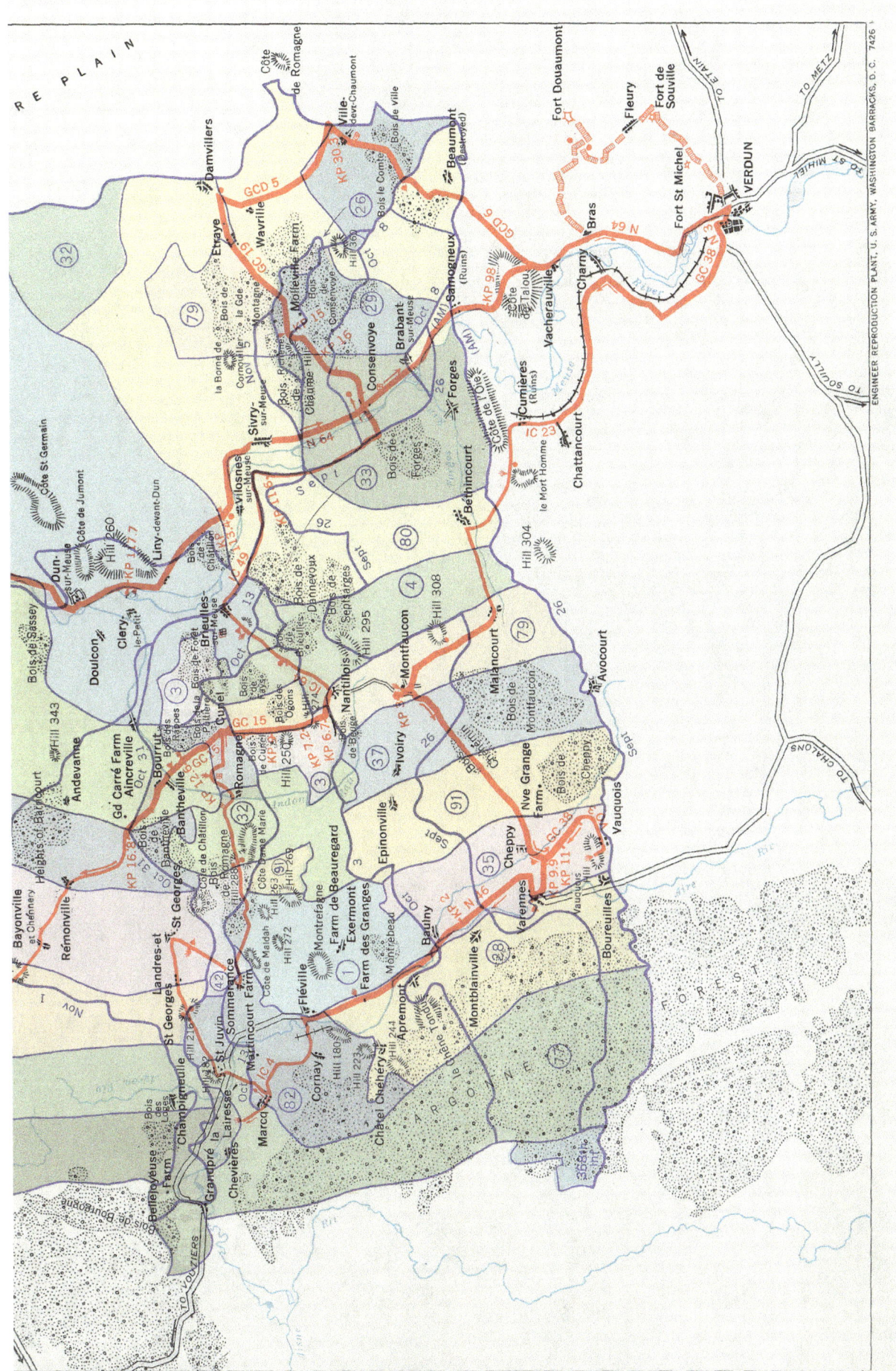

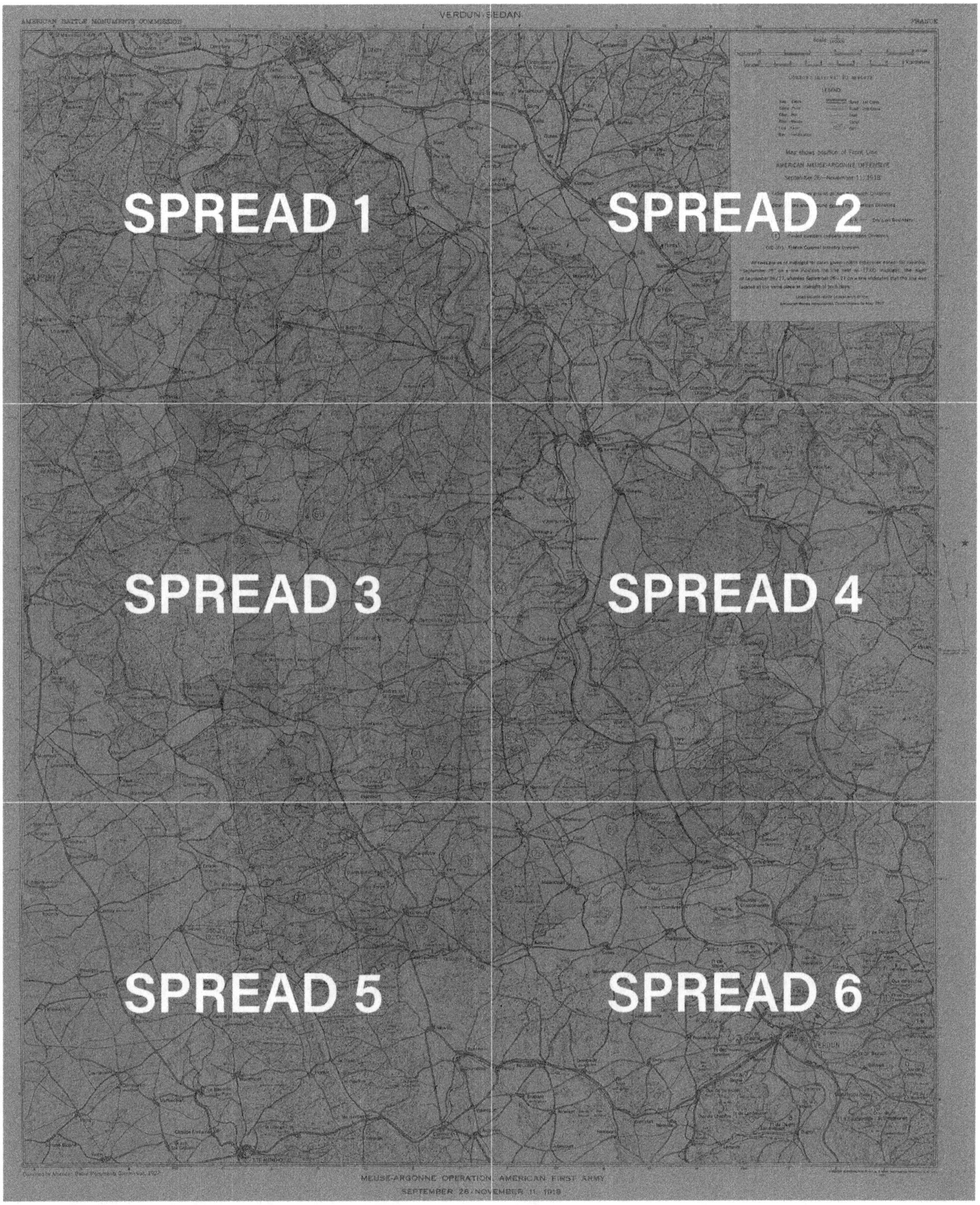
AMERICAN BATTLE MONUMENTS COMMISSION
VERDUN-SEDAN
FRANCE
SPREAD 1
SPREAD 2
SPREAD 3
SPREAD 4
SPREAD 5
SPREAD 6
MEUSE-ARGONNE OPERATION, AMERICAN FIRST ARMY
SEPTEMBER 26-NOVEMBER 11, 1918

SPREAD 1

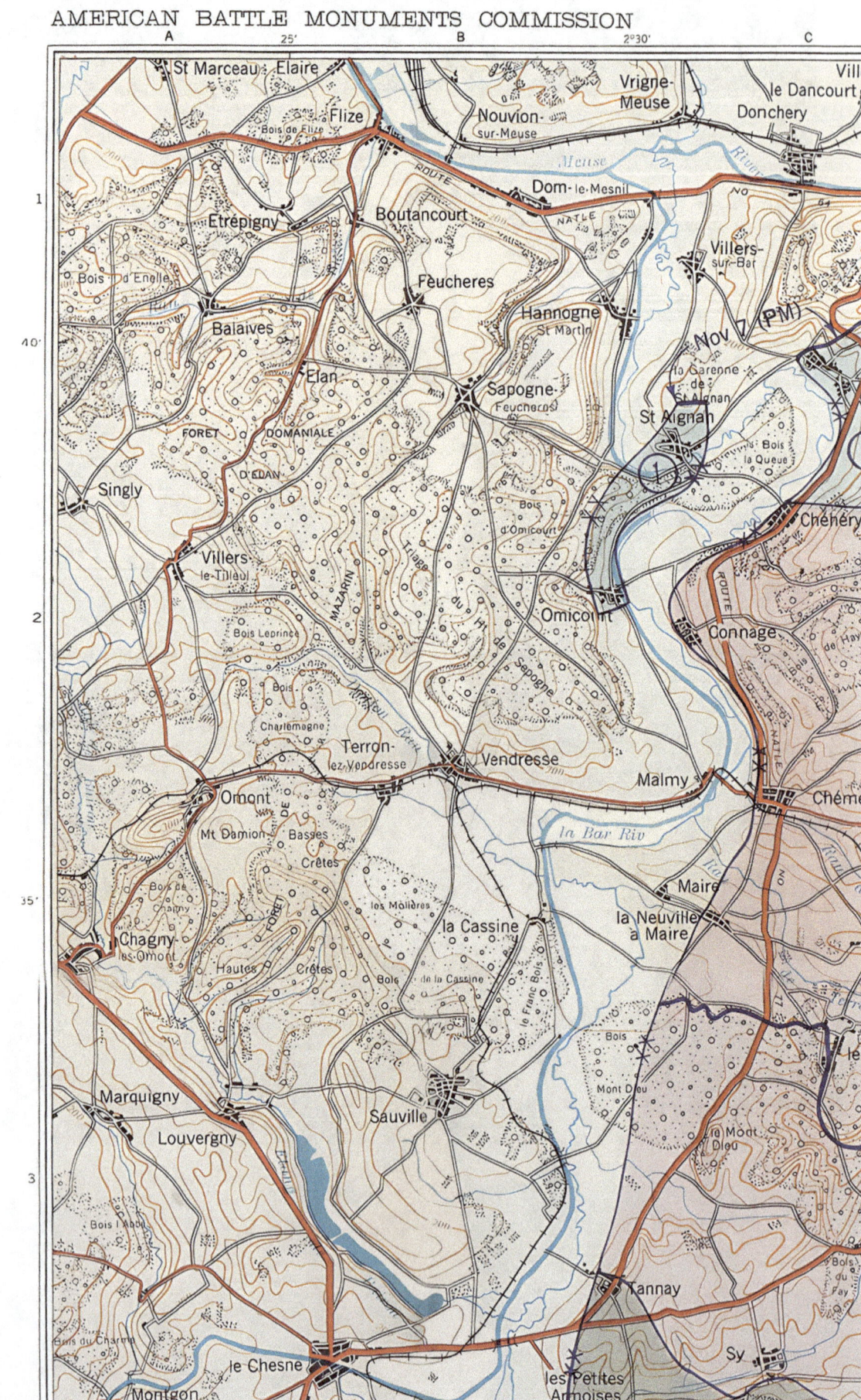

SPREAD 1

VERDUN-S

SPREAD 2

SEDAN

SPREAD 2

FRANCE

Scale $\frac{1}{100000}$

Contour interval 20 meters

LEGEND

Rau	Creek		Road 1st Class
Etang	Pond		Road 2nd Class
Côte	Hill		Trail
Bois	Woods		Canal
Fme	Farm		Fort
Ouv	Fortification		

Map shows position of Front Line

AMERICAN MEUSE-ARGONNE OFFENSIVE

September 26—November 11, 1918

Yellow color shows ground gained by French Divisions

Other colors show ground gained by American Divisions

———— Front Line   ——XX—— Division Boundary

(1)   Circled numbers indicate Americans Divisions

DIC (Fr)   French Colonial Infantry Division

All lines are as of midnight for dates given unless otherwise noted; for example, "September 26" on a line indicates the line held at 12:00 midnight, the night of September 26/27, whereas September 26—27 on a line indicates that the line was located at the same place at midnight of both days.

Lines include result of research of the
American Battle Monuments Commission to May 1927

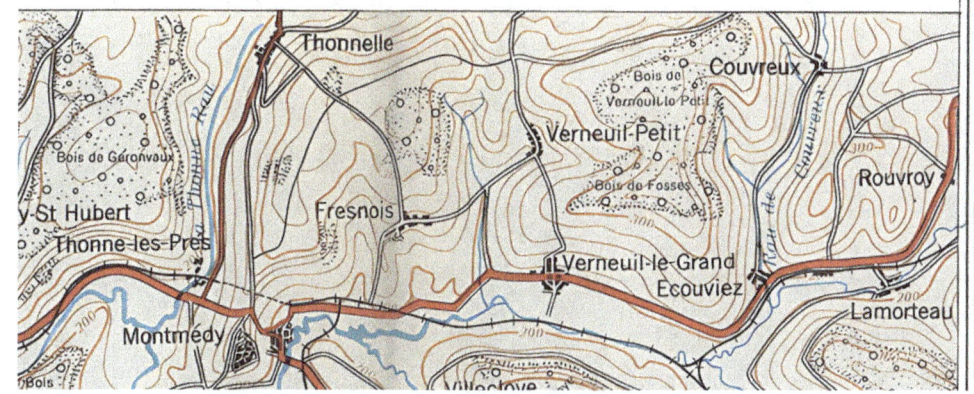

SPREAD 3

SPREAD 3

SPREAD 4

SPREAD 4

SPREAD 5

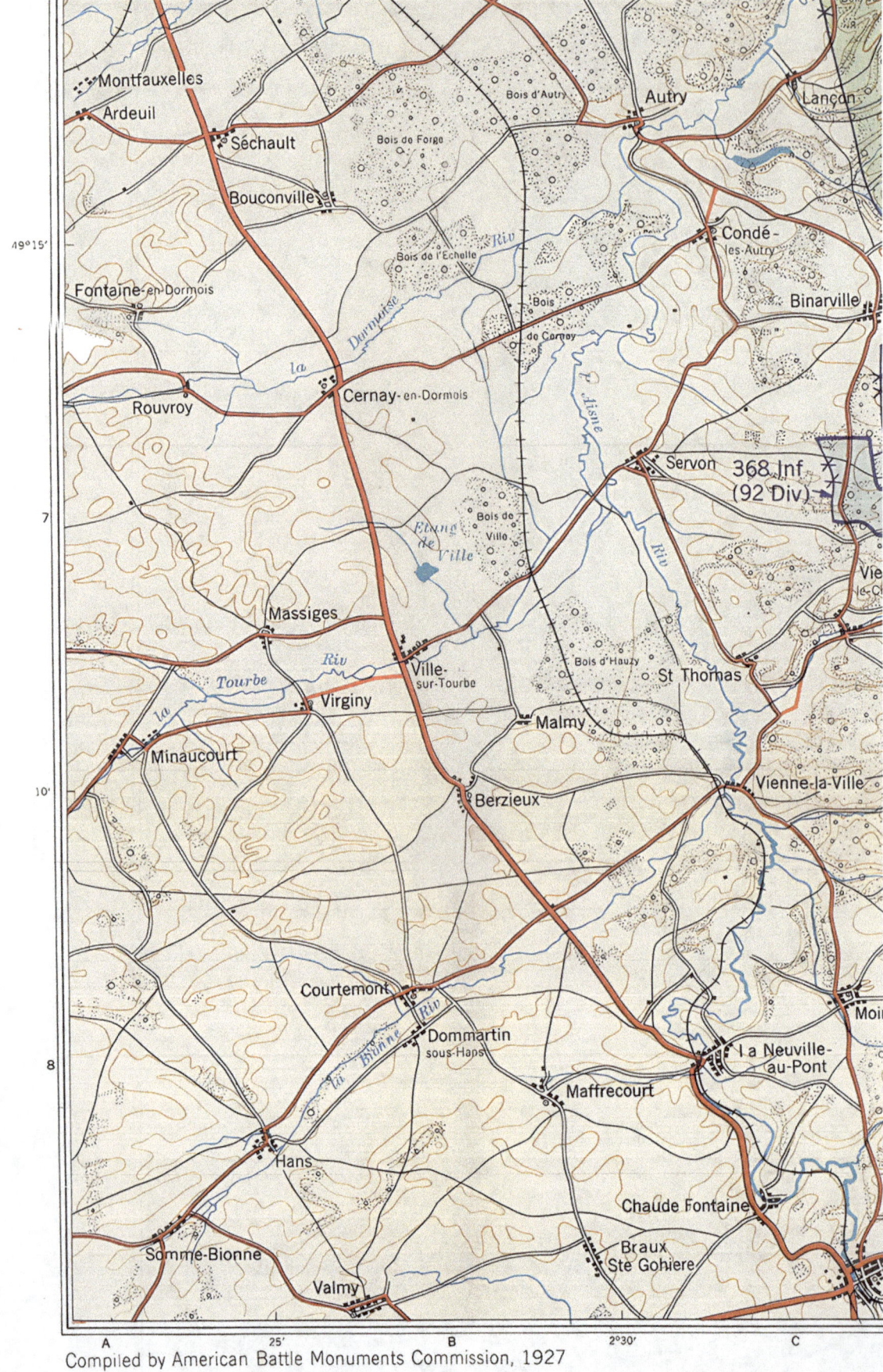

Compiled by American Battle Monuments Commission, 1927

SPREAD 5

MEUSE-ARGONNE OPERATION
SEPTEMBER 26 - NOV

SPREAD 6

, AMERICAN FIRST ARMY

'EMBER 11, 1918

SPREAD 6

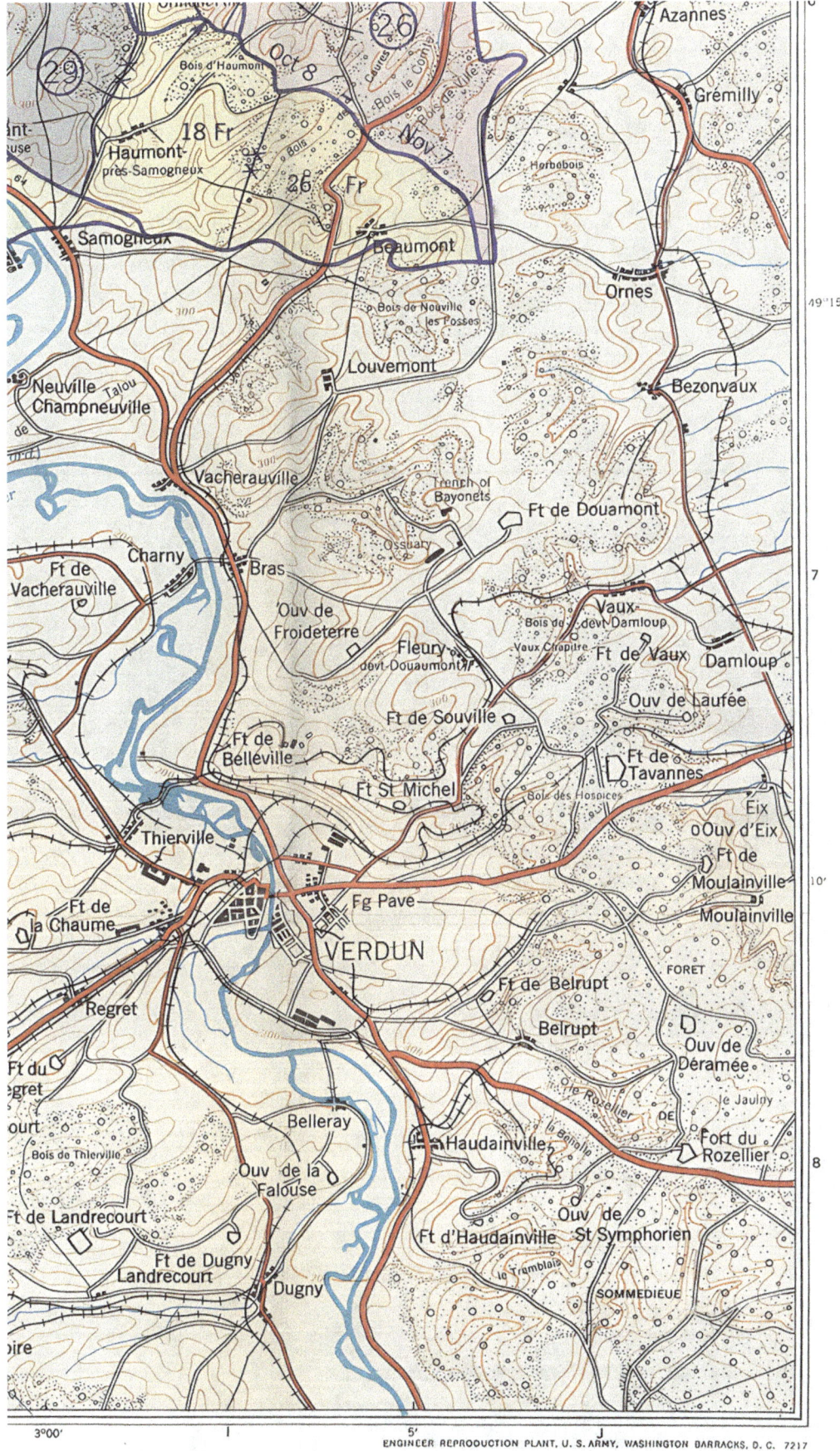

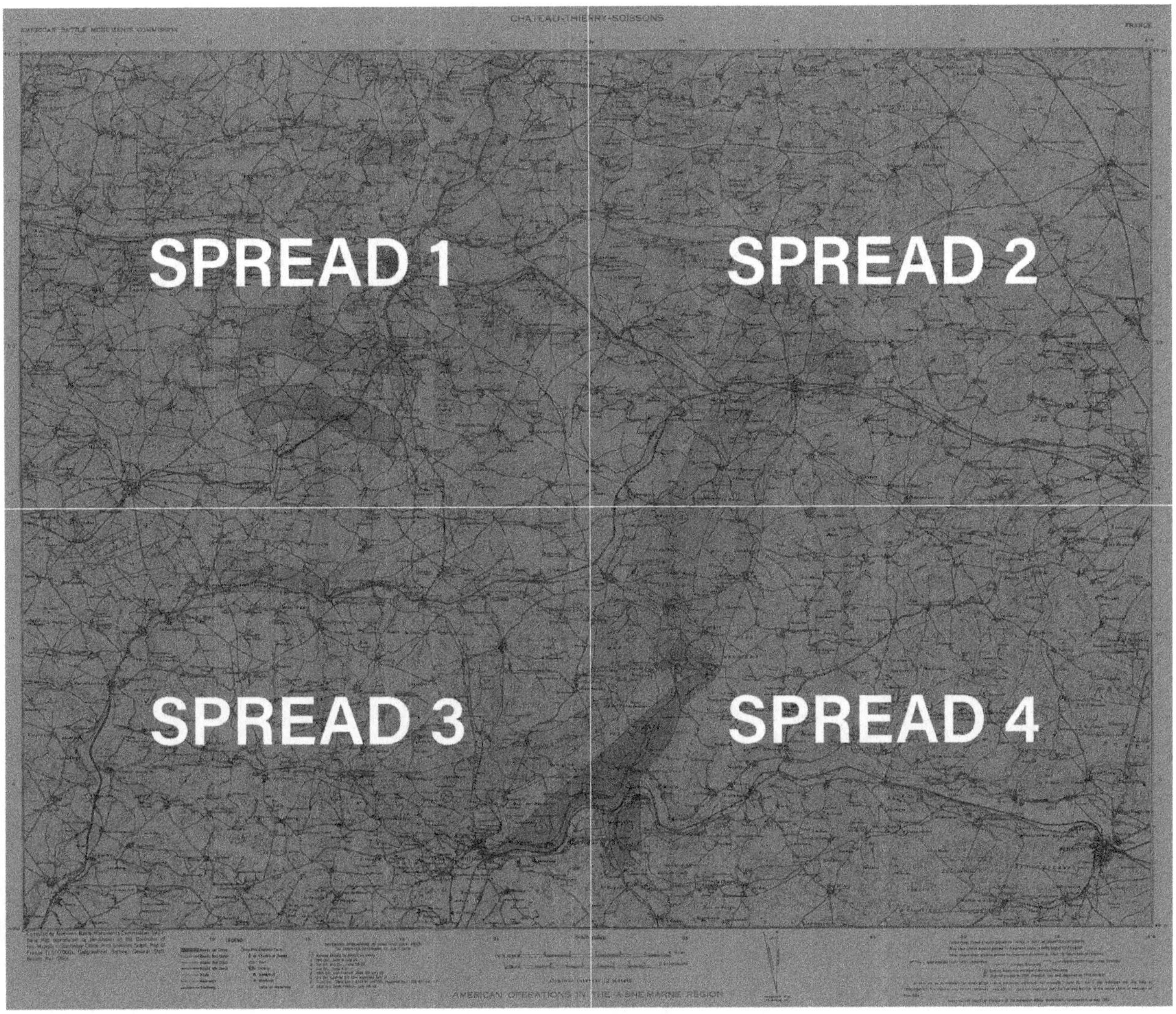
CHATEAU-THIERRY-SOISSONS
SPREAD 1
SPREAD 2
SPREAD 3
SPREAD 4
AMERICAN OPERATIONS IN THE AISNE-MARNE REGION

SPREAD 1

AMERICAN BATTLE MONUMENTS COMMISSION

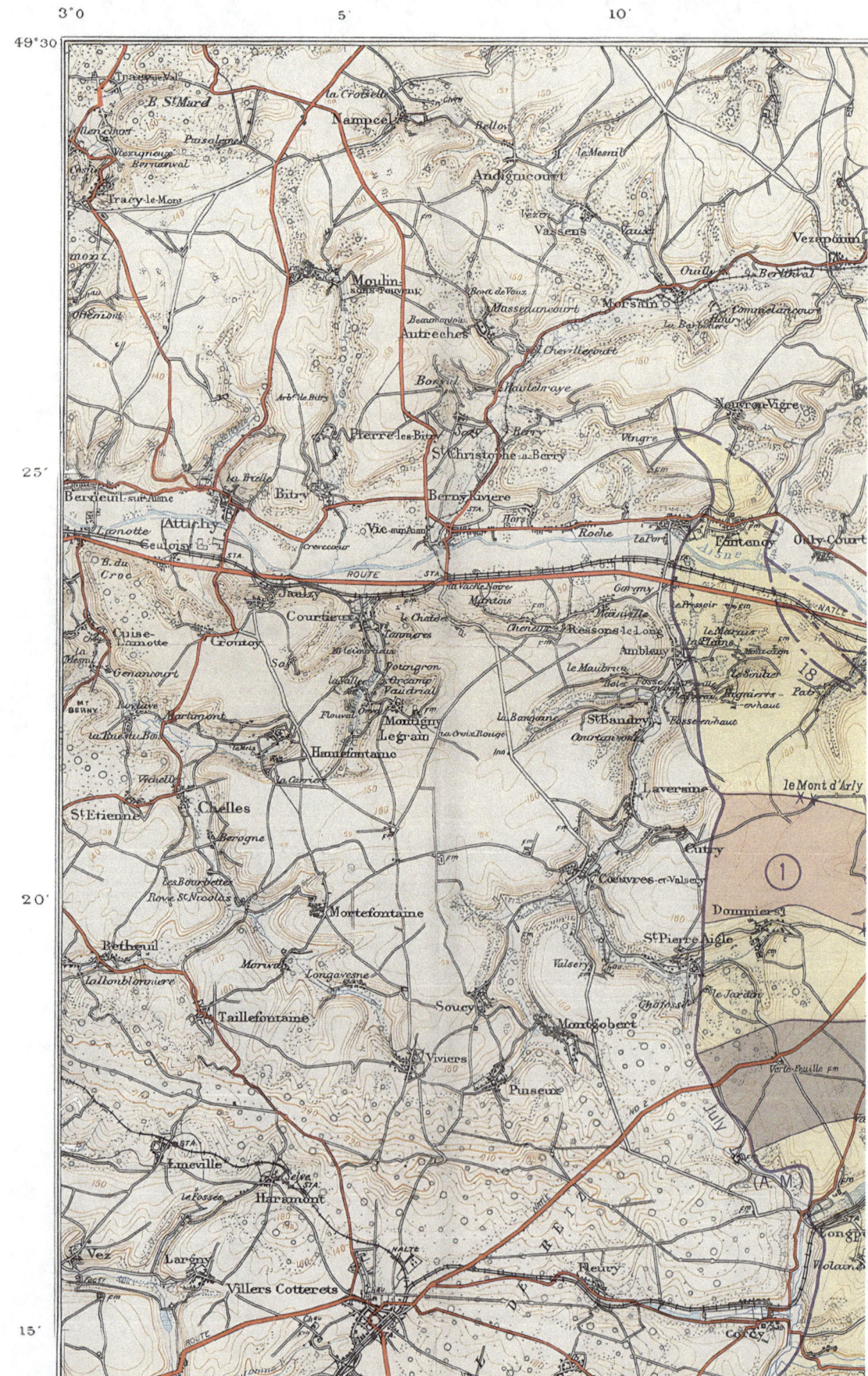

CHATEAU-THIE   SPREAD 1

SPREAD 2   RRY-SOISSONS

SPREAD 2

FRANCE

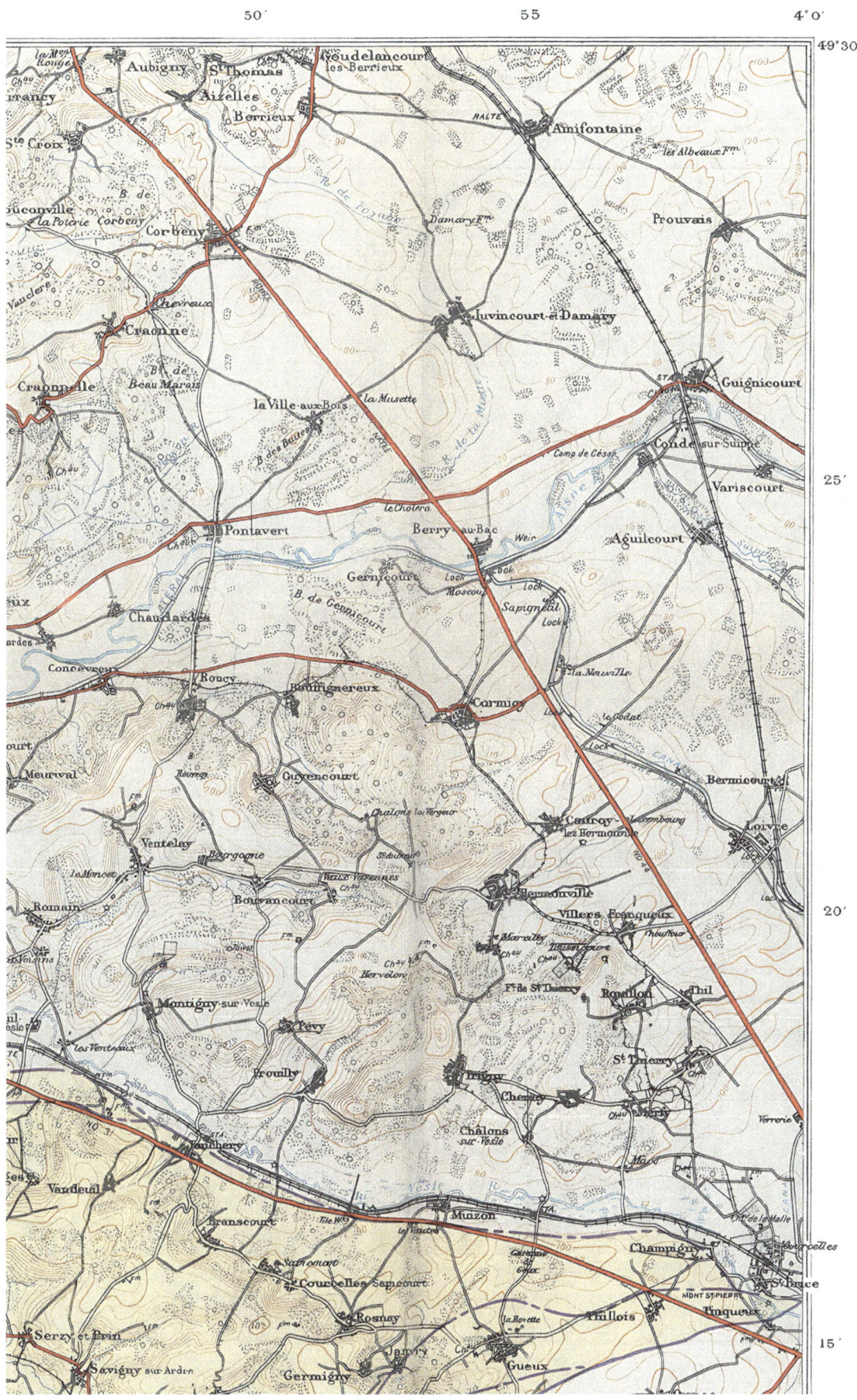

SPREAD 3

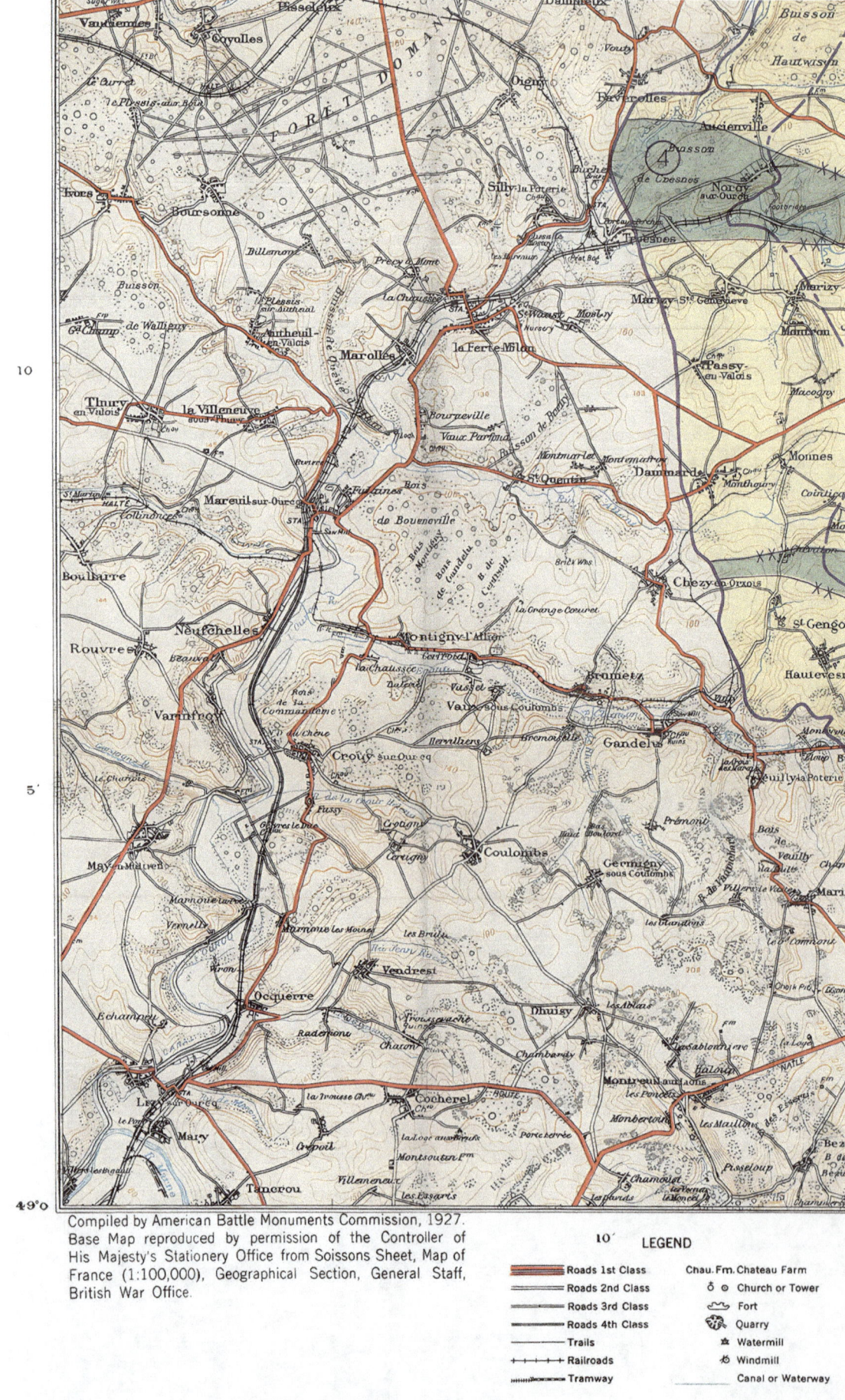

Compiled by American Battle Monuments Commission, 1927.
Base Map reproduced by permission of the Controller of
His Majesty's Stationery Office from Soissons Sheet, Map of
France (1:100,000), Geographical Section, General Staff,
British War Office.

LEGEND

- Roads 1st Class
- Roads 2nd Class
- Roads 3rd Class
- Roads 4th Class
- Trails
- Railroads
- Tramway
- Chau. Fm. Chateau Farm
- Church or Tower
- Fort
- Quarry
- Watermill
- Windmill
- Canal or Waterway

SPREAD 3

DEFENSIVE OPERATIONS IN JUNE AND JULY, PRIOR
TO COUNTER-OFFENSIVE OF JULY 18TH

▨ Ground gained by American Units
A 2nd Div., June 4-July 10
B 7th Inf. 3rd Div., June 18-23
C 3rd Div., June 6-9
D 28th Div. with French, June 30-July 18
E 3rd Div. Lost by 3rd Div. regained July 16
F 111th Inf. (28th Div.). Lost by 3rd Div. regained by 111th Inf. July 17
G 28th Div. (with French) July 16-18

AMERICAN OPERATIONS IN

SPREAD 4

THE AISNE-MARNE REGION

SPREAD 4

Yellow color shows ground gained by French in JULY 18 COUNTER-OFFENSIVE
Blue color shows ground gained by American units in OISE-AISNE OFFENSIVE
Other colors show ground gained by American divisions in JULY 18 COUNTER-OFFENSIVE

― Approximate Front Lines (American)   ― Division Boundary   ― Approximate Front Lines (French)
① Circled numerals indicate American Divisions
H Ground gained by 28th Division; lost and regained by 77th Division

All lines are as of midnight for dates given unless otherwise indicated; for example, "July 20" on a line indicates the line held at 12:00 midnight, the night of July 20/21, whereas "July 20—21" on a line indicates that the line was located at the same place at midnight of both days.

Lines include results of research of the American Battle Monuments Commission to May 1927

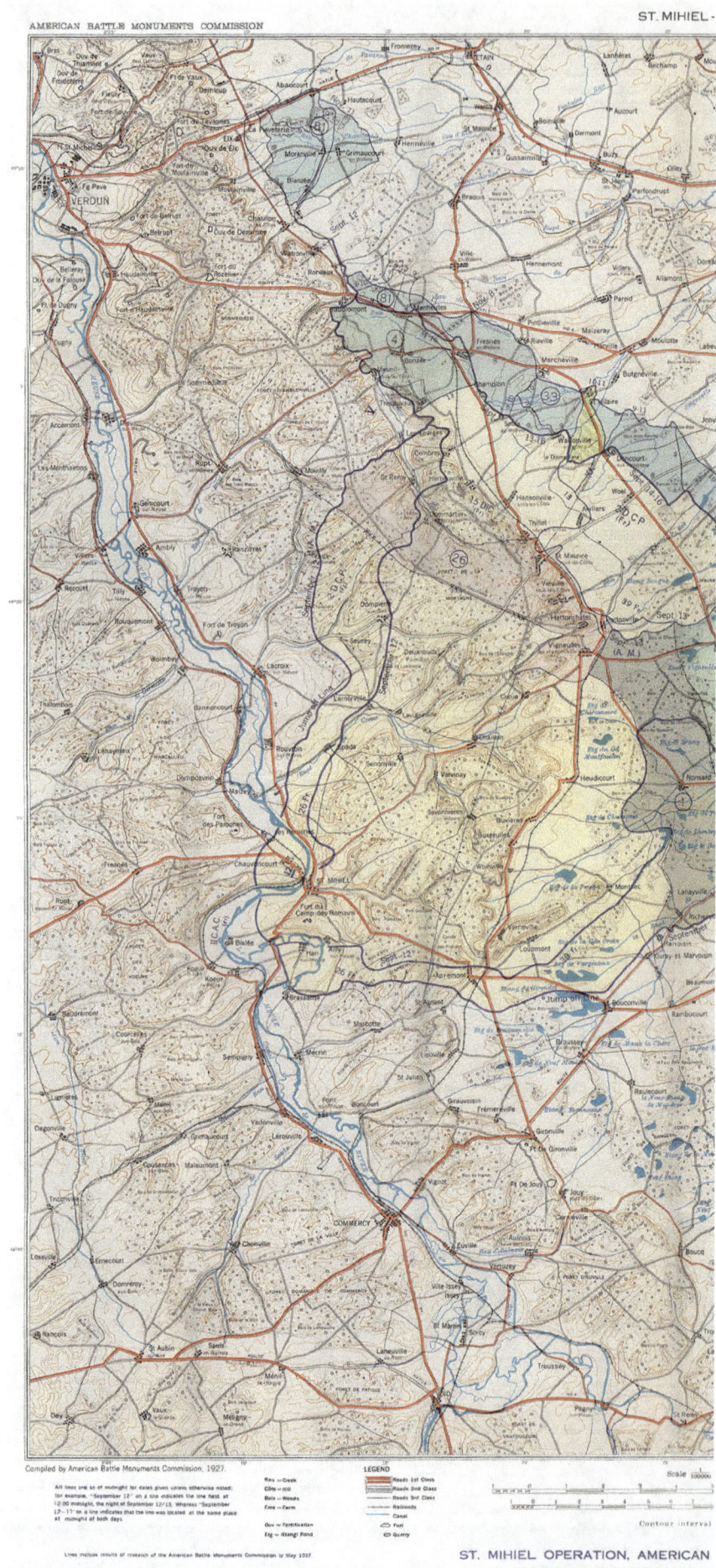

ST. MIHIEL OPERATION, AMERICAN
NOVEMBER 9-11 OPERATION,

FIRST ARMY, SEPTEMBER 12-16 AND
AMERICAN SECOND ARMY

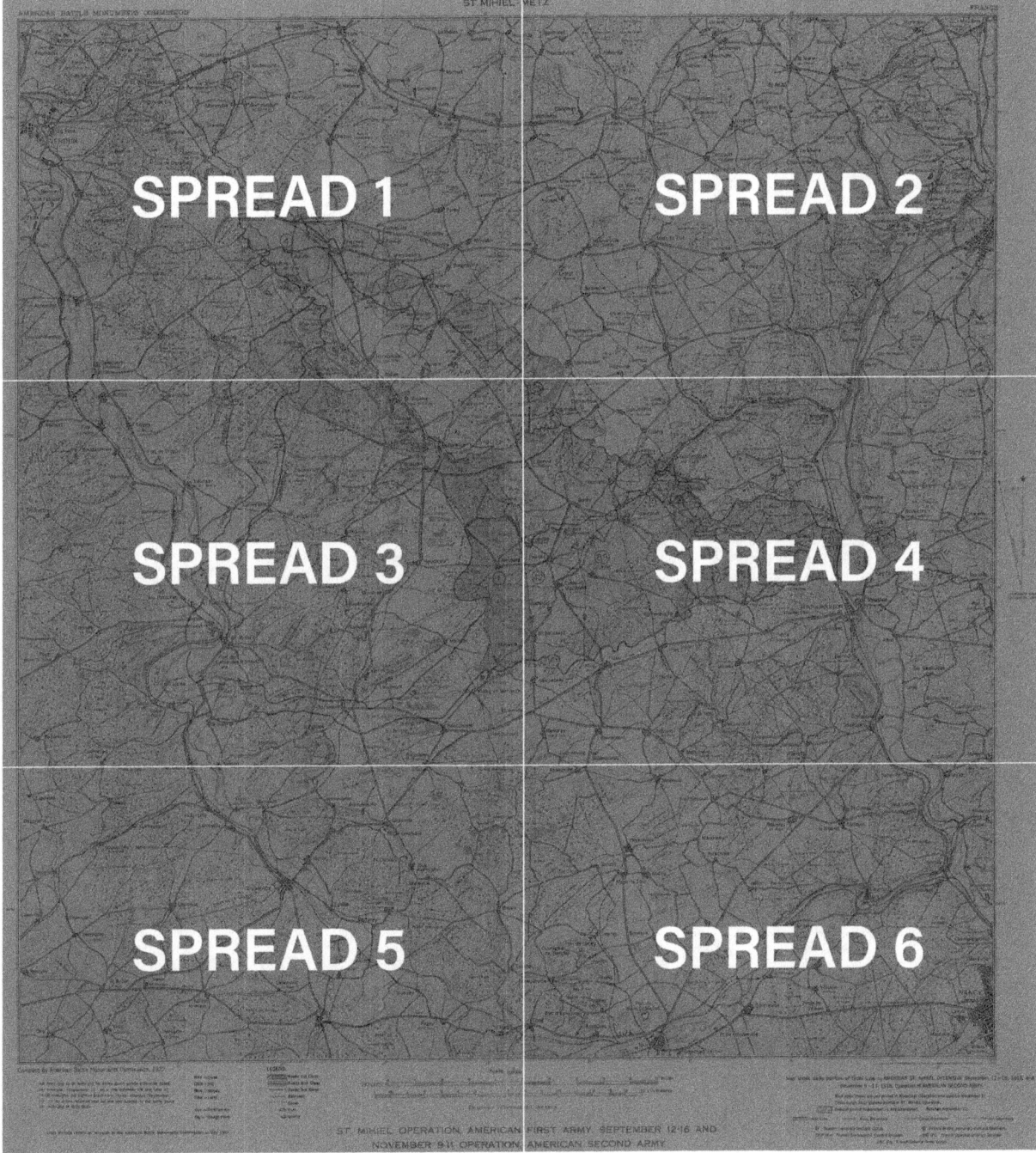

SPREAD 1

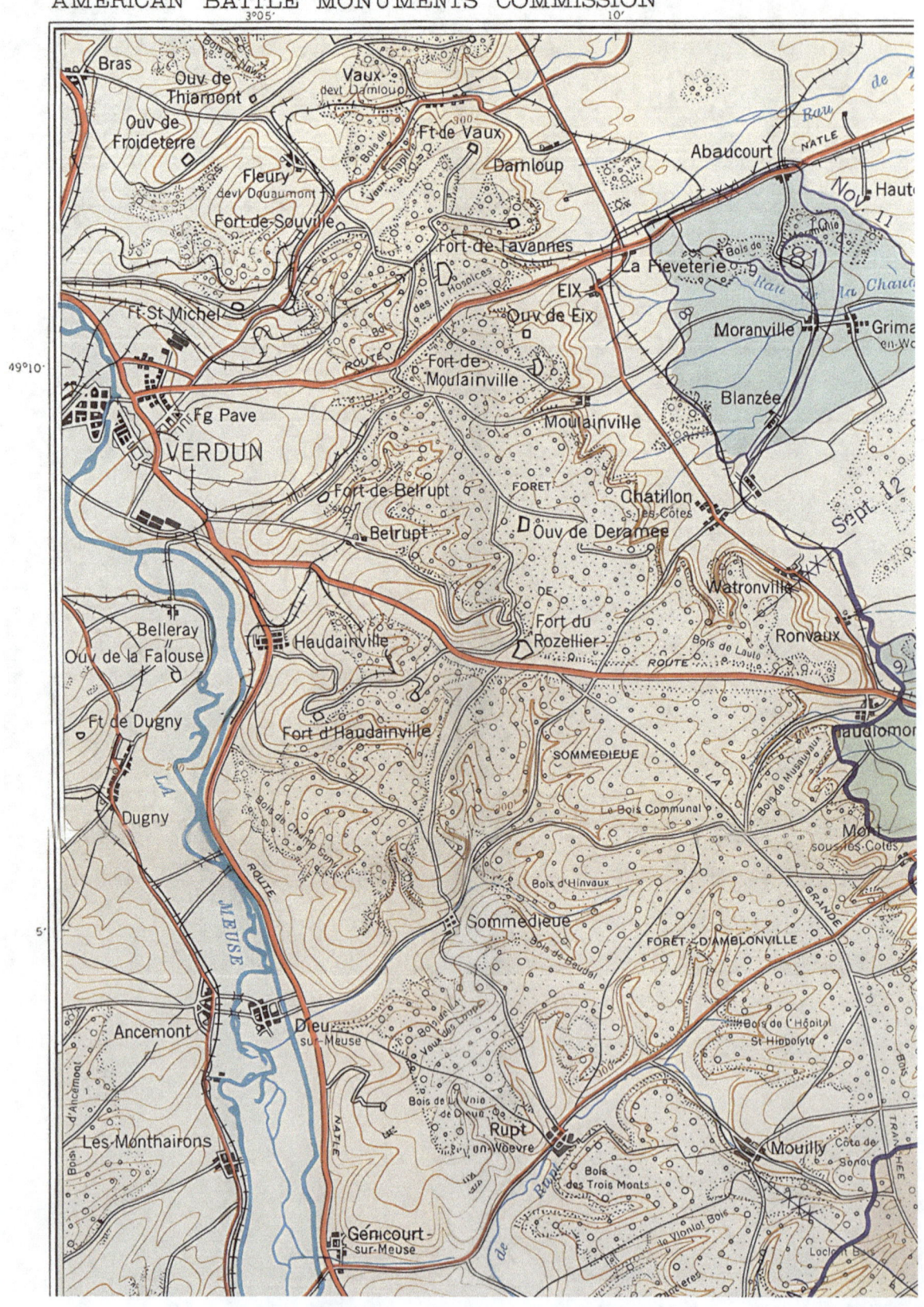

SPREAD 1

ST. MIHIEL -

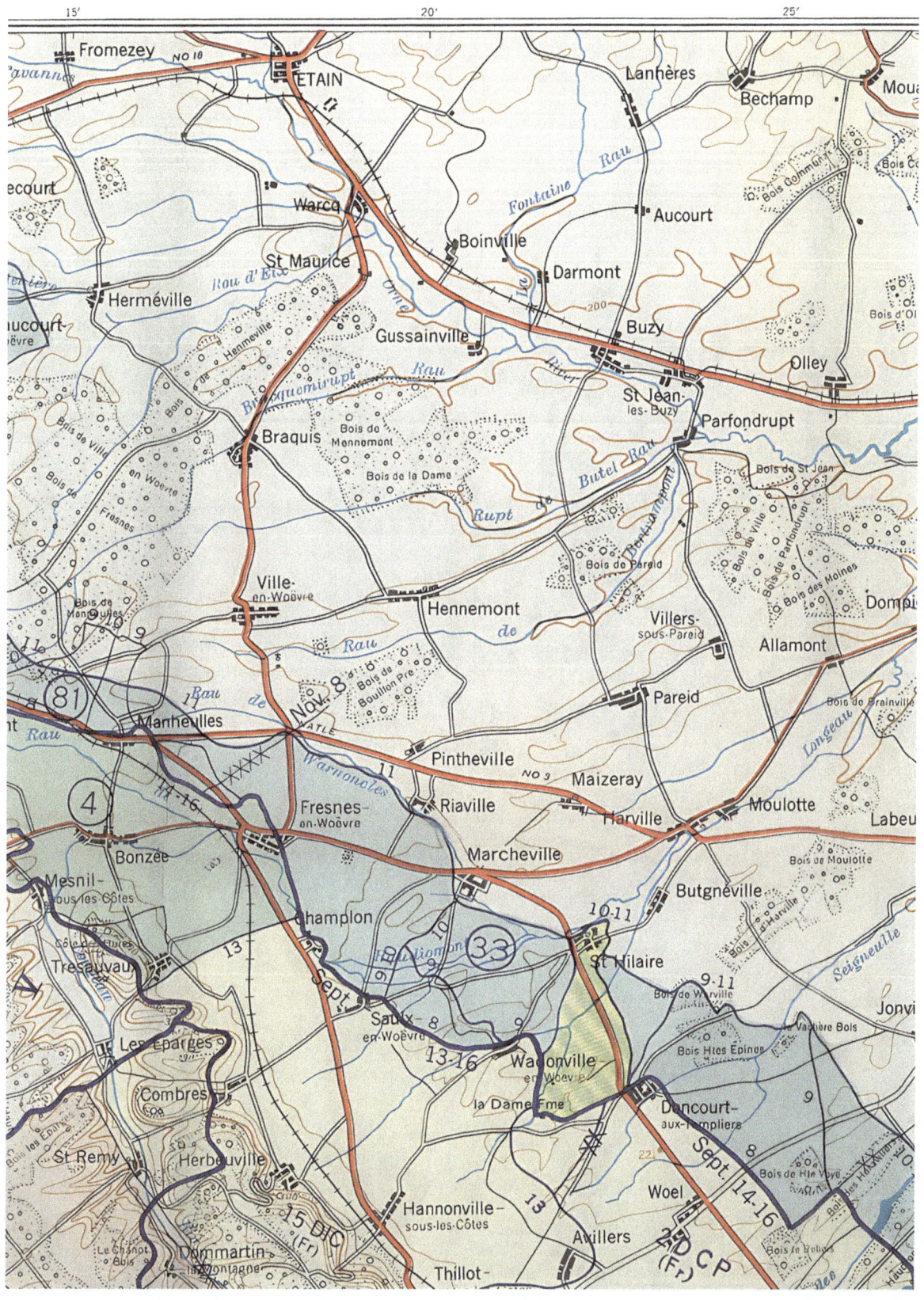

SPREAD 2

METZ

SPREAD 2

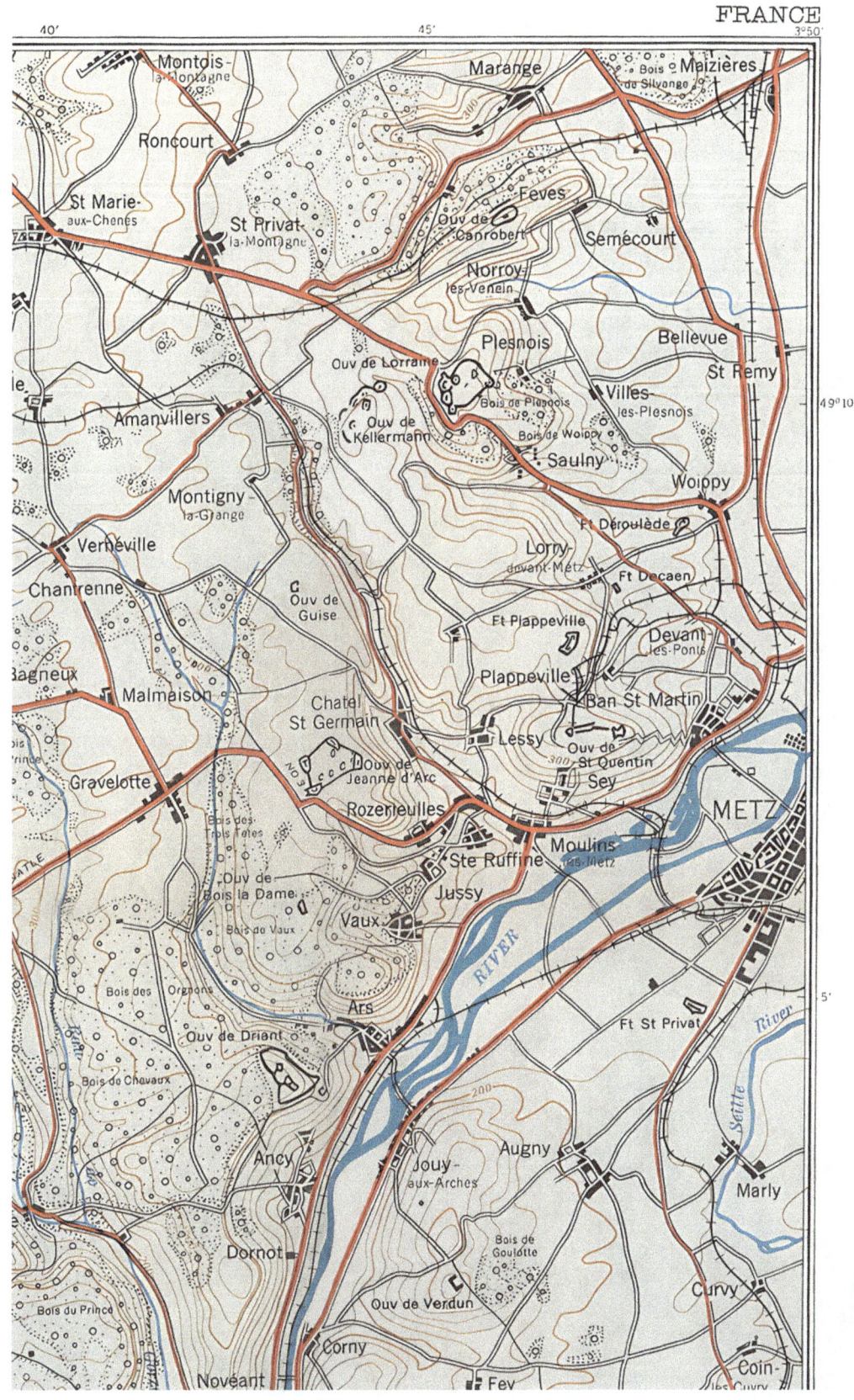

SPREAD 3

SPREAD 3

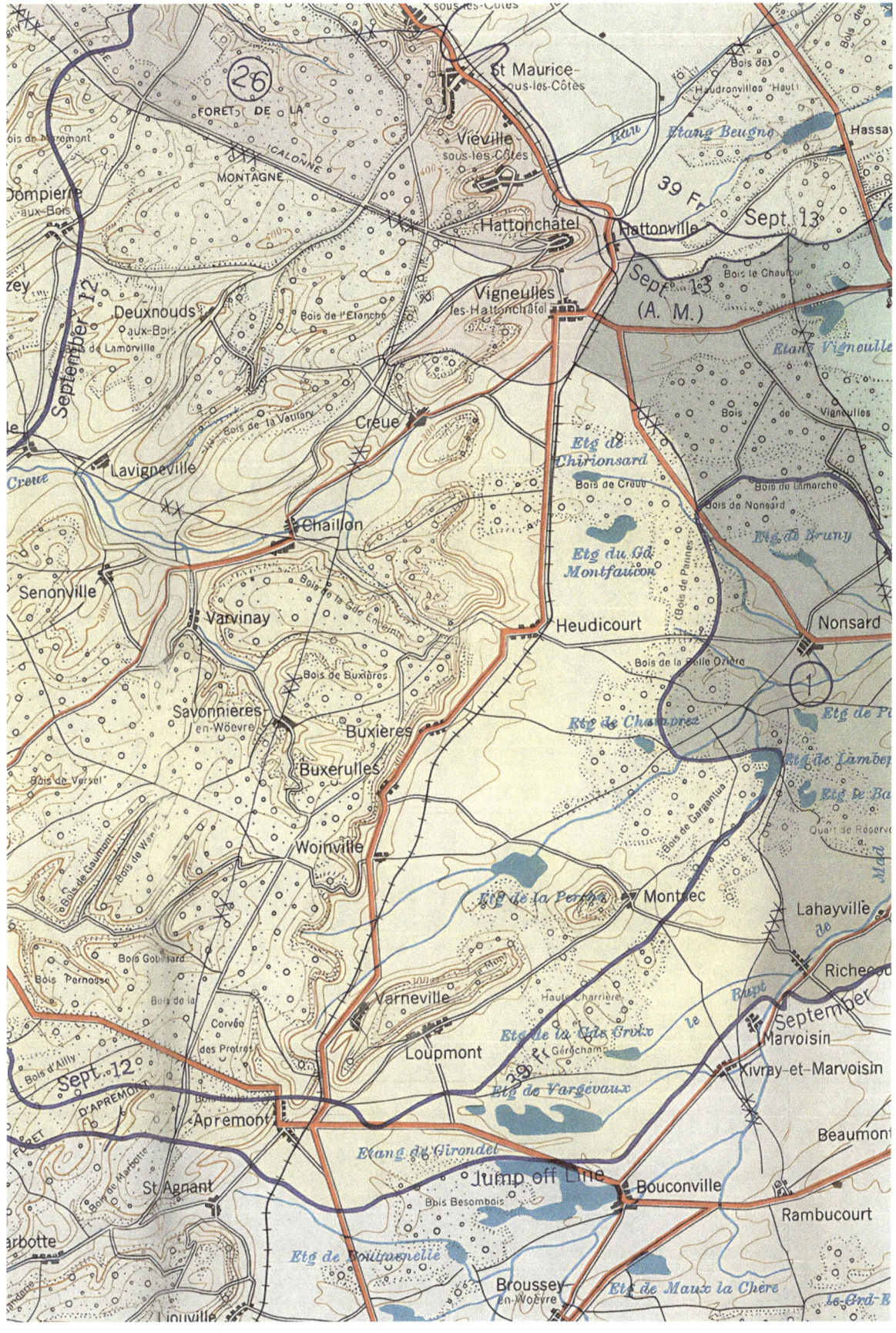

SPREAD 4

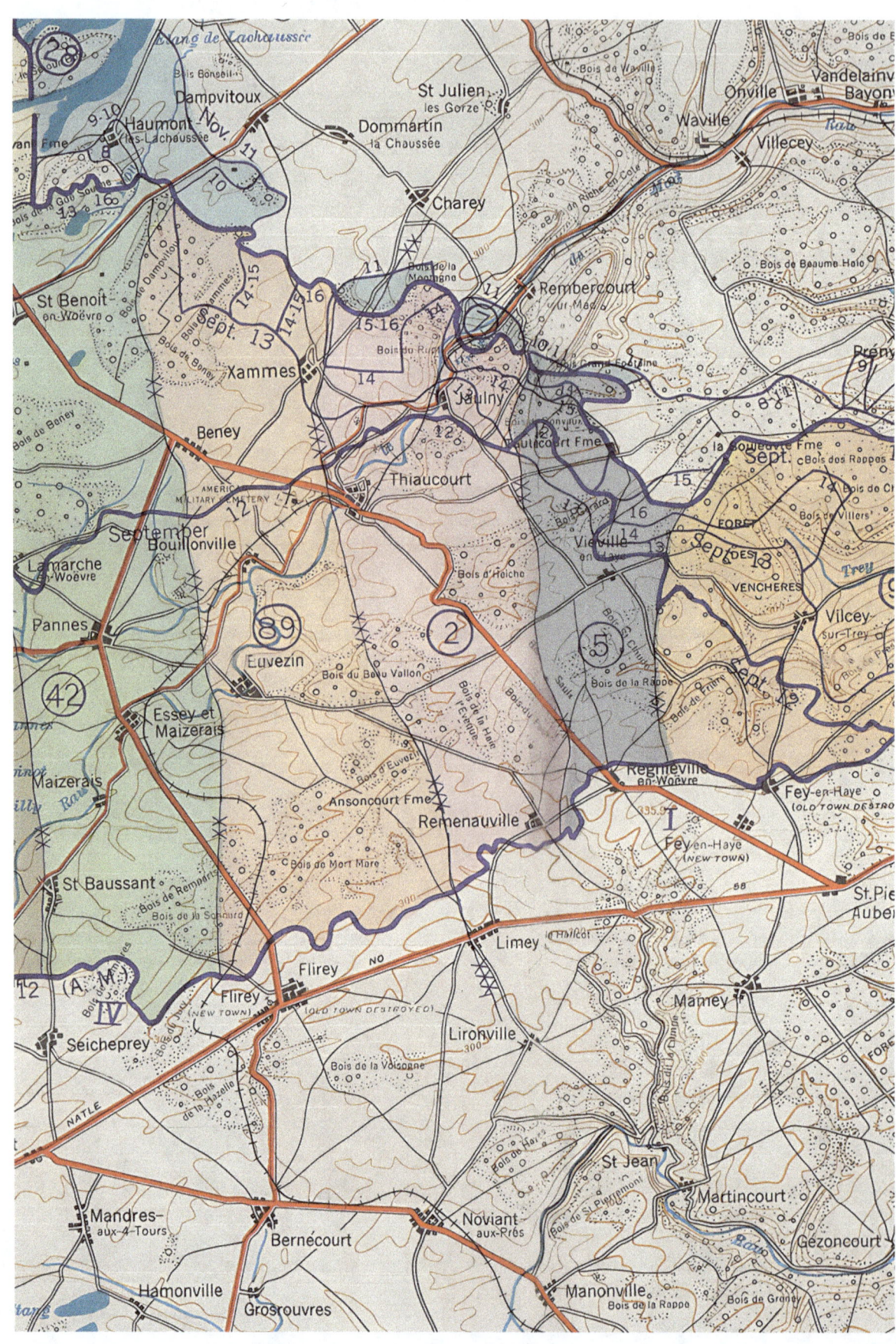

SPREAD 4

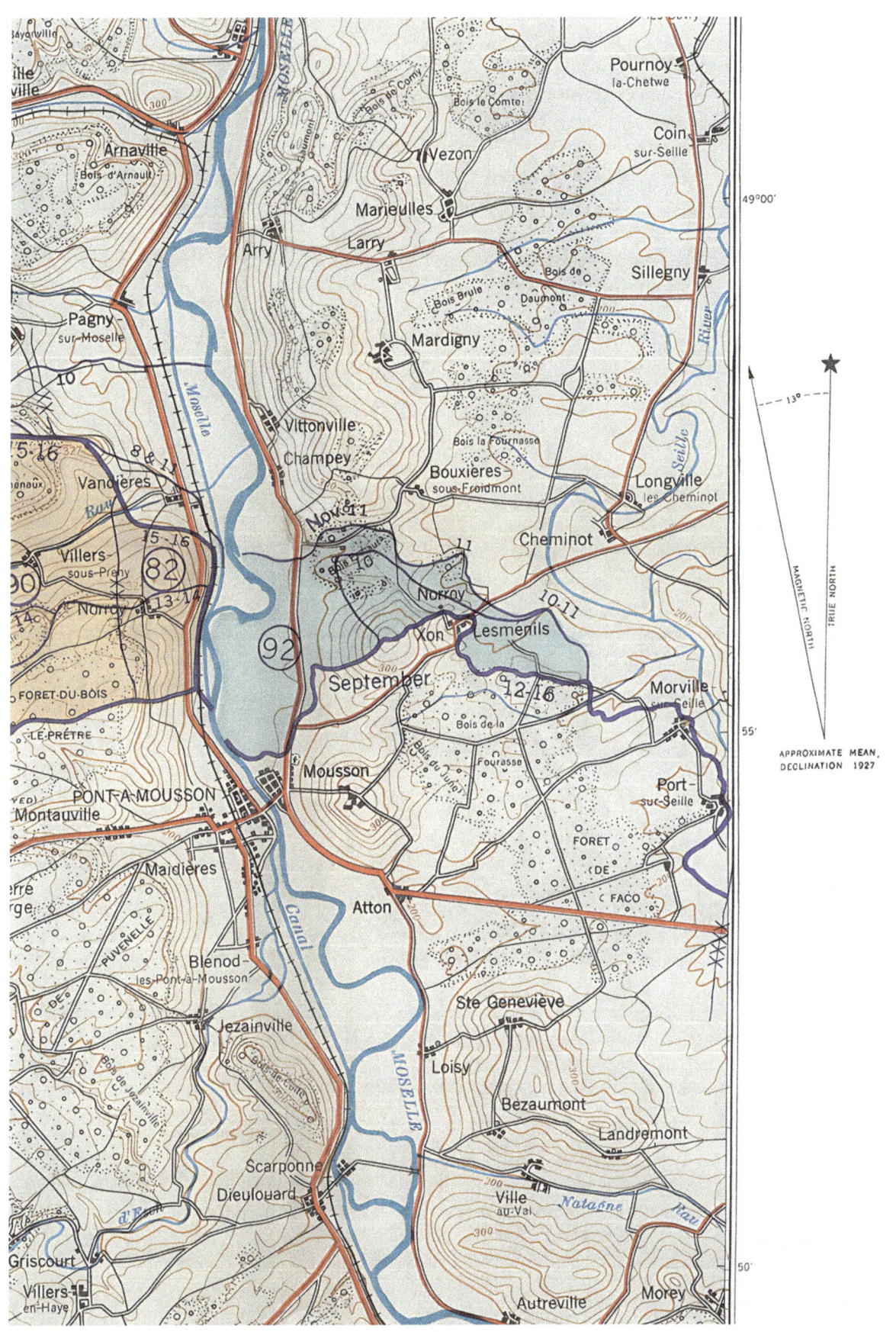

SPREAD 5

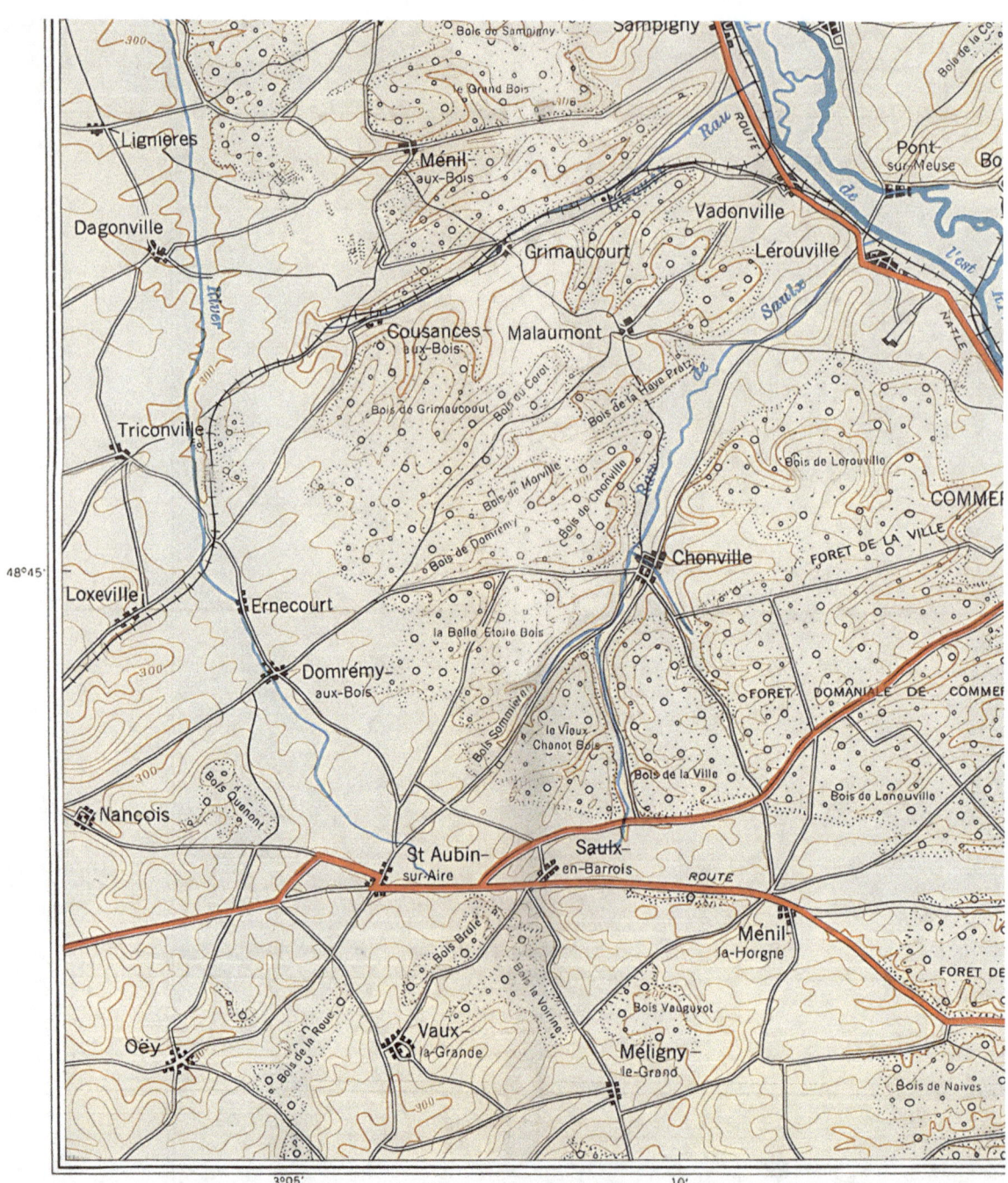

Compiled by American Battle Monuments Commission, 1927.

All lines are as of midnight for dates given unless otherwise noted; for example, "September 12" on a line indicates the line held at 12:00 midnight, the night of September 12/13. Whereas "September 12---13" on a line indicates that the line was located at the same place at midnight of both days.

Rau = Creek
Côte = Hill
Bois = Woods
Fme = Farm

Ouv = Fortification
Etg = (Etang) Pond

Lines include results of research of the American Battle Monuments Commission to May 1927.

SPREAD 5

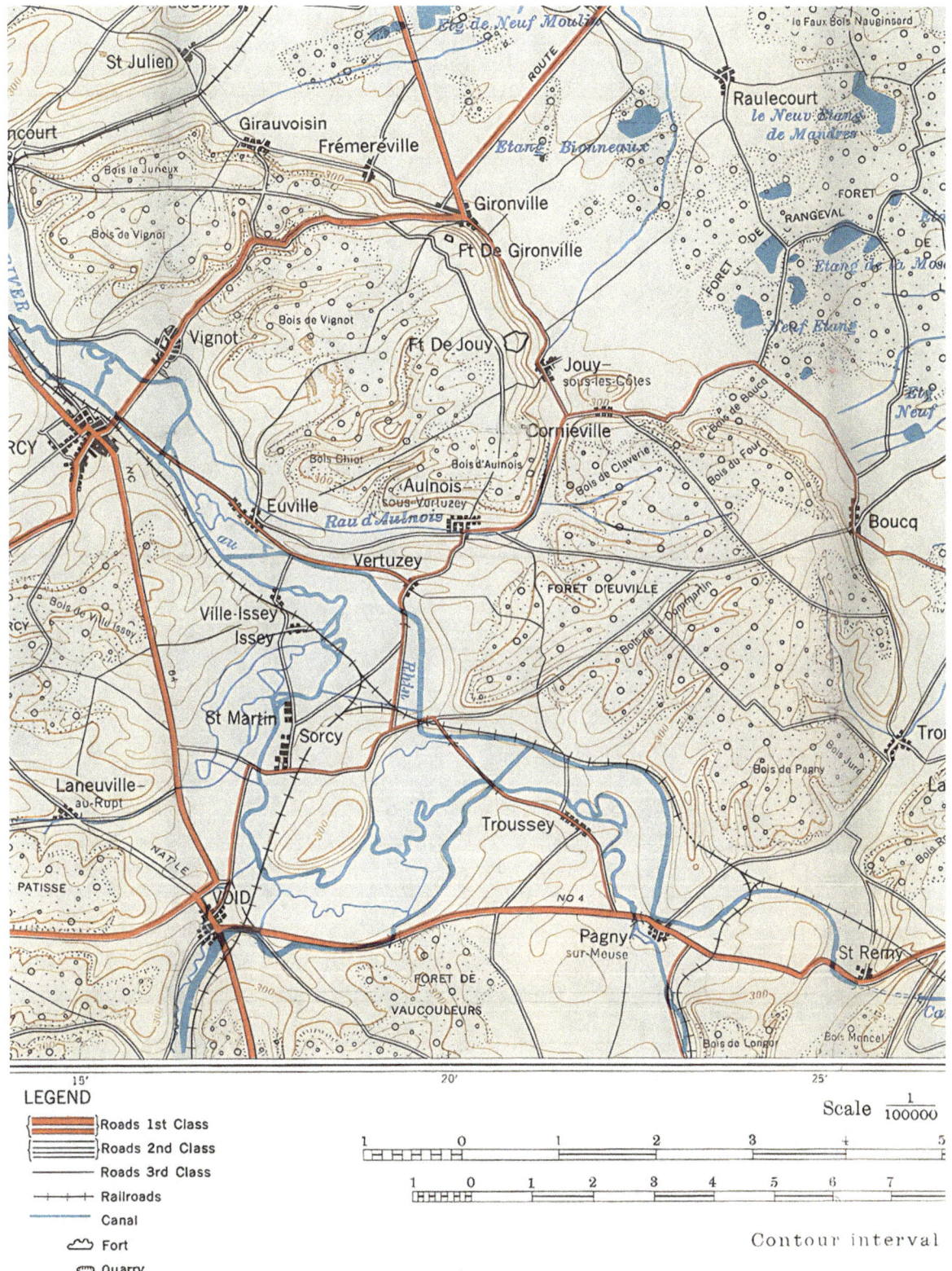

LEGEND
- Roads 1st Class
- Roads 2nd Class
- Roads 3rd Class
- Railroads
- Canal
- Fort
- Quarry

Scale $\frac{1}{100000}$

Contour interval

ST. MIHIEL OPERATION, AMERICAN
NOVEMBER 9-11 OPERATION,

SPREAD 6

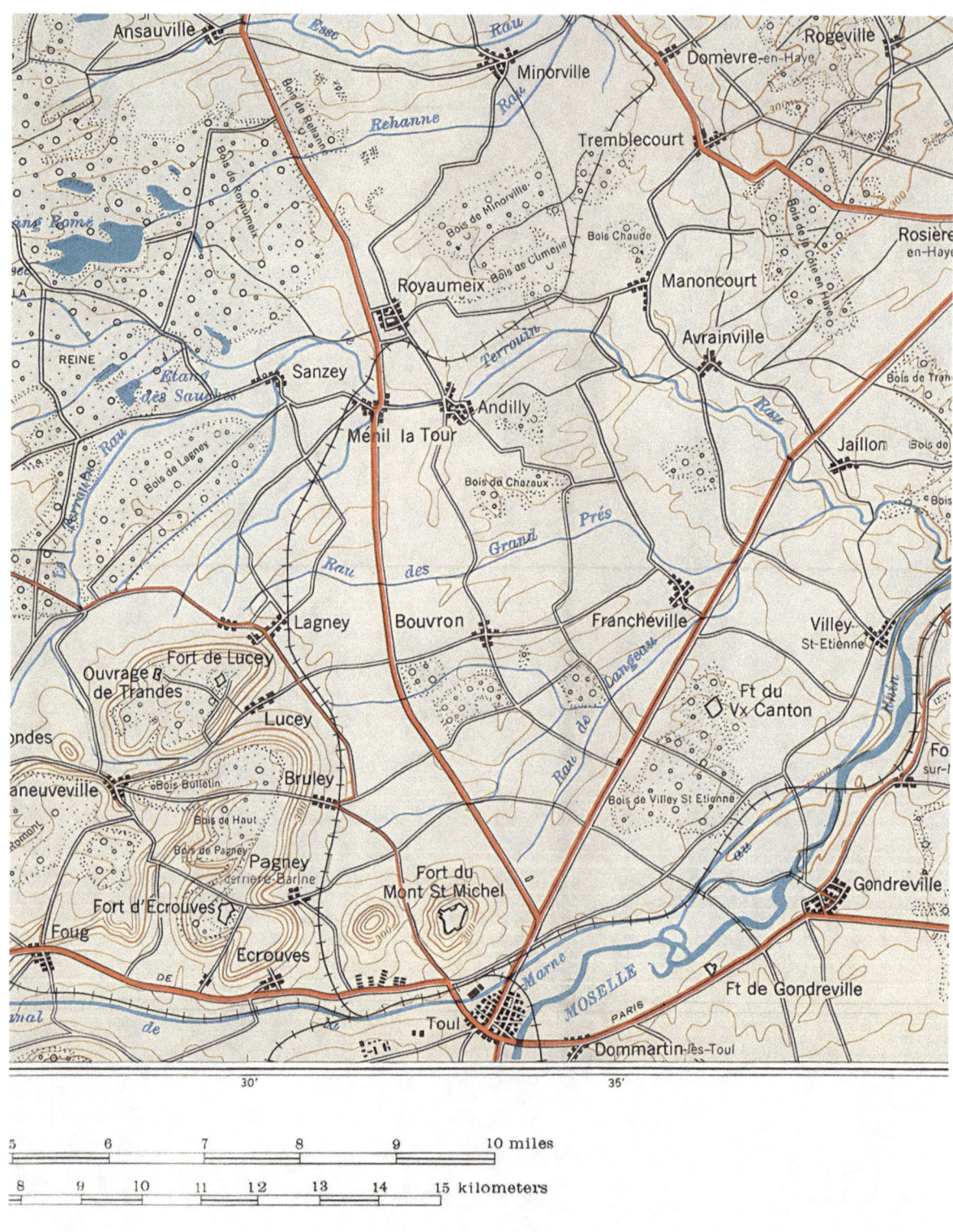

FIRST ARMY, SEPTEMBER 12-16 AND AMERICAN SECOND ARMY

SPREAD 6

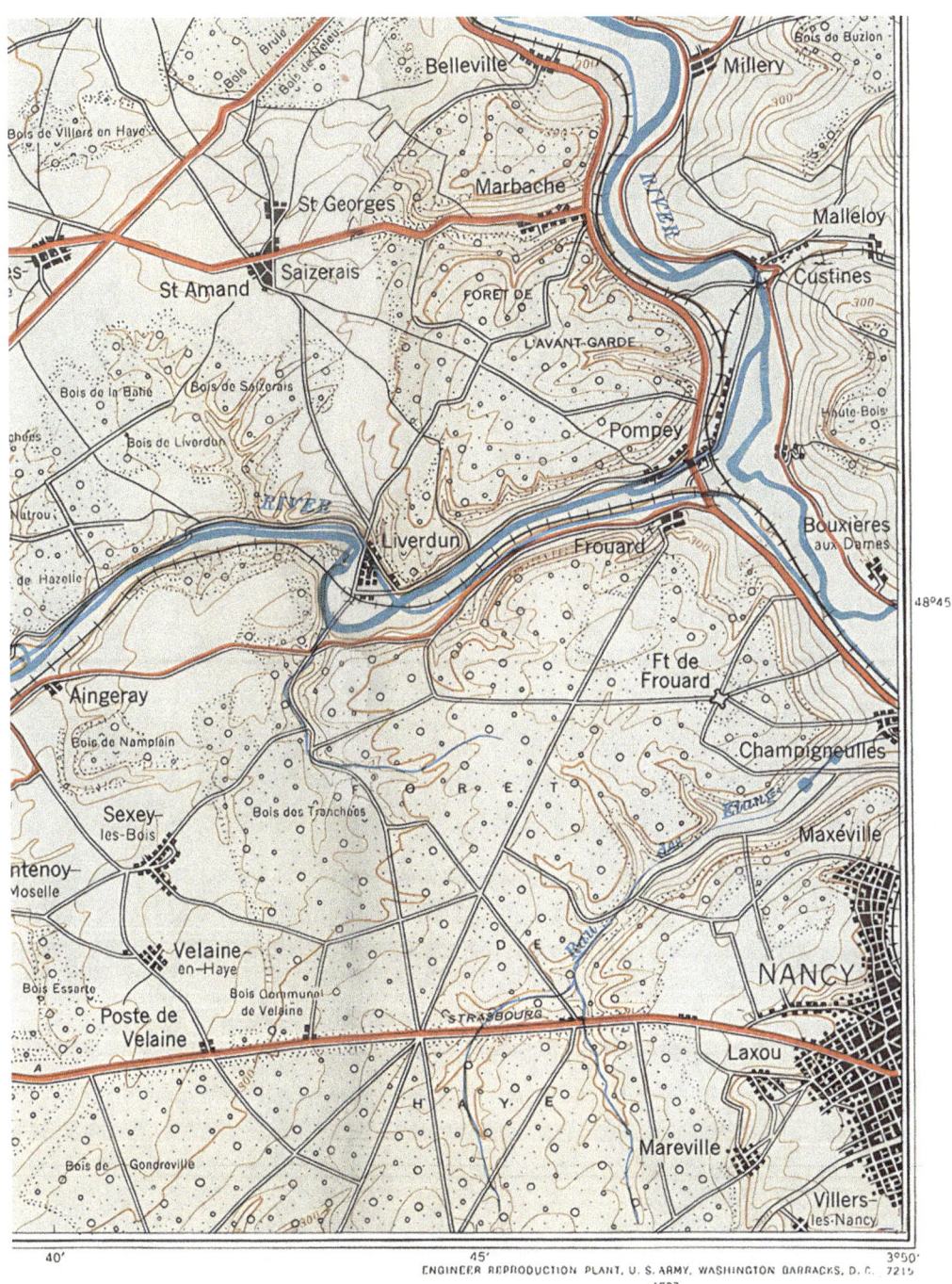

Map shows daily position of Front Line in AMERICAN ST. MIHIEL OFFENSIVE September 12—16, 1918, and November 9—11, 1918, Operation of AMERICAN SECOND ARMY.

Blue color shows ground gained in November Operation and held on November 11.
Other colors show ground gained in ST. MIHIEL Operation.
Ground gained September 14 and abandoned.   Retaken November 10.

Front Line   Army Boundary   Corps Boundary   Division Boundary

IV Roman numerals indicate Corps.   ① Circled Arabic numerals indicate Divisions.
DCP (Fr) French Dismounted Cavalry Division.   DIC (Fr) French Colonial Infantry Division.
CAC (Fr) French Colonial Army Corps.

www.naval-military-press.com

BOOKS FOR THE BATTLEFIELD TOURIST ALWAYS AVAILABLE ALWAYS IN PRINT

Works such as this guide formed the 'Roots of Remembrance' that 100+ years on still attract pilgrims in their droves to visit the Western Front and its memorials to the fallen.

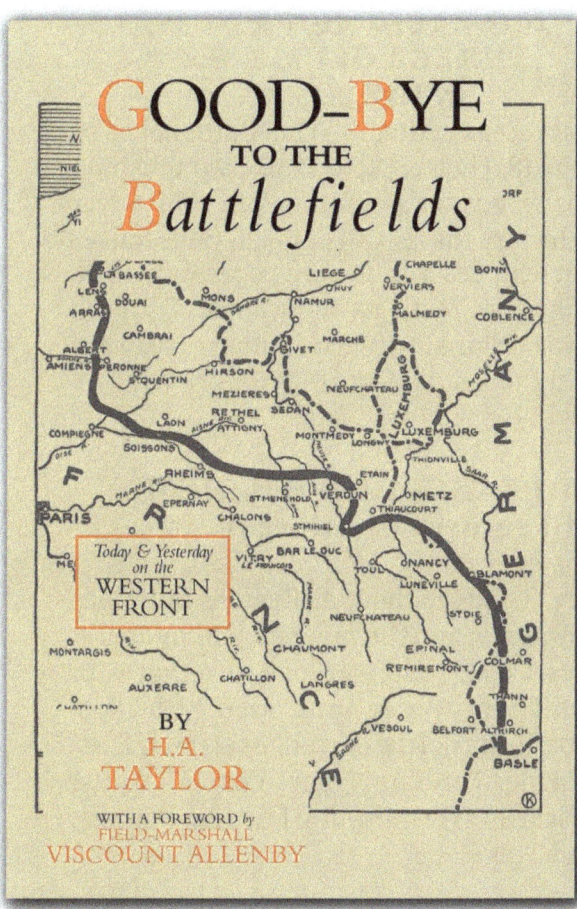

BRITISH MEMORIALS OF THE GREAT WAR
9781474537995

A historical and attractive guide to the various national, regimental and divisional memorials on the Western Front, with photographs and maps, and also notes on memorials further afield including Gallipoli. Published in the 1930s by pioneer travel agency and printing company Dean & Dawson, who conducted battlefield visits. An interesting contemporary tour prospectus is reprinted with this book that outlines the various tours to the Somme, Ypres, Arras etc, along with the maps that accompanied the original publication.

GOOD-BYE TO THE BATTLEFIELDS
Today and Yesterday
on the Western Front
9781474536967

Captain Taylor walks the battlefields of the Western Front 'as they are today (1928)', with good descriptions of the battlefields, relics and memorials during the inter-war period, along with 1920s photographs of towns and villages, cemeteries, memorials and battlefield areas during the period of post-war reconstruction.

With his reminiscences of events, that lend a real atmosphere, his memory and feet "follow our khaki-clad columns moving northward". This is definitely one book to add to your backpack when taking a pilgrimage to France.

THE PILGRIM'S GUIDE TO THE YPRES SALIENT
9781474536738

One of the earliest guidebooks to the Ypres Salient, stated by the author to be compiled for the ex-servicemen who may wish to visit the graves and battlefields of the Great War. Unusually, and interestingly, it includes essays on various aspects of service in the Salient: Hugh Pollard on infantry, Walter Gardiner on mining, F. Worthington on RAMC Work; Machine Guns in the Salient by 'Maxim', etc

TWENTY YEARS AFTER – THE BATTLEFIELDS OF 1914-1918 THEN & NOW THREE VOLUME SET
9781783315505

Twenty Years After – The Battlefields of 1914-1918 Then & Now' is not a publishing curiosity but a fascinating piece of Great War history that is still of much value today. Alongside the atmospheric images is an extensive text, describing many operations and locations on all Fronts, but mainly France & Flanders. With its thousands of superb photographs, this is a fine reference work that was originally issued in many parts but now much more convenient in this bound form.

GUIDE TO THE WAR REGIONS OF FRANCE AND BELGIUM
With the Best Routes & Chief Features of Interest
9781783319473

Published in the 1920s by Goodrich tyre company, 'Guide to the War Regions of France & Belgium' was aimed at the relatively new phenomenon and the independent motorist. Packed with useful information including coloured maps, photographs, together with advice for motorists and details of seventeen different war regions, each with map, route, hotels, historical and economic accounts, a short history of the operations and war facts. These war regions include: The Marne, Champagne, Verdun, Nancy, Vosges, Alsace, Lorraine, Ardennes, Belgium, Yser, Artois, Picardy, Chemin-des-Dames, Somme, Cambrai, Arras and Ypres.

YPRES: THE HOLY GROUND OF BRITISH ARMS
9781783317530

An important early Great War guidebook, written by a man who played a critical role in the Ypres we see today. Henry Beckles Willson was a fierce opponent of the rebuilding of Ypres, feeling that the horrific losses sustained there by the British Army meant that it should always remain a memorial. As Town Major of Ypres, he was instrumental in the development of Ypres as the focal point of Remembrance; he was also pivotal in the creation of the Ypres League.

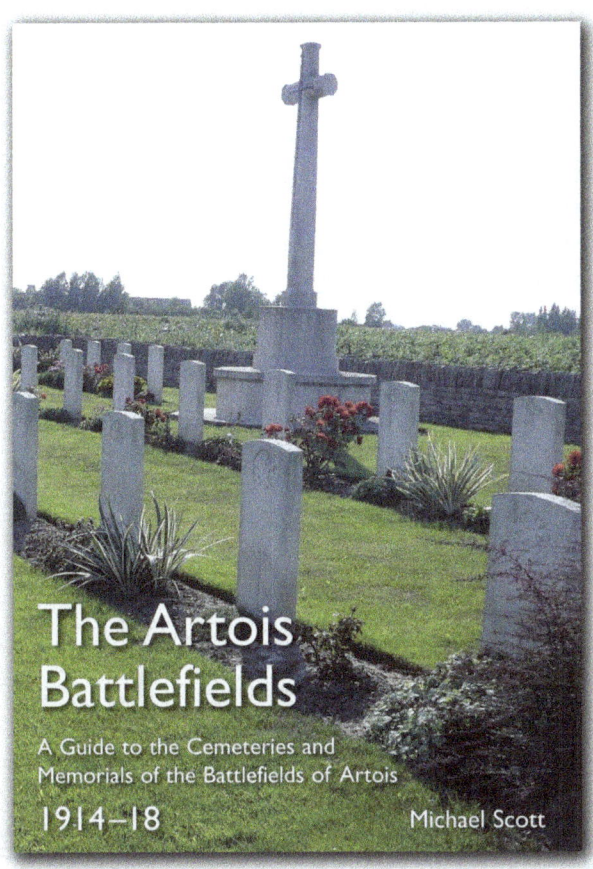

THE WHITE CROSS TOURING ATLAS OF THE WESTERN BATTLEFIELDS
9781783315758

An early historical Great War battlefield guide the whole Western Front, complete with 64 good colour maps, a descriptive text and a War Graves Index of over 1700 cemeteries. The main value to this book, that is now very scarce in it's original printing,is that it shows the locations of many of the British cemeteries that were later consolidated by the CWG.

THE ARTOIS BATTLEFIELDS
A Guide to the Cemeteries and Memorials of the Battlefields of Artois 1914–18
9781783314768

This introduction to the battlefields of Artois is told through the war cemeteries and those buried within. The story of the cemetery, local memorials and lives and war experiences of some of those buried in each cemetery are covered.

The Ypres Salient. A Guide to the Cemeteries and Memorials of the Ypres Salient 1914-18
9781783313518

An exciting new version of an earlier work, this introduction to the battlefields of the Ypres Salient is through the cemeteries and those buried within. The story of the cemetery, local memorials and lives and war experiences of some of those buried in each cemetery is told.

THE SOMME BATTLEFIELDS
A Guide to the Cemeteries and Memorials of the Battlefields of the Somme 1914-18
9781783312900

An introduction to the battlefields of the Somme through the cemeteries and the memorials. Every cemetery within which is buried a man recorded by the CWGC is covered. The story of the cemetery, the local memorials and information of the lives and war experiences of some of those buried in each cemetery is told.

ILLUSTRATED MICHELIN GUIDES
TO THE BATTLE-FIELDS (1914 1918)

THE AMERICANS IN THE GREAT WAR

VOLUME 3
MEUSE-ARGONNE BATTLE
(MONTFAUCON, ROMAGNE, St MENEHOULD.)

MICHELIN & Cie - CLERMONT-FERRAND.
MICHELIN TYRE Co Ltd - 81, Fulham Road. LONDON, S.W.
MICHELIN TIRE Co - MILLTOWN, N.J. U.S.A.

BYGONE PILGRIMAGE. THE AMERICANS IN THE GREAT WAR - VOL I
9781843421672

This admirable account of the part played by the American army on the Western Front is in three volumes. This first volume is concerned with the Second Battle of the Marne covering the period May - August 1918 and the first forty or so pages provides an historical background to the fighting, supported by good, clear maps and interesting photographs. The rest of the book is taken up with a three-day battlefield tour with a map for each day, taking in Chateau Thierry, Belleau Wood, Soissons, Fismes and all places of interest in between with an account of any actions. The tour ends back in Paris.

BYGONE PILGRIMAGE. THE AMERICANS IN THE GREAT WAR - VOL II
9781843421689

This volume is sub-titled The Battle of St Mihiel, and covers St Mihiel, Pont a Mouson and Metz. The first 18 pages provide the historical background, how the St Mihiel salient was formed in September 1914 and how it was eventually eliminated four years later, in September 1918. Details of the American forces (corps and divisions) involved are given with photos of some of their commanders. Then follow the outlines of three guided tours round the battlefields with comments on the scenes of interest and accounts of the fighting. The first tour covers Verdun to Commercy, via Calonne trench, Eparges, Apremont Forest, Ailly Wood and St Mihiel, including a visit to the latter. The next trip goes from Commercy to Metz, via Pont a Mousson and including a visit to Pretre Wood where there was heavy fighting from Sep 1914 to May 1915 when it finally passed into French hands and remained there. It ends with a tour of Metz. The third tour runs from Metz to Verdun via Etain, the main place of interest visited on this leg which does not take in the Verdun battlefield. Good maps and battlefield photos all make this an interesting piece of WWI history.

BYGONE PILGRIMAGE. THE AMERICANS IN THE GREAT WAR - VOL III
9781843421696

This final volume deals with the Meuse-Argonne battlefields. The background history goes back in time and gives a brief account of the Argonne campaign of 1792 against the Prussians before coming on to the Great War, covering the 1914-1918 fighting in the next twenty-two pages supported by good maps and battlefield photos. Then follow details of two guided tours round the scenes of the fighting, the first starts from Verdun and takes in Buzancy, Varennes, Vauquois, Clermont-en-Argonne and Sainte Menehould, some 155 km. The fighting at Vauquois is described in detail and the ravaged state of that battlefield is still very evident today. The next trip, 130 km, starts out from Sainte Menehould and goes on to Varennes, Montfaucon, Grandpre, Vienne-le-Chateau, La Gruerie Wood, Le Four de Paris, La Hayte Chevanchee and La Chalade. There are excellent accounts of the fighting in the areas covered by the tours.

**These three volumes together add up to a good,
well illustrated record of the Americans in France.**

www.ingramcontent.com/pod-product-compliance
Lightning Source LLC
Chambersburg PA
CBHW081144230426
43664CB00018B/2795